PERCEPTUAL AND COGNITIVE IMAGE OF THE CITY

PERSPECTIVES IN URBAN GEOGRPHY

VOLUME TWELVE

Concept's International Series in Geography

No. 1 Perspectives in Agricultural Geography (In Five Volumes)
Edited by NOOR MOHAMMAD

No. 2 Perspectives in Geomorphology (In Four Volumes)
Edited by H.S. SHARMA

No. 3 Perspectives in Urban Geography
Edited by C.S. YADAV

1. New Directions in Urban Geography
2. Comparative Urban Research
3. Comparative Urbanization : City Growth and Change
4.A Models in Urban Geography (Theoretical)
4.B Models in Urban Geography (Mathematical)
5. Urban Research Methods : Central Place, Hierarchical and City Size Models
6. Contemporary City Ecology
7. Slums, Urban Decline and Revitalization
8. Contemporary Urban (Issues)
9. Rural-Urban Fringe
10. Morphology of Towns
11. Cities and Housing
12. Perceptual and Cognitive Image of the City
13. Urban Economics
14. City Planning : Problems and Prospects
15. City Planning : Administration and Participation
16.A Urban Planning and Policies : Reorientation of Policy Norms
16.B Urban Planning and Policies : Cross-Cultural Urban Policies

Concept's International Series in Geography No. 3

PERSPECTIVES IN URBAN GEOGRAPHY

VOLUME TWELVE

PERCEPTUAL AND COGNITIVE IMAGE OF THE CITY

Edited by
C.S. YADAV

CONCEPT PUBLISHING COMPANY, NEW DELHI

First Published 1987

Published by
Naurang Rai
Concept Publishing Company
H-13, Bali Nagar
NEW DELHI-110015 (India)

Printed in India by
Ankur Composer
at Sunil Printers
CB-1067, 75/1 Ajay Palace, Naraina,
NEW DELHI-110028

PREFACE

NATURE OF URBAN GEOGRAPHY

THERE are several studies on urban geography which reveal that, as a major sub-discipline, it has a long tail but a short body. However, the 'spectrum' is so vast and broad that researchers are able to make general statements in defence of its conception, philosophy, nature and orientation. Urban geography today encompasses and interfaces with various disciplines which are interested in urban studies. As an introduction to this series, our task here is to make an attempt to briefly review the development of geographical interest in various aspects of cities.

There are several reviews of the early development of urban geography which have been dealt with by Berry and Harton (1970)[1] and Carter (1974).[2] Berry and Harton in their book, *Geographical Perspective on Urban System*, have made an attempt to introduce readers to its present-day status. They have clearly resolved that "the formative years of the social science in the late nineteenth century and early twentieth century were also the years in which urban studies first developed,"[3] thus providing the context for the geographer's emerging interest in cities. However, the emergence of urban studies dates back to the writing of Greek scholars, but as a sub-discipline, it has reached its present-day status only in the past 30 years.

In their historical perspective the works on urban geography show that the pre-20th century studies primarily concerned themselves with themes of location, size and shape of the cities. The initial findings were strongly subjective, descriptive and dependent more on observation such as the works of Hassert (1907)[4] and Blanchard (1911).[5] In the succeeding years the conceptual framework of site and situation was criticized by Aurousseau (1924)[6] and Crowe (1938)[7], their conception being that cities were not inanimate objects in landscape, but also organic elements which involved people and their movements. The morphologist, later in 1960, truly brought the indigenous line of evolution in the sphere of urban geography and studies on the build-up fabric of cities (Conzone, 1960).[8] Smails (1955)[9] constituted the prime base of urban geography, which remained articulated without any major conceptual change till early 1960s. The studies on the morphological aspects of the urban system were influenced by external forces, consequently the methodological frameworks got impetus within the discipline. At this juncture the evolution of concepts was not based on environment but took shelter under the umbrella of economics of location, and incorporated analysis of land values and rents, and the concept of nodality and accessibility. These concepts were derived from the economic theories of Cooley (1894)[10], Weber (1899),[11] and Hurd (1903).[12]

The Chicago School of Urban Ecology hastened the evolution of urban geography. In his monumental work Park (1925)[13] developed the idea of order and analysis of towns. Further, a powerful thrust and much of the rationale was provided to the studies of urban geography by the Central Place Theory of Christallar (1933).[14]

The impact of the statistical method was powerful and it brought rapid and enormous changes in the field of urban geography. It also brought new insights into the development and application of urban geography towards increased quantification. Brian J. Berry, pioneer in the field, analysed the spatial order, size and location of towns and cities. There was widespread use innovative techniques to explore the nature of urban problems, hypotheses were tested, new theories propounded and old theories remodelled. The statistical methods were put to a variety of uses. Smith (1965)[15] evaluated the classification of settlements ; Berry and Garrison (1956)[16] examined the utility of the rank-size rule for urban populations. The models of Park and Burgess (1925),[17] Harris and Ullman (1954)[18] and Homar Hoyt (1939)[19] were tested and re-examined by various geographers.

A new impetus to urban geography came from social area analysis which was initially propounded by Shevky and Bell (1955)[20] and later on this provided a basis for factorial ecology.

The collaboration of this stream in urban geography was offered by Berry (1971),[21] Herbert (1972)[22] and Johnston (1974).[23] As a consequence of these thrusts in geography after 1960, the techniques of investigation were sharpened and this has provided the basis for a scientific explanation of cities. Attempts were made to introduce new theories and frame laws to make the explanation of events more rational and logical. Sophisticated models were propounded as urban geography entered a new era of rationalizing the subject matter of urban studies on the basis of new philosophies, new concepts, new theories, new methodologies and applications.

However, the status of contemporary urban geography has been elevated only recently by the behavioural approach. The studies of perception and cognition which have a long tradition in physiology were first introduced into the field of geography by Lynch (1960),[24] Dowson and Stea (1973)[25] Gould and White (1974).[26] At present there is a sudden spurt in the studies on the subject with a new paradigm. But the full impact of behavioural approaches upon urbon geography has yet to be realized.

The aim of this series is to seek reorientation of the discipline strengthened by new philosophies, methodologies, subject matters or application. The series has been arranged in such a way that all contemporary view points are covered comprehensively. Hopefully, this series will inspire researchers to appreciate the work already done by geographers in studying cities. Geography by nature seems to be a synthesizing field of inquiry. As such we have made an endeavour to combine some of the otherwise disparate facts garnered by other disciplines in such a manner that we can gain a better understanding of the urban system. The study of urban geography is essential if we are to analyse the human consequences of the settlements in which we live. It is useful to planners, decision makers in government and corporations and also to each one of us as citizens. Finally, it gives us a perspective on what may be happening to our cities and to the nature.

To achieve the above goal only those contributions with originality and contrasting viewpoints were selected for inclusion in this series. In doing so the editor does not wish to compete with the journals in the field in which innovative research and methodological aspects are presented. But he does wish to convey, and convey with conviction, that significant researchers are being undertaken in the different branches of urban geography and in other allied disciplines. The present series is an attempt to provide a selective reappraisal and rigorous examination of the assumptions and the urge to disseminate new knowledge created by the mutual interaction. Emphasis is also placed on the conceptualization and theorization of the subject matter so that general laws may emerge. A conscious effort has been made to organize the series in such a way that it reflects the philosophical approach parallel to that of the behavioural school. Finally, a vigorous attempt has been made to demonstrate throughout the series how geographers are basically involved in solving the urban problems.

C.S. YADAV

REFERENCES

1. Berry and Harton, *Geographic Perspectives on Urban Systems : With Integrated Readings*, New Jersey, Prentice Hall, INC, Englewood Cliffs, 1970.
2. Carter, *The Study of Urban Geography*, Edward Arnold, London, 1974.
3. Berry and Harton, *op cit.*, 1970.
4. Hassert, K., *Die Stadte Geographisch Betrachect*, Leipzig, 1907.
5. Blanchard, R., *Grenoble : Etude De Geographic Urbanine*, Paris, 1911.
6. Aurousseau, M., "Recent Contributions to Geography : A Review," *Geographical Review*, 1924, 14, p. 444.
7. Crowe, P.R., "On Progress in Geography," *Scottish Geographical Magazine*, 1938, 54, pp. 1-19.
8. Conzone, M.R.G., "The Plan Analysis of an English City Centre," In Norkorg (Ed), *Proceedings of I.G.U. Symposium on Urban Geography*, C.W.K. Gleerup, Lund, 1962.
9. Smails, A.E., "The Urban Mess of England and Wales." *Transactions and Papers*, Institute of British Geographers, 1946, 11, 85, p. 101.
10. Cooley, C.H., "The Theory of Transportation," *Publications of the American Economic Association*, 1984, 9, pp. 5-7.
11. Weber, A.F., *The Growth of Cities in the Nineteenth Century : A Study in Statistics*, New York, 1899.

12. Hurd, R., *Principles of City Land Values : New York Record and Guide*, 1903, pp. 19-21.
13. Park, R.E., "Suggestions for the Investigation of Human Behaviour in an Urban Environment", in R.E. Park and R.D. Mackenzie (eds). *The City*, University of Chicago Press, 1925.
14. Christallar, W., *Central Place in Southern Germany*, Gustar Fischer, Teno, 1933.
15. Smith, R.M.T., "Method and Purpose in Functional Town Classification," *Annals of the Association of American Geographers*, 1965, 55, pp. 539-548.
16. Garrison, W.L., "Applicability of Statistical Inference to Geographical Research," *Geographical Review*, 1956, 46, pp. 427-429.
17. Burgess, E.W., "The Growth of City." in R.E. Park and R.D. Mackenzie (eds.), *The City*, University of Chicago Press, 1925.
18. Ullman, E.L., "The Nature of Cities," *Annals, American Academy of Political and Social Science*, 1945, 242, pp. 7-27.
19. Hoyt, H., *The Structure and Growth of Residential Neighbourhoods in American Cities*, Washington, Federal Housing Administration, 1939.
20. Shevky, E. and Bell, W., *Social Area Analysis*, Stanford University Press, Stanford, 1955.
21. Berry, B.J.L. (ed), "Comparative Factorial Ecology," *Economic Geographic (Supplement)*, 1971, p. 47.
22. Herbert, D.T., *Urban Geography : A Social Perspective*, David and Charles, Newton Abbot, 1972.
23. Johnston, *Urban Residential Pattern*, Bell, London, 1971.
24. Lynch, *Image of the City*, Massachusetts, Cambridge, 1960.
25. Dowson and Stea, "Image and Environment," Chicago and London, 1973.
26. Gould and White, R., *Mental Maps*, London, 1974.

ACKNOWLEDGEMENT

We Thank Editors Gerd-Michael Hellstern, Erithjof Spreer Hellmut Wollmann, *Heft 2*, *Vol. II* and *Vol. III*, for their permission to use material from "Applied Urban Research" Proceedings of the European Meeting on Applied Urban Research, Essen Oct. 2-4, 1981.

CONTENTS

PART THREE

IMAGES AND RESIDENTIAL ENVIRONMENT

PART FOUR

RURAL-URBAN MIGRATION

LIST OF CONTRIBUTORS

William Baer : Dean, School of Urban and Regional Planning, University of Southern California, Los Angeles, California-90007

Tridib Banerjee : Associate Professor, School of Urban and Regional Planning, University of Southern California, Los Angeles, California 90007

Yoram Bar-Gal : The University of Haifa, Mount Carmel, Haifa, Israel

Joel A. Diemer : New Mexico State University, Las Cruces, New Mexico 88003

Gary W. Evans : Program in Social Ecology, University of California, Irvine, California, 92717

Nathan Gale : Department of Geography, University of California Santa Barbara, California

Reginald G. Golledge : Department of Geography, University of California, Santa Barbara, California

Wilmer M. Harper : New Mexico State University, Las Cruces, New Mexico 88003

Emma Hooper : Department of Social Science and Administration, the London School of Economics, Houghton St., London, WC 2A 2AE

Joseph B. Juhasz : College of Environmental Design, University of Colorado, Boulder, Colorado 80302

James A. King : University of Toledo, Toledo, Ohio 43606, U.S.A.

William A. Muraco : University of Toledo, Toledo, Ohio 43606, U.S.A.

Mauro O'Brien-Marchand : U.S. Geological Survey, 345 Middlefield Road, Menlo Park, California 94025

G. Donald Richardson : Department of Geography, University of California, Santa Barbara, California

Vincent B. Robinson : Assistant Professor, Hunter College—CUNY 695, Park Avenue, New York, 10021 USA.

Linda C. Robinson : Environmental Planner, Vollmer's Associates, Inc. 62, Fifth Avenue, New York, 10011 USA.

Sally Ann Shumaker : University of California, Irvine, California

Peter F. Smith : University of Sheffield, U.K.

Daniel Stokols : Program in Social Ecology, University of California, Irvine, California 92717

Karl O. Vezner : University of Toledo, Toledo, Ohio 43606, U.S.A.

C.S. Yadav : Reader and Head, Department of Geography, Bhagat Singh College, University of Delhi, Kalkaji, New Delhi

Hermann Zinn : Mangoldweg 26, 6100 Darmstadt, Federal Republic of Germany

ONE

C.S. YADAV

INTRODUCTION

THE environmental psychologist suggests that man and environment interrelationship is a dynamic feature. Man lives in its environment which is a total milieu in terms of its physical, biotic and cultural attributes. Man is an active actor in this milieu who according to his capabilities, desires and activities makes an attempt to adapt himself to the environmental conditions prevailing in a particular region. As a matter of fact man act upon his environment and is in turn, influenced by it. The key variables in man-environment interaction are perception and cognition—"The internal mental processes by which individuals sense, perceive, interpret and make decision about their environment" (John R. Gold) 1980.[1] These processes have produced a unified paradigm of man environment relationships.

The term 'perception' and 'cognition' have been used in various ways by environmental psychologists. A historical examination of these terms indicates that in essence they are treated separate field of inquiry in experimental psychology, nevertheless their distinctiveness vanished over time. Proshansky (1976)[2] has rightly observed that 'some writers use one term, some the other and many use both, but the specific nature of the work done is relatively unrelated to the term chosen to describe it.' Many a scholars have argued that the difference between perception and cognition was mainly created by the reductionist tradition to experimental psychology. Thus any distinction between these two terms may be considered as a heuristic device rather than a fundamental dichotomy in mental process (Gold, 1980).[3] As a matter of fact cognition is a broad term which *interalia* includes perception. The frameworks of cognition include sensing, perceiving, remembering, imagining, judging, deciding and adopting or any other mental process. It is intimately related to knowledge, experience and behaviour of human beings. Whereas 'perception' by comparison is a more specific term. It is the physiological function that enables the individual to convert sensory stimulation into organized and coherent experience. Thus perception itself is a cognitive process" (Gold, 1980).[4]

Approaches to perception studies

Much has been written over last two decades about people's images of the cities. Most of the urban research scholars have implecitly agreed that city is a natural object, a phenomena in space which is perfectly perceived and easily comprehended by its residents or those who have established relations with it. Nevertheless for the citizen, the objective city does not exist. On the contrary, every resident has most appropriately a partial and most probably an idiosyncratic, view of the urban environment in which he or she lives (Carter).[5] Nevertheless a growing number of urban geographers are now focussing on the establishment and analysis of images of the city and they have chosen a specific line of action. The development of mental (Cognitive) maps which translate the images into a spatial framework. The cognitive maps or images of the urban environment are defined by Downs and Stea (1970)[6] as "... a process composed of a series of physiological transformations by which and individual acquires, codes, stores, recalls and decodes information about the relative locations and attributes of phenomena in his every day spatial environment." Downs in his attempt postulated three distinct approaches to analyse geographic space perception. First he advocated the structural approach which is concerned with the way in which the array of information about a place (city) is perceived. As a matter of fact, one cannot remember all elements perceived by an individual about an environment so, an individual follow a process of selection and ordering or he gives a structure to his sense perception. Thus it is evident that mental map of a city is constructed in which useless detail is discarded and predominant data set is detained.

Thus mental maps do not provide comprehensive picture of the environment rather internal representation of segments of the environment, which is based on sensory transformation of information about external environment. The second approach is known as evaluation approach, in which an individual after obtaining knowledge and experience of the environment, evaluates its distinct character so that he can make decisions and take action, according to the image held about a particular environment. The third approach preference approach. It is, the way in which preferences are developed among a set of objects distributed in space (Carter).[7]

Classification of urban perception

To obtain a comprehensive and precise account of how images of the townscape can be made, it is very necessary to get an insight into the typology of urban perception which explore the ways in which images are developed. Appleyard (1973)[8] has postulated a threefold rational classification.

1. *Operational perception* : When people move in a city, they gather familiarity about many elements in the city, because they use them as reference points in their every day life. They make an array through their sensory image about bus stops, traffic inter-section, key buildings or distinctive land marks. They notice them, remember and evaluate their importance and thus create a working mental structure of the city. They derive it through their repetitive activities.

2. *Responsive perception* : As a matter of fact people become more familiar with those places which are unique or unusual features which make an immediate impact on mans sensory image and generate response. The bright, isolated singular and distinct elements arouse more curiosity for search behaviour or catch the eyes of a amusing passenger. The advertising agencies, by using distinctive designs or colours, elicite a sort of response to easily remember the unusual features.

3. *Inferential perception* : When people move from one part of the city to another they remember their past experience and compare the environment of the city by inference from parallel situation.

4. *The image of the city* : The classification of urban perception is divised to provide an analytical system which reasonably

represented the way in which city images and the perception themselves, are structured. As it is evident that city images can be identified and represented in various ways. Nevertheless the seminal work of Lynch (1960)[9] solved the problem. Lynch in his book entitled, "The Image of the City", proposed five elements through which the physical structure of the city was analysed. His study created the paradigm with in which much subsequent research was carried out. As a matter of fact his principles supplied concepts and methods which could be accepted by other and more over provided some basic principles which are relevant for the various disciplines that are concern with urban analysis.

The content of the image of the city as described and evaluated by Lynch involved five elements which could be considered fundamental components of cognitive image of the city. These five elements were defined as paths, edges, districts, nodes and land marks. The paths were primarily the channels along which an individual normally move with in the city from his residence to place of work or he may commute to visit relations or attend social ceremonies. While he moves he observe places, make a mental map of these places or store the information in his memory. Edges are conceived as linear elements which characterise distinctive physical breaks with in the city. They can represent physical elements, such as breaks of lake, ridge, shoreline or river front. They can also be conceived of as man-made features such as breaks created by railways and motorways. Edges are considered barriers which differentiate one segment of the city from another. Districts are those areas of the city which are immediately identifiable to the residents. They are bounded by edges and usually have local names. They are delineated on the bases of distinctive activities, cultures or groups. Nodes were strategic points in the city. They are the physical identities, mostly consist of road junctions. Landmarks are easily identified physical elements, such as distinctive buildings or features, which are easily identified and easily stores in the memory. They are used in structuring the mental map of the city. They are also used to epitomize the whole city.

Lynch with the help of these five elements analysed the visual quality of three American cities. He examined the physical city landscape of these cities as perceived by small group of samples of their residents. In attempt Lynch tries to throw light upon the problem of urban design. In doing so he allowed the dominance of vision in spatial perception. It is a truism that Lynch analysed the visual component of urban schemata. However, the main objective of the analysis was to identify main elements in the city landscape and their structural relationship. It is also observed that residents were asked those questions which were "centered on a passive mode of perception examining the reaction of people to various contrasting environments rather than looking at more active modes of perception, where people impose meaning upon their urban environment" (Gold, 1980).[10] As it is evident that the central concept in the image of the city landscape which justifies that citizens are capable to organise the various elements of urban forms into coherent mental representations. Following the monumental work of Lynch, several distinguished scholars conducted research on imageability concept : such as Appleyard (1970),[11] Jonge (1962)[12] and Gallick (1963)[13] who conducted research in Venezuela, Netherlands and Lebnon respectively. They have defined the areal component of the basic Lynch structure and revealed why some landmarks should be incorporated into cognitive image of the city. Other pioneers in this field are Lee (1965),[14] Carr and Schissler (1969),[15] Downs (1970),[16] Golledge, Briggs and Demko (1969),[17] Orleans (1973),[18] Golledge and Zannaras (1973)[19] and Ladd (1970).[20] All of these scholars have made an attempt to further investigate visible components of the city image and postulated that mental maps could be viewed as an essential component of human adoption and use of a particular environment. All these scholars, have followed the concepts of legibility, imageability and the methods of collection of data and analysis as divised by Lynch. However the image of city provided viable research paradigm and it is considered to be an exploratory study. In subsequent years the followers of Lynch who applied his concepts and methods in their own studies of urban cognition, have not only extended the principles of Lynch but also modified the original version. While doing so, some researchers, identified four main deficiencies.

The first deficiency is related to methodology, which relates to free hand sketch maps. The appropriateness of this method depends upon the principle that map is a true representation of a person's cognition of the urban environment. According to Spencer (1973)[21] this preposition is not correct, because drawing sketch map require skill to draw them which can be possible from an experts hand every one cannot draw them, secondly several writers have postulated non-visual components of the city, according to them sight is not a prerequisite for spatial cognition, they emphasised more effective properties of the non visual senses. The study of Southward (1969)[22] was based on sonic environment which provided the analyses of auditory perception. The third criticism, is labelled against lack of functional and symbolic meaning to urban space, some of the critics like Steinitz (1968),[23] Appleyard (1973)[24] and Johns (1969),[25] postulated that recognition of symbols and functions involve a more active relationship between the individual perceiver and his environment. This is quite contrary to the implicit passive or responsive mode of perception studied by Lynch. Forthly the validity of Lynch's typology of five elements of spatial cognition has been challenged by Sarre (1972)[26] and Gooday (1972).[27]

Pocock (1975)[28] made a modification in original typology as proposed by Lynch because it has no underlying theoretical justification. He used a different data set, he proposed that city elements can be classified into three categories such as point features, linear features and areas which recognized as buildings, paths and areas respectively.

Buildings, he considered as monuments and landmarks which represent the physical unit of the city. The spatial cognition of buildings is derived from their functional use, from their territorial limitations, from their significance as monuments and as landmarks. As a matter of fact buildings, reflect the attitudes and values that were current in society at the time of their construction. Furthermore buildings play an important role in everyday life simply because they act as a repository of cultural values (Gold, 1980).[29] The buildings also serve as landmarks for orientation and way finding in the city.

The road system of the city is inevitably an important part of the modern city and play an important role in urban spatial cognition. It may be recalled the justification of Lynch (1960),[30] who considered paths of movements as structural element of urban schamat Acullen (1961)[31] examined the way the city landscapes was perceived by a moving observer. According to him the observer perceived the city landscape in a sequence which is manipulated as 'serial vision'. The visual image of the city based upon the vivid image can be divided into two elements : the 'existing view' and 'emerging view'.

The area, a portion of space that is identifiable by some particular set of characteristics is a fundamental unit of cognition of city landscape. The environmental complexity is easily comprehended by categorizing space into areas. Open spaces and residential neighbourhoods play an important role in the spatial cognition of the city land scape, open spaces in the city serves as symbolic functions. They are highly effective medium by which clues about the structure of the city are identified which allows the observer to discern spatial relationship. The open spaces in the form of parks and playgrounds, play an important role and convey a distinct character to the city. They some times constitute nationally and internationally, known symbols of the city.

The study of the image of the city are of practical utility in the field of planning. The geographers have come to the conclusion that circulatory image and behaviour not only interact with each other but also condition each other. It is an important thing that city image provide its residents an easy key to take decisions, where to shop, where to live and where to work and how to locate unknown places.

ABOUT THIS VOLUME

Although there was very little literature about people's preferences for places until late 1960. After the seminal work of Lynch, a number of scholars have thought about the images that men have of their local environments. Usually these environments are urban areas. There was a behavioural revolution in geography and quite a large number of urban geographers had focussed their interest in the way in which people perceive certain landmarks, routes, boundaries and neighbourhoods. The studies on people's perception of places were designed to understand the patterns of human activities in our cities are the result of man making locational decisions based on information that has come through perceptional filter.

The perception that people have of places and the mental images that are formed from filtered information flows, are two major themes of this volume. The study of the cognitive image of the city is a multidisciplinary outlook. Geographers have always looked to other disciplines to provide initial insight into behavioural process. It is in urban geography that important ideas have been derived from such subjects as sociology, anthropology, planning, architecture, psychology and ethology, all of which have their own framework to study the behavioural aspects of the city. Thus geographers have derived information from these disciplines about the mental storage of spatial information, mental map studies and action space studies. In essence therefore the present volume concerns itself to the process of decision making, choice theory analysis of space preference, spatial learning process environmental cognition and cognitive mapping.

For this reason the volume is divided into five parts. Part one of this volume sets out to provide foundation material upon which the later analysis can be established. It contains those articles which consider the major ways in which psychologists have traditionally viewed behaviour and the main emphasis is laid down on the emergence of an 'environmental psychology'. Part II deals cognitive Image of the City, which explicitly or implicitly includes the concepts of perception, cognition, motivation, emotion and attitudes. It includes those articles which reflect paradigm of individual spatial cognition and behaviour. Part three considers the images and residential environment. It includes those articles which reflect choice of the city dwellers where to live. So the constraints of residential desirability are explored. The fourth section on psychological implications of rural urban migration particularly focuss its attention on the way people perceived differences between various parts of the human settlements which generate movements of many different kinds. In this section authors have tried to assess the ways in which people build up images of other places and the section fourth highlights the symbolic and authentic judgement of the city landscape.

The scientific vitality of environmental psychology comprises of several active and focussed research domains. There has been substantial theoretical and empirical progress made with in the subareas of environmental psychology. Conceptual developments are evident in the field of spatial cognition proxemics, stress and ecological psychology. The author Daniel Stokols in his article "Environmental Psychology" analyses the major research domains of environmental psychology and tries vigorously to highlight some common assumptions or themes which eventually may provide the foundation for a general theory of environment, and behaviour. According to the author one such theme is the transactional or biodirectional nature of human environment relation, transactional views suggest that any attempt to conceptualize the relationship between environment and behaviour must account not only for the effects of the environment on people, but also for the reciprocal impact of people on their milieu. Another related theme is human environment optimization which suggests that various modes of transaction between people and their surroundings (*i.e.*, interpretive, evaluative, operative, and responsive modes) are organized in relation to prioritized goals and plans. The author emphasizes that the attempts of individuals and groups to create environments that are maximally supportive of their goals and activities. The author suggests that the concepts of transactionalism and optimization are relevant to one of the major tasks currently facing the behavioural sciences namely the development of a taxonomy of environments. In the final the author arrives at a conclusion that conceptualization of community planning as a goal oriented optimization process raises several questions for future research. For instance (a) On what dimensions do people attempt to optimize their environments ? (b) Do the salient dimensions of environmental optimization vary systematically in relation to the type of setting considered ? (c) What kinds of assessment criteria are appropriate for measuring optimization process and their outcomes at individual, group and community levels of analysis ? (d) What are the appropriate time intervals for assessing optimization cycles with in individuals, groups and communities ? (e) To what extent can competing goals be optimized both within and between systems ? (f) In what ways can empirical information concerning human environment optimization be translated to guidelines for environmental design ? The author advocates that analysis of these issues will require an integration of the concepts and tools of the environmental assessment with those from the other areas of the field.

A crucial challenge facing psychological research is to develop a theoretical basis for describing and categorizing the diverse settings of human behaviour. Only identifying the important dimensions and process of settings many assess the comparability of environments and ecological validity of the research findings and policy decisions. Guided by these concerns the authors Daniel Stokols and Sally Ann Shumaker in their article "People in Places : A Transactional View of Settings" reveal that their major purpose of the present paper is (1) to develop a conceptualization of settings emphasizing the cognitive and behavioural transactions between people and places (2) to delineate a set of theoretical dimensions for describing and categorizing settings and (3) to derive research hypotheses from the proposed taxonomic dimensions. The authors represent an ambitious attempt to develop a conceptualization of settings emphasizing the cognitive and behavioural transactions between people and places and to examine certain policy implications of this line of reasoning the key terms in Stokols and Shumakers analysis are 'place' and "transaction". This analysis is rich in substance involving for example a taxonomy of settings and represent in some sense all of the major concepts considered in our dialogue among cognitive, environmental and social psychologist. The authors in the paper have outlines eight distinct stages in the life cycles of settings and have offered a series of hypothesis concerning the antecedents add processes associated with setting emergence maintenance modification and termination. Although the authors feel that their analysis of the phenomena is preliminary and incomplete, it may provide a useful framework for future research on the transactions between people and places and a conceptual basis for designing and improving settings.

Human beings know a considerable amount about the content and location of information in real world settings they experience. Yet we know little about how this information is processed. Environmental psychologists studying the question have relied primarily on questionable methodologies such as hand drawing and small scale models. In addition theoretical development has been minimal with largely descriptive taxonomies of the geographic features contained in cognitive maps. The author Gary W. Evans in his article "Environmental Cognition" reviews research on human spatial cognition in real, every day settings. The cognitive mapping literature is organised into five empirical categories: age, familiarity, gender, class and culture and physical components of settings. The author discusses the methodological and conceptual issues in the environmental cognition literature. The author reveals the problems with hand drawn sketch map methodologies and theoretical ambiguities about the cognitive mapping process. In particular the lack of integration of pertinent cognitive research with the environmental psychology literature on cognitive mapping is noted. Finally, the potential applications of environmental cognition work to architecture, planning and education are discussed.

Although almost two decades of research have passed since Lynch's seminal work on city images was published, the academic investigation of this topic is still in its infancy. This is not surprising since, while many of the cognitive variables examined by researchers interested in the city of the mind had been developed, defined and measured at a micro-scale or in a laboratory, context, their verification, validation and measurement at a larger scale had not been achieved. In a very real sense, geographers had to start from scratch. Keeping this in mind, the authors Reginald G. Golledge ; G. Donald Richardson and Nathan Gale in their article "Cognitive Image of the City" have concentrated their efforts to a large extent on showing how to represent cognitive information cartographically. However the authors could not identified the full geometry of the cognitive representation. The authors reflect that many of the problems associated with representing cognitive information in cartographic form are the same problems that surfaced in interpreting the original sketch map suggested by early researchers as an appropriate way of obtaining information on city images. The author finally put a challenge before the researchers who are aiming to take up work on cognitive image of cities. According to the authors, the work on this phenomena should not be taken lightly. They cautioned that most of the work requires a very careful experimental design, the careful collection and monitoring of datasets, the selection of appropriate representational modes and the development and use of appropriate ways of representing cognitive information. The authors also reminds that research efforts in this area will take a lot of time and the researchers must be dedicated.

For many years a major concern of the discipline of geography has been the partitioning space as a procedure analogous to scientific classification. Emphasis was given to the classical taxonomy. Instead of an attempt to discover "natural" dimensions classification was seen as a research tool or device, that could be used to impose order on complex distribution. The authors Nathan Gole and Reginald G. Golledge in their article "on the subjective partitioning of space" try to comment on some fundamental concerns associated with the subjective partitioning of space. In particular they discussed some basic assumptions and epistemological positions that are both implicitly and explicitly assumed in the partitioning process. A brief discussion of the scale follows to make the point that the epistemological assumptions involved in the transitions from personal to cognitive space have not always been fully appreciated by geographic researchers. In the final section of the paper the authors discuss some major problems associated with subjective partitioning and briefly those references are selected that have logical application to fit in this research area.

City planners and designers have always had strong convictions about what constitute a residential environment, how it should be defined or how big it should be. These are implicit in the principles and standards expounded by the planning and design profession. What has not been fully explored is how the residential environment is actually perceived by the public and whether the public's perception matches that of the profession. Nor for that matter has it been known whether different segments of the public uniformally share the same perceptions of residential environment. The authors Tridip Banerjee and William Baer in their article "Variable Constructs and Images of the Residential Environment : Findings from Los Angels" have attempted to explore how people perceive and image their residential environment: and if variabilities in these images can be explained by social and physical factors. In seeking answers to these questions the authors have primarily focussed on the mental representation or 'cognitive maps' of the physical space. The authors have argued that image is part and parcel of the system of facts and values that mediate our preferences and satisfactions related to places where we live. It has also been authors' premise that how one images the environment is an important documentation of how one uses the environment. The authors have conducted empirical investigations in these questions.

During the last 20 years research on the interrelationships between the built environment and social behaviour has gradually emerges as a new field of scientific study. In this concern author Hermannzinn in his article "Interrelationship between Housing and Environment" finds that in most of the research work undertaken to date the relationship between man and his environment has been regarded as being merely equivalent to a straight forward stimulus response type of system. Man is depicted as an organism with relatively in variable behaviour patterns which are either biologically determined or else acquired in the process of socialization, and largely static needs. It is assumed that man is by no means an autonomous being with the freedom of choice to his relationship with his environment, but rather that he behaves largely reactively in response to stimuli of his social and physical environment to which he is more or less passively subjected.

The author finds that according to this approach man learns by positive and negative sanctions to adapt to environmental constraints. The author further illucidated the main object of this research which intentionally or unintentionally follows the tradition of behaviourism is consequently to determine by means of observation, standardized interview or experiment what rules there may be in the interplay of ecological variables and behavioural variables.

The process of converting vacant land to residential use is the result of a chain of decisions made by various individuals or groups guided by their own incentives. Pre-development land owners impelled by pecuniary and personal motives to sell, developers influenced by profit motives and Household consumers seeking their own housing needs and preferences are at the cost of the process while realtors, financiers, public officials, act as supporting agents. The leading role in the residential land development process is taken by the developer whose land purchase decision constitute the locational commitments to develop residential housing units on a specific plot of land. Although many studies have focussed upon the importance of various locational factors in the developers locational decision, few have studied developer attitudes in areas undergoing rapid land use change. The authors Vincent B. Robinson and Linde C. Robinson in their article "Dimensions of Residential Developer Decision Making in a Rapidly Urbanizing Region" focuss their attention on residential land developer attitudes towards locational information in his operational environment. The objective of this study is to identify and evaluate the major independent dimension of the locational decision of residential developers in a rapidly urbanizing region.

The realization and maintenance of some minimum standard of living or quality of life is integral to the social welfare goals of virtually all contemporary societies. This is amply manifest in the actions of national, subnational and local governments as they propose and initiate programmes to reduce unemployment. However, with few exceptions the measurement of the efficiency of such programmes in achieving improvements in perceived well being and quality of living has been particularly difficult.

The authors Wilmer H. Harper and Joel A. Diemer in their article "Quality of Life Assessment : A Methodology for Intra Regional Comparisons" postulate that quality of life depends on the following constraints : (1) economic security ; (2) family life ; (3) personal strengths ; (4) friendship ; (5) attractiveness of the physical environment.

The discussion addresses the problem of integrating economic and environmental variables into a quality of life measure which will yield economic welfare weights useful to decision makers and planners. Four partial approaches to quality of life measurement are examined and a conceptual framework for a generalized approach is presented. The generalized approach goes beyond traditional economic welfare measures and integrates a non-market environmental dimension into the consideration of personal well-being and quality of life.

These are numerous studies of migrants and migration movements, whose findings are complex and frequently contradictory. The author Emma Hooper in article "Behaviour and Perception : The Decision to Migrate" reveals those processes which help the migrants to take decision where to go. The author finds that a migrants choice of location is influenced by the presence of friends and relatives. The author arrives at a conclusion that economist and sociologist studying internal migration have always stressed the dominance of the economic motive in the decision to migrate. The author is of firm conviction that despite a multiplicity of factors being involved in a decision whether to migrate or not, people are not always consciously aware of all the variables influencing their decision.

The dynamics of inter and intra urban migration have long been of major interest to the urban geographers. It is through the nature of these population adjustments that the morphological character of the urban system is formed and transformed. Migration models have suggested that the decision to move and its subsequent behaviours are a result of multiple spatial "push" and "pull" factors. The models of spatial migration are generally based on the objective of maximising the place utility of the residential environment. Behavioural approaches to migration envision that residential stresses are exerted on individuals when the differential between residential aspirations widen relative to the place utility. The authors James A. Kind ; William A. Muraco ; Karl. O. Vezner in their article "Psychological and Environmental Implications of Intra-urban Migration : Community Adjustment and the Mental Patient" postulate that the decision to migrate represents an environmental adjustment which resolves the strain between unattained residential needs and the failure of the present residence to meet that need. The objective of the authors in this study is to investigate the impact that migration has on the psychological status of the migrants. Rather than focussing the research on the public in general, the study concentrates on mental patients who were recently released from a state mental hospital.

The author C.S. Yadav in his article "Physiological Implications of Rural-urban Migration : A Case Study of Delhi", highlights that in India, urbanization has been an enigma for many planners and policy makers, because it is accelerated by an unabated flow of migrants from the country side to primate cities. Two of the most serious problems facing India today are large and growing urban unemployment and shortages of housing in our primate cities. Migration contributes approximately 50 per cent increase in urban population which means, it is by far the most important component of urbanization and is the chief mechanism which has fostered the urbanization of large segments of peasants. In the present paper attempts are made to see whether rural-urban migration is one of the evils of urbanization or not and how adversities of rapid migration coupled with high rates of natural increase in both rural and urban areas have resulted in the skewed pattern of urbanization. To combat the problem of migration in Delhi some integrated rural and urban development strategies are suggested. The most promising alternative to solve the problem is to adopt decentralized urbanization policy which aims at lowering overall population growth rates, changing pattern of migration and increasing the productive capacity of rural areas by encouraging the growth of market towns, small cities and regional urban centers with an articulated national spatial hierarchy. The present paper is prepared to explore the magnitude, rate, incidence and process of migration. Vigorous attempts are made to explore how does the process of migration occur as a result of decision made by individuals in the light of what they perceive the objective world to be like. It is assumed that migrants held an enormous view of their environment that is acted upon rather than the objective real world situation. The process of migration will remain inevitable so long as migrants perceive better job opportunities higher wages in primate cities.

A reappraisal of the contact between man and landscape took place in geography during the decade of the seventies—marked by the appearance of the humanistic aspects, which have retreated during the previous decade, a period in which geography stressed the positivistic approach. The contact between man and landscape is frequently described by writers and artists in their creative work. The author

Yoram Bar Gal in his paper "The Birth Pangs of a City—From Jaffa to Tel Aviv" tries to demonstrate that the humanistic approach, as an intellectual method in geography, is helpful in revealing additional dimensions of the relations which exist between man and landscape. The author accepts that for the positivist the birth process of Tel Aviv is described with statistical data, maps and aerial photographs where as for the humanist the birth process of the city is the contact between man and landscape, a contact which creates feelings and a world of symbols which are passed on to the coming generations through paintings, sketching and literary descriptions. These artistic design reveal the hidden dimension of the transformation of a small group of buildings into houses, into neighbourhoods and than into a city. The author strongly proposed that this is the dimension of the sense of place that humanistic aims reveal as part of man's relationship with landscape.

Aesthetics is the study of the mind and emotions in relation to the sense of beauty. The term is used in discussing appreciation or criticism of beauty or in describing what is pleasing to the senses. Frequently the concepts of form, live, complexity, ambignity, dynamicism and balance interact in such a way as to influence one's aesthetic impression of an object or landscape. Landscape aesthetics are a synthesis of the physical and cultural characteristics of the landscape. The physical and cultural aspects strongly influence but do not wholly determine how a landscape may be aesthetically perceived by an individual. It is the complex intermeshing of physical and cultural factors which create a new entity, different from the sum total of its component parts, which then perceived through the mind of a person making an aesthetic judgement. The authors Mauro O' Brien-Marchant and Joseph B. Juhasz in their article "Aesthetic Judgements and Objective Characteristics of National Land Scapes" make an attempt to compare various techniques of aesthetic evaluation of natural landscape in a number of small central Pennsylvania water sheds. Scenic rating by socio economic groups is contrasted and the influence on aesthetic judgement of differing photographic media and photographic quality is examined. The paper also identifies and assesses the relative importance of some of the physical land characteristics which affect human aesthetic perception of the landscape. Quantitative techniques for evaluating physical and cultural aspects of the landscape and their use in conjunction with aesthetic ratings in an over all system of landscape are not discussed.

A top priority in the perception routine is the need to reduce the complexity of the sensory world by recognising patterns or systems of orderliness. The author Peter F. Smith in his article "The Harmonics of Information in Architecture", tries to demonstrate that a residence from our primordial past is the need to attempt to eliminate or at least reduce uncertainty in our environment. The author suggests that one way of doing this is to reduce the gross complexity of the milieu by organising data into patterns or schemes. The author further finds, one routine which the mind seems to favour is to arrange data into related pairs. This binary organizational routine is the simplest way of building up an orderly model of the world. As a matter of fact first we recognise the most obvious binary relationship say between the name and tower of church. Then we discern more discrete binary subsystems, such as the relationship between window and wall or decoration and plainness. The next point to note is that the mind somehow attaches weight to information systems and mind will make a value judgement according to the relative informational weight of aesthetic values.

FOOTNOTES

1. Gold, John R. *An Introduction to Behavioural Geography* (Oxford University Press), 1980.
2. Proshansky, H.M. et al. 1976.
   "Environmental Psychology. A Methodological Orientation" in H.M. Proshansky, W.H. Ittelson and L.G. Rivlin, eds. *Environmental Psychology* (second edition), New York : Holt Rinehart and Winston, 59-68.

3. John R. Gold, op. cit., page 20.
4. Ibid.
5. Carter, *The Study of Urban Geography*, Edward Arnold (London), 1977.
6. R.M. Downs (1970) *Geographic Space Perception : Past Approaches and Future Prospects in Progress in Geography*, 65-108.
7. Carter, op. cit.
8. D. Appleyard (1973) "Notes on Urban Perception and Knowledge" in R.M. Downs and D. Stea (eds), *Image and Environment*, 109-114.
9. Lynch (1980).
10. J.R. Gold, op. cit., p. 99.
11. D. Appleyard (1970) "Styles and Methods of Structuring a City", *Environment and Behaviour*, 2, 100-117.
12. Derek De Jonge (1962) "Images of Urban Areas : their Structure and Psychological Conditions", *A.I.P. Journal*, 28, 266-276.
13. J. Gallick (1963) "Images of an Arab City", *A.I.P. Journal*, 29, 179-198.
14. Lee (1964) "Psychology and Living Space", *Transactions of the Bartlet Society*, 2, 1136.
15. Carr and Schissler (1969) "The City as a Trip : Perceptual Selection and Memory in the View from the Road", *Environment and Behaviour*, 1, 7-35.
16. R.M. Downs (1970) The Cognitive Structure of the Shopping Center", *Environment and Behaviour*, 2, 13-39.
17. Golledge, Briggs, and Demko (1969) "The Configuration of Distance in Intra-urban Space", *Proceedings of the Association of American Geographers*, 1, 60-65.
18. P. Orleans (1973) "Differential Cognition of Urban Residents : The Effects of Social Scale on Mapping" in *Image and Environment Cognitive Mapping and Spatial Behaviour*, R.M. Downs and D. Stea (Eds).
19. Golledge and Zannaras (1973) "Cognitive Approaches to the Analysis of Human Spatial Behaviour" in *Environment and Cognition*, Willian A. Ittleson (Ed.).
20. F.C. Ladd (1970) "Black Users View Their Environment : Neighbourhood Maps", *Environment and Behaviour* 2, 74-79.
21. Spencer, D. (1973) An Evaluation of Cognitive Mapping in Neighbourhood Perception, Research Memorandum 23, Birmingham, Eng. Centre for Urban and Regional Studies.
22. Southward M. (1969) "The Sonic Environment of Cities", *Environment and Behaviour*, 1, 49-70.
23. Steinitz. C (1968) "Meaning and Congruence of urban Form and Activity", *Journal of the American Institute of Planners*, 34, 233-48.
24. Appleyard (1973), op., cit. 109-14
25. Johns E. (1969) "Symmetry and Asymmetry in the Urban Scene", *Area*, 2, 48, 57.
26. Sarre, P.V. (1972) "Perception", Unit 16 in New Trends in geography, Milton Keyness : Open University, 10-43.

27. Gooday, B. (1971) Perception of Environment, Occasional Paper 17, Birmingham, Eng., *Centre for Urban and Regional Studies*, University of Birmingham.
28. Pocock, D.C.D. (1975) Durham : Images of a Cathedral City, Occasional Publication (New series) 6, Durham : Department of Geography, University of Durham.
29. Gold, op. cit., 100.
30. Lynch (1960) op. cit.
31. Cullen, G. (1961) *Townscape*, London : Architectural Press.

PART ONE

EMERGENCE OF ENVIRONMENTAL PSYCHOLOGY

TWO

DANIEL STOKOLS

ENVIRONMENTAL PSYCHOLOGY

AT a time when environmentalists and economists are proclaiming that "small is beautiful" (383, 389), the research literature on human behavior in relation to its environmental settings continues to expand at a staggering rate. The rapid expansion of environmental psychology can be gauged by the diversity and sheer quantity of publications that have appeared since Kenneth Craik's 1973 review of this area in the present series (92). During the past 5 years (from early 1972 through early 1977), no fewer than ten text books (13, 72, 151, 194, 214, 271, 306, 307a, 344, 372) and six edited readers (160, 210, 320, 352, 360, 400) were published, all of which pertain to the interface between human behavior and the sociophysical environment. In addition, two multiple volume series designed to communicate significant theoretical and methodological advances in the field (15, 16, 41) were established, while more than 30 "state of the art" monographs and edited volumes on specific topics within the environment-and-behavior area appeared (5, 18, 33, 39, 42, 82, 89, 96, 102, 115, 116, 135, 157 172, 176, 179, 212, 259, 264, 276, 304, 305, 307, 315, 318, 324, 388, 389, 408, 415, 426, 433, 443, 453, 490, 494). Also during the same period, numerous reviews and programmatic analyses of environmental psychology were published in existing psychological, sociological, and geographical journals (11, 12, 38, 69, 95, 180, 234, 277, 349, 375, 407, 432, 437), as well as in several textbooks on social psychology (36, 158, 330, 390, 423).

Reprint from *Ann. Rev. Psychal.* 1978. 29 : 253-95

Environmental psychologists have maintained a vigorous level of professional and interdisciplinary contact as evidenced by the published proceedings of recent Environmental Design Research Association (EDRA) meetings (74, 204, 346, 347, 420, 445) and International Architectural Psychology Conferences (71, 258). As a further indication of the vitality of the field, the existing journal of *Environment and Behavior* (470), and newsletters on *Man-Environmental Systems* (133) and *Architectural Psychology* (270) were supplemented by the founding of a new journal entitled *Environmental Psychology and Nonverbal Behavior* (269). Moreover, the American Psychological Association (APA) established a Task Force on Environment and Behavior in 1974, which compiled an inventory of environment-behavioral researchers[a] and prepared a comprehensive report on curriculum and research developments in the environment-and-behavior field (455). The graduate curriculum chapter of this report, as of January 1977, listed more than 60 universities within Canada, the United States and Great Britain which provide either formal or informal graduate training programs in various subspecialities of human-environment studies (137). And as further testimony to the growing interest among psychologists in environmental research, APA now incorporates a formal division (Division 34) of "Population and Environmental Psychology". This group currently publishes a newsletter (144), and in March 1977 established a journal entitled *Population : Behavioral, Social, and Environmental Issues* (428), which will provide a new outlet for research on population and environmental psychology.

Though it is a simple matter to chart the quantitative growth of environmental psychology over the past 5 years, an assessment of the scientific quality and coherence of this area is considerably more difficult. A major complexity in this regard is that the boundaries of the field are not easily delimited. The study of human behavior in relation to the environment, broadly speaking, would seem to encompass all areas within psychology, let alone most of the behavioral sciences. To what extent then does environmental psychology comprise a unique domain of scientific inquiry ?

The present review assumes that the substantive concerns of environmental psychology are distinguishable from those of other areas of psychological research in some important respects, and can be framed within a broad interdisciplinary context. First, in contrast to most subareas of psychology, environmental psychology (and in particular, ecological psychology) brings an ecological perspective to the study of environment and behavior. Accordingly, the environment is construed in multidimensional, molar terms, and the focus of analysis generally is on the interrelations among people and their sociophysical milieu (11, 30, 212, 233, 350) rather than on the linkages between discrete stimuli and behavioral responses (167, 402, 446). It should be noted, though, that much of the research in this field has attempted to isolate physical dimensions (*e.g.*, noise, temperature, space) of the broader milieu in order to assess their specific effects on behavior.

Second, environmental psychology places greater emphasis on the utilization of scientific strategies in developing solutions to community-environmental problems than do most other areas within psychology.[b] This fusion of "basic" and "applied" perspectives, in the Lewinian tradition (278), is reflected in research on topics such as social impact assessment (480), perceived environmental quality (96), and urban stress (168). And third, owing to the complexity of the large-scale, sociophysical environment and the necessity of approaching it from different levels of analysis, much of the research in environmental psychology is interdisciplinary in both its scope and implementation.

In view of the above considerations, the research concerns and strategies subsumed under the rubric of "environmental psychology" (see outline of topical areas presented below) can perhaps be best represented as parts of an emerging interdisciplinary field of environment and behavior, or "human-environment relations" (21, 95, 131). This field encompasses several diverse perspectives on environment and behavior such as human ecology (331, 360, 438), environmental and urban sociology (76, 151, 307, 479, 490), architecture (375), planning (19), natural resources management (100, 494), and behavioral geography (172, 216, 433, 453). While closely related to these areas, environmental psychology diverges from them by placing relatively greater emphasis on basic psychological processes (*e.g.*, cognition, development, personality, learning) and on individual and group (vs. societal) levels of analysis.

The present discussion emphasizes the study of environment and behavior from a psychological perspective. Thus areas such as human ecology, environmental sociology, and behavioral geography are not given systematic coverage in the ensuing discussion.

ORIGINS AND DIRECTIONS OF ENVIRONMENTAL PSYCHOLOGY

Among psychologists, scientific interest in the effects of the ecological or "geographical" environment on people was expressed several decades ago by Koffka (246), Murray (321), Brunswik (61), Tolman (430), and Chein (80). Yet prior to the emergence of environmental psychology during the late 1960s and early seventies (352, 353), the only systematic attempt among psychologists to chart the ecological environment and its impact on human behavior was undertaken by Roger Barker[c] and his colleagues (30, 32, 34).[d] Most other "environmentally oriented" psychologists directed their attention away from the molar physical environment and toward either Lewin's (278) "life space"—the psychological situation as perceived by the individual (148, 192, 235, 368, 427)—or the microenvironmental "stimuli" of perceptual and operant psychology (167, 402).

During the past decade, the "doomsday" predictions of demographers (128, 303), the shrinkage of natural resources (including funding opportunities), and the deterioration of environmental quality prompted widespread concern about the constraints of the ecological environment. Suddenly psychologists "rediscovered" the large-scale physical environmental and, in collaboration with architects and planners, became increasingly involved in studying its impact on behavior.

As psychologists turned their attention to the study of behavior in relation to the built and natural environment, they encountered several engaging conceptual and methodological issues that had been left unresolved by the mainstream of behavioral science. Some of the more crucial of these issues or "gaps" were (*a*) the lack of an adequate taxonomy of environments (385) which made it difficult to assess the comparability of behavioral observations gathered in different situations and to gauge the ecological validity (62) of both laboratory and field studies ; (*b*) the lack of alternative theoretical perspectives from which to approach the complex, dynamic transactions between people and their everyday settings (save for Barker's ecological psychology) ; and (*c*) the restricted range of methodologies available for observing the behavior of individuals and groups within naturally occurring settings (465). Ongoing attempts by psychologists, design practitioners, and other researchers to confront these issues largely account for the current vitality and directions of environmental psychology (though environmentalist and societal concerns continue to play a role in shaping the course of research in this field).

At present, several trends can be discerned within environmental psychology and within the environment-and-behavior field at large. First, the interdisciplinary and problem-oriented nature of the field has fostered a high degree of methodological eclecticism (337, 364). A creative blend of observational, self-report, math-modeling, and simulation strategies has been employed in studying such issues as environmental cognition (115, 212, 315), environmental assessment (96, 302, 490, 494), and human response to environmental stressors (169, 369).

Second, environment-behavioral research reflects an increasing emphasis on the assessment of ecological validity, or the extent to which phenomena studies in one situation are representative of those occurring in other settings (62, 464). Recent studies of human crowding, for example, have been conducted within diverse laboratory and naturalistic settings and have emphasized the situation-specific nature of human reactions to high density (5, 13, 39, 42, 157, 414, 422).

Third, in their efforts to integrate diverse theoretical perspectives, researchers in the environment-and-behavior field have increasingly combined existing psychological theories of cognitive development, personality, interpersonal processes, and human learning with the assumptions of systems theory (129, 440). Altman's (12) "social-unit" approach to the study of environment and behavior, for instance, provides a synthesis of social psychological theory and the concepts of equilibrium, adaptation, stress, and coping. Other theorists (55, 212, 227, 238, 265a, 266, 291, 339, 429, 444) have called for the development of dynamic, "transactional" models which emphasize the bidirectional relationship between environment and behavior.

Fourth, increasing attention has been paid to the importance of psychological or "perceived" control over the environment and behavioral freedom as determinants of human well-being (23, 168, 227, 263, 272, 388, 485). A growing number of laboratory and naturalistic studies (84, 252, 361, 381, 393) suggests the existence of a pervasive human need for environmental control which plays a crucial role in determining the quality and intensity of people's reactions to their milieu. But the relative importance of different dimensions of control (*e.g.*, perceived vs. actual control, over physical vs. social features of the environment), as well as cross-cultural variations in the salience of these dimensions, remains to be examined in future research.

Fifth, the concept of "behavior-environment congruence" (220, 307a, 456) is becoming increasingly important as a theoretical and environmental design tool (255, 259, 305, 394, 415). To the extent that personal and cultural mediators of human response to the environment can be identified, it may be possible to develop criteria for designing environments that are maximally supportive of users' goals and activities.

While the eclectic nature of environmental research has, in many instances, promoted a creative synthesis of approaches, it also has resulted in widespread confusion and controversy over what should be the major concerns (*e.g.*, "applied" vs. "basic" issues) and theoretical orientation of the field. Environmental psychology has been racked by repeated arguments among architects, urban planners, and behavioral scientists as to whether design-oriented or theoretically focused approaches should be emphasized (11, 21, 95, 354, 419). And among proponents of the latter approach, heated debates have ensued over whether the environment should be construed in objective (30, 88, 99, 178, 475) or subjective terms, (115, 214, 227, 315, 355), and whether the occupants of behavior settings should be viewed as passive objects or active modifiers of environmental forces (213, 474).

Currently, environmental psychology is comprised of several diverse research areas which vary widely in their respective positions along the theoretical vs. applied continuum, their conceptualizations of the environment, and their emphases on alternative modes of human-environment interchange. The rather formidable task of the ensuing discussion is to assess the independent status of these research areas, as well as their present or potential linkages.

TOPICAL AREAS WITHIN ENVIRONMENTAL PSYCHOLOGY

There are a number of possible approaches that might be adopted in attempting to represent the diverse areas within environmental psychology. At one extreme, these areas could be viewed simply as an aggregation of unrelated and loosely defined research concerns whose only commonality is their joint relevance to the issue of human-environment relations. At the other extreme, they might be construed as integrated parts of an over-arching theory of environment and behavior—a scientific paradigm (257) characterized by a high degree of professional consensus regarding terminology, theory, methodology, and research priorities.

Environmental psychology at the present time appears to be more than an assortment of loosely defined problem areas but less than a comprehensive, coherent paradigm. Craik (95), for example, has characterized environmental psycho logy as an array of multiple scientific paradigms, each of which is organized around a set of exemplary achievements and an agreed-upon agenda of worthwhile puzzles for future research. Areas such as environmental cognition, environmental assessment, and ecological psychology are viewed as highly coh erent domains by virtue of either their firm grounding in the traditional paradigms of psychological research (*e.g.*, cognition, development, personality) of their exemplary and novel contributions (*e.g.*, Barker's analysis of behavior settings). As for the interrelations among these areas, Craik's analysis suggests that opportunities for "paradigm-merging" exist, but that the prospects of developing a comprehensive paradigm of human-environment relations are remote.

The present review, building upon Craik's (95), will emphasize those areas within environmental psychology that have achieved a considerable degree of progress and agreement regarding definitional, theoretical, and methodological matters. As indicated below, the relative coherence of the areas varies, and not all research in the field is area-specific. Nonetheless, an emphasis on the more active and focused research components should provide a reasonably representative view of the field's development and current concerns.

At the same time, an attempt will be made to identify certain conceptual continuities or common themes that are beginning to emerge across areas. These themes suggest several questions for future research whose eventual resolution may provide the basis for developing a more integrative perspective on environment and behavior than presently exists.

MODES OF HUMAN-ENVIRONMENT TRANSACTION

One theme which appears to underlie much of the research in environmental psychology is that of *human-environment optimization* (415). The concept of environmental optimization is based on a cyclical, feedback model of human cognition and behavior (60, 227, 310, 323) and pertains broadly to human transactions with the sociophysical environment. The optimization notion assumes that people ideally strive to achieve "optimal environments", or those that maximize the fulfillment of their needs and the accomplishment of their goals and plans. In actuality, people are often forced by situational constraints to accept undesirable environmental conditions, or at best to "satisfice" (399)—*i.e.*, to achieve less than optimal improvements in their surroundings. Although environmental optimization is never realized in its ideal form, the concept is heuristically useful in emphasizing the goal-directed and cyclical nature of human-environment transactions, and in suggesting certain processes by which these transactions occur.[6]

Specifically, the optimization theme suggests that people *orient* to the environment in terms of existing information, goals, and expectations ; they *operate* on the environment in an effort to achieve their goals and maintain desired levels of satisfaction ; they *are directly affected* by environmental forces (*e.g.*, situational supports, constraints) ; and they *evaluate* the quality of the environment as a context for future activity and goal attainment. These processes presumably occur within individuals, groups, and communities. This discussion places greatest emphasis on person-environment transactions, but also suggests the relevance of optimization processes to analyses of group and community-environment transactions.

The above processes can be characterized in terms of two basic dimensions : 1. *cognitive* (or symbolic) vs. *behavioral* (or physical) *forms* of transaction ; and 2. *active* vs. *reactive phases* of transaction. These dimensions essentially concern the extent to which cognitive representations (*e.g.*, beliefs, attitudes, cognitive maps) or physical and social features of the environment (*e.g.*, material objects, other people, rules) either influence or are themselves modified by the individual. Taken together, these dimensions yield four *modes* of human-environment transaction : 1. *interpretive* (active-cognitive) ; 2. *evaluative* (reactive-cognitive) ; 3. *operative* (active-behavioral) ; and 4. *responsive* (reactive-behavioral). The first mode involves the individual's cognitive representation or construction of the environment ; the second, his evaluation of the situation against predefined standards of quality ; the third, his movement through or direct impact on the environment ; and fourth, the environment's effects on the individual's behavior and well-being.

In the ensuing discussion, the various modes of human-environment transaction will be used as a basis for representing some of the major areas of environmental psychology in terms of their respective emphases. For instance, ecological psychology which emphasizes the impact of behavior-setting forces on people focuses most heavily on the responsive mode of human-environment interchange, whereas research on cognitive mapping places much greater emphasis on the interpretive mode (see Table 2.1).

TABLE 2.1 : **Modes of human-environment transaction and related areas of research**

		Form of Transaction	
		*Cognitive**	*Behavioral*
Phase of Transaction	*Active*	*Interpretive* Cognitive representation of the spatial environment Personality and the environment	*Operative* Experimental analysis of ecologically relevant behavior Human spatial behavior (Proxemics)
	Reactive	*Evaluative* Environmental attitudes Environmental assessment	*Responsive* Impact of the physical environment Ecological psychology

* In the present schema, the term "cognitive" refers to both informational and affective processes.

One implication of the proposed representation of the field is that most research areas typically have focused on a single mode (in some cases two or three, but rarely all four) of human-environment interchange.[f] Consequently, most theoretical orientations tend to overemphasize particular aspects of this interchange while ignoring or downplaying the possibility that the form and directionality of human-environment relations shift over time in a dynamic and cyclical pattern. Thus some important directions for future research are to link, conceptually and empirically, the various modes of human-environment transaction and to describe their patterns of occurrence both within and across different kinds of settings.

The proposed categorization of transactional modes is presented simply as a preliminary, descriptive schema rather than a predictive model. No assumptions are made about the sequence in which the different modes occur (at times two or more modes may occur simultaneously) or their relative duration in different situations. Also, it is recognized that the boundaries between the various modes are not always clear and distinct (hence the use of dotted rather than solid lines to separate the cells of the matrix in Table 2.1). For example, although attitudes toward the environment reflect judgments of environmental quality, they also mediate more active cognitive and behavioral processes. Thus the proposed categorization of research areas is somewhat arbitrary and at best representative of certain major emphases within each area.

With these qualifications stated, the following areas of human-environment research will be considered : (*a*) cognitive representation of the spatial environment and (*b*) personality and the environment (interpretive mode) ; (*c*) environmental attitudes and (*d*) environmental assessment (evaluative mode) ; (*e*) experimental analysis of ecologically relevant behavior and (*f*) human spatial behavior (operative mode) ; (*g*) impact of the physical environment and (*h*) ecological psychology (responsive mode). In reviewing each of these areas, an attempt is made to highlight theoretical and empirical trends, as well as priorities for future research.

Interpretive mode

Cognitive representation of the spatial environment

Perhaps spurred on by the so-called "cognitive revolution" in psychology (107), geography (172,432), and other fields, research on human comprehension of the molar environment has become one of the most active areas within environmental psychology. Recent work in this area reflects substantial progress in confronting definitional issues and in establishing a theoretical context for research. Basic distinctions have been drawn between *environmental cognition*, the perceptual, cognitive, and affective processes by which people come to know the sociophysical environment, and *cognitive mapping* (or spatial cognition), a more restrictive category involving those processes by which people acquire, code, store, recall, and decode information about the locations and attributes of phenomena within the spatial environment (115, 315). Also, *fundamental spatial cognition* (the perception of objects in space) has been distinguished from *macro-spatial cognition* (cognitive representation of the molar environment) (186, 212) ; and the hypothetical construct "cognitive map" (mental image of the spatial environment) has been differentiated from more encompassing "cognitive schemata" (*e.g.*, goals, beliefs, and attitudes) (323, 432),[g] and from externalized products or probes of cognitive representations (*e.g.*, sketch maps, repertory grids, verbal way-finding tasks) (115, 315).

Research on spatial cognition over the past 5 years has become increasingly anchored in psychological theories of cognitive development and functioning. Hart and Moore (186) and Siegel and White (397) provided comprehensive analyses of the development of spatial cognition based on the theories of Piaget (342) and Werner (452), while S. Kaplan (227) presented a conceptualization of cognitive mapping involving an integration of Darwinian assumptions and Hebb's (190) neural-net theory. And in line with the constructivist theories of Bruner (60), Kelly (236), and Neisser (323), an increasing emphasis has been placed on the interdependencies among perceptual and cognitive processes of environmental comprehension (212, 274, 314).

At a methodological level, several important developments can be noted. First, use of the sketch map as a probe of cognitive processes has been refined in several respects : (*a*) techniques for the measurement of relational and locational distortions in handdrawn maps have been devised (45, 367, 410, 435), though the relative validity and reliability of these techniques remain to be assessed ; (*b*) control measures pertaining to graphic ability and spatial aptitude have been added to the analysis of sketch maps (367) ; (*c*) Lynch's (289) taxonomy of environmental elements has been elaborated upon as exemplified by recent analyses of landmarks in terms of their visual and functional salience (2, 110, 146, 201, 225, 309) ; and (*d*) progress has been made toward the development of a cartographic mapping language (483) and the assessment of its effects on the graphic organization of spatial knowledge (45). At the same time, the use of sketch maps to assess spatial knowledge has been supplemented by a wide range of additional techniques including toy modeling (54, 410), photographic recognition (309), verbal wayfinding tasks (314), multidimensional and psychophysical scaling of subjective distance estimates, environmental ratings and activity patterns (58, 65, 70, 162, 171, 184, 251, 327), and factor analysis of repertory grid and semantic differential responses (185, 205, 418).

The current literature on spatial cognition reflects a number of substantive emphases and some emerging trends. First, the notion that spatial cognition develops ontogenetically from egocentric to coordinated-reference systems of orientation (186, 342) has received empirical support in recent studies (2, 146). Second, the microgenetic, or short-term development of spatial cognition has received increasing research attention, with several studies indicating that heightened familiarity with an area is associated with more detailed and hierarchically organized sketch maps (45, 110, 314, 435). An intriguing study by Wofsey, Rierdan & Wapner (472), however, emphasizes that the microgenesis of cognitive mapping and the form of successive sketch maps are strongly influenced by significant changes in the individual's orientation to the environment (*e.g.*, plans to move to a new area). Third, a variety of personal and cultural variables (sex, socioeconomic level, nationality, ethnic identity) appear to play an important role in the development and expression of cognitive mapping abilities (18, 154, 224, 298, 367, 410), but the possibility remains that these relationships can be accounted for by underlying covariates such as mobility patterns (18, 489) and relative proximity to various areas of the environment (90, 174, 175, 287, 372). And fourth, several studies have combined verbal, graphic, and behavioral assessments of spatial orientation and generally have found substantial overlap between these measures (70, 202, 208, 224, 327, 358).

Priorities for future research include the further assessment of: (*a*) sociocultural factors in spatial cognition (165, 356); (*b*) the effects of environmental surrogates and simulation techniques on the development of spatial cognition and behavior (115, 224, 435); (*c*) the validity and reliability of verbal, graphic, and behavioral assessments of environmental orientation (170, 207, 285); and (*d*) the cognitive and behavioral "spillover effects" (*e.g.*, on creativity, mood, empathy, altruism) of environmental simulations, and other exercises designed to broaden cognitive mapping abilities (115). The latter priority suggests the potential design and planning implications of research on spatial cognition which only recently have been subjected to empirical assessment (18). Also, the further extension of psychological research on various aspects of fundamental spatial cognition, including picture memory (293) and selective attention (51), to the study of macrospatial cognition remains as a promising avenue for future research.

Personality and the environment

Whereas the study of spatial cognition emphasizes the processes by which people in general construe the environment, research on personality and the environment focuses on the unique organization and expression of these processes within specific individuals. In recent reviews, Craik (92, 94, 95) noted at least two major thrusts of personality research in environmental psychology : (*a*) the conceptualization and measurement of environmental dispositions (personal styles of relating to the everyday physical environment) ; and (*b*) the utilization of established personality inventories to predict people's use and modification of the physical environment, as well as its reciprocal impact on them.

Several self-report inventories have been developed in recent years to assess environmental dispositions such as "pastoralism" and "urbanism" (301), "privacy preference" (296), "thing-person orientation" (282), "sensation-seeking" (496) and "arousal-seeking" (304, 305) tendencies, and sensitivity to noise (449). In addition, behavioral and projective measures of "close vs. far personal space" have been employed (6, 91, 114, 118). Some of the findings associated with this research are that high-arousal seekers react more pleasurably to complex situations than do low-arousal seekers (305), and that persons who characteristically maintain greater distance between themselves and others are more likely to experience physiological stress under conditions of high density (6) and to exhibit task-performance deficits following exposure to high-density situations (114), than are those who maintain close distances. While some measures of environmental dispositions have undergone considerably psychometric evaluation and refinement (296, 301), all of them must be tested in a wider variety of situations before their predictive and construct validity can be established.

In attempting to forecast individual behavior and experiences with regard to the environment, environmental psychologists have also utilized more established theories and measures of personality. For instance, the dimension of internal vs. external

(I-E) locus of control (368) has been found to be significantly related to individuals' engagement in ecologically relevant behavior. Specifically, internals were more likely to participate in antipollution activities (275, 431) and to implement birth control methods (3, 290), although at least one recent study failed to find a relationship between I-E and contraceptive success (386). And in a prospective study of Planned Parenthood clinic participants, a measure of future-time perspective (411) was found to be predictive of individuals' freedom from unwanted pregnancies (312).

With regard to the effects of the environment on individual experiences, several studies indicate that the dimensions of I-E and coronary-prone (Type A) behavior (497) may mediate the intensity of individuals' reactions to stressful situations (169, 273), but the reported relationships are highly complex and seem to depend on the situational context in which they are observed. In short-term laboratory situations, for example, external individuals as compared to internals required greater interpersonal distance between themselves and strangers (118) and were more susceptible to the experience of "learned helplessness" (388) following exposure to uncontrollable environmental events (86, 200). However, within longer-term residential situations, particularly where living conditions were perceived as cramped or constraining, internals manifested greater interpersonal distance requirements (37) and lower levels of adjustment and life satisfaction (147) than did externals. In regard to the coronary-prone behavior pattern, preliminary evidence (169, 252) suggests that Type A (impatient, job-involved, hard-driving) individuals strive harder to avoid loss of control over the environment, but under conditions of extreme or prolonged uncontrollability, they tend to relinquish their efforts to reassert control more readily than their Type B counterparts.

On the whole, the above findings reflect certain gaps in the existing literature and suggest priorities for future research. First, previous research on personality and the environment has been guided almost exclusively by trait models of human behavior, and consequently has failed to consider the situational modifiers of person-environment relationships (467). A shift of emphasis from trait-centered analyses toward "interactionist" models (55, 130, 291, 313), in which situational and personal antecedents of behavior are equally emphasized, might provide the basis for a more adequate understanding of the cross-situational variability in personality-environment linkages. The crucial dimensions of situations must be identified, however, before person-by-situation interactions can be adequately assessed. The tasks of dimensionalizing and codifying situations point towards the possible utility of linking personality-based analyses with other areas of environmental research, such as ecological psychology, in which attempts have been made to categorize situations in terms of their behaviorally relevant dimensions (33, 317, 348). In an initial attempt to link personality and ecological approaches, Eddy and Sinnett (124) studied the relationship between assessments of college students' introversion-extroversion and their participation in campus behavior settings. Results indicated that students' selection of settings and preferred activities varied in relation to personal orientations, with extroverts spending more time in settings offering opportunities for social contact.

Another priority for future research is the consideration of temporal and developmental mediators of personal orientation toward the environment. The importance of these factors is suggested by recent evidence that individual preference for environmental stimulation (477) and susceptibility to learned helplessness and depression (241) are related to the complexity and controllability of previously experienced environments; that hospitalization rates among certain clinical groups may be affected by the "supportiveness" of their home neighborhood (403); and that elderly persons are more likely to exhibit patterns of "environmental disengagement" (466) and preferences for lower levels of environmental stimulation (111) than younger individuals. Further elucidation of the situational and developmental determinants of personal orientations toward the environment may yield criteria for designing environments that are congruent with the goals and activities of diverse user groups (94, 284).

Evaluative mode

Environmental attitudes

Evaluation processes, or the ways in which people judge the quality of their surroundings, have been examined most directly in research on environmental attitudes and assessment. Like studies of cognitive mapping and personality, those pertaining to environmental attitudes and assessment have investigated people's internal (cognitive/affective) representations of the environment. But the latter studies have been more explicitly concerned with the evaluative and informational content of environmental perceptions, and with the role that these perceptions play in prompting behavioral attempts to improve the environment.

Research on environmental attitudes (*i.e.*, tendencies to respond favorably or unfavorably to one's milieu) has focused on two major issues : (*a*) public attitudes and knowledge regarding environmental problems (*e.g.*, pollution, depletion of resources) ; and (*b*) the degree of consistency among individuals' attitudes, beliefs and behavior relevant to the improvement of environmental conditions. Investigations of the first issue generally have employed survey research methods to assess public opinion about the environment and to identify the socio-economic and demographic correlates of environmental concern. Maloney, Ward and Braucht (292), for example, developed and refined a 45-item questionnaire to measure individual's ecological attitudes and knowledge. Other investigators, utilizing data from national opinion polls, have documented the upsurge of public concern about environmental problems (especially in the United States) during the mid-1960s (132, 281), and more recently, the increased resistance to environmental reforms voiced by certain segments of the population (9, 120, 398). The findings from both national and regional surveys conducted in the United States further suggest that environmental concern is most pronounced among people who are liberal and activist in their political orientation (119, 245), highly educated, and affluent (281, 311). Affluent individuals with vested interests in pollution-causing industries, however, are more likely to oppose rather than support proenvironmental reforms (10, 281).

During acute energy crises and resource shortages, expressions of environmental concern have been accompanied by increased conservationist behavior (98, 281). Nonetheless, most individuals (even those concerned about environmental quality) have expressed a general unwillingness to maintain reduced levels of resource conservation on a permanent basis (98, 281, 329). The discrepancy between environmental concern and individuals' reluctance to curb their consumption of resources has been attributed by some researchers either to mistaken beliefs or to insufficient knowledge about environmental problems. Donohue, Olien and Tichenor (113) found that people are overly optimistic about the ability of government and industry to solve current environmental problems. And a survey of ecological knowledge conducted in Britain. Hungary, and Yugoslavia (254) revealed that most respondents were unaware of the causes and health-related effects of atmospheric pollutants. Aso, research conducted by Heberlein (191) suggests that people are more likely to engage in ecologically responsible behavior when they are knowledgeable about the human consequences of pollution.

The degree of consistency among environmental attitudes, beliefs, and behavior has been examined in both correlational and experimental studies, many of which have been based on social psychological theories of attitude change. For instance, Crawford (97) and Davidson and Jaccard (103) examined the relationships between contraceptive attitudes, beliefs, and behavior in terms of Rosenberg's (363) affective-cognitive consistency theory and Fishbein's (153) model of behavioral intentions, respectively. Generally these studies found that the perceived consequences or beliefs about birth control were significantly correlated with attitudes toward contraception, intentions to engage in contraceptive behavior, and reported contraceptive use. A number of quasi-experimental studies also have been conducted in recent years (22a, 209, 447). In one such study, individuals' attitudes toward the Sierra Club were predictive of their willingness to join or support the club five months later (447). In other investigations, workers' attitudes toward recycling were predictive of their behavioral compliance with an experimental waste-paper sorting program sponsored by their company (209) ; and an environmental education program was found to promote conservation behavior among fifth-graders over a 2-year period (22a).

The future development of research in this area is likely to be facilitated by its integration with other paradigms and perspectives in environmental psychology. Attitudinal research has been widely utilized in the contexts of environmental design and assessment (see next section), but the potential linkages of this research with other approaches, including ecological psychology and operant analyses of proenvironmental behavior (see relevant sections below), have not been explored. For example, the combination of behavior-setting (29) and attitudinal surveys would yield a more comprehensive assessment of the interplay between environmental attitudes and behavior than would the use of either approach by itself. Also, informational and persuasive appeals might be effectively combined with reinforcement strategies to promote ecologically responsible behavior among community members (87). In the context of transportation planning, "market segmentation" techniques based on attitudinal surveys have been used to identify automobile commuters who would be most responsive to incentives for joining car pools (206) or for riding buses (357). These studies point toward the development of informational and incentive programs to promote ecological well-being that would be tailored to the needs, abilities, and preferences of specific community groups. Additional directions for research include the further analysis of attitude-behavioral consistency in relation to environmental issues (63, 447), and the development of transactional theories (238) which emphasize the reciprocal relationship between environmental attitudes and behavior.

Environmental assessment

Research on environmental assessment is concerned not only with people's attitudes toward their present surroundings, but also with their preferences regarding the shape of future environments. A basic assumption of this research is that people judge the adequacy of existing or potential settings in terms of predefined standards of environmental quality (96, 415, 427). To the extent that these standards are made explicit, the design of behaviorally supportive environments can be facilitated.

The expansion of assessment research in recent years coincides with increased public concern over environmental deterioration (see preceding section) and with the passage of legislation in various countries (*e.g.*, the 1969 National Environmental Policy Act in the United States and the 1971 Town and Country Planning Act in Britain requiring the evaluation of proposed environmental changes in terms of their potential community impact. The major thrusts of assessment research can be grouped according to their respective emphases on physical, social, or sociophysical dimensions of the environment. Physical assessments, for example, have focused on the perceived quality of buildings (1, 199), landscapes (17, 100, 222, 493, 494), and of air, water and noise (49, 77, 96). Social assessments have focused on the interpersonal "climate" within organizational and institutional settings (163, 166, 211, 217, 317, 318). And sociophysical assessments have involved appraisals of neighborhood and housing quality (64, 89, 294, 307a, 328, 403, 491), as well as forecasting community impacts resulting from technological and social interventions (52, 75, 478, 480).

In addition to categorizing and selecting environmental dimensions for study, assessment researchers have developed and compared various means of presenting environmental displays (*e.g.*, simulations) and of measuring observers' evaluative responses. Also, investigators have begun to examine the complex, interactive effects of setting properties, measurement techniques, and observer attributes on judgments of environmental quality (20, 93, 96). Substantial progress has been made in the area of environmental simulation. McKechnie (302) developed a useful typology of simulations distinguishing among those that are static (*e.g.*, photograph) vs. dynamic (*e.g.*, movie), and concrete (*e.g.*, scale model) vs. abstract (*e.g.*, computer modeling of environmental impacts). Much of the research on assessment of buildings and landscapes has utilized static simulations such as color photographs, and suggests that observers' responses to such displays are moderately predictive of their on-site reactions (100, 199, 392, 495).

Concurrently, dynamic simulations have been developed to study people's reactions to urban and rural landscapes (1, 20, 26, 228, 435). One such project (20) is equipped with a computer-guided video camera which provides simulated tours (via TV monitor and videotape) through a scale-model neighborhood.

Preliminary data from this project indicate a high degree of correspondence between observers' evaluations of the simulated and actual tours (93, 302). Another study utilized 16 mm films of beach areas in conjunction with tape recordings of ambient sounds to simulate an oceanfront setting (26).

The development of dynamic simulation procedures has been accompanied by additional methodological innovations. First, semantic differential measures of perceived environmental quality (1, 199) have been supplemented by a wide array of behavioral and perceptual techniques, including Q-sort and paired comparison tasks for the assessment of scenic quality (198, 495), and psychophysical scaling procedures for the judgment of noise, temperature, air quality, and landscape value (26, 49, 77). Also, behavioral-mapping procedures (215) have been used to assess occupants' reactions to residential environments (44, 203, 491), playgrounds (189) and specialized work settings (197, 488).

A second methodological trend reflected in recent research is the systematic sampling of different respondent groups. The data from this research suggest, for example, that inhabitants tend to rate their surroundings more favorably than visitors (1) ; that environmental design specialists and nonexpert groups of comparable income and social status are quite similar in their appraisals of landscape quality (495) ; and that adolescents and young adults are more critical in their evaluations of urban beach areas than middle-age people (26).

At present, there appear to be at least two major gaps in environmental assessment research. First, the work in this area has been predominantly atheoretical. As Weinstein (450) and Wohlwill (473) have noted, there has been an overemphasis on the construction of empirically derived models of preference (*i.e.*, factor analyses, multiple regression procedures) and too little attention paid to the development of theory. Exceptions to this trend include Wohlwill's (473) extension of Berlyne's (50) theory of aesthetics to the realm of environmental assessment, and S. Kaplan's (225) model for the prediction of landscape preference. These theories are useful in that they suggest critical determinants of environmental preference (*e.g.*, complexity, coherence, mystery) and may help to explain the observed relationship between perceived environmental quality and variables such as naturalism (229, 494), landuse compatibility (198), familiarity, and spaciousness (222). To predict the generalizability of these relationships across different settings, however, it will be necessary to extend current models through the development of a theoretically based taxonomy of environments.

A second major gap in assessment research is the lack of data concerning the relative validity of different simulation and measurement procedures (99). Obtaining validity data will require the incorporation of multiple forms of measurement in assessment studies (334) and the systematic comparison of alternative displays, respondents, and response criteria (96, 450, 473). Along these lines, a recent experiment (150) found that observers' perceptions of room size and crowding varied significantly under three different modes of environmental display (actual room, video tape, scale model).

As these problems are resolved, environmental assessment strategies should become increasingly important in the context of community planning. Potential applications of research in this area include : (*a*) the incorporation of Perceived Environmental Quality Indices (PEQIs) as a standard component of environmental impact analyses (96, 478, 480) ; (*b*) the use of social climate scales to gauge the psychological impact of architectural interventions (203, 461) ; and (*c*) the use of environmental simulation procedures in predicting users' response to alternative future environments (20, 302). Finally, the unexplored relationships between cognitive mapping processes, personality variables, and environmental preference suggest several opportunities for "cross-paradigm" research.

Operative mode

Experimental analysis of ecologically relevant behavior

While the above areas of research emphasize interpretive and evaluative processes in human-environment transactions, the four remaining sections focus on the ways in which people physically modify or respond to their surroundings. Until recently, environmental psychologists had given very little attention to the consequences of human activity in the environment (*e.g.*, litter, pollution, resource scarcities) or to those behaviors that produce or eliminate such products (88, 434).

The relative lack of "product-oriented" studies (88) has been in marked contrast to what some observers (99) view as an over-abundance of research focusing on the role of psychological processes in mediating environment-behavior relationships. Within the past few years, efforts to redress this imbalance have yielded one of the newest areas within environmental psychology, namely, the behavioral analysis of environmental/ecological problems. The conceptual and methodological underpinnings of this area are derived primarily from Skinnerian (402) learning theory and the techniques of applied behavioral analysis (24), but also reflect the concerns of environmental assessment research. Further integration of these perspectives may eventually lead to significant extensions of the operant paradigm in psychology. As a step in that direction, Willems's (462) critique of behavioral technology from an ecological point of view highlights the pitfalls (*e.g.*, unintended side effects) of behavioral interventions that are too narrowly conceived and illustrates the advantages of linking operant perspectives with those of ecological psychology and environmental assessment.

Comprehensive reviews of empirical work in this area have been provided by Cone and Hayes (88) and Tuso and Geller (434). As these authors note, a combination of within- and between-subjects experimental designs has been used to assess the behavioral dimensions of two major community problems: environmental degradation and resource management. Overall, the findings from this research clearly indicate that environmental problems can be reduced through behavioral modification strategies. Littering, for example, has been decreased in various settings through antilitter prompts (*e.g.*, printed messages on disposable materials (164) and by providing rewards for the proper disposal of trash (81, 188, 247, 345). Also, prompting and reward strategies have been implemented to promote newspaper recycling (288, 359), the use of public transportation systems (141-143), and energy conservation in private households (187, 248, 468, 469).

As for the relative impact of alternative interventions, the provision of cash rewards or special privileges on a response-contingent basis appears to be the most potent means of encouraging proenvironmental behavior (141, 187), whereas the mere dissemination of information (*e.g.*, energy conservation manuals) has been the least effective strategy (187, 248). Moreover, in the absence of material contingencies, social praise (384) and the provision of verbal or written feedback to families about their rate of electricity usage (187, 248, 387, 468, 469) have been moderately effective in reducing levels of energy consumption. The independent effects of reward and feedback on patterns of energy use have been demonstrated both within self-selected (volunteer) and randomly chosen households (187).

If these and related experimental findings are to be implemented at a community level, then several practical and theoretical issues must be addressed in future research. First, unlike short-term demonstration studies, community interventions must be cost-effective. Possible strategies for developing economically feasible programs are suggested by (*a*) the proven impact of social reinforcement and feedback on conservation behavior ; (*b*) evidence that intermittent levels of reinforcement may be as effective as continuous schedules in promoting proenvironmental behavior (108, 247) ; (*c*) successful development of automated and remote reinforcement systems (345) ; and (*d*) current efforts to pretest community interventions via simulation procedures (143).

Second, criteria for defining acceptable levels of environmental quality and energy consumption must be derived largely from nonbehavioral or "reactive" studies (88) incorporating attitudinal, perceptual, and physiological measures. Also, preintervention assessment of perceived environmental quality (96) might make proposed programs more congruent with citizens' needs and ultimately more acceptable to them. Third, the extension of an ecosystems perspective (419, 462) to the design of behavioral interventions might help to avoid certain desirable outcomes such as the reinforcement of trash production (78) or the promotion of bus ridership among pedestrians rather than automobile drivers (142). Finally, the effectiveness of small-scale experimental interventions in promoting environmental quality and resource conservation suggests the value of approaching other environmental problems, such as overpopulation (492), from an applied behavioral perspective.

Human spatial behavior

The central concern of *proxemics* (181, 406) is the matter in which people use space as a means of regulating social interaction. This issue has been examined in relation to at least four basic phenomena : (*a*) ***privacy***, the control of others' access to oneself ; (*b*) ***personal space***, the maintenance of an intrusion-resistant zone around oneself ; (*c*) ***territoriality***, the personalization, ownership, and defense of areas and objects ; and (*d*) ***crowding***, the desire for reduced contact with others arising from spatial and/or social interferences.[h]

The quantitative growth of proxemic research is reflected in recent literature reviews, one of which (13) cites over 200 empirical studies of personal space as of 1975, while another (422) reviews nearly 100 studies of human crowding, most of which were completed during 1974-76. This prodigious research effort has been accompanied by several conceptual developments. First, attempts have been made to refine existing proxemic concepts, to develop new ones, and to examine their interrelationships. For example, the differences between personal space and territory, and between animal and human territoriality, have been considered (13, 126); physical density has been distinguished from the experience of crowding (13, 109, 134, 413, 436) ; and the concept of "group space", an analogue of personal space, has been developed (243, 244). At the same time, the conceptual linkages between privacy, territoriality, personal space, and crowding have been emphasized (13, 139, 336). Altman's (13) model of proxemic behavior, for example, views personal space and territoriality as "boundary-regulation" mechanisms designed to maintain a balance between desired and achieved levels of privacy, and crowding as an experience in which desired privacy exceeds achieved privacy.

Second, recent analyses (13, 39, 126, 336, 424) place greater emphasis on the cognitive, psychological, and social underpinnings of human spatial behavior than did earlier biologically oriented theories (181). The dimension of "perceived control" over the environment (23, 168, 272, 388), for instance, has become a central unifying concept in contemporary formulations of spatial behavior (295, 361, 362, 393, 394, 396, 414).

Additional conceptual and methodological developments include greater attention to the situation-specificity or proxemic phenomena (230, 336, 414, 481), increased methodological eclecticism in studying these phenomena (13, 39), and preliminary tests of the design implications of spatial research (42, 104, 109, 136, 325, 377, 394, 408, 417). Specific developments pertaining to privacy, personal space, territoriality, and crowding are briefly noted below. More thorough discussions of these trends can be found in the review articles cited under each topic.

Privacy: Three major conceptualizations of privacy have been proposed (13, 239, 261). Kelvin's (239) model defines privacy as the perceived limitation of others' power over oneself. This is distinguished from isolation, the lack of social relations imposed upon, rather than chosen by, the individual. The analysis developed by Laufer, Proshansky & Wolfe (261) emphasizes the psychological functions of privacy as they emerge throughout the life cycle and are affected by situational factors. Research derived from this model indicates age-related shifts in people's ability to define privacy (482) and the impact of institutionalization on children's privacy experiences (481). Altman's (13) boundary-regulation model focuses on behavioral strategies used to maintain desired levels of privacy. The relationship between privacy-regulation capabilities and the well-being of institutionalized elderly persons has been examined by Pastalan (333), while individual differences in preferences for privacy have been assessed by Marshall (296). Additional developments in this area are reviewed by Margulis (295).

Territoriality: Recent analyses have emphasized the cognitive and social-organizational functions of human territoriality rather than its biological (reproductive and survival-related) aspects (13, 126, 324, 425). A classification of territories based on their association with primary, secondary, and reference group functions was developed (13). Empirical findings indicate a positive correlation between occupants' use of territorial markers and their degree of attachment to an area (125, 183), reduced fear of crime (335), and respect of proprietary rights by outsiders (46). Other studies have examined the situationally determined relationship between secial dominance and territorial behavior (106, 424). Design principles have been derived from theories of territoriality (13, 325) but have received only preliminary empirical assessment (104, 324). [See (13, 126) for detailed reviews.]

Personal space : According to Argyle & Dean's (22) equilibrium theory, desired levels of involvement with others are maintained through a delicate interplay of verbal and nonverbal behaviors. Given a comfortable level of intimacy, changes in one behavioral component (*e.g.*, eye contact) will prompt compensatory changes along other dimensions (*e.g.*, interpersonal distance). While some studies have found evidence of compensation (337, 382), others have observed either reciprocal (57) or equivocal relationships (4, 73, 371) between eye contact and distance. Recently Patterson (336) proposed that the behavioral consequences of increased intimacy are mediated by arousal and emotional labeling. Thus the occurrence of either compensatory or reciprocal responses may depend on the perceived meaning of the approacher's behavior. "Inappropriate" proximity with strangers, for example, has been found to induce both physiological (308) and self-reported (127) arousal.

Hall's (181) theory of spatial zones and his empasis on cultural antecedents of personal space have received substantial empirical support (14, 182). Ethnicity, however, has been found to interact with such variables as age, gender, and family income in predicting spatial behavior (218). A variety of other individual, interpersonal, and situational determinants of personal space (*e.g.*, physical attractiveness, degree of acquaintance, standing vs. sitting) have been examined (14), but the influence of architectural factors on personal space (376) has received little empirical attention. [See (140, 280, 339, 424) for additional reviews.]

Crowding : Substantial progress has been made in refining terminology and in developing preliminary theoretical analyses of crowding. The distinction between physical density and the experience of crowding, mentioned above, as well as analyses of density in terms of its spatial, social, and perceptual components (25, 37, 40, 54a, 161, 283, 355, 373, 378, 439) exemplify definitional refinements. Recent theoretical analyses reflect both physicalistic and psychological conceptions of crowding. According to the "density-intensity" model (157) density serves merely to intensify the prevailing quality of social situations. Alternatively, psychological theories posit that high density can at times independently impair the quality of situations by promoting behavioral constraints (351, 380 412, 421), stimulation overload (42, 109, 134, 373), reduced privacy (13), overmanning (457, 458), and negatively labelled arousal resulting from personal space violation (138, 336, 484). The assumption that crowding involves a reduction of personal control over the environment is central in psychological analyses (361, 362, 393, 414), but the conditions under which reduced spatial or social control are most salient have not been identified. A recent typology suggests that crowding experiences will be most intense and difficult to resolve in primary (psychologically important) vs. secondary environments and in the context of perceived threat to personal security (413, 414). The predictive utility and design implications of the above theories, however, remain to be established empirically.

Significant empirical developments include the findings that short-term exposure to high density (with group size held constant) can heighten physiological arousal (6, 7, 138, 308) and can induce both immediate and delayed task-performance deficits (114, 138, 195, 338, 374, 393, 484). Negative effects of prolonged residential density on health and behavior have also been observed, particularly among confined or low-status groups (8, 37, 42, 54a, 101, 105, 299, 361). In addition, recent studies suggest that sex differences in reactions to crowding may be mediated by temporal and social factors, with females responding more positively to proximity with strangers in short-term situations (159, 364, 416) and more negatively under conditions of prolonged residential density (8), though normative factors may be more critical than duration of exposure in mediating these differences (231). Also, the relationship between personality and crowding sensitivity appears to be time-dependent (37). [See (39, 84, 152, 262, 380, 422) for additional reviews.]

Responsive mode

Human response to the physical environment

Research in this area has focused on the behavioral and health consequences of (*a*) environmental stressors (*e.g.*, noise, heat, pollution, high density), (*b*) the built environment (*e.g.*, housing, urban design), and (*c*) the natural environment (*e.g.*, climate, topography). Theoretical and empirical work on stress has been most extensive and therefore receives greatest emphasis in this section.

Environmental stressors : Environmental conditions operate as stressors to the extent that they tax or exceed the individual's adaptive resources (265, 389). Several studies have documented the direct effects of stressors such as noise (84, 168), extreme temperature (35, 177, 369), air pollution (319, 340, 370, 441), and high density (see preceding section) on human physiology and behavior. Noise, for example, has been found to be associated with elevated blood pressure (219), adrenalin secretion (155), skin conductance (59, 168, 256), and impaired task performance (168, 396, 448).

The major thrust of recent research has been to identify cognitive and psychological factors that mediate the impact of stressors on people. The research of Glass & Singer (168) has been particularly important in identifying the role of predictability and perceived control as determinants of response to stressors. Specifically, their research indicates that although people are able to adapt (physiologically and behaviorally) to high-intensity noise in the short run, they frequently exhibit post-noise "aftereffects" such as decreased tolerance for frustration and impaired task performance. Furthermore, when noise is predictable (periodic) or perceived as controllable, its negative aftereffects are reduced.

The differential effects of controllable and uncontrollable stressors have been documented in numerous laboratory and field investigations (23, 84, 272, 388). In lab settings, uncontrollable noise has been found to produce greater aggression (112), less helping behavior (395), and lower tolerance for frustration (168, 396) than controllable noise. Similarly, exposure to high density resulted in fewer negative aftereffects when subjects believed that they were free (vs. not free) to leave a crowded room if they so desired (393). Also, the detrimental impact of prolonged exposure to environmental stressors has been demonstrated in field investigations of the relationship between highway noise and reading ability in children (85), railroad commuting and physiological stress among urban workers (401), and the controllability of individuals' life events and their susceptibility to coronary heart disease (169).

Several theories have been proposed to account for the relationship between perceived control and response to stressors (23, 83, 168, 297, 388, 396). Cohen's (83) theory of attentional overload assumes that individuals' capacity for attention is limited (see also 221) and that uncontrollable or unpredictable stimuli require more extensive monitoring (due to their novelty, complexity) than controllable events. The former stimuli are, therefore, more likely to deplete attentional resources and to result in impaired task performance and interpersonal relations. Consistent with this theory, Wohlwill & Heft (476) found children from noisy homes to be less proficient on a selective attention task and less sensitive to auditory distraction than children from quieter homes. And in two related studies, pedestrians in noisy areas were observed to be less helpful to strangers than those in quieter areas (250, 297). These findings, while subject to arousal-based (122) as well as cognitive interpretations, are at least consistent with the notion that excessive environmental inputs result in decreased attentiveness to others' needs.

Seligman's (388) theory of learned helplessness provides an alternative explanation for the beneficial effects of perceived control. Helplessness involves a syndrome of cognitive, motivational, and emotional disturbances stemming from repeated encounters with uncontrollable events. Through exposure to such events, the individual comes to believe that personal outcomes are independent of his behavior and consequently reduces his attempts to influence the environment. Experimental studies indicate that personal expectancies for control (200, 485) and the extent to which one attributes lack of control to either task difficulty or insufficient effort (121, 241, 486) are crucial determinants of susceptibility to learned helplessness. Moreover, the amount of exposure to uncontrollable events (252, 361, 365), the aversiveness of these events (48) and the psychological importance of the situation (365, 485) have been identified as important mediators of helplessness effects. Two recent studies of the institutionalized aged (260, 381) further suggest that helplessness may be reduced and possibly reversed by providing persons greater control over various aspects of their environment (*e.g.*, the predictability of visitors).

The existing literature, while documenting the importance of cognitive and psychological determinants of stress, reveals several conceptual and empirical gaps. First, most studies have been guided by a single theoretical perspective and have not been designed to assess the relative validity of alternative models [see (396) for a notable exception]. Because the predictions of certain theories are quite similar, it becomes difficult to isolate rival explanatory mechanisms, especially when some studies focus on attentional measures, others emphasize motivational indices, and still others rely on measures of affect and arousal. The use of multiple levels of measurement and the comparative assessment of alternative theories in future research are prerequisites for developing a more comprehensive understanding of human stress than presently exists.

Second, the persistence and generalizability of stress responses across situations have not been adequately examined. The use of postexperimental assessments in field settings would be crucial in studies attempting to distinguish learned helplessness from temporary states of hyperarousal or attentional fatigue. Longitudinal research designs also would permit an assessment of broader theoretical issues that have been virtually ignored in previous research. For instance, what are the potential *costs* of perceived and actual control (*e.g.*, frustration arising from disconfirmed expectancies for control ; premature depletion of adaptive resources in the quest for *too much* control) ? Also, what are the long-term benefits of temporary exposure to unpredictable or uncontrollable situations ? In this regard, transactional theories of stress (265a, 266) and of human development (444, 452, 454) emphasize the positive relationship between environmental challenge and personal growth.

Impact of the built environment : Several studies have examined the impact of residential environments on interpersonal relations. The influence of spatial proximity on friendship patterns, observed earlier by Festinger, Schachter and Back (149), was corroborated in two recent investigations. In one study, the degree of similarity among friends was inversely related to the proximity of their apartments (322).

In the other, residential proximity was predictive of both friendly and unfriendly relations among neighbors (123).

Studies of university housing have assessed the behavioral effects of high- and low-rise dormitories on students (193). In at least two investigations, high-rise dorms were associated with less favorable evaluations of social climate (461) and with lower levels of altruistic behavior (53) than were smaller dorms. Within urban housing projects, Newman (324) found the size and height of buildings to be jointly predictive of crime rates. These data were attributed to the limited opportunities for establishing defensible space in high-rise apartment buildings, although alternative interpretations of the findings have been offered (334). And on a more positive note, Weckerle (451) observed high levels of neighboring and residential satisfaction among the inhabitants of a high-rise singles complex, presumably due to their age similarity and shared preference for establishing social contact with neighbors.

The impact of interior design on building occupants also has been demonstrated in several studies (42, 104, 203, 242, 436). Valins and Baum (436) found that the residents of corridor-design dorms were more likely to complain about crowding and forced interaction than were those living in suite-design dorms, presumably because the former design provides less shielding from unwanted social contacts. Other investigations have examined the effects of architectural renovations on residents of rehabilitative institutions (203, 242). In one study (203), the provision of increased opportunities for privacy through physical remodeling of a psychiatric ward resulted in decreased passivity and more positive social interactions among residents.

Additional areas of research include the analysis of environments from a human factors perspective (332), the effects of traditional and "open" learning environments on children (79, 82, 253, 255, 366), the effects of housing quality on health (232), and the impact of residential relocation on the elderly (333, 379). [For additional reviews, see (27, 72, 214, 249, 375).]

Impact of the natural environment: While much research has been conducted on landscape assessment (see preceding section on Environmental Assessment), the behavioral consequences of exposure to elements of the natural environment have received very little attention. Preliminary evidence suggests that involvement in the care-taking of plants may be associated with unique psychological and behavioral benefits (223, 260, 279). In one study (279), the implementation of gardening programs in low-income housing projects was associated with reduced vandalism and increased social contact among residents. In another investigation (260), nursing home residents who were assigned personal responsibility for the care-taking of a plant exhibited increased alertness and participation in social activities relative to those who did not assume this responsibility.

Researchers have begun to assess the effects of meteorological variables on behavior, but the findings from this work are quite preliminary and inconsistent (66, 319, 320). Behavioral geographers have examined motivational aspects of outdoor recreation (306a) as well as the impact of perceived natural hazards on human migration patterns (37?, 453). Also the emotional impact of natural and built environments was conceptualized by Mehrabian and Russell (305) in terms of three basic dimensions : pleasure, arousal, and dominance.

Relative to other areas of the field, research on human response to the natural environment has been sparse. The development of a theoretical framework for empirical work in this area, and the derivation of planning criteria from such research, remain as important priorities for the future.

Ecological psychology

The basic unit of analysis in ecological psychology is the *behavior setting*, a recurring pattern of human activity that takes place within specific time and space boundaries (*e.g.*, colloquium, concert, baseball game). In comparison with other areas of environmental psychology, ecological psychology places considerably greater emphasis on setting-specific rather than person-specific determinants of people's reactions to the environment. The groundbreaking efforts of Roger Barker and his colleagues (29-32, 34) identified the major features of behavior settings (*e.g.*, action patterns, personnel requirements, physical milieu) and traced the behavioral and psychological consequences of *undermanning*, a condition in which available participants are fewer than the number typically required to maintain the setting at an optimal level (*e.g.*, three rather than five persons per team in a basketball game). An important finding of this research was that students attending small schools (assumed to be more undermanned than large schools) were more likely to perform leadership and supportive roles in extracurricular activities and to experience feelings of responsibility and importance than were those enrolled in large schools (32).

The conceptualization and measurement of behavior settings have undergone considerable refinement in recent years. The concepts of "setting capacity" and "maintenance minimum", proposed by Wicker, McGrath and Armstrong (460) provide criteria for specifying conditions of *under*, *adequate*, and *overmanning* within settings, irrespective of the size of the institutions (*e.g.*, schools, churches, hospitals) in which these settings occur. Also, the distinction between "performer" and "non-performer" (or staff vs. client) roles has permitted an assessment of manning levels for different groups within the same setting (458, 460). And at a community level of analysis, Barker and Schoggen (33) developed several innovative measures for assessing the extent, variety, and productivity of human habitats. One of these measures, the "urb", is based on the number, occurrence, and duration of a town's behavior settings and reflects the range of behavioral opportunities available or "at hand" to members of a community each year. Another measure, the "productivity index" of a community, reflects the "person hours" of participation required to operate and maintain community settings for a one-year period, and the extent to which inhabitants are engaged in crucial roles (*i.e.*, "claim operations") within those settings. These and other theoretical refinements evolved from a comprehensive comparison of an English and an American town involving two year-long behavior setting surveys, conducted at each locale during 1954-55 and 1963-64.

Recent research in ecological psychology reflects significant empirical and methodological advances. First, the effects of under and overmanning on participants' behavior and experiences have been examined experimentally (183a, 341, 459).

The findings from this research indicate that members of overmanned groups feel less needed, less important, and less helpful to their group than do those of undermanned or adequately manned groups, and that these effects occur with group size held constant. Second, the influence of manning levels previously observed within schools and churches has also been found in more recent investigations of hospitals and rehabilitation centers (409), shopping areas (286), temporary environments in cold regions (44), and a national park (458). Third, progress has been made toward the empirical classification of environments based on analyses of data obtained through community-wide behavior setting surveys (33, 348). Barker and Schoggen (33), for example, suggest that behavior settings and whole communities might be categorized in terms of the major action patterns or behavioral "genotypes" (*e.g.*, professional, educational, recreational) found within them.

An important trend reflected in recent studies is the use of behavior setting surveys in developing habitability criteria, as well as social or physical interventions designed to improve behavior-environment fit. For instance, Lozar (286) attempted to increase the number of responsible staff roles within a grocery store to reduce pilferage and to increase levels of customer-staff interaction. Willems (463) measured levels of behavioral "independence" and "complexity" among paraplegic patients to assess their rehabilitative progress and the effectiveness of the therapeutic setting. Also, Wicker and Kirmeyer (458) installed a queing device at tram stops in Yosemite National Park for the purpose of reducing overmanning and stress among park visitors. Thus, while earlier conceptualizations of the behavior setting (29, 30) emphasized the natural "synomorphy" or congruence among its physical and behavioral components, more recent analyses have attempted to identify conditions of inadequate fit between people and their environments, and to develop strategies for enhancing behavior-milieu synomorphy.

The expanding interface between ecological psychology and environmental design suggests several intriguing directions for future policy-oriented research, including (*a*) the use of manning theory to resolve problems of crowding and congestion in situations where population size cannot be reduced (457);

(*b*) the intentional undermanning of organizations and institutions to increase their efficiency and productivity (43, 409) ; and (*c*) the enhancement of desired manning levels through architectural interventions [*e.g.*, the establishment of legible territorial boundaries and accessible nodes of interaction within settings ; see (267, 268, 286)]. Before the design relevance of ecological concepts and methods can be fully realized, however, major theoretical questions must be addressed. For example : (*a*) Under what conditions are settings established, modified, or terminated by their occupants ? (*b*) Do the effects of manning conditions vary in relation to personality and cultural factors (404, 459) ? (*c*) Are the effects of manning mediated by population size, architectural features, and specific action patterns (286, 341, 458) ? The resolution of these and related questions most likely will require a more complete integration of ecological theory with cognitive and motivational constructs (300, 458), as well as more extensive laboratory and field experimentation. In addition, the development of a taxonomy of settings based not only on their modal action patterns, but also on their relative psychological salience for different individuals and groups, would provide a more adequate basis for designing and evaluating environments than is now available. [See also (405) for an extensive bibliography of research in this area.]

CONCLUSIONS

Research developments over the past 5 years demonstrate that environmental psychology is no mere fad of the 1960s – a short-lived product of environmentalist and political activism. Instead, this field has taken hold both conceptually and empirically and is now comprised of several active and focused research domains. Each of these domains is oriented not only to the resolution of environmental problems but also to the development of a more adequate conceptualization of human-environment interchange than presently exists.

The scientific vitality of environmental psychology is reflected in the substantial theoretical and empirical progress that has been made within many of its major subareas. Conceptual developments are especially evident in the literature on spatial cognition, proxemics, stress, and ecological psychology. Research in these areas has moved beyond simple application of established psychological theories (*e.g.*, of cognitive development, information processing) to the derivation of new concepts and models pertaining to environment and behavior (*e.g.*, fundamental vs. macrospatial cognition, boundary-regulation processes, the crowding construct, under vs. overmanning). Furthermore, empirical advances have been made in these areas as well as in the measurement of environmental dispositions and attitudes, the assessment of environmental quality, and the analysis of ecologically relevant behavior. To be sure, most of these developments await further validation and refinement. Also, preliminary research on certain issues (*e.g.*, the impact of the natural environment on behavior) has been particularly sparse. But on the whole, engaging scientific questions have been discovered within the major areas of environmental psychology, and these have prompted considerable theoretical and empirical progress in recent years.

Though the major research areas of the field are rooted in diverse theoretical traditions and emphasize different modes of human-environment transaction, a number of linkages among these areas have been drawn. Such linkages are evident in the combination of behavior setting analysis with the concerns of environmental assessment ; the analysis of personality variables as they mediate proxemic behavior and the intensity of stress reactions ; and the combined use of cognitive and behavioral mapping strategies in studies of human response to the physical environment. As for the future, several of the most exciting and promising opportunities for research can be found at the interface of the major substantive areas of the field (*e.g.*, the further integration of ecological and operant perspectives on the analysis of environmentally relevant behavior).

The major research domains of environmental psychology reflect certain common assumptions or themes which eventually may provide the foundation for a general theory of environment and behavior. One such theme is the transactional or bidirectional nature of human-environment relations (13, 130, 212, 266, 313, 415). Transactional views suggest that any attempt to conceptualize the relationship between environment and behavior must account not only for the effects of the environment on people, but also for the reciprocal impact of people on their milieu. The related theme of human-environment optimization suggests that the various modes of transaction between people and their surroundings (*i.e.*, interpretive, evaluative, operative, and responsive modes) are organized in relation to prioritized goals and plans. The optimization theme emphasizes the attempts of individuals and groups to create environments that are maximally supportive of their goals and activities.

The concepts of transactionalism and optimization are relevant to one of the major tasks currently facing the behavioral sciences : namely, the development of a taxonomy of environments (130, 266, 313, 385, 415). Specifically, the personal and group goals underlying human-environment transactions offer a basis for defining environments in terms of (*a*) their *salience*, or the extent to which they are associated with psychologically important goals and plans ; and (*b*) their *congruence*, or the extent to which they permit behavioral opportunities for realizing salient goals and plans [see also Michelson's (307a) notion of intersystem congruence]. In combination, these dimensions predict environmental *quality*, an index of the proportion of salient goals and plans that are supported by a particular environment. For instance, residential settings are typically highly salient environments that can vary widely in terms of their congruence and desirability (*e.g.*, high-income housing vs. slum dwelling or prison cell).

The above dimensions of environments are "transactional terms" (265a, 266) in the sense that they reflect the interplay of human and environmental forces. The salience dimension, for example, emphasizes the range and importance of cognitive representations associated with a particular setting, whereas the congruence notion reflects what Chein (80) referred to as environmental "supports" or "constraints".

The description of settings in transactional terms may extend earlier attempts to categorize environments either in terms of their behavioral (33, 156, 348) or perceptual dimensions (211, 305, 317). By considering the behavioral (or functional) features of settings in conjunction with their psychological salience, it becomes possible to move from purely descriptive to predictive taxonomies. For example, the impact of environmental stressors on people is likely to depend on both the importance (salience) and controllability (congruence) of the setting in which these stressors occur (see preceding sections on crowding and environmental stressors).[j] And at a more general level, predicting the generalizability of research findings from one setting to another may be facilitated by knowing the extent to which the settings are of comparable salience and congruence.

Future refinement and operationalization of environmental dimensions such as salience, congruence, and quality may be advantageous at the practical level as well. Several areas of environment-behavioral research, including urban planning (19, 316), environmental design (82, 264, 375), environmental decision-making (28, 173, 391), and population psychology (145, 326) are explicitly concerned with the creation of environments that are congruent with occupants' goals and activities. The specification and measurement of salient goals at the community level are prerequisites for designing behaviorally supportive environments and for deriving criteria of environmental quality (96, 415).

The conceptualization of community planning as a goal-oriented optimization process raises several questions for future research. For instance : (*a*) On what dimensions do people attempt to optimize their environments ? (*b*) Do the salient dimensions of environmental optimization vary systematically in relation to the type of setting considered ? (*c*) What kinds of assessment criteria are appropriate for measuring optimization processes and their outcomes at individual, group, and community levels of analysis (66, 68, 442) ? (*d*) What are the appropriate time intervals for assessing optimization cycles within individuals, groups, communities (68) ? (*e*) To what extent can competing goals be optimized both within and between systems (56, 343) ? (*f*) In what ways can empirical information concerning human-environment optimization be translated into guidelines for environmental design ?

Analysis of these issues will require an integration of the concepts and tools of environmental assessment with those from other areas of the field. Thus future research in environmental psychology is likely to reflect a consolidation of theory and data within its major substantive areas, as well as the further development of cross-paradigm research (95) as a basis for community planning and design.

ACKNOWLEDGEMENT

I would like to thank the following persons who offered helpful comments on an earlier version of this chapter : Irwin Altman, Mark Baldassare, Roger Barker, Sheldon Cohen, Barry Collins, Kenneth Craik, Joseph DiMento, Gary Evans, Stephen Kaplan, Harold Kelley, Vladimir Konecni, Richard Lazarus, Burton Mindick, Lyman Porter, Dru Sherrod, David Stea, Peter Stringer, Carol Whalen, Allan Wicker, and Jack Wohlwill. Also, thanks are due to Alicia Gomez for her able assistance in the preparation of the manuscript : and a special note of appreciation to Jeanne Stokols for several constructive readings of the paper and for her valuable support throughout all phases of this project.

FOOTNOTES

[a] See also the directory of behavior and design researchers published by the Association for the Study of Man-Environment Relations (47).

[b] Community psychology (196, 237, 240) is explicitly concerned with the development and evaluation of community intervention strategies, but the emphasis of this field is on the prevention or reduction of psychological and behavioral disorders at the community level, rather than on the more general assessment of environment-behavioral relationships.

[c] Additional historical treatments of environmental psychology are provided by Altman (18), Canter & Stringer (72), Smith (404), Stokols (415), and Willems (464).

[d] The development of an ecological perspective within sociology was signaled by the establishment of human ecology during the mid-1920s by Park & Burgess (331). Although human ecology and ecological psychology are based on similar theoretical assumptions, these areas have essentially developed in isolation from each other.

[e] A distinction can be drawn between adaptation (117) and optimization. Adaptation refers to people's attemps (behavioral, cognitive, physiological) to cope with existing environmental conditions. Optimization involves a more planful and cyclical process whereby individuals not only adapt to the existing situation, but also opt to maintain or modify their milieu in accord with specified goals. Optimization subsumes adaptation but places an equal emphasis on man's reciprocal control over the environment. See also Wohlwill's (474) discussion of adaptation and adjustment.

[f] Certain research areas within the environment-and-behavior field, such as those represented by the literature on family planning (145, 326), case studies of the urban planning process (18, 19, 89), and research on the evaluation of social and environmental programs (66, 68, 487) would seem to encompass all four modes of human-environment transaction as they are explicitly concerned with successive cycles of environmental optimization.

[g] Although affective processes clearly play a role in spatial cognition, research specifically pertaining to evaluative dimensions of environmental cognition (*e.g.*, attitudes, preferences) is reviewed in a subsequent section concerning the "Evaluative Mode" of human-environment transactions.

[h] The conceptualization of crowding as a stressful experience suggests that this area of research might have been reviewed more appropriately in the section on environmental stressors (see below). The discussion of crowding in the context of proxemics, however, reflects the shift in emphasis in recent research from the behavioral effects of high density per se to the development of a comprehensive model of human spatial behavior in which individuals' attempts to regulate privacy and personal space are of central importance.

[i] In general, it is assumed that environmental conditions will exert greatest impact on people where situational constraints are inflexible (*i.e.*, where the operative mode of transaction is restricted) and/or where occupants are of low competence (263, 414, 471).

REFERENCES

1. Acking, C.-A., Kuller, R. 1973, Presentation and judgment of planned environment and the hypothesis of arousal. See Ref. 346, pp. 72-83.
2. Acredolo, L.P., Pick, H.L., Olsen, M.G., 1975, Environmental differentiation and familiarity as determinants of children's memory for spatial location, *Dev. Psychol*, 11: 495-501.
3. Adler, N.E., 1974, *Factors affecting contraceptive use*, Presented at 82nd Ann. Conv. APA, New Orleans.
4. Aiello, J.R., 1977, A further look at equilibrium theory : Visual interaction as a function of interpersonal distance, *Environ. Psychol. Nonverb. Behav.*, 1: 122-40.
5. Aiello, J.R., Baum, A., eds. 1978, *Residential Crowding and Design*. New York : Plenum. In press.
6. Aiello, J.R., DeRisi, D.T., Epstein, Y.M., Karlin, R.A., 1977, Crowding and the role of interpersonal distance preference, *Sociometry* 40. In press.
7. Aiello, J.R., Epstein, Y.M., Karlin, R.A., 1975, Effects of crowding on electrodermal activity, *Sociol. Symp.* 14 : 43-58.

8. Aiello, J.R., Epstein, Y.M., Karlin, R.A., 1977, *Field experimental research on crowding*, Presented at Ann. Conv. EPA, New York.
9. Albrecht, S.L., 1976, Legacy of the environmental movement, *Environ. Behav.*, 8 : 147-68.
10. Althoff, P., Grieg, W.H., 1974, Environmental pollution control policy-making : An analysis of elite perceptions and preferences, *Environ. Behav.* 6 : 259-88.
11. Altman, I., 1973, Some perspectives on the study of man-environment phenomena, *Rep. Res. Soc. Psychol.*, 4 : 109-26.
12. Altman, I., 1976, Environmental psychology and social psychology, *Pers. Soc. Psychol. Bull.*, 2 : 96-113.
13. Altman, I., 1975, *The Environment and Social Behavior*, Monterey, Calif : Brooks-Cole, 256 pp.
14. Altman, I., Vinsel, A.M., 1977, Personal space : An analysis of E.T. Hall's proxemics framework, See Ref. 16. In press.
15. Altman, I., Wohlwill, J., eds. 1976, *Human Behavior and Environment : Advances in Theory and Research*, Vol. I, Now York : Plenum, 301 pp.
16. Altman, I., Wohlwill, J., eds. 1977, *Human Behavior and Environment : Advances in Theory and Research*, Vol. 2, New York : Plenum. In press.
17. Anderson, T.W., Zube, E.H., MacConnell, W.P., 1976, Predicting scenic resource values, In *Studies in Landscape Perception*, *Publ. No. R-76-1*, ed. E.H. Zube, pp. 6-69, Amherst Mass : Inst. Man Environ., 169 pp.
18. Appleyard, D., 1976, *Planning a Pluralist City : Conflicting Realities in Ciudad Guayana*, Cambridge, Mass : MIT Press, 312 pp.
19. Appleyard, D., 1977, A planner's guide to environmental psychology : A review essay, *J. Am. Inst. Plann.*, 43 : 184-89.
20. Appleyard, D., Craik, K.H., 1974, The Berkeley Environmental Simulation Project : Its use in environmental impact assessment. In *Environmental Impact Assessment : Guidelines and Commentary*, ed. T.G., Dickert, K.R. Domeny, pp. 121-26, Berkeley : Univ. California Extension.
21. Archea, J., 1975, Establishing an inter-disciplinary commitment, See Ref. 204, pp. 285-302.
22. Argyle, M., Dean, J., 1965, Eye-contact, distance, and affiliation, *Sociometry*, 28 : 289-304.
22a. Asch, J., Shore, B.M., 1975, Conservation behaviour as the outcome of environmental education, *J. Environ. Educ.* 6 : 25-33.
23. Averill, J.R., 1973, Personal control over aversive stimuli and its relationship to stress, *Psychol. Bull.*, 80 : 286-303.
24. Baer, D.M., Wolf, M.M., Risley, T.R., 1968, Some current dimensions of applied behavior analysis, *J. Appl. Behav. Anal.*, 1 : 91-97.
25. Baldassare, M., 1976, *Residential crowding in urban America*, PhD. thesis, Univ. California, Berkeley, Calif. 260 pp.

26. Banerjee, T., Gollub, J., 1976, The public view of the coast : Toward aesthetic indicators for coastal planning and management, see Ref. 445, pp. 115-22.

27. Barbey, G., Gelber, C., 1973, *The relationship between the built environment and human behavior : A survey and analysis of the existing literature*, Lausanne, Switzerland : Fed. Inst. Technol. 410 pp.

28. Barker, M.L., 1974, Information and complexity : The conceptualization of air pollution by specialist groups, *Environ. Behav.* 6 : 346-77.

29. Barker, R.G., 1968, *Ecological Psychology : Concepts and Methods for Studying the Environment of Human Behavior*, Stanford, Calif. : Stanford Univ. Press, 242 pp.

30. Barker, R.G., 1960, Ecology and motivation, *Nebr. Symp. Motiv.* 8 : 1-48.

31. Barker, R.G., 1963, On the nature of the environment, *J. Soc. Issues* 19 : 17-34.

32. Barker, R.G., Gump, P.V., 1964, *Big School, Small School*, Stanford, Calif : Stanford Univ. Press, 250 pp.

33. Barker, R.G., Schoggen, P., 1973, *Qualities of Community Life*, San Francisco: Jossey-Bass, 562 pp.

34. Barker, R.G., Wright, H.F., 1955, *Mid-west and its Children*, Evanston, Ill: Row Peterson, 532 pp.

35. Baron, R.A., Bell, P.A., 1976, Aggression and heat : The influence of ambient temperature, negative affect, and a cooling drink on physical aggression, *J. Pers. Soc. Psychol.* 33 : 245-55.

36. Baron, R.A., Byrne, D., 1977, *Social Psychology : Understanding Human Interaction*, Boston : Allyn & Bacon, 656 pp., 2nd ed.

37. Baron, R.M., Mandel, D.R., Adams, C.A., Griffen, L.M., 1976, Effects of social density in university residential environments, *J. Pers. Soc. Psychol*, 34 : 434-46.

38. Bass, B.M., Bass, R., 1976, Concern for the environment : Implications for industrial and organizational psychology, *Am. Psychol.* 31 : 158-66.

39. Baum, A., Epstein, Y., eds. 1978, *Human Response to Crowding*, Hillsdale, NJ : Erlbaum. In press.

40. Baum, A., Korman, S., 1976, Differential response to anticipated crowding : Psychological effects of social and spatial density, *J. Pers. Soc. Psychol.* 34 : 526-36.

41. Baum, A., Singer, J.E., Valins, S., eds. 1978. *Advances in Environmental Psychology*, New York : Erlbaum. In press.

42. Baum, A., Valins, S., 1977, *The Social Psychology of Crowding : Studies of the Effects of Residential Group Size*, Hillsdale, NJ : Erlbaum. In press.

43. Bechtel, R.B., 1975, The undermanned future, See Ref. 204, pp. 269-76.

44. Bechtel, R.B., Ledbetter, C.B., 1976, *The temporary environment : Cold regions habitability*, *U.S. Army Corps Eng. Tech. Rep. 76-10*, U.S. Army Cold Regions Res. Eng. Lab., Hanover, N.H.

45. Beck, R., Wood, D., 1976, Comparative developmental analysis of individual and aggregated cognitive maps of London. See Ref. 315, pp. 173-84.
46. Becker, F.D., 1973, Study of spatial markers, *J. Pers. Soc. Psychol.* 26 : 439-45.
47. Beckman, R., Conway, D., Esser, A.H., Preiser, W., eds., 1974, *International Directory of Behavior and Design Researchers,* Orangeburg, NY: Assoc. Study Man-Environ. Relat. 100 pp.
48. Benson, J.S., Kennelly, K.J., 1976, Learned helplessness : The result of uncontrollable reinforcements or uncontrollable aversive stimuli ? *J. Pers. Soc. Psychol.* 34 : 138-45.
49. Berglund, B., 1977, Quantitative approaches in environmental studies, *Int. J. Psychol.* 12. In press.
50. Berlyne, D.E., 1971, *Aesthetics and Psychobiology*, New York : Appleton-Century-Crofts, 336 pp.
51. Berlyne, D.E., Ditkofsky, J., 1976, Effects of novelty and oddity on visual selective attention, *Br. J. Psychol.* 67 : 175-80.
52. Bharucha-Reid, R.P., 1975, *Environmental Psychology, NEPA, and the challenge of the real world*. Presented at 83rd Ann. Conv. APA, Chicago.
53. Bickman, L., Teger, A., Gabrielle, T., McLaughlin, C., Berger, M., Sunaday, E., 1973, Dormitory density and helping behavior, *Environ. Behav.*, 5 : 465-89.
54. Blaut, J.M., Stea, D., 1974, Mapping at the age of three, *J. Geogr.* 73 : 5-9.
54a. Booth, A., 1976, *Urban Crowding and Its Consequences*, New York : Praeger, 139 pp.
55. Bowers, K.S., 1973, Situationism in psychology : An analysis and a critique, *Psychol. Rev.*, 80 : 307-36.
56. Brechner, K.C., 1978, An experimental analysis of social traps, *J. Exp. Soc. Psychol.* In press.
57. Breed, G., 1972, The effect of intimacy : Reciprocity or retreat ? *Br. J. Soc. Clin. Psychol.* 11 : 135-42.
58. Briggs, R., 1976, Methodologies for the measurement of cognitive distance. See Ref. 315, pp. 325-34.
59. Broadbent, D.E., 1971, *Decision and Stress*, New York : Academic, 522 pp.
60. Bruner, J.S., 1957, On perceptual readiness, *Psychol. Rev.* 64 : 123-52.
61. Brunswik, E., 1943, Organismic achievement and environmental probability, *Psychol. Rev.* 50 : 255-72.
62. Brunswik, E., 1956, *Perception and the Representative Design of Experiments,* Berkeley : Univ. California Press, 154 pp.
63. Bruvold, W.H., 1973, Belief and behavior as determinants of environmental attitudes, *Environ. Behav.* 5 : 202-18.
64. Burby, R.J., Weiss, S.F., 1976, *New Communities, U.S.A.*, Lexington, Mass : Heath, 593 pp.

65. Cadwallader, M.T., 1976, Cognitive distance in intra-urban space, see Ref. 315, 316-24.
66. Campbell, D.E., 1976, Evaluation of the built environment : Lessons from program evaluation, see Ref. 445, 227-34.
67. Campbell, D.E., Beets, J.L., 1977, Meteorological variables and behavior : An annotated bibliography, *JSAS Cat. Sel. Doc. Psyhol.* In press.
68. Campbell, D.T., 1969, Reforms as experiments, *Am. Psychol.* 24 : 409-29.
69. Canter, D., 1974, Empirical research in environmental psychology : A brief review, *Bull. Br. Psychol. Soc.*, 27 : 31-37.
70. Canter, D., 1975, *Behavioral maps or cognitive maps : A camparison for children's hospital ward ecology*, Surrey, Engiand : Univ. Surrey.
71. Canter, D., Lee, T.R., eds. 1974, *Psychology and the Built Environment*, New York : Halstead, 213 pp.
72. Canter, D., Stringer, P., 1975, *Environmental Interaction*, New York : Int. Univ. Press, 374 pp.
73. Carr, S.J., Dabbs, J.M. Jr., 1974. The effects of lighting, distance and intimacy of topic on verbal and visual behavior, *Sociometry* 37 : 592-600.
74. Carson, D.H., ed. 1974, *Man-Environment Interactions : Evaluations and Applications*, Vols. 1-12, *Proc. 5th Int. Environ. Design Res. Assoc. Conf.*, Washington DC : Environ. Design Res. Assoc.
75. Catalano, R., Simmons, S., Stokols, D., 1975, Adding social science knowlege to environmental decision making, *Nat. Res. Lawyer*, 8 : 41-59.
76. Catton, W., Dunlap, R.E., 1978, Environmental sociology, *Ann. Rev. Sociol.* In press.
77. Cermak, G.W., Cornillion, P.C., 1976, Multidimensional analyses of judgements about traffic noise, *J. Acoust. Soc. Am.*, 59 : 1412-20.
78. Chapman, C., Risley, T.R., 1974, Anti-litter procedures in an urban high density area, *J. Appl. Behav. Anal.* 7 : 377-83.
79. Chase, R.A., 1974, Information ecology and the design of learning environments, see Ref. 82, pp. 282-96.
80. Chein, I., 1954, The environment as a determinant of behavior, *J. Soc. Psychol.* 39 : 115-27.
81. Clark, R.N., Burgess, R.L., Hendee, J.C., 1972, The development of anti-litter behavior in a forest campground, *J. Appl. Behav. Anal.* 5 : 1-5.
82. Coates, G.J., ed. 1974, *Alternative Learning Environments.* Stroudsburg, Pa : Dowden, Hutchinson & Ross, 387 pp.
83. Cohen, S., 1978, Environmental load and the allocation of attention, see Ref. 41. In press.
84. Cohen, S., Glass, D.C., Phillips, S., 1977, Environment and health, *Handbook of Medical Sociology*, ed. H.E. Freeman, S. Levine, L.G. Reeder, Englewood Cliffs, NJ : Prentice-Hall. In press.

85. Cohen, S., Glass, D.C., Singer, J.E., 1973, Apartment noise, auditory discrimination, and reading ability in children, *J. Exp. Soc. Psychol.* 9 : 407-22.
86. Cohen, S., Rothbart, M., Phillips, S., 1976, Locus of control and the generality of learned helplessness in humans, *J. Pers. Soc. Psychol.* 34 : 1049-56.
87. Cone, J.D., Hayes, S.C., 1977, Applied behavior analysis and the solution of environmental problems, see Ref. 16. In press.
88. Cone, J.D., Hayes, S.C., 1976, *The submerged discipline of environmental psychology*, Presented at Ann. Conv. Mid-west. Assoc. Behav. Anal., Chicago.
89. Cooper, C., 1975, *Easter Hill Village : Some Social Implications of Design*, New York : Free Press, 337 pp.
90. Coren, S., Porac, C., 1976, Distance makes the heart grow fonder : Attributes and metrics in cognitive macromaps, see Ref. 445, pp. 81-85.
91. Cozby, P.C., 1973, Effects of density, activity, and personality on environmental preferences, *J. Res. Pers.* 4 : 45-60.
92. Craik, K.H., 1973, Environmental psychology, *Ann. Rev. Psychol.*, 24 : 403-22.
93. Craik, K.H., 1975, Individual variations in landscape description, see Ref. 494, pp. 130-50.
94. Craik, K.H., 1976, The personality research paradigm in environmental psychology, see Ref. 443, pp. 55-79.
95. Craik, K.H., 1977, Multiple scientific paradigms in environmental psychology, *Int. J. Psychol.* 12, In press.
96. Craik, K.H., Zube, E.H., eds. 1976, *Perceiving Environmental Quality*, New York : Plenum. 310 pp.
97. Crawford, T.J., 1973, Beliefs about birth control : A consistency theory analysis, *Represent. Res. Soc. Psychol.*, 4 : 53-65.
98. Curtin, R.T., 1975, *Consumer adaptation to energy shortages*, Presented at 83rd Ann. Conv. APA, Chicago.
99. Danford, S., Willems, E.P., 1975, Subjective responses to architectural displays : A question of validity, *Environ. Behav.*, 7 : 486-516.
100. Daniel, T.C., Boster, R.S., 1976, *Measuring landscape esthetics : The scenic beauty estimation method, USDA For. Serv. Res. Pap. RM-167*, Rocky Mt. Forest Range Exp. Sta., Ft. Collins, Colorado, 66 pp.
101. D'Atri, D.A., 1975, Psychophysiological responses to crowding, *Environ. Behav.*, 7 : 237-52.
102. David, T., Wright, B., eds. 1974, *Learning Environments*, Chicago, Ill : Univ. Chicago Press, 233 pp.
103. Davidson, A.R., Jaccard, J.J., 1975, Population psychology : A new look at an old problem, *J. Pers. Soc. Psychol.* 31 : 1073-82.
104. Davis, G., Altman, I., 1976, Territories at the work-place : Theory into design guidelines, *Man-Environ. Syst.* 6 : 46-53.

105. Dean, L.M., Pugh, W.M., Gunderson, E., 1975, Spatial and perceptual components of crowding : Effects on health and satisfaction, *Environ. Behav.* 7 : 225-36.

106. DeLong, A.J., 1973, Territorial stability and hierarchical formation, *Small Group Behav.* 4 : 56-63.

107. Dember, W.N., 1974, Motivation and the cognitive revolution, *Am. Psychol.* 29 : 161-68.

108. Deslauries, B.C., Everett, P.B., 1978, The effects of intermittent and continuous token reinforcement on bus ridership, *J. App. Psychol.* In press.

109. Desor, J., 1972, Toward a psychological theory of crowding, *J. Pers. Soc. Psychol.* 21 : 79-82.

110. Devlin, A.S., 1976, The "small town" cognitive map : Adjusting to a new environment, see Ref. 315, pp. 58-70.

111. Dibner, A.S., 1973, *Behavioral correlates of preference for complexity in aged*, Presened at Ann. Conv. Gerontol. Soc., Miami.

112. Donnerstein, E., Wilson, D.W., 1976, Effects of noise and perceived control on ongoing and subsequent aggressive behavior, *J. Pers. Soc. Psychol.* 34 : 774-81.

113. Donohue, G.A., Olien, C.N., Tichenor, P.J., 1974, Communities, pollution, and the fight for survival, *J. Environ. Educ.* 6 : 29-37.

114. Dooley, B., 1974, Crowding stress : *The effects of social density on men with "close" or "far" personal space*. PhD. thesis. Univ. California, Los Angeles, Calif. 146 pp.

115. Downs, R.M., Stea, D., 1973, Cognitive maps and spatial behavior : Process and products. In *Image and Environment*, ed. R.M. Downs, D. Stea, pp. 8-26, Chicago : Aldine, 439 pp.

116. Downs, R.M., Stea, D., 1977, *Maps in Minds : Reflections on Cognitive Mapping*. New York : Harper & Row. 284 pp.

117. Dubos, R., 1965, *Man Adopting*, New Haven, Conn : Yale Univ. Press, 527 pp.

118. Duke, M.P., Nowicki, S., 1972, A new measure and social-learning model for interpersonal distance, *J. Exp, Res. Pers.* 6 : 119-32.

119. Dunlap, R.E., 1975, The impact of political orientation on environmental attitudes and actions, *Environ Behav.* 7 : 428-54.

120. Dunlap, R.E., Dillman, D.A., 1976, Decline in public support for environmental protection: Evidence from a 1970-74 panel study, *Rural Sociol.* 41 : 382-90.

121. Dweck, C.S., Reppucci, N.D., 1973, Learned helplessness and reinforcement responsibility in children, *J. Pers. Soc. Psychol.*, 25 : 109-16.

122. Easterbrook, J.A., 1959, The effect of emotion on cue utilization and the organization of behavior, *Psychol. Rev.* 66 : 183-201.

123. Ebbesen, E.B., Kjos, G.L., Konecni, V.J, 1976, Spatial ecology : Its effects on the choice of friends and enemies, *J. Exp. Soc. Psychol.* 12 : 505-18.

124. Eddy, G.L., Sinnett, E.R., 1973. Behavior setting utilization by emotionally disturbed college students, *J. Consult. Clin. Psychol.* 40 : 210-16.
125. Edney, J.J., 1972. Property, possession, and permanence : A field study in human territoriality, *J. Appl. Soc. Psychol.*, 2 : 275-82.
126. Edney, J.J., 1974, Human territoriality, *Psychol. Bull.* 81 : 959-75.
127. Efran, M.G., Cheyne, J.A., 1974, Affective concomitants of the invasion of shared space : Behavioral, physiological, and verbal indicators, *J. Pers. Soc. Psychol.*, 29 · 219-26.
128. Ehrlich, P.R., 1968, *The Population Bomb.*, New York : Ballantine, 223 pp.
129. Emery, F.E., ed. 1969, *Systems Thinking*, Hardmondsworth, England : Penguin, 398 pp.
130. Endler, N.S., Magnusson, D., eds. 1976, *Interactional Psychology and Personality*, Washington DC : Hemisphere, 663 pp.
131. Epstein, Y.M., 1976, Comment on environmental psychology and social psychology, *Pers. Soc. Psychol. Bull.* 2 : 346-49.
132. Erskine, H., 1972, The polls : Pollution and its costs, *Public Opin. Q.* 36 : 120-35.
133. Esser, A.H., ed. 1969-present, *Man-Environment Systems*, Orangeburg, NY : Assoc. Study Man-Environ. Relat.
134. Esser, A.H., 1973, Experiences of crowding : Illustration of a paradigm for man-environment relations. *Represent. Res. Soc. Psychol.*, 4 : 207-18.
135. Esser, A.H., Greenbie, B.B., eds. 1978, *Design for Community and Privacy*, New York : Plenum. In press.
136. Evans, G.W., 1978, Design implications of spatial research. See Ref. 5. In press.
137. Evans, G.W., 1978, Graduate programs in environment and behavior, see Ref. 455. In press.
138. Evans, G.M., 1978, Human spatial behavior : The arousal model. See Ref. 39. In press.
139. Evans, G.W., Eichelman, W., 1976, Preliminary models of conceptual linkages among proxemic variables, *Environ. Behav.* 8 : 87-116.
140. Evans, G.W., Howard, R., 1973, Personal space, *Psychol. Bull.* 80 : 334-44.
141. Everett, P.B., Deslauries, B.C., Newsom, T.J., Anderson, V.B., 1978, Increasing the effectiveness of free transit, *Transit J.* In press.
142. Everett, P.B., Hayward, S.C., Meyers, A.W., 1974, The effects of a token reinforcement procedure on bus ridership, *J. Appl. Behav. Anal.* 7 : 1-10.
143. Everett, P.B., Studer, R.G., Douglas, T.J., 1978, Gaming simulation to pretest operant-based community interventions : An urban transportation example, *Am. J. Community Psychol.* In press.
144. Falbo, T., ed., 1976-present, *Population and Environmental Psychology Newsletter* ,Washington DC : Div. 34, APA.

145. Fawcett, J.T., ed. 1973, *Psychological Perspectives on Population*, New York : Basic Books, 522 pp.
146. Fehr, L.A., Fishbein, H.D., 1976, The effects of an explicit landmark on spatial judgments, see Ref. 445, pp. 86-93.
147. Felton, B., Kahana, E., 1974, Adjustment and situationally-bound locus of control among institutionalized aged. *J. Gerontol,* 29 : 295-301.
148. Festinger, L.. 1975, *A Theory of Cognitive Dissonance*, Stanford, Calif : Stanford Univ. Press, 291 pp.
149. Festinger, L., Schachter, S., Back, K., 1950, *Social Pressures in Informal Groups*, Stanford, Calif : Stanford Univ. Press, 197 pp.
150. Firestone, I.J., Karuza, J., Greenberg, C., Kingman, K., 1977, *The perception of crowding : Modality, perspective, and feedback effects*. Presented at 8th Ann. Conv. Environ. Des. Res. Assoc., Champaign, Iii.
151. Fischer, C.S., 1976, *The Urban Experience*, New York : Harcourt, Brace, Jovanovich, 309 pp.
152. Fischer, C.S., Baldassare, M., Ofshe, R.J., 1975, Crowding studies and urban life : A critical review, *J. Am. Inst. Plann.* 41 : 406-18.
153. Fishbein M., 1967, Attitude and the prediction of behavior, In *Readings in Attitude Theory and Measurement*, ed. M. Fishbein, pp. 477-92, New York : Wiley, 499 pp.
154. Francescato, D., Mebane, W., 1973, How citizens view two great cities : Milan and Rome. See Ref. 115, pp. 131-47.
155. Frankenhaeuser, M., Lundberg, U., 1977, The influence of cognitive set on performance and arousal under different noise loads, *Motiv. Emotion*. In press.
156. Frederickson, N., 1972, Toward a taxonomy of situations, *Am. Psychol.* 27 : 114-23.
157. Freedman, J.L., 1975, *Crowding and Behavior,* San Francisco : Freeman, 177 pp.
158. Freedman, J.L., Carlsmith, J.M., Sears, D.O., 1974, *Social Psychology*, Englewood Cliffs, NJ : Prentice Hall, 526, pp. 2nd ed.
159. Freedman, J.L., Levy, A.S., Buchanan, R.W., Price, J., 1972, Crowding and human aggressiveness, *J. Exp. Soc. Psychol.* 8 : 528-48.
160. Friedman, S., Juhasz, J.B., eds. 1974. *Environments : Notes and Selections on Objects, Spaces and Behavior,* Monterey, Calif : Brooks-Cole, 275 pp.
161. Galle, O.R., Gove, W.R., McPherson, J.M., 1972, Population density and pathology : What are the relations for man ? *Science* 176 : 23-30.
162. Garling, T., 1976, The structural analysis of environmental perception and cognition : A multidimensional scaling approach, *Environ. Behav.* 8 : 385-415.
163. Gavin, J.F., Howe, J.G., 1975, Psychological climate : Some theoretical and empirical considerations, *Behav. Sci.* 20 : 228-40.

164. Geller, E.S., Witmer, J.F., Orebaugh. A.L., 1976, Instructions as a determinant of paper-disposal behaviors, *Environ. Behav.* 8: 417-39.

165. Gerson, E.M., Gerson, M.S., 1976, The social framework of place perspectives. See Ref. 315, pp. 196-205.

166. Gerst, M.S., Moos, R.H., 1974, *University Residence Environment Scale, Form R.* Palo Alto, Calif : Consult. Psychol. Press.

167. Gibson, J.J., 1960, The concept of the stimulus in psychology, *Am. Psychol.* 15 : 694-703.

168. Glass, D.C., Singer, J.E., 1972, *Urban Stress*, New York : Academic, 182 pp.

169. Glass, D.C., Singer, J.E., Pennebaker, J.W., 1977, Behavioral and physiological effects of uncontrollable environmental events, see Ref. 415, pp. 131-51.

170. Golledge, R.G., 1976, Methods and Methodological issues in environmental cognition research. See Ref. 315, pp. 300-13.

171. Golledge, R.G., 1977, Multidimensional analysis in the study of environmental behavior and environmental design. See Ref. 16. In press.

172. Golledge, R.G., Rushton, G., eds. 1976, Spatial Choice and Spatial Behavior : *Geographic Essays on the Analysis of Preference and Perceptions*, Columbus : Ohio State Univ. Press, 320 pp.

173. Goodey, B., 1973, *The state of the art and a review of literature on the perception of environmental quality* : *Working paper No. 3*, Center for Urban and Regional Studies, Univ. Birmingham, England, 23 pp.

174. Gould, P.R., 1973, The black boxes of jonkoping : Spatial information and preference. See Ref. 115, pp. 235-43.

175. Gould, P.R., White, R., 1974, *Mental Maps*, Middlesex, England : Penguin, 204 pp.

176. Greenbie, B.B., 1976, *Design for Diversity*, New York : Elsevier. 209 pp.

177. Griffiths, I.D., 1976, The thermal environment. See Ref. 72, pp. 21-52.

178. Gump, P.V., 1975, Environmental psychology and the behavior setting. See Ref. 204, pp. 152-63.

179. Gutman, R., ed. 1972, *People and Buildings*, New York : Basic Books, 471 pp.

180. Gutman, R., 1975, Architecture and sociology, *Am. Sociol.* 10 : 219-28.

181. Hall, E.T., 1966, *The Hidden Dimension*, New York : Doubleday, 217 pp.

182. Hall, E.T., 1974, *Handbook for Proxemic Research*, Washington DC : Soc. Anthropol. Visual Commun. 124 pp.

183. Hansen, W.B., Altman, I., 1976, Decorating personal places : A descriptive analysis, *Environ. Behav.* 8 : 491-504.

183a. Hanson, L., Wicker, A.W., 1973, *Effects of overmanning on group experience and task performance*, Presented at Ann. Conv. West. Psychol. Assoc., Anaheim.

184. Harman, E.J., Betak, J.F., 1976, Behavioral geography, multidimensional scaling, and the mind. See Ref. 172, pp. 3-20.

185. Harrison, J., Sarre, P., 1976, Personal construct theory, the repertory grid, and environmental cognition. See Ref. 315, pp. 375-84.

186. Hart, R.A., Moore, G.T., 1973. The development of spatial cognition. See Ref. 115, pp. 246-88.

187. Hayes, S.C., Cone, J.D., 1978, Reducing residential electrical energy use : Payments, information, and feedback, *J. Appl. Behav. Anal.* In press.

188. Hayes, S.C., Johnson, V.S., Cone, J.D., 1975. The marked item technique : A practical procedure for litter control, *J. Appl. Behav. Anal.* 8 : 381-86.

189. Hayward, D.G., Rothenberg, M., Beasley, R.R., 1974, Childrens' play and urban playground environments : A comparison of traditional, contemporary, and adventure playground types, *Environ. Behav.* 6 : 131-68.

190. Hebb, D.O., 1949, *The Organization of Behavior : A Neuropsychological Theory*, New York : Wiley, 319 pp.

191. Heberlein, T.A., 1975, Social norms and environmental quality, Presented at Ann. Conv. Am. Assoc. Adv. Sci., New York.

192. Heider, F., 1958, *The Psychology of Interpersonal Relations*, New York : Wiley, 322 pp.

193. Heilweil, M., 1973, The influence of dormitory architecture on resident behavior, *Environ. Behav.* 5 : 377-412.

194. Heimstra, N.W., McFarling, L.H., 1974, *Environmental Psychology*, Monterey, Calif : Brooks-Cole, 210 pp.

195. Heller, J.F., Groff, B.D., Solomon, S.H., 1977, Toward an understanding of crowding : The role of physical interaction, *J. Pers. Soc. Psychol.* 35 : 183-90.

196. Heller, K., Monahan, J., 1977, *Psychology and Community Change*, Homewood, Ill. : Dorsey, 433 pp.

197. Helmreich, R., 1974, Evaluation of environments : Behavioral observations in an undersea habitat. See Ref. 259, pp. 274-85.

198. Hendrix, W.G., Fabos, J.G., 1975, Visual land use compatibility as a significant contributor to visual resource quality, *Int. J. Environ. Stud.* 8 :21-28.

199. Hershberger, R.G., Cass, R.C., 1974, Predicting user responses to buildings. See Ref. 74, 4 : 117-34.

200. Hiroto, D., 1974, Locus of control and learned helplessness, *J. Exp. Psychol.* 102 : 187-93.

201. Hochberg, J., Gellman, L., 1977, The effect of landmark features on mental rotation times, *Mem. Cognit.* 5 : 23-26.

202. Holahan, C.J., Dobrowolny, M.B., 1978, Cognitive and behavioral correlates of the spatial environment : An interactional analysis, *Environ. Behav.* In press.

203. Holohan, C.J., Saegert, S., 1973, Behavioral and attitudinal effects of large-scale variation in the physical environment of psychiatric wards, *J. Abnorm, Psychol.* 82 : 454-62.

204. Honikman, B., 1975, *Responding to social change, Proc. 6th Int. Environ. Design Res. Assoc. Conf.* Stroudsburg, Pa : Dowden, Hutchinson & Ross, 311 pp.

205. Honikman, B., 1976, Personal construct theory and environmental meaning. See Ref. 315, pp. 88-98.

206. Horowitz, A.D., Sheth, J.N., 1976, *Ridesharing to work : A psychological analysis,* Presented at 84th Ann. Conv. APA, Washington DC.

207. Howard, R.B., Chase, S.D., Rothman, M., 1973, An analysis of four measures of cognitive maps. See Ref. 346, pp. 254-64.

208. Hudson, R., 1974, *Consumer spatial behavior : A conceptual model and empirical investigation,* PhD. thesis, Univ. Bristol, Bristol, England.

209. Humphrey, C.R., Bord, R.J., Hammond, M.M., Mann, S.H., 1977, Attitudes and conditions for cooperation in a paper recycling program, *Environ. Behav.* 9 : 107-24.

210. Insel, P.M., Moos, R.H., eds. 1974, *Health and the Social Environment,* Lexington, Mass : Heath : 460 pp.

211. Insel, P.M., Moos, R.H., 1974, Psychological environments : Expanding the scope of human ecology, *Am. Psychol.* 29 : 179-88.

212. Ittelson, W.H., 1973. Environment perception and contemporary perceptual theory, In *Environment and Cognition*, ed. W.H., Ittelson, pp. 1-19, New York : Seminar, 187 pp.

213. Ittelson, W.H., 1974, Some issues facing a theory of environment and behavior. See Ref. 252, pp. 51-59.

214. Ittelson, W.H., Proshansky, H.M., Rivlin, L.G., Winkel, G., 1974, *An Introduction to Environmental Psychology,* New York : Holt, Rinehart & Winston, 406 pp.

215. Ittelson, W.H., Rivlin, L.G., Proshansky, H.M., 1976, The use of behavioral maps in environmental psychology. See Ref. 352, pp. 340-51.

216. Jackle, J.A., Brunn, S., Roseman, C., 1976, *Human Spatial Behavior : A Social Geography,* North Scituate, Mass : Duxbury, 315 pp.

217. James, L.R., Jones, A.P., 1974, Organizational climate : A review of theory and research, *Psychol. Bull.* 81 : 1096-1112.

218. Jones, S.E., Aiello, J.R., 1973, Proxemic behavior of black and white first, third and fifth grade children, *J. Pers. Soc. Psychol.* 25 : 21-27.

219. Jonsson, A., Hansson, L., 1977, Prolonged exposure to a stressful

stimulus (noise) as a cause of raised blood pressure in man, *Lancet* 1 : 86-87.

220. Kahana, E., 1975, A congruence model of person-environment interaction. See Ref. 467, pp. 181-214.
221. Kahneman, D., 1973, *Attention and Effort*, Englewood Cliffs, NJ : Prentice-Hall, 246 pp.
222. Kaplan, R., 1977, Preference and everyday nature : Method and application. See Ref. 415, pp. 235-50.
223. Kaplan, R., 1973, Some psychological benefits of gardening, *Environ. Behav.* 5 : 145-62.
224. Kaplan, R., 1976, Way-finding in the natural environment. See Ref. 315, pp. 46-57.
225. Kaplan, S., 1976, Adaptation, structure and knowledge. See Ref. 315, pp. 32-45.
226. Kaplan, S., 1975, An informal model for the prediction of preference. See Ref. 494, pp. 92-101.
227. Kaplan, S., 1973, Cognitive maps in perception and thought. See Ref. 115, pp. 63-78.
228. Kaplan, S., 1977, Participation in the design process : A cognitive approach. See Ref. 415, pp. 221-33.
229. Kaplan, S., Kaplan, R., Wendt, J.S., 1972, Rated preference and complexity for natural and urban visual material, *Percept, Psychophys.* 12 : 354-56.
230. Karlin, R.A., Epstein, Y.M., Aiello, J.R., 1977, A setting specific analysis of crowding. See Ref. 39. In press.
231. Karlin, R.A., McFarland, D., Aiello, J.R., Epstein, Y.M., 1976, Normative mediation of reactions to crowding, *Environ. Psychol. Nonverb Behav.* 1 : 30-40.
232. Kasl, S.V., 1974, Effects of housing on mental and physical health, *Man. Environ. Syst.* 4 : 207-26.
233. Kates, R.W., Wohlwill, J.F., eds. 1966, *Man's Response to the Physical Environment*, Special issue of *J. Soc. Issues* 22 : 1-140.
234. Kaye, S.M., 1975, Psychology in relation to design : An overview, *Con. Psychol. Rev.* 16 : 104-10.
235. Kelley, H.H., 1973, The processes of casual attribution, *Am. Psychol.* 28 : 107-28.
236. Kelly, G., 1955, *The Psychology of Personal Constructs*, 2 vols, New York : Norton, 1218 pp.
237. Kelly, J.G., Snowden, L.R., Munoz, R.F., 1977, Social and community interventions, *Ann. Rev. Psychol.* 28 : 303-61.
238. Kelman, H.C., 1974, Attitudes are alive and well and gainfully employed in the sphere of action, *Am. Psychol.* 29 : 310-24.
239. Kelvin, P., 1973, A social-psychological examination of privacy, *Br. J. Soc. Clin. Psychol.* 12 : 248-61.
240. Kessler, M., Albee, G.W., 1975, Primary prevention, *Ann. Rev. Psychol.* 26 : 557-91.

241. Klein, D.C., Fencil-Morse, E., Seligman, M.E.P., 1976, Learned helplessness, depression, and the attribution of failure, *J. Pers. Soc. Psychol.* 33 : 508-16.

242. Knight, R.C., Zimring, C.M., Weitzer, W.H., Wheeler, H.C., 1977, *Social development and normalized institutional settings : A preliminary research report*, Amherst : Univ. Mass. Inst. Man Environ. 102 pp.

243. Knowles, E.S., 1973, Boundaries around group interactions : The effects of group size and member status on boundary permeability, *J. Pers. Soc. Psychol.* 26 : 327-31.

244. Knowles, E.S., 1978, The gravity of crowding : Application of social physics to the effects of others, see Ref, 39. In press.

245. Koenig, D.J., 1975, Additional research on environmental activism, *Environ. Behav.* 7 : 472-85.

246. Koffka, J., 1935, *Principles of Gestalt Psychology*, New York : Harcourt, Brace & World, 720 pp.

247. Kohlenberg, R., Phillips, T., 1973, Reinforcement and rate of litter depositing, *J. Appl. Behav. Anal.* 6 : 391-96.

248. Kohlenberg, R., Phillips, T., Proctor, W., 1976, A behavioral analysis of peaking in residential electrical energy consumers, *J. Appl. Behav. Anal.* 9 : 13-18.

249. Korte, C., 1978, Helpfulness in the urban environment. See Ref. 41. In press.

250. Korte, C., Ypma, I., Toppen, A., 1975, Helpfulness in Dutch society as a function of urbanization and environmental input level, *J. Pers. Soc. Psychol.* 32 : 996-1003.

251. Kosslyn, S.M., Pick, H.L., Fariello, G.R., 1974, Cognitive maps in children and men, *Child Dev.* 45 : 707-16.

252. Krantz, D.S., Glass, D.C., Synder, M.L., 1974, Helplessness, stress level and the coronary-prone behavior pattern, *J. Exp. Soc. Psychol.* 10 : 284-300.

253. Krasner, L., Krasner, M., 1973, Token economies and other planned environments. In *Seventy-second Yearbook of the National Society for the Study of Education*, pp. 351-84.

254. Kromm, D.E., Probald, F., Wall, G., 1973, An international comparison of response to air pollution, *J. Environ. Man*, 1 : 363-75.

255. Krovetz, M.L., 1977, Who needs what when : Design of pluralistic learning environments. See Ref. 415, pp. 251-72.

256. Kryter, K.D., 1970, *The Effects of Noise on Man*, New York : Academic, 639 pp.

257. Kuhn, T., 1962, *The Structure of Scientific Revolutions*, Chicago : Chicago Press, 210 pp. 2nd ed.

258. Kuller, R., ed. 1973, *Architectural Psychology : Proc. Conf. Lund, Sweden*, Stroudsburg, Pa : Dowden, Hutchinson & Ross, 450 pp.

259. Lang, J., Burnette, C., Moleski, W., Vachon, D., eds. 1974, *Designing for Human Behavior : Architecture and the Behavioral Sciences*, Stroudsburg, Pa : Dowden, Hutchinson & Ross, 353 pp.

260. Langer, E.J., Rodin, J., 1976, The effects of choice and enhanced personal responsibility for the aged : A field experiment in an institutional setting, *J. Pers. Soc. Psychol.* 34 : 191-98.

261. Laufer, R.S., Proshansky, H.M., Wolfe, M., 1973, Some analytic dimensions of privacy. See Ref. 258, pp. 353-72.

262. Lawrence, J.E., 1974, Science and sentiment : Overview of research on crowding and human behavior, *Psychol. Bull.* 81 : 712-20.

263. Lawton, M.P., 1975, Competence, environmental press, and the adaptation of older people. See Ref. 467, pp. 13-83.

264. Lawton, M.P., Newcomer, R.J., Byerts, T.O., eds. 1976, *Community Planning for an Aging Society*. Stroudsburg, Pa : Dowden, Hutchinson & Ross, 340 pp.

265. Lazarus, R.S., 1966, *Psychological Stress and the Coping Process*, New York : McGraw-Hill, 466 pp.

265a. Lazarus, R.S., Cohen, J.B., 1977, Environmental stress. See Ref. 16. In press.

266. Lazarus, R.S., Launier, R., 1978, Stress-related transactions between person and environment. In *Internal and External Determinants of Behavior*, ed. L.A., Pervin, M. Lewis, New York : Plenum. In press.

267. LeCompte, W.F., 1974. Behavior settings as data-generating units for the environmental planner and architect. See Ref. 259, pp. 183-93.

268. Ledbetter, C.B., 1974, Undermanning and architectural accessibility. See Ref. 74, 8 : 281-88.

269. Lee, R.M., ed. 1976-present, *Environmental Psychology and Nonverbal Behavior*, New York : Human Sci. Press.

270. Lee, S.A., ed. 1969-present. *Architectural Psychology Newsletter*, Surrey, England : Kingston Polytechnic.

271. Lee, T.R., 1976, *Psychology and the Environment*, London : Methuen : 143 pp.

272. Lefcourt, H.M., 1973, The function of the illusions of control and freedom, *Am. Psychol.* 28 : 417-25.

273. Lefcourt, H.M., 1976, Locus of control and the response to aversive events, *Can. Psychol. Rev.* 17 : 202-9.

274. Leff, H.L., Gordon, L.R., Ferguson, J.G., 1974, Cognitive set and environmental awareness, *Environ. Behav.* 6 : 395-447.

275. Levenson, H., 1974, Activism and powerful others : Distinctions within the concept of internal-external control, *J. Pers. Assess.* 38 : 377-83.

276. Levi, L., Anderson, L., 1975, *Psychosocial Stress : Population, Environment and Quality of Life*, New York : Spectrum, 142 pp.

277. Levy-Leboyer, C., 1976, La psychologie de l'environment recherches actuelles aux Etats-Unis. *Res. Psychol. Appl.* 26 : 609-16.

278. Lewin, K., 1936, *Principles of Topological Psychology*, Transl. F. and G. Heider, New York : McGraw-Hill, 231 pp.

279. Lewis, C.A., 1976, People/plant proxemics : A concept for human design. See Ref. 445, pp. 102-7.

280. Linder, D.E., 1974, *Personal Space*, Morristown, NJ : General Learn, Press Modular Stud. 23 pp.

281. Lipsey, M.W., 1977, Attitudes toward the environment and pollution. See Ref. 330, pp. 360-79.

282. Little, B.R., 1976, Specialization and the varieties of environmental experience. See Ref. 443. pp. 81-116.

283. Loo, C., 1977, Beyond the effects of crowding : Situational and individual differences. See Ref. 415, pp. 153-68.

284. Lounsburg, J.W., 1974, Patterns and correlates of environmental design preference. See Ref. 74, 9 : 69-76.

285. Lowenthal, D., 1972, Research in environmental perception and behavior : Perspectives on current problems, *Environ. Behav.* 4 : 333-42.

286. Lozar, C.C., 1974, Application of behavior setting analysis and undermanning theory to supermarket design. See Ref. 74, 8 : 271-79.

287. Lundberg, U., 1973, Emotional and geographical phenomena in psychophysical research. See Ref. 115, pp. 322-37.

288. Luyben, P.D., Bailey, J.S., 1975, Newspaper recycling behaviors : The effects of reinforcement versus proximity of containers, Presented at Ann. Conv. Mid-west, Assoc. Behav. Anal., Chicago.

289. Lynch, K., 1960, *The Image of City*, Cambridge, Mass : MIT Press, 194 pp.

290. MacDonald, A.P., 1970, Internal-external locus of control and the practice of birth control, *Psychol. Rep.* 27 : 206.

291. Magnusson, D., Endler, N.S., 1977, Interactional psychology : Present status and future prospects. In *Personality at the Crossroads : Current Issues in Interactional Psychology*, ed. D. Magnusson, N.S. Endler, Hillsdale, NJ : Erlbaum. In press.

292. Maloney, M.P., Ward, M.P., Braucht, G.N., 1975, A revised scale for the measurement of ecological attitudes and knowledge, *Am. Psychol.* 30 : 787-90.

293. Mandler, J.M., Parker, R.E., 1976, Memory for descriptive and spatial information in complex pictures, *J. Exp. Psychol : Hum. Learn. Mem.* 2 : 38-48.

294. Marans, R.W., 1976, Perceived quality of residential environments : Some methodological issues. See Ref. 96, pp. 123-47.

295. Margulis, S.T., 1974, Privacy as a behavioral phenomenon. See Ref. 74, 6 : 101-23.

296. Marshall, N.J., 1974, Dimensions of privacy preferences. *Multivar. Behav. Res.* 9 : 255-72.

297. Mathews, K.E., Canon, L.K., 1975, Environmental noise level as a determinant of helping behavior, *J. Pers. Soc. Psychol.* 32 : 571-77.

298. Maurer, M., Baxter, J.C., 1972, Images of the neighborhood and city among Black, Anglo, and Mexican-American children, *Environ. Behav.* 4 : 351-88.

299. McCain, G., Cox, V.C., Paulus, P.B., 1976, The relationship between illness complaints and degree of crowding in a prison environment, *Environ. Behav.* 8 : 283-90.

300. McGrath, J.E., 1976, Stress and behavior in organizations, In *Handbook of Industrial and Organizational Psychology*, ed. M.D., Dunnette, pp. 1351-95, Chicago : Rand-McNally, 1740 pp.

301. McKechnie, G.E., 1974, *Manual for the Environmental Response Inventory*, Palo Alto, Calif : Consult, Psychol. Press, 26 pp.

302. McKechnie, G.E., 1977, Simulation techniques in environmental psychology. See Ref. 415, pp. 169-89.

303. Meadows, D.H., Meadows, D.L., Randers, J., Behrens, W.W., 1972, *The Limits to Growth*, New York : Universe Books, 205 pp.

304. Mehrabian, A., 1976, *Public Places and Private Spaces : The Psychology of Work, Play, and Living Environments,* New York : Basic Books, 354 pp.

305. Mehrabian, A., Russell, J.A., 1974, *An Approach to Environmental Psychology*, Cambridge, Mass : MIT Press, 206 pp.

306. Mercer, C., 1975, *Living in Cities,* Harmondsworth, England : Penguin.

306a. Mercer, D.C., 1976, Motivational and social aspects of recreational behavior. See Ref. 15, pp. 123-61.

307. Michelson, W., ed. 1975, *Behavioral Research Methods in Environmental Design*, Stroudsburg, Pa : Dowden, Hutchinson & Ross, 307 pp.

307a. Michelson, W., 1976, *Man and His Urban Environment : A Sociological Approach*, Reading, Mass : Addison-Wesley, 273 pp. 2nd ed.

308. Middlemist, R.D., Knowles, E.S., Matter, C.F., 1976, Personal space invasions in the lavatory : Suggestive evidence for arousal, *J. Pers. Soc. Psychol.* 33 : 541-46.

309. Milgram, S., Jodelet, D., 1976, Psychological maps of Paris. See Ref. 352, pp. 104-24.

310. Miller, G.A., Galanter, E., Pribram, K.H., 1960, *Plans and the Structure of Behavior*, New York : Holt, Rinehart & Winston, 226 pp.

311. Mindick, B., 1977. Attitudes toward population issues. See Ref. 330, pp. 380-403.

312. Mindick, B., Oskamp, S. 1975. Population, planfulness, and the environment. *Man-Environ. Syst.* 5 : 311-12.

313. Mischel, W., 1977. On the future of personality measurement. *Am. Psychol.* 32 : 246-54.

314. Moore, G.T., 1976, Theory and research on the development of environmental knowing. See Ref. 315, pp. 138-64.

315. Moore, G.T., Golledge, R.G., 1976, Environmental knowing : Concepts and theories. In *Environmental Knowing : Theories,*

Research, and Methods, ed. G.T., Moore, R.G., Golledge, pp. 3-24. Stroudsburg, Pa : Dowden, Hutchinson and Ross. 441 pp.

316. Moore, R.C., 1974, Childhood city : Some orientations and foci. See Ref. 74, pp. 103-6.

317. Moos, R.H., 1973, Conceptualizations of human environments. *Am. Psychol.* 28 : 652-65.

318. Moos, R.H., 1975, *Evaluating Correctional and Community Settings*, New York : Wiley, 377 pp.

319. Moos, R.H., 1976, *The Human Context*, New York : Wiley, 444 pp.

320. Moos, R.H., Insel, P.M., eds. 1974, *Issues in Social Ecology : Human Milieus*, Palo Alto, Calif : National Press, 616 pp.

321. Murray, H.A., 1938, *Explorations in Personality*, New York : Oxford, 761 pp.

322. Nahemow, L., Lawton, M.P., 1975, Similarity and propinquity in friendship formation, *J. Pers. Soc. Psychol.* 32 : 205-13.

323. Neisser, U., 1976, *Cognition and Reality : Principles and Implications of Cognitive Psychology.* San Francisco : Freeman. 230 pp.

324. Newman, O., 1973, *Defensible Space*, New York : MacMillan, 264 pp.

325. Newman, O., 1975, *Design Guidelines for Creating Defensible Space*, Washington DC : GPO, 213 pp.

326. Newman, S., Thompson, V.D., eds. 1976, *Population Psychology : Research and Educational Issues.* Washington DC : Center for Population Research, Dep. HEW. 234 pp.

327. Olshavsky, R.W., MacKay, D.B., Sentell, G., 1975, Perceptual maps of supermarket locations, *J. Appl. Psychol.* 60 : 80-86.

328. Onibokun, A.G., 1974, Evaluating consumers' satisfaction with housing : An application of a systems approach, *J. Am. Inst. Plann*, 40 : 189-200.

329. O'Riordan, T., 1976, Attitudes, behavior, and environmental policy issues. See Ref. 15, pp. 1-36.

330. Oskamp, S., 1977, *Attitudes and Opinions*, Englewood Cliffs, NJ : Prentice Hall, 466, pp.

331. Park, R.. Burgess, E., eds. 1925. *The City*, Chicago : Univ. Chicago Press, 239 pp.

332. Parsons, H.M., 1974, Why human factors research in environmental design ? See Ref. 74, pp. 1-13.

333. Pastalan, L.A., 1974, Privacy preferences among relocated institutionalized elderly. See Ref. 74, 6 : 73-82.

334. Patterson, A.H., 1977, Methodological developments in environment-behavioral research. See Ref. 415, pp. 325-44.

335. Patterson, A.H., 1978, Territorial behavior and fear of crime in the elderly, *Hum. Ecol.* In Press.

336. Patterson, M.L., 1976. An arousal model of intimacy. *Psychol. Rev.* 83 : 235-45.

337. Patterson, M.L., 1973, Compensation and nonverbal immediacy behaviors : A review, *Sociometry* 36 : 237-53.
338. Paulus, P.B., Annis, A.B., Seta, J.J., Schkade, J.K., Matthews, R.W., 1976, Density does affect task performance. *J., Pers. Soc. Psychol.* 34 : 248-53.
339. Pedersen, D.M., Shears, L.M., 1973, A review of personal space research in the framework of general system theory. *Psychol. Bull.* 80 : 367-88.
340. Peterson, R.L., 1975, *Air Pollution and attendance in recreation behavior settings in the Los Angeles Basin,* Presented at 83rd Ann. Conv. APA, Chicago.
341. Petty, R.M., 1974, Experimental investigation of undermanning theory. See Ref. 74, 8 : 259-69.
342. Piaget, J., Inhelder, B., 1967, *The Child's Conception of Space.* New York : Norton, 490 pp.
343. Platt, J., 1973, Social traps. *Am. Psychol.* 28 : 641-51.
344. Porteous, J.D., 1977, *Environment and Behavior : Planning and Everyday Urban Life.* Reading, Mass : Addison-Wesley. 446 pp.
345. Powers, R.B., Osborne, J.G., Anderson, E.G., 1973, Positive reinforcement of litter removal in the natural environment. *J. Appl. Behav. Anal.* 6 : 579-86.
346. Preiser, W.F.E., ed. 1973, *Environmental Design Research : Vol. 1, Selected Papers. Proc. 4th Int. Environ, Design Res. Assoc. Conf.* Stroudsburg, Pa : Dowden, Hutchinson and Ross. 557 pp.
347. Preiser, W.F.E., ed. 1973, *Environmental Design Research : Vol. 2, Symposia and Workshops, Proc. 4th Int. Environ. Design Res. Assoc. Conf.* Stroudsburg, Pa : Dowden, Hutchinson and Ross. 545 pp.
348. Price, R., Blashfield, R.K., 1975, Explorations in the taxonomy of behavior settings : Analysis of dimensions and classification of settings. *Am. J. Community Psychol.* 3 : 335-51.
349. Proshansky, H.M., 1976, Comment on environmental and social psychology. *Pers. Soc. Psychol. Bull.* 2 : 359-63.
350. Proshansky, H.M., 1976, Environmental psychology and the real world, *Am. Psychol.* 31 : 303-10.
351. Proshansky, H.M., Ittelosn, W.H., Rivlin, L.G., 1970, Freedom of choice and behavior in a physical setting. See Ref. 352, pp. 170-81.
352. Proshansky, H.M., Ittelson, W.H., Rivlin, L.G., eds. 1976, *Environmental Psychology : People and their Physical Settings,* New York : Holt, Rinehart and Winston, 632, pp. 2nd ed.
353. Proshansky, H.M., O'Hanlon, T., 1977, Environmental psychology : Origins and development. See Ref. 415, pp. 101-29.
354. Rapoport, A., 1973, An approach to the construction of man-environment theory. See Ref. 347, pp. 124-35.
355. Rapoport, A., 1975, Toward a redefinition of density *Environ. Behav.* 7 : 133-58.

356. Rapoport, A., 1976, Environmental cognition in cross-cultural perspective. See Ref. 315, pp. 220-34.

357. Recker, W.W., Golub, T.F., 1976, An attitudinal modal choice model, *Transp. Res.* 10 : 299-310.

358. Regnier, V.A., 1974, Matching older persons' cognition with their use of neighborhood areas. See Ref. 74, 11 : 19-40.

359. Reid, D.H., Luyben, P.D., Rawers, R.J., Bailey, J.S., 1976, Newspaper recycling behavior : The effects of prompting and proximity of containers. *Environ. Behav.* 8 : 471-82.

360. Richerson, P.J., McEvoy, J., eds., 1976, *Human Ecology : An Environmental Approach.* North Scituate, Mass : Duxbury, 370 pp.

361. Rodin, J., 1976, Density, perceived choice, and response to controllable and uncontrollable outcomes. *J. Exp. Soc. Psychol.* 12 : 564-78.

362. Rodin, J., Baum, A., 1977, Crowding and helplessness : Potential consequences of density and loss of control. See Ref. 39. In press.

363. Rosenberg, M.J., 1956, Cognitive structure and attitudinal affect. *J. Abnorm. Soc. Psychol.* 53 : 367-72.

364. Ross, M., Layton, B., Erickson, B., Schopler, J., 1973, Affect, facial regard, and reactions to crowding, *J. Pers. Soc. Psychol.* 28 : 69-76.

365. Roth, S., Kubal, L., 1975, Effects of non-contingent reinforcement on tasks of differing importance : Facilitation and learned helplessness, *J. Pers. Soc. Psychol.* 32 : 680-91.

366. Rothenberg, M., Rivlin, L.G., 1975, *An ecological approach to the study of open classrooms.* Presented at Conf. Int. Soc. Study Behav. Dev., Surrey, England.

367. Rothwell, D., 1976, Cognitive mapping of the home environment. See Ref. 445, pp. 71-74.

368. Rotter, J.B., Chance, J., Phares, E., 1972, *Applications of a Social Learning Theory of Personality.* New York : Holt, Rinehart and Winston, 624 pp.

369. Rule, B.G., Nesdale, A.R., 1976, Environmental stressors, emotional arousal, and aggression. In *Stress and Anxiety* : ed. I.G., Sarason, C.D., Spielberger, 3 : 87-103. Washington DC : Hemisphere, 365 pp.

370. Russell, R.W., 1978, Behavioral adjustment and the physical environment. *Int. J. Psychol.* In Press.

371. Russo, N.F., 1975, Eye contact, interpersonal distance, and the equilibrium theory. *J. Pers. Soc. Psychol.* 31 : 497-502.

372. Saarinen, T., 1976, *Environmental Planning Perception and Behavior,* Boston : Houghton-Mifflin, 262 pp.

373. Saegert, S., 1973, Crowding : Cognitive overload and behavioral constraint. See Ref. 347, pp. 254-60.

374. Saegert, S., Mackintosh, E., West, S., 1975, Two studies of crowding urban public spaces, *Environ. Behav.* 7 : 159-84.

375. Sanoff, H., 1974, Integrating human needs in environmental design, *CRC Crit. Rev. Environ. Control* 4 : 507-34.

376. Savinar, J., 1975, The effect of ceiling height on personal space, *Man-Environ. Syst.* 5 : 321-24.

377. Schiffenbauer, A.I., Brown, J.E., Perry, P.L., Shulack, L.K., Zanzola, A.M., 1977, The relationship between density and crowding : Some architectural modifiers, *Environ. Behav.* 9 : 3-14.

378. Schmidt, D.E., Goldman, R.D., Feimer, N.R., 1976, Physical and psychological factors associated with perceptions of crowding : An analysis of subcultural differences. *J. Appl. Psychol.* 61 : 279-89.

379. Schopler, K.K., 1976, Environmental change and the elderly. See Ref. 15, pp. 265-98.

380. Schopler, J., Stokols, D., 1976, *A psychological approach to human crowding*. Morristown, NJ : Gen. Learn. Press Modular Study. 26 pp.

381. Schulz, R., 1976, Effects of control and predictability on the physical and psychological well-being of the institutionalized aged. *J. Pers. Soc. Psychol.* 33 : 563-73.

382. Schulz, R., Barefoot, J., 1974, Non-verbal responses and affiliative conflict theory, *Br. J. Soc. Clin. Psychol.* 13 : 237-43.

383. Schumacher, E.F., 1973, *Small is Beautiful : Economics, as if People Mattered*, New York : Harper and Row. 305 pp.

384. Seaver, W.B., Patterson, A.H., 1976, Decreasing fuel-oil consumption through feedback and social commendation. *J. Appl. Behav. Anal.* 9 : 147-52.

385. Secord, P.F., 1977, Social psychology in search of a paradigm, *Pers. Soc. Psychol. Bull.* 3 : 41-51.

386. Seeley, O.F., 1976, Field dependence independence, internal-external locus of control, and implementation of family-planning goals. *Psychol. Rep.* 38 : 1216-18.

387. Seligman, C., Darley, J.M., 1978, Feedback as a means of decreasing energy consumption. *J. Appl. Psychol.* In Press.

388. Seligman, M.P., 1975, *Helplessness : On Depression, Development, and Death.* San Francisco : Freeman, 250 pp.

389. Selye, H., 1976, *Stress in Health and Disease.* Woburn, Mass : Butterworths, 1500 pp.

390. Severy, L.J., Brigham, J.C., Schlenker, B.R., 1976, *A Contemporary Introduction to Social Psychology.* New York : McGraw-Hill, 462 pp.

391. Sewell, W.R.D., 1974, The role of perceptions of professionals in environmental decision-making, In *Environmental Quality*, ed. J.T., Coppock, C.B., Wilson, pp. 109-31. Edinburgh : Scottish Academic Press.

392. Shafer, E.L., Richards, T.A., 1974, A comparison of viewed reactions to outdoor scenes and photographs of those scenes. See Ref. 71, pp. 71-79.

393. Sherrod, D.R., 1974, Crowding, perceived control, and behavioral after effects. *J. Appl. Soc. Psychol.* 4 : 171-86.

394. Sherrod, D.R., Cohen, S., 1978, Density, personal control, and design. See Ref. 5. In press.

395. Sherrod, D.R., Downs, R., 1974, Environmental determinants of altruism : The effect of stimulus overload and perceived control on helping, *J. Exp. Soc. Psychol.* 10 : 468-79.

396. Sherrod, D.R., Hage, J.N., Halpern, P.L., Moore, B.S., 1977, Effects of personal causation and perceived control on responses to an adversive environment : The more control, the better, *J. Exp. Soc. Psychol.* 13 : 14-27.

397. Siegel, A.W., White, S.H., 1975, The development of spatial representations of large-scale environments, *Adv. Child Dev. Behav.* 10 : 9-55.

398. Sills, D.L., 1975, The environmental movement and its critics, *Hum. Ecol.* 3 : 1-41.

399. Simon, H.A., 1957, *Models of Man : Explorations in the Western Educational Tradition*, New York : Wiley, 470 pp.

400. Sims, J.H., Baumann, D.D., eds., 1974. *Human Behavior and the Environment*, Chicago : Maaroufa, 354 pp.

401. Singer, J.E., Lundberg, U., Frankenhaeuser, M., 1978, Stress on the train : A study of urban commuting, See Ref. 41. In press.

402. Skinner, B.F., 1953, *Science and Human Behavior*. New York : Macmillan, 461 pp.

403. Smith, C.J., 1976, Residential neighborhoods as humane environments. *Environ Plann. A* 8 : 311-26.

404. Smith, M.B., 1977, Some problems of strategy in environmental psychology. See Ref. 415, pp. 289-301.

405. Sobal, J., 1976, Ecological psychology : An introduction and bibliography, *Man-Environ. Syst.* 6 : 201-7.

406. Sommer, R., 1969, *Personal Space*. Englewood Cliffs, NJ : Prentice-Hall, 177 pp.

407. Sommer, R., 1973, Evaluation yes, research maybe. *Represent. Res. Soc. Psychol.* 4 : 127-33.

408. Sommer, R., 1974, *Tight Spaces : Hard Architecture and How to Humanize It*. Englewood Cliffs, NJ : Prentice Hall, 150 pp.

409. Srivastava, R.K., 1974, Undermanning theory in the context of mental health care environments. See Ref. 74, 8 : 245-58.

410. Stea, D., Taphanel, S., 1974, Theory and experiment on the relation between environmental modeling ('Toy Play') and environmental cognition. See Ref. 71, pp. 170-78.

411. Stein, K.B., Sarbin, T.R., Kulik, J.A., 1968, Future time perspective, *J. Consult. Clin. Psychol.* 32 : 257-64.

412. Stokols, D., 1972, On the distinction between density and crowding : Some implications for future research. *Psychol. Rev.* 79 : 275-77.

413. Stokols, D., 1975, Toward a psychological theory of alienation. *Psychol. Rev.* 82 : 26-44.

414. Stokols, D., 1976, The experience of crowding in primary and secondary environments. *Environ. Behav.* 8 : 49-86.
415. Stokols, D., 1977, Origins and directions of environments-behavioral research. In *Perspectives On Environmental and Behavior : Theory, Research, and Application*, ed. D., Stokols, pp. 5-36, New York : Plenum, 360 pp.
416. Stokols, D., Rall, M., Pinner, B., Schopler, J. 1973, Physical, social, and personal determinants of the perception of crowding, *Environ. Behav.* 5 : 87-115.
417. Stokols, D., Smith, T.E., Prostor, J.J., 1975, Partitioning and perceived crowding in a public space. *Am. Behav. Sci.* 18 : 792-814.
418. Stringer, P., 1976, Repertory grids in the study of environmental perception. In *The Measurement of Intrapersonal Space by Grid Technique, Volume 1 : Explorations of Intrapersonal Space*, ed. P. Slater, pp. 183-208, New York : Wiley, 258 pp.
419. Studer, R.G., 1973, Man-environment relations : Discovery or design ? See Ref. 347, pp. 136-51.
420. Suedfeld, P., Russell, J.A., Ward, L.M., Szigeti, F., Davis, G., eds. 1977. *Book 2 : Invited Addresses Symposia, and Workshops*. In *The Behavioral Basis of Design : Proc. 7th Int. Environ. Design. Res. Assoc. Conf.*, ed. P. Suedfeld, J.A., Russell, Stroudsburg, Pa : Dowden, Hutchinson and Ross. In press
421. Sundstrom, E., 1975, An experimental study of crowding : Effects of room size, intrusion, and goal-blocking on nonverbal behavior, self-disclosure and self-reported stress. *J. Pers. Soc. Psychol.* 32 : 645-54.
422. Sundstrom, E., 1977, Crowding as a sequential process : Review of research on the effects of population density on humans. See Ref. 39. In press.
423. Sundstrom, E., 1977, Interpersonal behavior and the physical environment. In *Social Psychology*, ed. L., Wrightsman, pp. 511-49. Monterey, Calif : Brooks-Cole. 767 pp., 2nd ed.
424. Sundstrom, E., Altman, I., 1976, Interpersonal relationships and personal space : Research review and theoretical model. *Hum. Ecol.* 4 : 47-67.
425. Suttles, G.D., 1972, *The Social Construction of Communities*. Chicago : Univ. Chicago Press, 278 pp.
426. Swan, J., Stapp, W., eds. 1974, *Environmental Education : Strategies Toward a More Livable Future*. New York : Wiley, 349 pp.
427. Thibaut, J.W., Kelley, H.H., 1959. *The Social Psychology of Groups*, New York : Wiley, 313 pp.
428. Thompson, V.D., ed. 1977-present, *Population : Behavioral, Social, and Environmental Issues*. New York : Human Sciences Press.
429. Tibbetts, P., Esser, A.H., 1973, Transactional structures in man-environment relations. *Man-Environ. Syst.* 3 : 441-68.

430. Tolman, E.C., 1948, Cognitive maps in rats and men. *Psychol. Rev.* 55 : 189-208.

431. Trigg, L.J., Perlman, D., Perry, R.P., Janisse, M.P., 1976, Anti-pollution behavior : A function of perceived outcome and locus of control. *Environ. Behav.* 8 : 307-13.

432. Tuan, Y.F., 1975, Images and mental maps. *Ann. Assoc. Am. Geogr.* 65 : 205-13.

433. Tuan, Y.F., 1974, *Topophilia : A Study of Environmental Perception, Attitudes and Values.* Englewood Cliffs, NJ : Prentice-Hall. 260 pp.

434. Tuso, M.A., Geller, E.S., 1978, Behavior analysis applied to environmental/ecological problems : A review, *J. Appl. Behav. Anal.* In press.

435. Tzamir, Y., 1978, Internal representation of the spatial structure of simulated urban networks. *Environ. Behav.* In press.

436. Valins, S., Baum, A. 1973, Residential group size, social interaction, and crowding, *Environ, Behav.* 5 : 421-39.

437. Valsiner, J., Heidmets, M., 1976, Density and spatial behavior : On some problems of environmental psychology (Parts 1 and 2). *Est. Nat.* 19 : 33-37, 89-95.

438. Vayda, A.P., ed. 1972-present, *Human Ecology*, New York : Plenum.

439. Verbrugge, L.M., Taylor, R.B., 1976, *Consequences of population density : Testing new hypotheses.* Presented at 84th Ann. Conv. APA, Washington DC.

440. Von Bertalanffy, L., 1950, The theory of open systems in physics and biology, *Science* 111 : 23-29.

441. Waldbott, G.L., 1973, *Health Effects of Environmental Pollutants.* St. Louis : Mosby, 316 pp.

442. Wandersman, A., 1976, Applying humanism, behaviorism, and a broader social developmental view to understanding and researching the design process. See Ref. 445, pp. 9-20.

443. Wapner, S., Cohen, S.B., Kaplan, B., eds. 1976, *Experiencing the Environment.* New York : Plenum, 244 pp.

444. Wapner, S., Kaplan, B., Cohen, S.B., 1973, An organismic-developmental perspective for understanding transactions of men in environments. *Environ. Behav.* 5 : 255-89.

445. Ward, L.M., Coren, S., Gruft, A., Collins, J.B., eds. 1976, *Book 1 : Selected Papers, EDRA 7.* In *The Behavioral Basis of Design : Proc. 7th Int. Environ. Design Res. Assoc. Conf.* ed. P. Suedfeld, J.A., Russell, Stroudsburg, Pa : Dowden, Hutchinson and Ross. 381 pp.

446. Watson, J.B., 1913, Psychology as the behaviorist views it. *Psychol. Rev.* 20 : 159-77.

447. Weigel, R.H., Vernon, D.T., Tognacci, L.N., 1974, Specificity of the attitude as a determinant of attitude-behavior congruence. *J. Pers. Soc. Psychol.* 30 : 724-28.

448. Weinstein, N.D., 1974, Effect of noise on intellectual performance. *J. Appl. Psychol.* 59 : 548-54.

449. Weinstein, N.D., 1977, *Individual differences in reactions to noise : A longitudinal investigation.* Presented at Ann. Conv. East. Psychol. Assoc., New York.

450. Weinstein, N.D., 1976, The statistical prediction of environmental preferences : Problems of validity and application. *Environ. Behav.* 8 : 611-26.

451. Wekerle, G.R., 1976, Vertical village : Social contacts in a singles highrise complex. *Sociol. Focus.* 9 : 299-315.

452. Werner, H., 1957, The concept of development from a comparative and organismic point of view. In *The Concept of Development*, ed. D.B. Harris, pp. 125-48. Minneapolis : Univ. Minnesota Press, 287 pp.

453. White, G.F., 1974, *Natural Hazard : Local, National, and Global.* New York : Oxford Univ. Press, 288 pp.

454. White, R.W., 1959, Motivation reconsidered : The concept of competence, *Psychol. Rev.* 66 : 297-333.

455. White, W.P., ed. 1978. *Resources in Environment and Behavior.* Washington DC : APA. In press.

456. Wicker, A.W., 1972, Processes which mediate behavior-environment congruence, *Behav. Sci.* 17 : 265-77.

457. Wicker A.W., 1973, Undermanning theory and research : Implications for the study of psychological and behavioral effects of excess populations. *Represent. Res. Soc. Psychol.* 4 : 185-206.

458. Wicker, A.W., Kirmeyer, S.L., 1976, From church to laboratory to national park : A program of research on excess and insufficient populations in behavior settings. See Ref. 443, pp. 157-85.

459. Wicker, A.W., Kirmeyer, S.L., Hanson, L., Alexander, D., 1976, Effects of manning levels on subjective experiences, performance, and verbal interaction in groups. *Organ. Behav. Hum. Perform,* 17 : 251-74.

460. Wicker, A.W., McGrath, J.E., Armstrong, G.E., 1972, Organization size and behavior setting capacity as determinants of member participation, *Behav. Sci.* 17 : 499-513.

461. Wilcox, B.L., Holahan, C.J., 1976, Social ecology of the megadorm in university student housing, *J. Educ. Psychol.* 68 : 453-58.

462. Willems, E.P., 1974, Behavioral technology and behavioral ecology. *J. Appl. Behav. Anal.* 7 : 151-64.

463. Willems, E.P., 1976, Behavioral ecology, health status and health care : Applications to the rehabilitation setting. See Ref. 15, pp. 211-63.

464. Willems, E.P., 1977, Behavioral ecology. See Ref. 415, pp. 39-68.

465. Willems, E.P., Raush, H.L., eds. 1969, *Naturalistic Viewpoints in Psychological Research.* New York : Holt, Rinehart and Winston, 294 pp.

466. Windley, P.G., 1973, Measuring environmental dispositions of elderly females. See Ref. 346, pp. 217-28.

467. Windley, P.G., 1975, Environmental dispositions: A theoretical and methodological alternative. In *Theory Development in Environment and Aging.* ed. P.G., Windley, T.O., Byerts, F.G., Ernst, pp. 127-41, Washington DC : Gerontol. Soc. 294 pp.

468. Winett, R.A., Kaiser, S., Haberkorn, G., 1977, The effects of monetary rebates and daily feedback on electricity conservation. *J. Environ. Syst.* 6 : 327-39.

469. Winett, R.A., Nietzel, M.T., 1975. Behavioral ecology : Contingency management of consumer energy use. *Am. J. Community Psychol.* 3 : 123-33.

470. Winkel, G.H., ed. 1969, present, *Environment and Behavior*. Beverly Hills, Calif : Sage.

471. Winkel, G.H., 1977, Some human dimensions of urban design. In *On Streets*, ed. S. Anderson, Cambridge, Mass : MIT Press. In press.

472. Wofsey, L., Rierdan, J., Wapner, S., 1978, Changes in representation of the currently inhabited environment as a function of planning to move to a new environment. *Environ. Behav.* In press.

473. Wohlwill, J.F., 1976, Environmental aesthetics : The environment as a source of affect. See Ref. 14, pp. 37-86.

474. Wohlwill, J.F., 1974, Human adaptation to levels of environmental stimulation. *Hum. Ecol.* 2 : 127-47.

475. Wohlwill, J.F., 1973. The environment is not in the head. See Ref. 347, pp. 166-81.

476. Wohlwill, J.F., Heft, H., 1978, Environments fit for the developing child. In *Ecological Factors in Human Development*, ed. H. McGuirk. Amsterdam : North Holland. In press.

477. Wohlwill, J.F., Kohn, I. 1976, Dimensionalizing the environmental manifold. See Ref. 443, pp. 19-45.

478. Wolf, C.P., 1974, Social impact assessment : The state of the art. See Ref. 74, 2 : 1-44.

479. Wolf, C.P., ed. 1974-1977. *Environmental Sociology Newsletter*, Washington DC : Am. Sociol. Assoc.

480. Wolf, C.P., ed. 1975, Special issue on social impact assessment. *Environ. Behav.* 7 : 259-404.

481. Wolfe, M., Golan, M.B., 1977, Privacy and institutionalization. See Ref. 420. In press.

482. Wolfe, M., Laufer, R., 1974, The concept of privacy in childhood and adolescence. See Ref. 74, 6 : 29-54.

483. Wood, D., Beck, R., 1976. Talking with environmental A, an experimental mapping language. See Ref. 315, pp. 351-61.

484. Worchel, S., Teddlie, C., 1976, The experience of crowding : a two factor theory. *J. Pers. Soc. Psychol.* 34 : 30-40.

485. Wortman, C.B., Brehm, J.W., 1975. Responses to uncontrollable

outcomes : An integration of reactance theory and the learned helplessness model. *Adv. Exp. Soc. Psychol.* 8 : 277-336.

486. Wortman, C.B., Panciera, L., Shusterman, L., Hibscher, J., 1976, Attributions of causality and reactions to uncontrollable outcomes. *J. Exp. Soc. Psychol.* 12 : 301-16.
487. Wortman, P.M., 1975. Evaluation research : A psychological perspective, *Am. Psychol.* 30 : 562-75.
488. Wortz, E.C., Nowlis, D.P., 1975. The design of habitable environments. *Man-Environ. Syst.* 5 : 280-88.
489. Zannaras, G., 1976, The relationship between cognitive structure and urban form. See Ref. 315, pp 336-50.
490. Zeisel, J., 1975, *Sociology and Architectural Design.* New York : Sage. 57 pp.
491. Zeisel, J., Griffen, M., 1975. *Charlesview Housing : A Diagnostic Evaluation.* Cambridge, Mass : Harvard Grad. Sch. Design. 131 pp.
492. Zifferblatt, S.M., Hendricks, C.G., 1974. Applied behavioral analysis of societal problems : Population change, a case in point. *Am. Psychol.* 29 : 750-61.
493. Zube, E.H., 1976. Perception of landscape and land use. See Ref. 15, pp. 87-121.
494. Zube, E.H., Brush, R.O., Fabos, J.G., eds. 1975. *Landscape Assessment : Values, Perceptions,* and *Resources.* Stroudsburg, Pa : Dowden, Hutchinson and Ross. 367 pp.
495. Zube, E.H., Pitt, D.G., Anderson, T.W., 1975, Perception and prediction of scenic resource values of the Northeast. See Ref. 494, pp. 151-67.
496. Zuckerman, M., Bone, R.N., Neary, R., Mangelsdorff, D., Brustman, B., 1972, What is the sensation seeker ? Personality trait and experience correlates of the sensation-seeking scales. *J. Consult. Clin. Psychol.* 39 : 308-21.
497. Zyzanski, S.J., Jenkins, C.D., 1970, Basic dimensions within the coronaryprone behavior pattern. *J. Chronic Dis.* 22 : 781-95.

THREE

DANIEL STOKOLS AND SALLY ANN SHUMAKER

PEOPLE IN PLACES: A Transactional View of Settings

INTRODUCTION

ALTHOUGH the behavioral relevance of the molar environment is widely recognized, systematic studies of the transactions between people and their sociophysical settings have been sparse (see Barker and Associates, 1978; Bronfenbrenner, 1979; and Moos, 1976, for notable exceptions). A major difficulty facing such research is the staggering complexity of the large-scale environment. Unlike the discrete stimuli and cues comprising the microenvironment (cf. Gibson, 1960; Skinner, 1953), the architectural, geographical, and sociocultural components of the molar environment are interdependently arrayed in the form of dynamic, ecological systems (cf. Barker, 1968). In the face of this complexity, it becomes difficult to demarcate the appropriate units of environmental analysis, and to assess their implications for behavior and health.

A crucial challenge facing psychological research is to develop a theoretical basis for describing and categorizing the diverse settings of human behavior. Only by identifying the important dimensions and processes of settings can we begin to assess the comparability of environments and the ecological validity of our research findings and policy decisions (cf. Secord, 1977). Guided by these concerns, the major purposes of the present chapter are (1) to develop a conceptualization of settings emphasizing the cognitive and behavioral transactions between people and places ; (2) to delineate a set of theoretical dimensions for describing and categorizing settings ; and (3) to derive research hypotheses from the proposed taxonomic dimensions.

The term setting, as it has been used in the psychological literature, typically refers to a common set of interrelated elements—namely, a particular place in which specific individuals share recurring patterns of activity and experience (cf. Argyle, 1977 ; Barker, 1968 ; Bronfenbrenner, 1977 ; Magnusson, 1981 ; Pervin, 1978 ; Wicker, 1979b). Among the most comprehensive psychological analyses of settings are Barker's (1960, 1968) theory of "behavior settings" and Bronfenbrenner's (1977, 1979) analysis of the ecology of human development. Although their analyses focus on different psychological and developmental questions, both Barker and Bronfenbrenner construe settings as units of the ecological environment that are characterized by the high degree of interdependence among their physical, social-structural, and personal components.

The conceptualization of settings presented in this chapter extends earlier analyses in at least three respects. First, it gives explicit consideration to the concept of "place"—the geographical and architectural context of behavior. Previous analyses of settings have emphasized the social and behavioral aspects of settings (*e.g.*, processes of under- and overmanning in Barker's theory ; transcontextual social networks in Bronfenbrenner's analysis), while neglecting to consider the relationships between these dimensions and the architectural geographical milieu.[1] Second, a transactional perspective is emphasized in the present analysis, highlighting the reciprocal influence between people and places. Places, thus, are viewed not only as a composite of behaviour-shaping forces, but also as the material and symbolic product of human action. Third, our analysis distinguishes among settings that are oriented toward and occupied by single individuals, coacting aggregates, and/or interactive groups. This strategy is in contrast to earlier analyses that have not differentiated among settings in terms of the composition and organization of their occupants. Our approach is based on the assumption that a categorization of settings, reflecting the different levels of social organization and interdependence among occupants offers theoretical leverage for understanding the complex transactions between people and places.

We should note, however (as becomes apparent in the latter sections of the chapter), that our analysis gives greatest attention to group-occupied settings. We have chosen to emphasize this category of settings because people spend so much of their waking time in groups, and because group-occupied settings afford an opportunity to assess the interrelationships among a wider range of environmental dimensions (*e.g.*, social-structural and organizational as well as psychological and physical dimensions) than do individual- and aggregate-occupied settings.

As a basis for developing the proposed theoretical analysis, it is first necessary to examine in detail the two major components of settings : their physical milieu (places) and their occupants (individuals, aggregates, and groups). Theoretical terms for describing and analyzing the physical milieu and occupants of settings are delineated in the next two sections of the chapter. Throughout these sections, the artificiality of rigidly separating the components of settings becomes apparent as our analysis arrives at a taxonomy of settings based on transactional or relational terms. Places, for example, are characterized in terms of the predominant orientation of their human functions (*e.g.*, individual-, aggregate-, or group-oriented), whereas people are distinguished by their association or lack of association with particular places (*e.g.*, place-specific and place-nonspecific) and their perceived attachments to those environments (*e.g.*, place-dependent and place-independent). In the final section of the chapter, the proposed taxonomic terms are utilized as a basis for developing a theoretical analysis of the group-environment interface and for deriving hypotheses about the dynamic relationships between people and places.

PLACES : THE PHYSICAL AND SYMBOLIC CONTEXT OF HUMAN ACTION

In 1943, Clark Hull, a leading proponent of behavioral psychology, commented that ". . . as the behavior sciences evolve the relationships where multiple causes are involved will be expressed more and more precisely in the form of equations ; . . . It is hardly to be doubted that the behavior sciences are rapidly moving in this direction [p. 288]." Hull's statement summarizes the lofty aspirations of American psychologists during the

1940's, 1950's, and early 1960's—the heyday of behaviorism and the golden age of experimentation—as they rushed into their laboratories in quest of discovering the laws of human behavior.

The experimental search for enduring behavioral laws posed some important implications regarding the proper definition of the environment, on the one hand, and its behavioral consequences on the other. First, the environment had to be construed in terms of discrete, separable units—that is, *stimuli*—that were amenable to systematic observation within the laboratory. Second, these environmental elements, or stimuli, had to be isolated—that is, examined singly or in small clusters—so that their functional relationships with specific *responses* of the organism could be discerned through experimental manipulation. In the words of Benton Underwood (1957), a highly regarded methodologist, "One may vary more than one stimulus condition in a given experiment . . . but to draw a conclusion about the influence of any given variable, that variable must have been systematically manipulated alone, somewhere in the design [p. 35]."

As psychologists pursued the laws of behavior, their experimentalist fervor gradually gave way to concerns about the external validity or generalizability of laboratory findings (cf. Campbell and Stanley, 1963), and the simplicity of stimulus-response models vis-a-vis the complexity of behavior within naturalistic settings (cf. Gergen, 1973 ; Ring, 1967 ; Smith, 1972 ; Willems and Raush, 1969). In light of these concerns, many psychologists shifted their theoretical focus from the micro to the molar environment in the hope of identifying the contextual moderators of environment-behavior relationships (*e.g.*, Barker, 1963 ; Chein, 1954 ; Craik, 1973 ; Gibson, 1960 ; Lewin, 1936).

With the emergence of environmental psychology during the late 1960's and early 1970's (cf. Craik, 1973 ; Wohlwill, 1970), several programs of research emphasizing the large-scale environment were implemented. Research in the areas of environmental cognition, spatial behavior, and stress exemplify this changing research strategy. In the area of environmental cognition, Lynch (1960) developed a conceptualization of cognitive mapping within humans, drawing upon Tolmon's (1938) pioneering (but initially neglected) research on "cognitive maps" in rats. Also, Ittelson (1973) contributed a comprehensive analysis of the differences between environment (place) and object (stimulus) perception.

In the areas of spatial behavior and stress, researchers have examined several dimensions of the large-scale environment as they affect human performance and well-being. Studies of personal space, territoriality, and crowding, for example, have established the behavioral and health relevance of variables such as residential density and architectural design (cf. Altman, 1975 ; Baum and Valins, 1977 ; Gove, Hughes, and Galle, 1979 ; Newman, 1973). Other studies have demonstrated the impact of stressors such as community noise, ambient temperature, and air pollution on behavior (cf. Baron and Bell, 1976 ; Cohen, Glass, and Singer, 1973).

These studies of spatial behavior and stress reflect some significant trends in current research on environment and behavior. First, investigations of the molar environment typically proceed by isolating (via laboratory or field experiments) specific dimensions of the sociophysical milieu—for example, architectural design, noise, density, ambient temperature—and examining their relationships with behavior and health. Although this strategy is consistent with the sequential, experimental strategy favored by Underwood (see the previous quote), it fails to capture the interdependencies among multiple dimensions of the environment and their joint relationships with behavior. One objective of the present analysis is to highlight the interconnections among social-structural and architectural-geographical components of settings.

Second, psychologists typically construe the environment either in terms of its objective, material features or in terms of the individual's subjective impressions of those features. Rarely are the objective and subjective elements of environments considered within the same analysis.[2] In our view, the sociophysical environment is a composite of material and symbolic features. Thus, an attempt is made to integrate the objectivist and subjectivist perspectives within the proposed conceptualization of places. More specifically, the degree to which a place has been transformed by its occupants from a melange of material elements into a symbolically meaningful setting serves as an important criterion for describing and comparing diverse environments.

Finally, whereas most research on environmental cognition has emphasized the individual's perception of the environment (cf. Moore and Golledge, 1976), the present analysis encompasses the phenomena of social perception—that is, the processes by which setting members collectively perceive and ascribe meaning to their sociophysical milieu. By focusing on the common or widely recognized meanings that become associated with the molar environment, our analysis offers a "middle ground" between subjectivist perspectives, which construe environmental perception as essentially a personal, idiosyncratic phenomenon, and objectivist views of the environment, which avoid reference to perceptual processes altogether.

It is apparent from the preceding discussion that places can be characterized in terms of numerous criteria, including their overt physical attributes, individuals' perceptions of those attributes, and occupants' collective interpretation of place meanings. We have chosen to develop a categorization of places based on their functional, motivational, and evaluative meanings, as reflected in the collective appraisals of their occupants. We believe that an analysis of collectively held place meanings offers conceptual leverage for understanding phenomena such as the degree to which occupants feel dependent on or attached to a particular place, their reactions to abrupt environmental change or relocation, and the conditions under which residents and users will be motivated to improve or withdraw from a given place.

As a basis for identifying the functional, motivational, and evaluative meanings of places, it is necessary to examine the processes of collective perception in more detail. Our discussion of these phenomena builds upon an earlier analysis of group-place transactions presented by Stokols (1981).

The social perception of places

The widely recognized images or meanings conveyed by places constitute the non-material properties of the physical milieu—the sociocultural "residue" or residual meaning that becomes attached to places as the result of their continuous association with specific patterns of activity. Just as environments can be described in terms of the imageability (or memorability) of their physical elements (Lynch, 1960), they also can be characterized in terms of their *Social Imageability*—that is, their capacity to evoke vivid and collectively held social meanings among the occupants and users of a place.[3] The sociocultural meanings associated with a place can be thought as a kind of "glue" that binds individuals and groups to a particular environment.

Not all places can be characterized as socially imageable, due to the absence of certain circumstances that foster the development of social imageability. One such factor is the regularity with which places are occupied. We can distinguish between *patterned-activity* (*i.e.*, regularly occupied) and *non-patterned-activity* (*i.e.*, unoccupied or sporadically occupied places). Examples of the former include homes, schools, public parks and beaches, and entire array of behavior settings that have been investigated by Barker and his colleagues (cf. Barker and Associates, 1978). Examples of the latter include empty fields or dilapidated buildings that are neither inhabited nor used by people on a regular basis. A central assumption of this analysis is that places acquire social imageability to the extent that they are regularly and predictably associated with particular patterns of individual and/or collective behavior.

For those places that are associated with recurring patterns of activity, several additional factors may mediate the development of social imageability. For example, the frequency with which community members used a particular place, the number of people in the community who use or know about the place, and the degree to which inhabitants or users of the place communicate with each other about the sociocultural meanings of their environment are all potential determinants of social imageability.

The imageability of a place refers to those features of the environment that are highly salient to its occupants. Kevin Lynch's (1960) discussion of the physical imageability of places, for example, emphasizes the dimension of *perceptual salience*—that is, the number and intensity of highly noticeable features within an environment (cf. Stokols, 1979 ; Taylor and Fiske, 1978). Among the factors that heighten the perceptual salience of environments are stimulus contrast, novelty, and complexity (cf. Berlyne, 1960 ; Kaplan, 1975 ; Wohlwill, 1976).

The concept of social imageability, as used in this analysis, refers not to the perceptual prominence of environments, but rather to their *functional, motivational*, and *evaluative significance*. These dimensions of environmental salience encompass collectively held images that relate, respectively, to three basic facets of places : (1) their *functions*—that is, individual or group-specific activities that occur within places on a regular basis, the norms associated with these activities, as well as descriptive information regarding the identities and social roles of setting members ; (2) personal and collective *goals* and purposes, each of which is weighted by its relative importance to the inhabitants or regular users of a place ; and (3) *evaluations* of occupants, physical features, and/or social functions typically associated with a place (*e.g.*, the negative stereotypes connected with certain neighborhoods regarding the presumed dangerousness of their occupants ; cf. Suttles, 1968).[4]

The actual content of those meanings associated with particular places is referred to in this discussion as the perceived social field of the physical environment. More specifically, the *perceived social field of a place is defined as the totality of functional, motivational, and evaluative meanings conveyed by the physical environment to current or prospective occupants of the place.* This matrix of meanings is essentially a set of collectively held images that evolve as the result of direct or indirect interaction with a particular place.

The evolution of socio-cultural meanings within organizations and cultural groups generally has been investigated by sociologists and anthropologists (cf. Agar, Chapter 2 in this volume ; Berger and Luckmann, 1966 : Garfinkel, 1967 ; Gerson and Gerson, 1976 ; Mead, 1934 ; Tyler, 1969), though more recently psychologists have begun to apply ethnographic methods to the study of social interaction and group structure (*e.g.*, Harre, 1977 ; Harre and Secord, 1972). The present analysis diverges from these earlier investigations by focusing on place-related meanings (*i.e.*, those attached to a particular environment or category of environments) rather than on the broader set of social rules and meanings (*e.g.*, ethical norms) that are widely held by the members of a community but are not necessarily attached to a specific place.

The notion that physical environments convey information about the sociocultural functions associated with them is similar to Gibson's (1977) "affordance" concept. The affordance of an object or place refers to the potential uses or activities it suggests to observers by virtue of its physical properties (cf. Kaplan, 1978). Gibson has distinguished among physical affordances (those associated with objects and places) and social affordances—the potential forms and consequences of interpersonal encounters available within a social situation (cf. Baron, Chapter 4 in this volume). Whereas physical affordances are presumed to be recognizable by most members of a species, many categories of social affordances are more likely to be perceived by the members of a particular group than by outsiders.

In the present analysis, the concept of social field subsumes only those social affordances (*i.e.*, functional meanings) that become associated with specific places (*e.g.*, having a drink with one's friends at a local tavern), while excluding those that are not restricted to particular places or types of places (*e.g.*, having a friendly chat). At the same time, it should be noted that the imageability of a place is determined not only by the social affordances it subsumes, but also by those that it precludes (*e.g.*, difficulty of informal social interaction at a religious service).

The specific meanings associated with places can be described in terms of their content, complexity, clarity, heterogeneity, distortions, and contradictions (cf. Stokols, 1981). For example, the *content* of the social field can be assessed by having a representative sample of occupants list those functional, motivational, and evaluative meanings associated with a given place. This open-ended procedure is similar to Harre and Secord's (1972) notion of "accounting" (*i.e.*, the explication of social action in terms of shared social meanings reflected in individuals' accounts of their social experiences) but pertains more specifically to the sociocultural images attached to the physical environment.

The *complexity* of the social field can be indexed in terms of the number of shared meanings that emerge from the independent listings provided by the different users of a place. The more often a particular meaning is cited by the occupants and users of a place, the greater its *clarity*. An additional criterion for judging the relative clarity of place meanings is the extent to which they are rated by occupants as being highly or slightly characteristic of a particular place.[5]

In some situations, the content and clarity of place meanings may vary according to subgroup membership. Thus, the perceived social field can be characterized in terms of its *heterogeneity*, or the number of subgroups within an environment for whom distinguishable patterns of meaning can be discerned. The social field also can be analyzed in terms of its *distortions*. Distortions are unrecognized discrepancies between the sociocultural images of a place and the nature of the social activities and experiences that actually occur there. Distortions can arise as the result of insufficient exposure to a place (*e.g.*, among outsiders who have never visited the area or among group members who are minimally involved in its activities) or from misinformation about the place.

Finally, we can characterize place meanings in terms of their *contradictions*—that is, their consistency with or contradiction of the preferences of occupants. Discrepancies between the actual and preferred meanings of a place are exemplified by situations in which people's images of a place are negatively toned as a result of earlier, unpleasant experiences there, or where the actual uses of a place are contradictory to its intended functions (*e.g.*, the presence of a noisy group in a reading room at the library).

The proposed dimensions and measures of place meanings, outlined, previously offer a basis for categorizing environments and for analyzing the reciprocal relationships between people and places. In the remainder of this section, we develop a categorization of place in terms of their functional meanings ; in subsequent sections, we examine the processes by which the motivational and evaluative salience of places prompt their occupants to enact structural modifications of the environment.

The functional orientation of places

Our analysis of the perceived social field suggests that places can be categorized in terms of their predominant functional orientations. Earlier, we distinguished between nonpatterned activity (irregularly occupied) and patterned-activity (regularly occupied) places. In the former, the absence of recurring activity patterns precludes the association of unambiguous, widely recognized functional meanings with the environment. Such places, because they exclude the possibility of occupation or are structured in ways that inhibit the development of sustained activity, remain ambiguous in their functional meanings. Rugged mountain terrains, desert areas, and open fields, for example, are all unlikely places for the development of patterned behaviors. Although people may climb a mountain, explore a desert, or wander through an open field, the probability is low that these behaviors will be repeated or exist independently of a particular person or group. Only in those cases in which people have intervened in these natural environments and have implemented design changes that foster, for instance, hiking, exploring, or wandering (*e.g.*, natural park trails) will clear-cut, functional meanings become associated with the place. In such instances, the places are linked with patterned activities and fall within our second category of place types.

Considering the wide array of functional meanings that evolve within patterned-activity places, it is apparent that such meanings can be categorized according to several different strategies. One such strategy involves a straightforward description of the kinds of activities and behaviors that occur within an environment (*e.g.*, eating, socializing, parenting, political events ; cf. Price and Blashfield, 1975). An alternative taxonomic approach is to subsume specific categories of behavior within a smaller set of broader categories (*e.g.*, Moos, 1976). Our analysis reflects the second general strategy. Specifically, we categorize the functional meanings of places in terms of the composition and organization of occupants. An advantage of this approach, we believe, is that it provides transactional terms for describing environments that reflect the linkages between physical and social-structural features of places.

Patterned-activity places, thus, are categorized according to whether occupants and users perceive them to be functionally oriented toward single individuals, coacting aggregates, or organized groups. (We are assuming, for the time being, a correspondence between the actual and perceived functional orientations of places. Possible discrepancies between the actual functions and the perceived functional meanings of environments are discussed in a subsequent section of the chapter.)

Individual-oriented places are those typically occupied by a single individual. A private study room or carrel within a library, an individual's bedroom, or the bathroom in a family dwelling exemplify such places. The physical structure and normative properties of these environments either preclude or discourage occupancy by more than one person at a time.

Aggregate-oriented places are those typically occupied by coacting individuals—that is, by collectivities comprised of strangers or minimally related people. Examples of these environments include public subway stations, beaches, pedestrian malls, or parking lots. In these locations. activities are performed by several individuals who are usually unrelated to each other.

Group-oriented places, in contrast with the first two categories of environments, are usually occupied by people who know and interact with each other on a regular basis—that is, by organized groups. The secret meeting place of a neighborhood gang, the headquarters of a business or religious group, the back-yard of a family residence, and the practice field of an athletic team exemplify group-oriented places. In each instance, the predominant functions of the environment are geared toward the presence of organized groups (see Fig. 3.1). (The distinguishing features of groups vis-a-vis coacting aggregates are discussed in the following section of the chapter.)

For several of the examples just mentioned, it is apparent that the main functions associated with a place can be performed by either the same occupants or by different occupants on different occasions. Library study rooms, for instance, might be reserved for use by a specific person, or could be used by several individuals on a rotating basis. Similarly, an athletic practice field might be reserved for use by one team only or could be utilized by different groups at various times. Environments whose functions are performed by the same people on a regular basis we label *same-occupant places* ; those whose functions are carried out by different people on a rotating basis we refer to as *variable-occupant places.* The implications of occupant variability for understanding the dynamic relationships between people and their environments are examined in the section of this chapter focusing on settings.

The proposed categories of individual-, aggregate-, and group-oriented places are intended as "ideal types" and, as such, reflect oversimplifications of the actual environment. The meaning and applicability of the proposed place types, therefore, should be qualified in relation to several conceptual issues. First, the suggested categorization of places might imply that environments have singular, rather than multiple, functional orientations. Yet, the constituency of many environments varies over time, as illustrated by offices that support the simultaneous activities of individuals and small groups, or by classrooms that are sometimes used as a study place by individuals and, at other times, as a meeting place by the people enrolled in a course. Thus, a distinction can be drawn between *single-function* and *multiple-function* places. This distinction suggests that any attempt to characterize the functional orientation/s of a place must be carefully bounded with respect to specific time and space coordinates (*e.g.*, the use of Room 432 on Thursday from 1:00 to 2:00 P.M. ; the conference meeting area within the executive suite of ACME corporation).

Closely related to the issue of single versus multiple functions of places is the nested or *hierarchical structure of environments* (cf. Barker, 1968). Library study rooms, for example, are located within broader territorial and administrative systems (*e.g.*, the library building, the campus environment). Thus, such places can be characterized not only in terms of the functional meanings associated with individual study, but also with those reflecting the administration of the library (*e.g* , the maintenance schedule dictating the times at which study rooms must be vacated by readers to permit floor mopping, or the opening and closing hours of the library building).

The functional meanings associated with library study rooms can be assessed from the perspective of individual users or from that of library administrators. In general, our analysis of place meanings emphasizes the perspective of performers within places, but it is important to note that the images-of environments can be assessed from the vantage point of administrators and managers, or from the perspective of potential occupants who have had minimal direct exposure to the environment under consideration.

An additional distinction between *geographical* versus *generic places* should be noted.[6] The former refers to a particular geographical area whereas the latter refers to a category of places that are functionally similar. For instance, in attempting to ascertain the functional orientations of Bar-B-Que restaurants, we can query current or potential customers of Bar-B-Que restaurants in general, or we can ask them about "Shorty's Bar-B-Que on Dixie Highway in South Miami, Florida". The level of specificity of the environment poses a number of implications regarding the complexity, clarity, and heterogeneity of place meanings reflected in the respondents' comments. The composite of functional meanings associated with a particular place is likely to be more complex (detailed) than that conveyed by a generic category of environments. Moreover, the place meanings perceived by actual versus potential users of an environment are more likely to diverge when they consider a specific place rather than a more general category of places. For example, people who have never been to a restaurant are more likely to have encountered indirect information about restaurants in general, via the media and friends, than about a specific eating place.

Finally, the relationship between environmental specificity and the characteristics of place meanings (*e.g.*, their complexity, clarity) suggests the importance of distinguishing among *personal*, *common*, and *shared meanings* of environments. Personal meanings are impressions about places (*i.e.*, their functional, motivational, and evaluative meanings) that are held by single individuals. Personal meanings can be arrived at on an idiosyncratic basis (*i.e.*, through intuition alone), through direct experience with an environment, or through communication with others about their experiences with a place. Personal meanings become part of the perceived social field, described earlier, to the extent that they closely resemble (or are cross-validated by) the place meanings perceived by other users of the environment.

Considering those meanings that are subsumed under the perceived social field (*i.e.*, are jointly held by current or potential occupants of the place), we can distinguish between common and shared meanings. The key difference between these categories of meanings is that the former do not presuppose communication among place users (that is, the commonly held meanings do not arise, intensify, or change as the result of such communication), whereas the latter do. The functional meanings associated with public beaches may arise as the result of each bather's personal experiences with the beach or through communication about the beach with sources other than fellow bathers at the time of occupancy. By contrast, the meanings that become attached to the "turf" of a neighborhood gang arise through the joint use of and communication about the area by members of the gang.

Summary

In this section, we have divided places into two general categories : (1) unoccupied or irregularly occupied ; (2) regularly occupied. When places are occupied on a recurring basis, they become associated with widely recognized, sociocultural meanings. These collectively held images of a place—its perceived social field—evolve from the sustained interactions that occur within it. The major components of the perceived social field are the functional, motivational, and evaluative meanings of places.

The patterned activities that occur in regularly occupied places can be oriented toward single individuals, coacting aggregates, or organized groups. These functional orientations are reflected in the physical and normative properties of places. The characterization of places in terms of their functional orientations is proposed as a very general classification scheme ; several factors that qualify the proposed categorization are discussed (*e.g.*, variability among occupants). Having outlined and qualified some of the functional properties of places, we turn now to a more explicit analysis of the composition and organizational attributes of the occupants within places.

OCCUPANTS : THEIR COMPOSITION, ORGANIZATION, AND RELATIONSHIP TO PLACE

The number of ways people vary, both as individuals and in commerce with others, has been studied extensively by social scientists. The results of many of these investigations could be usefully applied to a description of place occupants. Any attempt on our part to review this literature here, however, would both tax our expertise and take the reader far beyond the scope and intended focus of this chapter. Instead, we highlight two features of occupants that critically influence the types of transactions that occur between people and places and are, therefore, particularly relevant to our development of a setting taxonomy. We first consider the composition and organization of occupants, and then discuss the types and degrees of associations that exist between places and people. Our distinctions along occupants along these two dimensions are, primarily, descriptive. However, in the following section of this chapter, the dynamic implications of these distinctions are developed.

Composition and organization

One of the first things that is obvious when viewing place occupants is simply the number of people present. Is an accupant alone, or are there more than one occupant present in the same place ? And, when there is more than one person present, how do the occupants relate to one another ? That is, are they individuals who appear to behave independently of one another (*e.g.*, an audience at a Broadway play) or are they more of a unit (*e g.*, a family picnicking together ?). These initial observations produce an unambiguous classification of occupants. People in places act alone, as part of an aggregate, or as members of a group (see Fig. 3.2). Before discussing some of the implications of this classification scheme, we would like to clarify our distinction between groups and aggregates.

Definitions of groups are numerous and range from general, inclusive descriptions to very elaborate, precise delineations. This range comes from the number of characteristics used to describe groups, including : internal structure, reciprocal influence of members, amount and form of interaction, degree of real and perceived boundedness, objectives (*e.g.*, work, therapy), size, level of formality, and activities performed (cf. Cartwright and Zander, 1968 ; Hare, Borgatta, & Bales, 1965 ; Kelley and Thibaut, 1978 ; McGrath, 1964 ; Shaw, 1976 ; Steiner, 1972). Because of this variety, and our emphasis on group-occupied places in the next section of this chapter, it is important that we make explicit our meaning of grougs *vis-a-vis* aggregates. Shaw (1976) defines a group as : "... two or more persons who are interacting with one another in such a manner that each person influences and is influenced by each other person [p. 11]." We would like to add to this definition the criterion that members are aware of their interdependence. This expanded definition complements our goal of clearly differentiating groups from aggregates, while simultaneously allowing us flexibility and leverage in our discussion of setting dynamics in the following section. In that section, we discuss a number of group characteristics (*e.g.*, boundedness, formation, structure, *etc.*) that are not explicitly reflected in the foregoing definition.

Although the classification of occupants by number (single versus multiple) and organization (aggregate versus group) is straightforward, each occupant category has complex implications when the transaction with place is considered. When acting alone, an individual brings to a place a number of personal factors (*e.g.*, values and attitudes, dispositions, history, and behavioral style) that will influence his or her perception and use of the resources within that place. Thus, in conjunction with "collectively held images", there are a number of differences among individuals that impact on the transaction between person and place.

As soon as two more people transact with the same place at the same time, a number of social factors, in addition to the individual issues, become relevant. For example, social facilitation (Zajonc, 1965), privacy (Altman, 1975), personal space (Evans and Howard, 1973), distribution of resources (Wicker, 1979a, 1979b), and complementarity in personality styles (Altman, 1977) are issues that may influence the person-place interface. When the occupants are a group, these individual and social issues are further complicated by the features that distinguish groups from aggregates (*i.e.*, the interaction and interdependency of members), as well as by other characteristics that are specific to groups (*e.g.*, internal structure and cohesiveness).

On a very general level, variations in occupant numbers and organization influence the sources and kinds of information available to the occupants. The perceived place meaning for a person acting alone derives from his or her personal experience with the place, shared norms, and the widely known and collectively held images of the place. A member of an aggregate has the same sources of information, with the additional input acquired from observing the transactions of others with the place ; and, group members' experience is further augmented by the explicit sharing among members of place impressions and images.

One example of the possible impact of information differences on person-place transactions comes from viewing a person who enters a place for the first time and is faced with the immediate task of determining what behaviors are appropriate and how to best use the resources available. If alone, this occupant has no social cues and, therefore, must rely on the physical cues (*i.e.*, affordances) provided by the place, and whatever he or she knows from general norms. If others are present in the place, social cues are available ; and, if there is a group of friends present, the individual can enhance his or her commerce with the place by asking them relevant questions.

This example suggests a further nuance in a person's commerce with place that differs because of the number and organization of occupants. Though the presence of others may provide additional information about behaviour, it also may restrict behavior. When alone, inappropriate behavior cannot be judged or evaluated by others. However, when in the presence of others, a degree of conformity is a probable outcome and pressures toward conformity are even stronger within a group (cf. Cartwright & Zander, 1968). Thus even though movement from individual to group increases information, it may concomitantly decrease one's freedom of self expression.

Relationship to places

Objective properties of association : *Place specificity.* Whether occupants are acting alone or in the presence of others, their association with place can vary considerably. An individual may walk alone along a beach, join a crowd of people who are watching a sailboat race, and by chance meet some friends who are discussing sailing. In each of these situations, the association between person and place is short-lived and impromptu. Furthermore, the probability is low that the same or similar activities will predictably recur in the same places. When people occupy particular places on a sporadic basis, we discribe them in these situations as being *place nonspecific.*

Another situation in which people are place nonspecific is one in which they are members of organizations that rarely (or, perhaps never) meet in particular place on a regular basis. Members of unions and professional organizations, for example, may be place nonspecific. For them, there is no shared image of a physical place, and though recurring behaviors may occur (*e.g.*, voting by mail for leaders), they do so independently of place.

It is important to emphasize that when we use the term place nonspecific (or, later in this section, place specific), we are not talking about trans-situational traits. Certainly, there are different styles among people in their associations with places and one difference may be the recurring nature of an occupant's association with place. That is, some people may more frequently be place nonspecific than others. However, our application of this term is limited to particular activities associated with distinct places. Limiting the term to a description of specific situations promotes a more ecological perspective than viewing it as a trait. That is, it forces us to consider the multiple factors (including individual differences) that would produce a place-nonspecific (or place-specific) association.

We describe people as *place specific* when they perform particular activities in the same location or in categories of places, on a regular, predictable, basis. To distinguish among situations in which occupants are associated with particular places versus categories of places, we use the terms *geographical* and *generic place specificity,* respectively. Examples of *geographical place specificity* are : the student working in a library carrel over a school year, the business person who works in an office each day, the secretary who performs his or her job-related activities at the same desk, and the football team that practices on its home field each week. These associations between people and places are predictable and they recur on a regular basis.

If people perform particular activities at differently located, but functionally similar, places, we describe their association to place as *generically place specific.* For example, a group of friends may meet for lunch, every Monday, but rotate their meeting places among restaurants. Or, a scientific organization might rotate annual convention sites among a number of university campuses. In both of these examples, the people are place specific—that is, the places they occupy are alike in characteristics that are essential to the activities in question (in these examples, eating lunch and exchanging information and ideas).

There are several possible reasons why people are place specific or place nonspecific. For example, activities vary in terms of how place specific the resources are that they require. An individual can hike in a number of places, but playing tennis requires a court, net, and so on. Activities may also differ by how acceptable their performance is in particular places (cf. Price & Bouffard, 1974). Some, for example, may require more privacy or solitude than others. People also differ in how flexible they are in their use of the environment. These variations could evolve from personality traits (*e.g.*, a rigid versus open style), or economic realities including income and mobility (cf. Michelson, 1977). Whatever the antecedents or causes, people do develop different modal styles in their associations with particular activities and places. These styles can be classified into the two broad categories of place specific and place nonspecific. In most instances, this classification is easily done and is based on objectively observable events. Within the set of place-specific occupants, there are two further objective properties of association that merit consideration. These are *endurance* and *frequency*.

A farmer who has worked the same land all of his or her life has an association with place (*i.e.*, the farmland) that has persisted over a lifetime. If the farmer's family has owned and worked this same land for several generations, one might argue that the association that has existed between the family and place has a quality of endurance that goes beyond the experience of the one, current family member. That is, the farmer's sense of endurance is based on his or her actual transactions with the land, and is amplified by the ancestral ties.

The example of the farmer represents one end on a continuum ranging from enduring to transitory place specificity. Individuals, however, may associate with places in less enduring ways. A student's relationship to his or her dormitory room will probably not persist beyond 1 year. Even shorter associations occur between groups that form to solve specific problems in a given period of time and that use the same place for their problem-solving activities. Thus, endurance might range from a lifetime to a few days. In all cases, the people are place specific ; but, the quality of their transactions with the environment varies considerably as a function of endurance.

Although frequency of association may relate to endurance, it is not the same property. That is, people may have an infrequent, but enduring association with a place. For example, a group of college alumni may annually reconvene for the homecoming football game. Their transaction with place may endure for several decades, but it occurs only once per year. The problem-solving group described in the earlier example may meet six times per day for 1 month, or only three times during their existence as a group. For the farmer and dormitory student, frequency of transaction with place is very high. Endurance, however, ranges from 1 year to one lifetime.

Subjective properties of association : Place dependence. In addition to the objective properties of association (*i.e.*, specificity, endurance, and frequency), there is a subjective quality to the relationship between occupants and places. Individuals have differing perceptions of their associations with places—the same person may feel an intense or compelling connection to some places, and very little linkage to others. When occupants perceive themselves as having a strong association with a place, we describe them as *place dependent.* In contrast, when occupants observe a weak connection between themselves and a place, they are characterized as *place independent.* Thus, *place dependence describes an occupant's perceived strength of association between him or herself and specific places.*[7]

This perceived strength of association can occur at any level of analysis with respect to place. That is, a person may be place dependent on a home, a neighborhood, or an entire city. Furthermore, the same person may be place dependent for some associations, and place independent for others, (*e.g.*, a person may feel a strong attachment to his or her home, but not to the office in which he or she works).

The place-dependence dimension is descriptive of individuals' (as in the preceding example), aggregates', and groups' relationships to places. A number of surfers, for example, may feel a strong attachment to a beach that they consider the "best" in their area. Though they behave fairly independently of one another (*i.e.*, constitute an aggregate), their perceived association with the place is common. They are all place dependent with respect to that beach. Their commonality in place dependence could produce behaviors that derive strength from the aggregate, as opposed to an individual, perception—a kind of surrogate social support system (cf. Jacobs, 1961). Territorial behavior exemplifies this point. The surfers may have a tacit agreement among themselves as to who has "rights" to use of "their" beach area, and who is an outsider. This implicit understanding could bolster both their coactive and their individual responses to potential encroachments.

Groups have perceived associations with places that transcend the place dependence of individual members. The San Francisco Giants, for example, may, as a team, be place dependent on Candlestick Park. This strong association could evolve from a number of factors. Team members may share perceptions of place meanings, the park may uniquely support the team's activities, they may have a higher success rate at "home", and there may be little opportunity for relocation. Whatever the contributing elements, the outcome is a strong link to a specific place.

Our definition and examples of place dependence provide a general characterization of the concept. In order for place dependence to be usefully applied to settings, however, it is important that we go beyond this imprecise and static description to a more systematic and dynamic analysis. That is, we need to focus on the factors that underlie individual or group assessments of dependency on place. These factors can be organized within a two-component process. Briefly, they include an occupant's assessment of : (1) *the quality of current place* ; and (2) *the relative quality of comparable alternative places.*

Before expanding on these components, we should note that although we are conceptualizing place dependence as evolving from occupants' assessments of the quality of places, we are not suggesting that people are continuously and self consciously monitoring their transactions with places. Place dependence is not always salient to occupants. Rather, it becomes relevant when circumstances occur that heighten the occupants' awareness of their associations to places. Periods of abrupt environmental change, relocation, and very pleasant or unpleasant experiences with places are all circumstances that could bring issues of place dependence to the fore (cf. Fried, 1963 ; Michelson, 1977). Our two components, therefore, merely model the process undergone by occupants when relevant levers cause place dependence to become prominent.

Whatever the particular triggering incident, once people become aware of their association to a place, they will likely assess the place's quality, and the quality of relevant alternatives, in order to determine the strength of their association (*i.e.*, how dependent they are on a particular place). In evaluating the quality of a place, individuals judge how well the place facilitates their goals and activities. This is particularly true of those goals and activities that are most important to them. The result of this evaluation determines an occupant's satisfaction with a place—the better a place meets one's goals, the greater one's satisfaction. This kind of assessment is necessarily subjective and based on some internal standard of the occupant's as to how well a place should meet one's goals. That is, people expect certain outcomes in their transactions with places. These expectations, derived from a person's direct or vicarious experiences with possible outcomes, produces his or her Comparison Level (CL) for places (Thibaut & Kelley, 1959). Thus, degree of satisfaction with place is indexed by the extent to which an existing place's quality diverges from the occupants' CL for places (*i.e.*, their expected level of place quality.)

A number of factors contribute to an assessment of place quality. As noted, a person's CL develops from his or her previous experiences with places. The valence of these experiences will determine current CL. Thus, for example, if individuals historically have had relatively negative outcomes, their CL will be low and they will have lower expectations in their evaluation of place quality. In contrast, a history of positive outcomes with current or comparable, previously experienced places will raise their CL and, concomitantly, the expectations imposed upon their current situation.

Several features of the resources available within a place can affect whether a place facilitates or inhibits goal attainment and, thereby, assessments of place quality. These include the amount of resources in an area, their caliber, and the degree to which they fit the needs of the occupant. The impact of each of these resource characteristics on assessments may vary considerably, and is dependent on the goal in question. For example, a hospital patient whose goal is to become healthier would be more concerned with the caliber or expertise of his or her doctor than with the number and variety of doctors available within that particular hospital.

The value or salience of the goals that are met in a particular place also influence judgments of quality. Although the thwarting of any goal is frustrating, the more important the goal, the more upsetting its blockage (cf. Stokols, 1979 ; Wortman & Brehm, 1975). Similarly, the achievement of highly valued goals will produce more positive feelings than the attainment of minor ones. Therefore, the value of goals or needs will mediate an occupant's assessment of place quality by influencing the strength of an occupant's reactions to goal facilitation or thwarting.

The second component in the process of assessing place dependence involves the occupants' evaluation of the relative quality of their current situation vis-a-vis alternative comparable places. That is, occupants compare the environment they presently occupy with places that they view as potential locations for their activities. Following Thibaut and Kelley's (1959) formulation of the construct Comparison Level for Alternatives (CLalt), occupants assess the quality of expected outcomes among suitable alternative places. Thus, the issue of place dependence goes beyond a simple assessment of the place currently occupied by focusing on the quality differentials among present place and relevant options.

The identification and evaluation of alternatives is affected by several factors. First, a comparison of possible options is predicated on an occupant's *awareness*, and to a lesser degree *familiarity*, with existing alternatives. Awareness refers to an individual's knowledge of relevant options. Familiarity extends awareness to actual experiences in different places. The more individuals and groups use a variety of places for similar activities, the better able they are to make informed judgments about the relative quality of places. Both awareness and familiarity of potential locations can vary considerably among people. Differences in personality styles may explain why some people are more willing to learn about locational alternatives than others. For example, one couple moving into a new home might actively explore the environment, seeking out accessible recreational facilities and service organizations. Another couple, in the same situation, might be reluctant or uninterested in searching for options, settling quickly on single places for specific activities and never becoming cognizant of other possibilities.

Mobility is another factor that can influence an evaluation of the quality of alternative places. The elderly, physically handicapped, and the poor are often severely limited in their access to different environments and are forced to perform most of their activities in places located within the immediate vicinity of their homes. Although this limited mobility can decrease knowledge of alternatives, this is not necessarily the case. People who lack mobility may be aware of and familiar with alternatives, and even recognize higher quality in places other than the ones they currently occupy. However, as long as places are inaccessible, they are nonviable alternatives.

The resources needed for the performance of some activities may be more specific than for others, thereby limiting the number of alternative places available. Sports activities like golfing and tennis are considerably more *resource specific* than jogging or bicycling. Even more limiting are the resources required by certain types of business establishments. Saw mills, ship builders, and ski resorts all are economically dependent on particular features of the environment.

Our consideration of the elements that influence assessments of current place quality (*i.e.*, CL, resource characteristics, and value of goals), and the quality of relevant options (*i.e.*, awareness of alternatives, mobility, and resource specificity) is not meant to represent an exhaustive list. Rather, these elements are reasonable representations of the kinds of issues that contribute to the two-component process involved in an occupant's assessment of place dependence. In addition to these specific factors, there are a number of more subtle considerations that relate to both components of the assessment process, and account for variations in the essential *character of place dependence.* We consider these variations in place dependence because of their potential implications for the dynamics of settings.

As we have mentioned, place dependence is partially evaluated in terms of how well current and alternative places facilitate the attainment of important goals. The *number and range of needs* met by a particular place will affect judgments of the character of place dependence. Places that satisfy several needs (*e.g.*, primary environments) probably lead to a type of place dependence that can be described as being more embedded, extensive, or deep-seated for the occupants than places in which possible activities (and, therefore, attainable goals) are narrowly defined (cf. Stokols, 1979). In such situations, satisfaction with current place is based on a number of expected outcomes and represents a kind of weighted averaging of all possible effects (*i.e.*, all needs met in one place weighted by value, and averaged across expected outcomes). In addition, the range of possible alternatives may narrow as the range of needs met in one's current environment increases.

The *type of needs* that are met within a particular place can also influence the nature of place dependence. The place dependence that occurs in environments where basic survival needs are met will undoubtedly differ from that that emerges in places where less crucial (*e.g.*, recreational) needs are met (cf. Maslow, 1968). These differences would be most salient when place dependence is strong and occupants are threatened with a loss or disruption of place. The repercussions and impact of such threats would be considerably more serious in places meeting basic subsistence needs than in those associated with less central goals.

Place dependence can occur in situations in which outcomes are ***above or below CL***. That is, occupants can be place dependent when their experiences with places are either satisfying or nonsatisfying. In some instances, people will perceive themselves as place dependent when they are satisfied with the quality of their transaction with a particular place, and they believe that this same level of satisfaction cannot be derived from their best comparable alternatives (CLalt). Occupants also can perceive themselves as being strongly linked to a particular place when their transactions with the place are unsatisfactory (below CL) but their best relevant alternative (CLalt) is perceived to be even more negative, or when they feel they have no other alternatives. For example, institutionalized people or those who lack mobility might be dissatisfied with their current place transactions, yet they may still perceive themselves as place dependent because alternatives are inaccessible.

There are several implications for the kind of place dependence that evolves in these very different circumstances. For example, when outcomes are below CL but options are worse or nonexistent, people may react against their environments (*e.g.*, vandalism ; cf. Zeisel, 1976 ; Sommer, 1974), or they may develop a sense of helplessness (Seligman, 1975) and feel unable to act in ways that will improve their lives. Conversely, place dependence that develops because of very positive outcomes may cause people to be very protective of their situations, unwilling to seek out alternatives, and/or resistant to any changes, even those that might improve their current situations (Burton, Kates, and White, 1978).

There are two ways in which the *temporal component* of place dependence affects its general character. As noted, place dependence can occur because of a paucity of relevant options. This lack of alternatives, however, may result from very different factors. In some situations, there may be, from the onset of transaction with place, a limited number of places in which the activity can be performed (*e.g.*, saw mills and ski resorts). In other cases, options may decrease over time. That is, there may have been, initially, a number of viable alternatives for a particular activity but, as occupants spend more time in one place, a narrowing of known alternatives occurs.

A second temporal feature of place dependence relates to the associations people sometimes feel toward places they do not currently occupy. For example, people who are relocated because of business transfers or urban renewal projects may still perceive themselves as strongly linked to their previous or past environment. As long as this perception persists, adaptation to their new environment will most likely be slow. Similarly, people may feel a compelling association toward prospective places. Members of the Palestinian Liberation Organization exemplify this temporal quality of place dependence. That is, they perceive themselves to be linked to, and dependent on, a land that they do not currently occupy. A strong future-oriented place dependence may influence an individual's willingness to adapt to his or her current place transactions, and his or her motivation to alter current activity locations.

In assessing place dependence, occupants evaluate the quality of *perceived place options.* For a variety of reasons (*e.g.*, awareness), there may be discrepancies between these perceived options and *actual place options.* Such inconsistencies would not affect the perception of place dependence, per se. They could, however, have major implications if the occupants become cognizant of the discrepancies. The sudden recognition that one's formerly perceived options do not really exist, or the awareness that more options exist than were initially realized, potentially could affect the long-range survival of settings as well as the short-term stress and well-being of occupants.

A final nuance of place dependence to consider here represents an extension of the CLalt construct, as developed by Thibaut and Kelley (1959). CLalt is the occupant's assessed quality of the single, best alternative. In determining strength of association between oneself and a place, the *number of available* alternatives, as well as the quality of the best alternative, are considered by the occupant. A person perceiving him or herself to have several, qualitatively similar options will probably feel less place dependent than the individual who recognizes only one alternative. Thus, the evaluation of place dependence derives from an assessment of the range or richness of options available, and the quality differentials among all viable options.

Consistent with our earlier distinction between geographical and generic place specificity, it follows that people can be dependent on either a particular place or on a category of places (*geographical* versus *generic place dependence*). People may care deeply about a place that they have never seen and probably never will—because of what it (like generically similar areas) affords. Thus, bird watchers may fight for the preservation of remote, relatively inaccessible places (an example suggested by Stephen Kaplan in a personal communication). People are motivated to preserve their generically similar place options—they care about alternatives that are attractive to them in principle, irrespective of whether they have experienced them in the past or are likely to do so in the future.

We have endeavored to define and characterize place dependence because we consider the concept to be critical in understanding several issues related to settings. Occupants' willingness to alter existing settings or establish new ones, and the impact of settings' termination on occupants, are mediated by the strength of association between place and occupant (cf. Firey, 1945 ; Fried, 1963). Moreover, the subtle variations in place dependence (*e.g.*, its temporal quality) can be expected to affect the dynamics of settings in several ways. The Palestine Liberation Organization provides an interesting example of how these variations manifest themselves.

The PLO, as a group, is dependent on its current environment (*i.e.*, settlements outside of Israel) because (1) this environment meets the subsistence needs of the members ; and (2) the locational alternatives of the group are severely limited. At the same time, the group is dependent on an unrealized future place (*i.e.*, a Palestinian state) that represents an ideal in which the member's subsistence, higher-order personal (*e.g.*, self respect) and group (*e.g.*, collective autonomy as a nation) needs can be met. The incongruity between the outcomes achieved in the current setting (below CL) and those believed to be attainable in the ideal setting (above CL) is stressful, motivating the group to resist adaptation to their current setting and continually strive for their ideal. The PLO is, perhaps, an extreme example of the possible variations in place dependence and the impact of these variations on settings. The more typical ways in which dependence might influence settings are discussed in the following section of this chapter. Before discussing the dynamic interface between people and places i.e., settings), a brief review of our categorization of occupants may be helpful to the reader.

Summary

People occupy places individually, or as a part of aggregates and groups. The relationship between people and places may be regular or sporadic. When people occupy a particular place on a predictable basis, we describe them as *place specific.* When their relationship to place is irregular, we describe them as *place nonspecific.* Regular relationships between people and places vary objectively with respect to the frequency and enduring nature of the transactions. Subjectively, there may be differences in the degree to which occupants perceive themselves as linked to a particular place (*i.e., place-dependent* versus *place-independent* people).

SETTINGS : THE TRANSACTIONS AMONG PEOPLE AND PLACES

The preceding discussion offers a set of dimensions for categorizing people and places. In general, places have been characterized in terms of their predominant functional orientations, and people in terms of their organization and the type and degree of their associations with places. Although the proposed dimensions are transactional—that is, they reflect the inherent interrelatedness of people and places—we have yet to examine explicitly the dynamic relationships implied by those dimensions. To this point in the discussion, we have neglected questions such as the following : Under what conditions do places acquire a particular functional orientation ? To what extent does place dependence mediate people's reactions to abrupt environmental change and to life events involving residential or occupational relocation ? What factors prompt people to actively modify their sociophysical environment ?

To address these and related questions pertaining to people-place transactions, we begin by delineating a taxonomy of settings based on the dimensions presented in earlier sections of this chapter. Having designated the various types of settings included in our taxonomy, we proceed to examine the dynamic relationships among people and places that are associated with those settings. Our analysis of people-place transactions is organized around a broad set of issues relating to the "life cycles of settings" (cf. Devereux, 1977 ; Stokols, 1978 ; Wicker, 1979a)—that is, the conditions under which settings are established, maintained, modified, and/or terminated.

A taxonomy of settings

The intersection between categories of places (see Fig. 3.1) and categories of people (see Fig. 3.2) illustrates the distinction between *settings*—that is, patterned-activity places occupied by place-specific people—and *nonsettings*—that is, nonpatterned-activity places that are either unoccupied or sporadically occupied by place-nonspecific people (see Fig. 3.3). Moreover, settings can be partitioned into six major categories on the basis of the composition and organization of their occupants (individuals, aggregates or organized groups) and the predominant functional meanings associated with their physical milieu (individual, aggregate, or group oriented), as depicted in Fig. 3.4. Thus, the composition and organization of occupants can be either consistent with the predominant, widely recognized orientation of the setting (*e.g.*, an individual studying in a library carrel) or inconsistent with that orientation (*e.g.*, a raucous group that appropriates a library study area as a regular meeting place).

Because the proposed categories of settings represent "ideal types", they necessarily oversimplify a number of inherently complex issues, including situations in which settings are associated with multiple functional orientations (*e.g.*, a large company office containing individual work stations, aggregate-oriented reception areas for visitors, and group-oriented conference rooms), and are occupied simultaneously by individuals, aggregates, and groups. Clearly, then, the boundaries between the proposed categories should not be viewed as rigid and impermeable.

The utility of the proposed taxonomy of settings, we believe, resides not so much in its descriptive capacity but rather in the

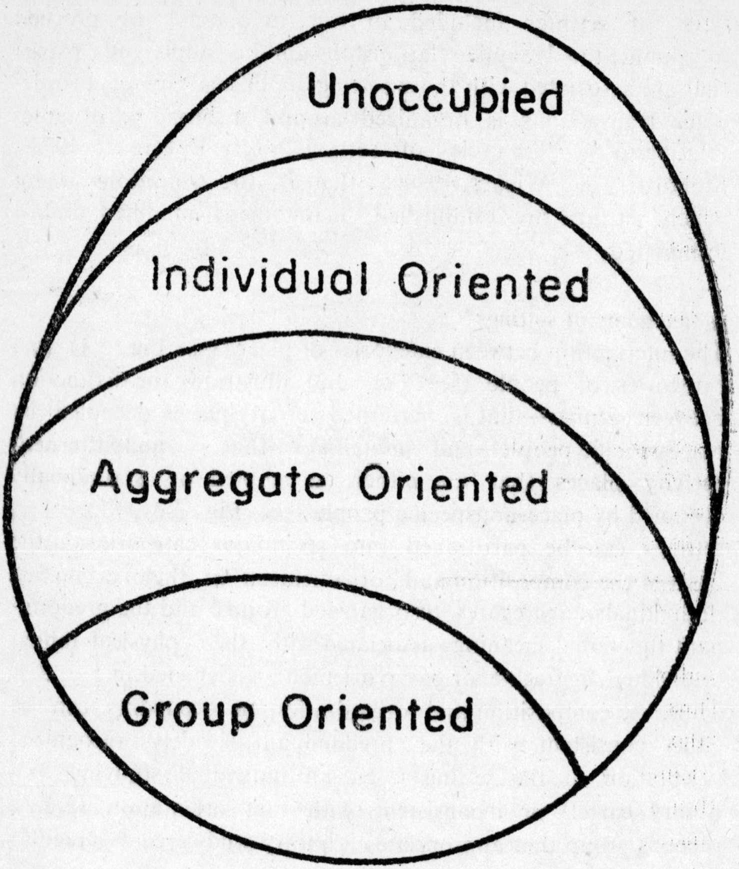

PLACES

FIG. 3.1 : *Categories of places according to their functional orientation*

range of theoretical questions and hypotheses that it suggests. As oversimplified as the proposed categories of settings may be, they nonetheless suggest several intriguing questions concerning the etiology, maintenance, modification, and demise of settings. For instance, in what ways do the consistencies or discrepancies among place orientations and occupant organization predispose settings to stability or instability, to internal cohesion or conflict ?

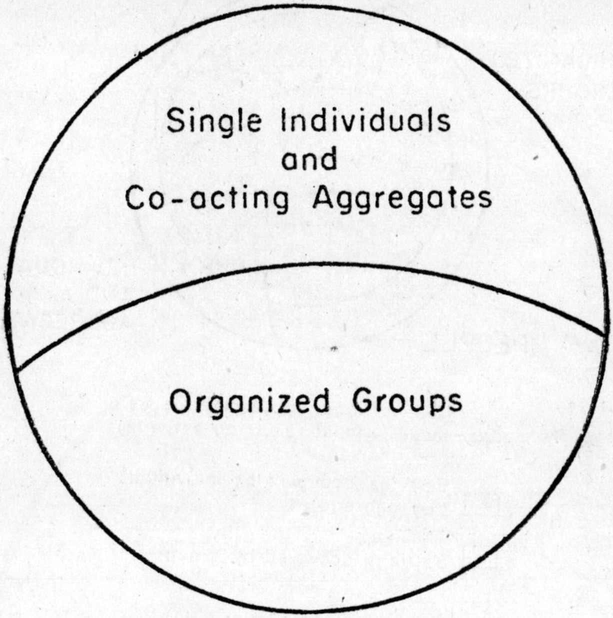

PEOPLE

FIG. 3.2 : *Categories of people according to their composition and organization*

It is with these kinds of transactional phenomena that we are concerned throughout the remainder of this chapter.

Before turning to an analysis of the life cycle of settings, we should note once again that our discussion focuses on group-occupied rather than on individual- or aggregate-occupied settings. Our reasons for focusing on this subset of our taxonomy are threefold. First, people spend an inordinate amount of their daily routine within group-occupied places, be they family dwellings, classrooms, company offices, or friends' homes. Second, the analysis of group-occupied settings affords the consideration of social-structural as well as personal and architectural-geographical elements of settings. And third, due to space limitations, it is not possible in this discussion to provide a more comprehensive treatment of the full range of settings included within our taxonomy.

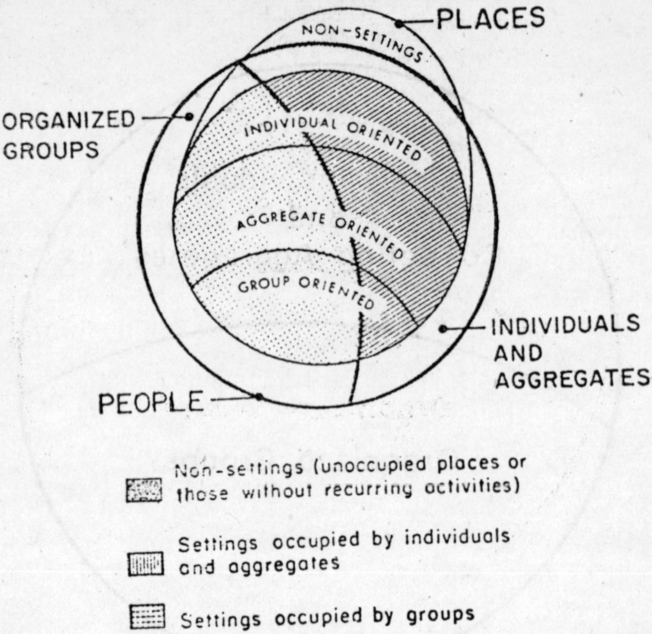

FIG. 3.3 : *The intersection of people and place categories*

The life cycles of settings

Factors affecting the emergence of settings. Edward Devereux, in a recent discussion of the life cycles of settings (Devereux, 1977), has stated that "Behavior settings are nothing more than the swirls and eddies in the flow of motivated human behavior which have become, to some degree, organized, stabilized, localized, recurrent and institutionalized [p. 13]." But what is the nature of those processes by which behavioral "swirls and eddies" are transformed into organized and enduring settings? As a preliminary basis for addressing this question, we distinguish between settings that emerge within previously unoccupied (nonpatterned-activity) places and those that develop within occupied (patterned-activity) areas. Moreover, we distinguish among situations in which the emergence of a setting coincides with the gradual development of a group within a particular place, and those in which a setting emerges as the result of territorial migration or invasion on the part of a pre-existing

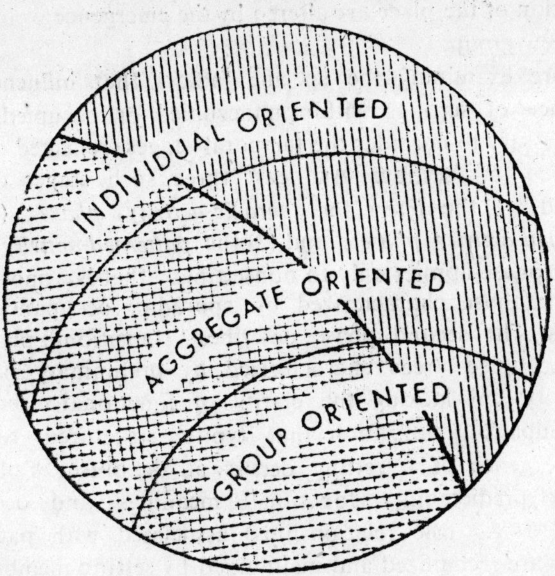

SETTINGS

Settings occupied by individuals and aggregates

Settings occupied by groups

FIG. 3.4 : *A taxonomy of settings*

group. These antecedents of setting development are interrelated but not wholly overlapping, and their interaction yields four different sets of conditions under which settings evolve : *unoccupied areas* that either (1) foster the development of a group and, potentially, a setting ; or (2) are abruptly appropriated by a preexisting group ; and *occupied areas* that either (3) permit or encourage the development of a new group ; or (4) are invaded by (or peacefully merge with) an already existing, outside group. In the third and fourth instances, the previous meanings and orientation of the place are altered by the emergence or invasion of the new group.

Before examining the specific factors that influence the emergence of settings within unoccupied or occupied areas, it is necessary to consider the temporal stages reflected in the emergence of settings. At least three such stages can be identified : (1) the *intert* (*or sporadic-activity*) *phase* ; (2) the *transitional-activity phase* ; and (3) the *patterned-activity phase.* The first phase applies only to nonsettings—that is, unoccupied places or those characterized by sporadic occupancy and activities. The second phase describes "transitional places"—that is, occupied areas characterized by preliminary patterns of activity but lacking the clarity of functional orientation and occupant organization that typify structured settings. The emergence of a setting occurs at the outset of phase 3, once the predictability, functional meanings, and occupant structure (*e.g.*, role relationships) associated with patterned activities are recognized and maintained by setting members.

Note that patterned-activity places (*i.e.*, settings) are conceptualized in this analysis as more than the objective "social facts" described by Durkheim (1964). That is, the emergence of settings in our analysis presupposes a subjective dimension involving the recognition among occupants (including previous, current, or prospective occupants) of the stable, functional meanings associated with a place, and of the organizational requirements for maintaining the setting intact. Thus, settings are construed as a category of "perceived social facts"—objective social forces whose existence and impact are collectively recognized.

Having outlined some of the spatial and temporal patterns of setting emergence, we now consider a number of specific circumstances that foster the establishment of settings within unoccupied and occupied areas. Our analysis focuses, first, on conditions favoring the transformation of an initially unoccupied place from a composite of purely physical elements into an organized setting—a mixture of social as well as physical affordances. Second, we consider factors contributing to the evolution of new settings within already existing ones, such that the symbolic meanings (*e.g.*, functional orientation) previously associated with the place undergo fundamental change.

We begin with the assumptions that unoccupied places are differentially suitable for the establishment of settings, and that those areas of greatest latent value to prospective occupants will be most likely to evolve into organized settings. The *latent value of a place* refers to its as-yet unrecognized capacity for accommodating the preferred goals and activities of prospective occupants. To the extent that this supportive capacity of an environment is recognized and, in some cases, actualized by occupants, its value becomes manifest rather than latent. Our earlier discussion of perceived environmental quality and place dependence, for example, emphasized the *manifest value* of environments. That is, environmental quality is judged in terms of the degree to which places are viewed by occupants as congruent or incongruent with their preferred goals and activities (see also the definition of environmental congruence in the glossary of this chapter and in Stokols, 1981). Thus, the distinction between manifest and latent value relates to whether or not potential or current occupants *recognize* the place as congruent with their needs.

The same kinds of factors that determine assessments of manifest value (*e.g.*, the perceived fit between physical affordances of an environment and the activities of its users) offer a basis for estimating the latent value of places. For example, an out-of-the-way, undiscovered pond that remains frozen throughout winter has latent potential value as an outdoor recreational area. Once the pond is discovered by ice-skating enthusiasts, its potential value is recognized and transitional (presetting) activity develops in the area. To the extent that manifest or recognized value is high, the likelihood of a setting emerging (*e.g.*, an outdoor skating rink) is enhanced. Note than in some instances, the recognized potential value of places is not actualized due to physical barriers or normative constraints (*e.g.*, the presence of "no trespassing" signs near the pond).

Any attempt to assess the latent or manifest value of places requires consideration of the potential or actual match between place characteristics and the attributes of a particular set of occupants. The present discussion is not intended to provide a comprehensive listing of the determinants of place value, but it is possible to suggest certain environmental and occupant factors that are relevant to this issue. For instance, places whose supportive physical features are unique (*i.e.*, few comparable areas exist elsewhere or are accessible) are likely to be of high value to prospective or current occupants. Such features might include the aesthetic quality of a place, its proximity to transportation and communication facilities, and the degree to which its geographical characteristics offer physical protection and well-demarcated group territory. Among the occupant attributes that are likely to contribute to assessments of place value are the range of alternative environments available to occupants, and the kinds of environmental supports that are required for their accomplishment of desired goals and activities.

Considering the three phases of setting emergence proposed earlier (*i.e.*, inert, transitional activity, and patterned activity), we thus hypothesize that : (1) unoccupied places high in latent value for prospective occupants are more likely to attract and sustain transitional activity than those of low latent value ; and that (2) the higher the manifest value of a place either prior or subsequent to occupancy, the greater the probability that patterned activities will be established and a setting will form.

We further hypothesize that : (3) the occupants of settings that emerge gradually within unoccupied areas will ascribe greater symbolic meaning to place than will the members of preexisting groups that migrate to the area. This heightened symbolic meaning of the physical milieu for locally formed versus migratory groups is assumed to result from the greater experience of local groups with a place prior to setting emergence, and the temporal linkage of group formation processes (*e.g.*, the development of cohesion) with the establishment of a setting. At the outset of the patterned-activity phase, then, members of locally formed groups will manifest greater clarity and consensus in their perception of place meanings than will those of migratory groups. Thus, for locally formed groups, the physical environment will be viewed as symbolic of group identity. Accordingly, we predict that : (4) within newly formed settings, assessments of place dependence or independence will be more extreme among local versus migratory groups due to the former's relatively greater experience with the place. Moreover, (5) the direction of occupants' assessments toward either place dependence or independence will be mediated by the quality of their cumulative experiences within that environment.

As our analysis of setting development shifts from initially unoccupied to already-occupied areas, additional conceptual issues arise. Most importantly, the establishment of new settings in occupied areas involves not only a transformation of physical affordances into symbolic meanings, but also the modification of the existing, symbolic meaning by the new occupants. This alteration in the perceived social field of the environment introduces the potential for social conflict, particularly when place meanings associated with the original and newly formed settings are contradictory. Differing perceptions of territorial jurisdiction and ownership rights exemplify sources of conflict among occupant groups who lay claim to the same area.

In many situations, the establishment of a new setting within an already-existing one occurs without social conflict. This is particularly the case when members of a preexisting setting decide voluntarily to subdivide into smaller settings or to merge with the members of an outside group. Examples of subdivision within settings and mergers between them can be found in the research literature of ecological psychology (*e.g.*, Bechtel, 1977 ; Lozar, 1974 ; Srivastava, 1974 ; Wicker and Kauma, 1974). This literature also provides evidence for the impact of subdivisions and mergers on organizational effectiveness and member well-being.

The establishment of a new setting within an occupied area, however, often raises the potential for social conflict, especially when members of the original setting view the impending subdivision or merger as unwanted and involuntary. An attempt by an alienated faction of a teenage gang to develop an alternative setting within an existing one, or the appropriation and alteration of a setting by another gang, exemplify the involuntary or imposed establishment of settings in occupied areas.

The preceding discussion suggests the following, additional hypotheses :

6. The likelihood of a new setting developing within the territorial domain of an already-existing one decreases as the potential for conflict between members of the two settings increases.

7. The potential for intergroup conflict is heightened to the extent that the original setting undergoes involuntary subdivision or merger (particularly when territorial resources are limited and the place meanings perceived by members of the original and new settings are contradictory).

8. Given a high level of potential conflict, active attempts to establish new settings within existing ones will promote overt, intergroup aggression to the degree that the relative power (*e.g.*, membership size, economic resources) of the opposed occupant groups is comparable. Differential power among occupant groups is expected to reduce the likelihood and duration of overt violence, following nonvoluntary subdivisions and mergers of settings (cf. French and Raven, 1959).

Because of our focus on group-occupied settings in this discussion, we have emphasized the role of intergroup conflict as a concomitant of setting emergence in certain situations. We should note, however, that attempts to establish new settings are sometimes accompanied by conflict arising among different categories of occupants (*i.e.*, groups, aggregates, and individuals). The earlier mentioned examples of a noisy group "hanging out" in a library study area, or a youth gang whose "turf" includes the parking lot of a shopping center, illustrate situations involving potential group-versus-individual and group-versus-aggregate conflicts. Thus, in relation to our proposed typology of settings (see Fig. 3.4), we hypothesize that : (9) the likelihood of a new setting developing within an occupied area decreases to the extent that its membership structure (*e.g.*, group organization) is discrepant with the predominant functional orientation (*e.g.*, individual or aggregate orientation) of the original setting. In those instances in which functionally discrepant settings do emerge, their stability and duration are likely to depend on the rigidity and enforcability of functional meanings associated with the original setting.

Factors affecting the maintenance and modification of settings. The three stages of setting emergence previously discussed—that is, the sporadic, transitional, and patterned-activity phases—precede the appearance of those processes by which existing settings are maintained, modified, and terminated. The present section considers some of those processes by focusing on three additional stages in the life cycle of settings namely ; (4) the *stability-maintenance phase* ; (5) the *deviation phase* ; and (6) the *structural-transformation phase.* In the subsequent section, we examine the (7) *crisis* and (8) *termination phases* marked by the occurrence of events within settings that lead to their deterioration and eventual demise. Crisis events are viewed as a category of severe deviations and transformations whose detrimental impact on the setting is irreversible.

Most conceptualizations of settings deemphasize the emergence, transformation, and termination phases, focusing instead on the ways in which on-going settings maintain their stability and cope with environmentally induced deviations. Barker's (1968) analysis of behavior settings, for example, highlights the synomorphy or fit between recurring patterns of human activity and the sociophysical environment. Deviations from optimal fit between human and environmental resources (*e.g.*, undermanning) are counteracted by setting-protective strategies (*e.g.*, the recruitment of additional members). Thus, the behavior setting is construed as an open system (cf. Katz and Kahn, 1966 ; von Bertalanffy, 1950) that strives to maintain a stable (equilibrium-like) relationship between itself and the broader environment through internal organization and negative feedback mechanisms.

Our analysis builds upon earlier discussions of setting maintenance and deviation-countering processes. We assume, for example, that settings develop mechanisms for maintaining their stability (*e.g.*, the norms and role structure associated with group-oriented settings), and for resisting internal and external threats to setting operations. The stability-maintenance phase previously mentioned is characterized by the smooth and predictable recurrence of organized activity patterns within the setting. To the extent that perceived or actual departures from typical activity patterns occur, the setting is said to be in a deviation phase. The structural-transformation phase is marked by the occurrence of deviations that result in significant and enduring changes in the setting's activity structure and/or physical milieu.

The present analysis, however, differs from earlier discussions of setting maintenance and deviation in some important respects. First, whereas previous analyses of behavior settings and group dynamics (cf. Barker and Associates, 1978; Cartwright and Zander, 1968) emphasize deviation-countering mechanisms, which serve to preserve equilibrium within groups, we give equal attention to the deviation-amplifying processes (Maruyama, 1963) by which settings are structurally transformed. The phenomenon of overmanning, for example, could be analyzed in terms of occupants' efforts to reduce population pressure by admitting fewer-than-usual new members to the setting (deviation counteraction) or, alternatively, in terms of their initial decision to expand the physical size of the setting, thereby attracting larger numbers of applicants, creating overmanning and stimulating further efforts to expand the physical dimensions of the setting (deviation amplification). We view both of these perspectives as crucial to the analysis of setting maintenance, deviation, and transformation.

Second, earlier discussions of deviations within settings have emphasized the predominant role of the environment in altering stable patterns of setting activities—for example, through the sudden influx of new occupants from outside the setting (cf. Wicker & Kauma, 1974) or through abrupt architectural-geographical changes (cf. Bechtel, 1977). In the face of these events, occupants are usually portrayed as passive responders to environmental problems. Yet, it is often the case that setting members act spontaneously and decisively to refine their activities and surroundings, even in the absence of pressing environmental problems. Thus, we distinguish between *occupant-induced* and *environment-induced deviations* to highlight both the active and responsive roles played by occupants in creating and coping with setting deviations.

Finally, unlike earlier discussions of disequilibrium within settings (*e.g.*, Barker & Associates, 1978), our analysis emphasizes anticipated as well as actual deviations. Whereas the anticipation of deviations will often lead to their actual occurrence, this is not necessarily the case. A company's plans for relocation to a larger office building, for instance, may be delayed or even abandoned due to resource constraints. We, therefore, treat *anticipated* and *actually occurring deviations* within settings as separable phenomena. In the ensuing discussion, we are particularly concerned with those circumstances that prompt occupants first to devise plans for transforming and improving the setting and, subsequently, to actively implement their plans.

Under what conditions are settings likely to shift from stability to deviation and transformation phases ? Our attempt to identify some of these conditions begins with an assessment of the *transformational potential* of settings (cf. Stokols, 1981). Transformational potential refers to the motivation of occupants to modify the physical or social structure of their setting in accord with collective preferences. Transformational potential will be high to the degree that existing levels of occupant-environment congruence are lower than the potential level of congruence thought to be available in the best alternative setting. The "best alternative setting" can be either a transformed version of the existing setting or a completely different setting that has not yet been established or experienced.

We noted earlier that when preferred, alternative settings are thought to be available outside of the existing situation, occupants will tend to be place independent rather than place dependent. We, therefore, hypothesize that : (10) when the existing level of environmental congruence is perceived to be low, place-independent occupants will be more motivated to leave rather than attempt to improve the existing setting, whereas place-dependent occupants will be more motivated to transform rather than leave the immediate setting.

In our discussion of place dependence and perceived environmental quality, we mentioned a variety of factors that may contribute to occupants' assessments of actual and potential levels of congruence (*e.g.*, the unique goals and activities of setting occupants ; the degree to which these goals are supported by the environment ; occupants' awareness of and exposure to alternative settings). The same diversity of factors influences the transformational potential within settings at a given point in time. Changes in the particular goals pursued by occupants, for example, may prompt them to search for more congruent, alternative settings or to restructure their existing environment (occupant-induced deviations). At the same time, sudden shifts in the form and quality of the physical environment may decrease perceived levels of congruence (environment-induced deviations), thereby promoting dissatisfaction with the setting and efforts to improve or withdraw from it.

In general, the perceived gap between actual and potential congruence will be greater to the extent that occupants possess clear images of preferred future environments. Images of preferred settings arise from the collective imagination of occupants within the context of existing environmental conditions. But the salience of preferred environmental arrangements (*i.e.*, a high level of transformational potential) does not necessarily promote structural modification of the setting, even when attractive alternative settings are thought to be unavailable. For, the accomplishment of environmental change requires not only salient images of the future, but also sufficient levels of environmental flexibility, social organization, and behavioral competence among occupants. Thus, assuming that setting members are motivated to improve their environment, the greatest amount of change would be initiated by imaginative individuals and groups within flexible settings, whereas the least change would be accomplished by unimaginative occupants within rigid settings.

The preceding discussion suggests the following specific hypotheses regarding the determinants of setting stability, deviation, and transformation.

11. Place-dependent groups located within group-oriented areas will, in general, maintain settings of greater stability and endurance than will place-independent groups located within group-oriented, aggregate-oriented, or individual-oriented areas. Also, settings established by place-dependent groups within agregate or individual-oriented areas will be less stable than those consisting of place-dependent groups within group-oriented areas.

12. Group-oriented places whose physical characteristics favor the development of group identity and cohesion (*e.g.*, "defensible spaces" with well-defined boundaries ; cf. Newman,

1973) will be more congruent and, therefore, stable than group-oriented places that do not offer architectural or geographical supports for maintaining group solidarity.

13. Group-occupied settings that have emerged gradually within initially unoccupied areas, or were established voluntarily within previously occupied areas, will manifest greater stability than those whose establishment was non-voluntary (*i.e.*, contrary to the preferences of occupants within the original setting).

14. Environmentally induced deviations (*e.g.*, sudden geographical changes or the appearance of unwanted stimuli such as noise and congestion) will be more disruptive to place-dependent than to place-independent groups, due to the former's lack of attractive place options and (consequently) their greater psychological investment in the immediate situation.

15. Deviations from optimal staffing levels within settings (*e.g.*, undermanning and overmanning ; cf. Wicker, McGrath, & Armstrong, 1972) will induce greater stress and deviation-countering efforts among place-dependent than among place-independent occupants. In the face of membership shortages, for example, place-independent occupants might be more willing to allow their setting to deteriorate or to merge with other undermanned settings.[8]

16. Given a high level of transformational potential and the lack of better alternative settings elsewhere, structural modifications will more likely be implemented by organized and cohesive groups than by occupants whose disorganization preludes their ability to agree upon and to implement a remedial course of action.

To this point in our analysis, we have ignored the question of whether deviations and transformations within settings are functional or dysfunctional from the occupants' point of view. This issue raises additional, complex questions such as : "functional or dysfunctional in the short run or long run, and for individual occupants or the setting as a whole ?" In the remainder of our analysis, we employ two basic criteria for gauging the effectiveness of occupant-induced deviations and transformations within settings—namely, the degree to which these changes raise perceived levels of environmental congruence among occupants, and the degree to which the modifications enacted within settings promote its renewed stability or its eventual demise. The former criterion is essentially one of occupant well-being whereas the latter is more a matter of organizational survival. Depending on the situation, these criteria can be directly, inversely, or negligibly related to each other.

Factors affecting the termination of settings. The present section focuses on the circumstances leading to an irreversible deterioration in the activity patterns of a setting (the *crisis phase*) and, ultimately, to the disappearance of such patterns altogether (the *termination phase*). Our emphasis in this portion of the chapter is on settings of undefined rather than defined duration. *Undefined-duration settings*, such as neighbourhood restaurants, churches, and movie theaters, can persist indefinitely, whereas *defined-duration settings*, such as college classes, the campaign headquarters of a presidential candidate, and the yearly convention of a professional group, have prescribed termination dates—for example, the closing of the semester, the presidential election, and the national convention, respectively. Our principal concern, then, is to identify factors that affect the longevity of settings whose duration is indefinite.

Among the various circumstances that can prompt the abrupt and unexpected termination of settings are severe environmental perturbations (*e.g.*, earthquakes and floods forcing migration to safer areas) and events relating to the life cycles of occupants (*e.g.*, increased family size or the death of a spouse necessitating residential relocation). In our analysis of setting crises and termination, we are more concerned with the interplay of environmental and occupant factors than with either of these categories considered alone. For instance, we are more interested in the relative impact of environmental change on place-dependent versus place-independent groups than in the impact of such change on groups in general.

We begin with a series of hypotheses derived from our earlier discussion of environmental congruence, place dependence, and transformational potential.

17. To the extent that occupants' efforts to improve their setting fail to enhance perceived levels of environmental congruence, the setting is more likely to enter the crisis and term-

ination phases, particularly when dissatisfaction among occupants has been prolonged.

18. The abrupt termination of settings following environmental crises and/or occupants' life events will induce greater stress (*e.g.*, mental and physical disorder, social disorganization) among place-dependent *vis-a-vis* place-independent occupants.

19. Due to their greater psychological ties to their setting, place-dependent groups will take longer to establish new settings following geographical relocation than will place-independent groups.

The concept of place dependence, defined earlier, reflects the perceived strength of association between occupants and their environments. Throughout our analysis, we have emphasized the role of place dependence in affecting the maintenance, modification, and termination of settings. Just as it is possible to assess the dependence of individuals and groups on their environments, it is also conceivable that settings are differentially dependent on particular occupants for maintaining their efficiency and very survival. Prosperous companies, for example, may collapse precipitously following the departure of key executives. Similarly, a neighborhood tennis club may face premature closing as increasing numbers of its members shift their allegiance to raquetball and resign from the club.

Occupant-dependent settings, thus, are defined as those whose continued existence requires the presence of specific occupants or a subset of occupants. *Occupant-independent settings* are those that do not require the presence of specific members for their continuation. In general, variable-occupant settings (or those whose membership varies over time) will be less dependent on specific occupants for their survival than will same-occupant settings (see our earlier discussion of place categories).

On the basis of the preceding definitions, we hypothesize that : (20) occupant-dependent settings are more likely to terminate following the departure of setting members than are occupant-independent settings. Moreover, (21) group-occupied settings characterized by constant rather than rotating members will be more likely to terminate following the departure of key individuals (*e.g.*, charismatic leaders, persons occupying important roles in the organization) than following the loss of less crucial personnel.

In addition to the dimensions of place dependence and occupant dependence, we introduce a final factor into our analysis of setting termination. Emery and Trist (1965) suggest that the environments of organizations vary with respect to their relative "turbulence"—that is, their complexity and unpredictability. Consistent with their discussion of environmental turbulence, we hypothesize that : (22) the prospects for prolonged survival decrease to the extent that settings exist within turbulent environments. For instance, a housing construction firm may find it increasingly difficult to survive in an economy beset by wildly fluctuating interest rates, spiraling inflation, and a global energy crisis. Furthermore, we predict that : (23) within turbulent environments, settings whose internal organization enables members to forecast environmental changes and to actively initiate self-protective strategies prior to the occurrence of environmental crises (rather than simply responding passively to such events) will be more likely to survive than will less organised and sophisticated settings (cf. Terreberry, 1968 ; Weick, 1979).

Summary

In this section of the chapter, we have presented a taxonomy of settings based on the intersection of place-specific people and functionally organised places. Additionally, we have outlined eight distinct stages in the life cycles of settings and have offered a series of hypotheses concerning the antecedents and processes associated with setting emergence, maintenance, modification, and termination. Although our analysis of these phenomena is preliminary and incomplete, it may provide a useful framework for future research on the transactions between people and places, and a conceptual basis for designing and improving settings.

SUMMARY AND CONCLUSIONS

In recent years, the focus of psychological research has shifted increasingly from the micro to the molar (ecological) environment. This expanded frame of reference stems from the recognition among social scientists that models based solely on intrapersonal processes and/or social interaction do not adequately explain human behavior. Instead, behavior must be viewed within the context in which it occurs. In this chapter, we have developed a classification framework for describing the sociophysical milieu of behavior. This taxonomy of settings is derived theoretically, and serves as a basis for : (1) conceptualizing the complex transactions between people and their environment ; (2) conducting theory-guided research that focuses on the molar environment ; and, (3) developing criteria for assessing the ecological validity of research findings and policy recommendations.

Our theoretical analysis of settings began with a detailed examination of their two major components : places (the physical context of behavior) and occupants (the people who transact with places). After distinguishing between regularly and irregularly occupied places, we discussed aspects of the former that contribute to their social imageability among current and prospective occupants. We further classified regularly occupied places in terms of their predominant functional orientation (*i.e.*, individual, aggregate, and group oriented), and noted certain qualifications of this categorization scheme.

Occupants were described as acting alone, as part of an aggregate, or as members of organized groups. They can be sporadically associated with some places (*i.e.*, place non-specific), while predictably associated with others (*i.e.*, place specific). When place specific, occupants may develop strong subjective attachments to particular locations. We termed this phenomenon place dependence and discussed, in some detail, its antecedents, subtle qualities, and its role in mediating occupants' reactions to environmental change.

In the last section of the chapter, we examined the interface of place and occupant categories as the basis for developing our taxonomy of settings. We then discussed eight distinct stages in the life cycle of settings and presented several hypotheses derived from our analysis.

Even though the present chapter has not been explicitly policy oriented, we do believe that our analysis of settings is germane to contemporary environmental and political problems. The concept of place dependence, for example, offers a basis for understanding and altering the behavior of people living in hazardous areas who refuse to resettle in different regions, despite the potential for disaster within their current locations. And, in the context of international politics, the place-dependence concept suggests why the fervor of terrorist groups is heightened rather than neutralized by the perception that they have been denied a desired geographical area, or that they have been thwarted in their attempts to transform a currently occupied area into a new setting. These phenomena are exemplified by the efforts of revolutionary groups, such as the PLO and the IRA, to establish independent nations. In these and other instances of social conflict, the place dependence of groups and the collectively perceived contradictions between existing and preferred qualities of an area can have enormous political ramifications.

We have attempted in this chapter to develop a conceptualization of settings that reflects the reciprocal relationship between people and places. Framing behavior within this multicausal model is, admittedly, complex. We believe, however, that taxonomic efforts at describing the large-scale environment, which necessarily reflect the complexity of that environment, are crucial if psychological research is to move effectively from micro to more molar levels of behavioural analysis. As a first step in submitting our conceptualization to empirical test, we are currently evaluating the reliability and validity of an index of place dependence.

DESCRIBING AND CLASSIFYING THE TRANSACTIONS BETWEEN PEOPLE AND PLACES : A GLOSSARY

1. *Aggregate-oriented places* (*or settings*). Places (or settings) that are typically designed for and occupied by aggregates of strangers or minimally related people.
2. *Character of place dependence*. Subtle variations in occupants' perception of their attachment to place/s derived from differences on dimensions such as (1) the number and range of needs met by a particular place ; (2) temporal aspects of place dependence ; and (3) the perceived availability of alternative place options. See also *place dependence*.
3. *Crisis events*. Severe deviations within settings whose detrimental impact on the setting is irreversible. Such

events lead to the deterioration and eventual demise of the setting.

4. *Crisis phase of settings.* A stage within the life cycle of settings marked by the occurrence of events that lead to the deterioration and eventual demise of the setting.
5. *Defined-duration settings.* Settings that have a prescribed termination date.
6. *Deviation phase of settings.* A phase within the life cycle of settings marked by the occurrence of perceived or actual changes in the typical activity patterns and/or physical structure of a setting.
7. *Deviations within settings.* Anticipated or actual departures from the typical activity patterns and/or physical structure of a setting.
8. *Environmental congruence.* The degree to which the environment enables occupants to meet their needs and attain their valued goals. (A method for quantifying congruence is presented by Stokols [1979, 1981]. See also Michelson, 1976, for an analysis of environmental congruence).
9. *Environment-induced deviations.* Alterations in the typical activity patterns or physical arrangement of a setting arising from changes in the external or internal environment of the setting (*e.g.*, abrupt geographical changes within or adjacent to the setting).
10. *Generic place dependence of occupants.* The degree to which occupants perceive themselves to be strongly associated with and dependent on a category of functionally similar places. See also *geographical place dependence of occupants.*
11. *Generic place specificity of occupants.* The degree to which the activities of people are associated with a category of functionally similar places on a regular and predictable basis. See also *geographical place specificity of occupants.*
12. *Geographical place dependence of occupants.* The degree to which occupants perceive themselves to be strongly associated with and dependent on a particular place. See also *place dependence* and *generic place dependence of occupants.*
13. *Geographical place specificity of occupants.* The degree to which the activities of people are associated with a parti-

cular place on a regular and predictable basis. See also *place specificity of occupants* and *generic place specificity of occupants*.

14. *Group*. Two or more individuals whose activities and goals are interdependent, and who are aware of their interdependence. See also the definitions of group presented by Cartwright and Zander (1968); Hare, Borgatta, and Bales (1965); McGrath (1964); and Shaw (1976).
15. *Group-oriented places (or settings)*. Places (or settings) whose predominant functions are geared toward people who know and interact with each other on a regular basis.
16. *Individual-oriented places (or settings)*. Places (or settings) whose physical and normative properties either exclude or discourage occupancy by more than one person at a time.
17. *Inert (or sporadic-activity) phase*. A stage in the life cycle of settings marked by the absence of occupants or by sporadic occupancy and activities.
18. *Irregularly occupied places*. Places characterized by sporadic occupancy and human activities. See also *nonsettings* and *nonpatterned-activity places*.
19. *Latent value of places*. The unrecognized capacity of places to accommodate the preferred goals and activities of prospective or current occupants.
20. *Life cycle of settings*. Processes associated with the establishment, maintenance, modification, and termination of organized settings. As conceptualized in this analysis, the life cycle of settings incorporates the following distinct stages: (1) *inert* (or *sporadic-activity*) *phase*; (2) *transitional-activity phase*; (3) *patterned-activity phase*; (4) *stability-maintenance phase*; (5) *deviation phase*; (6) *structural-transformation phase*; (7) *crisis phase*; and (8) *termination phase*. See also Devereux's (1977) and Wicker's (1979a) discussions of the life cycle of behavior settings.
21. *Local groups*. Groups whose development coincides with the emergence of an organized, environmental setting. See also *migratory groups*.
22. *Manifest value of places*. The recognized (and sometimes actualized) capacity of places to support the preferred goals and activities of prospective or current occupants.

See also *environmental congruence* and *potential congruence.*

23. *Migratory groups.* Preexisting groups that move into a new area and establish a setting there. See also *local groups.*
24. *Nonpatterned-activity places.* Areas characterized by the absence of occupants or by sporadic occupancy and association with human activities. See also *irregularly occupied places* and *nonsettings.*
25. *Nonsettings.* Nonpatterned-activity places that are either unoccupied or sporadically occupied by place-nonspecific people. Nonsettings are characterized by the absence of recurring patterns of behavior and the lack of a clear functional orientation. See also *irregularly occupied places, nonpatterned-activity places,* and *place-specificity of occupants.*
26. *Occupant dependence of settings.* The degree to which a setting requires the presence of particular occupants, or a subset of occupants, for its continued existence.
27. *Occupant-induced deviations.* Alterations in the typical activity patterns or physical arrangement of a setting arising from the spontaneous and voluntary actions of setting members.
28. *Patterned-activity phase of settings.* A stage in the life cycle of settings marked by the establishment of stable, recurring patterns of activity and widely recognized place meanings (*e.g.*, the functional orientation of the setting).
29. *Patterned-activity places.* Places in which recurring and predictable patterns of behavior occur. The predominant, functional orientation of such places can be classified as individual oriented, aggregate oriented, or group oriented. See also *settings.*
30. *Perceived social field of the physical environment.* The totality of functional, motivational, and evaluative meanings conveyed by the physical milieu to current or prospective occupants of a place. The specific meanings associated with a place can be described in terms of their content, complexity, clarity, heterogeneity, distortions, and contradictions. (Strategies for quantifying these dimensions are discussed in Stokols, 1981.)

31. *Place.* A geographically and/or architecturally delimited area. Places in this analysis are categorized as unoccupied (or sporadically occupied) and regularly occupied. The latter category includes three types of places : individual oriented, aggregate oriented, and group oriented, depending on the predominant functional orientation associated with the place.
32. *Place dependence.* The degree to which occupants perceive themselves to be strongly associated with and dependent on a particular place, or a category of functionally similar places. The perception of place dependence derives from a two-component process by which occupants assess the quality of their current place, and the relative quality of comparable alternative places. These assessments are influenced by factors such as the importance of occupants' goals, the kinds of resources available within an area, and occupants' awareness of and familiarity with relevant alternative places. See also *geographical place dependence of occupants* and *generic place dependence of occupants.*
33. *Place meanings.* Functional, motivational, and evaluative information and impressions associated with particular places. *Personal meanings* are those held by single individuals. Personal meanings become part of the perceived social field of an environment to the extent that they are held in common with other occupants (*common meanings*), and/or are shared through the interaction and communication among members of organized groups (*shared meanings*). See also the *perceived social field of the physical environment* and *social imageability.*
34. *Place options.* Geographical areas that are perceived by occupants as comparable to their present location and as realistic (accessible) alternatives to their current place. The perceived availability of place options is a crucial factor in determining occupants' assessments of place dependence. See also *place dependence.*
35. *Place specificity of occupants.* The degree to which the activities of people are associated with a particular place, or with a category of functionally similar places, on a regular and predictable basis. See also *geographical place*

specificity of occupants and *generic place-specificity of occupants*.

36. *Potential congruence*. The level of goal facilitation perceived by the occupants of a place to be available within their best alternative setting. The best alternative setting can be either a transformed version of the existing setting or a different setting that has not yet been experienced or established.
37. *Regularly occupied places*. Places characterized by stable patterns of occupancy, human activity, and functional orientation. See also *patterned-activity places* and *settings*.
38. *Same-occupant places* (*or settings*). Places or settings whose functions are performed by the same people on a regular basis. See also *variable-occupant places* (*or settings*).
39. *Settings*. Patterned-activity places occupied by place-specific people. Settings are characterized by recurring patterns of behavior and by widely recognized place meanings (*e.g.*, functional orientation). The functional orientation of the physical milieu and the composition and organization of its occupants are used in this analysis to develop a taxonomy of settings. See also the analyses of behavior settings presented by Barker (1968), Barker and Associates (1978), and Wicker (1979b). See also *patterned-activity places, regularly occupied places*, and *place specificity of occupants*.
40. *Social imageability*. The capacity of a place to evoke vivid and collectively held social meanings among its occupants. Places acquire social imageability to the extent that they are regularly and predictably associated with patterns of individual and/or collective behavior. See also the *perceived social field of the physical environment*.
41. *Stability-maintenance phase of settings*. A stage in the life cycle of settings characterized by the smooth and predictable recurrence of organized activity patterns.
42. *Structural-transformation phase of settings*. A stage in the life cycle of settings marked by the occurrence of deviations that result in significant and enduring changes in the setting's activity structure and/or physical milieu. See also *deviations within settings* and *transformations within settings*.

43. *Termination phase of settings.* A stage within the life cycle of settings marked by the cessation of organized activity patterns within an area. See also *crisis events* and the *crisis phase of settings.*
44. *Transformational potential.* The motivation of occupants to modify the physical or social structure of their setting in accord with personal and collective preferences. The actual accomplishment of desired transformations depends not only on motivational factors but also on occupant resources (*e.g.*, imagination, organization) and environmental circumstances (*e.g.*, rigidity or flexibility of the environment).
45. *Transformations within settings.* A category of deviations within settings that result in significant and enduring alterations of the activity structure and/or physical milieu of the setting.
46. *Transitional-activity phase of settings.* A stage in the life cycle of settings maked by the preliminary occurrence of patterned activity within an area that is not yet associated with a clear, functional orientation.
47. *Transitional places.* Occupied areas characterized by preliminary patterns of activity but lacking the clarity of functional orientation and occupant organization associated with structured settings.
48. *Undefined-duration settings.* Settings that do not have a prescribed termination date. See also *defined-duration settings.*
49. *Unoccupied places.* Places that either preclude the possibility of occupation or are structured in ways that inhibit the development of sustained activity, and, thereby, remain ambiguous in their functional meaning.
50. *Variable-occupant places* (*or settings*). Places or settings whose functions are performed by different people on a rotating basis.

ACKNOWLEDGEMENTS

We thank Michael Agar, Baruch Fischhoff, Alan Levy, Kelly Shaver, Perry Thorndyke, and Abe Wandersman for their comments on the conference presentation of this manuscript. Also, we are grateful to Irwin Altman, Roger Barker, Dorwin Cartwright, Stephen Kaplan, Joseph McGrath, and Allan Wicker for their helpful suggestions on earlier portions of this chapter. The preparation of this manuscript was supported by funding from the Focused Research Program in Human Stress at the University of California, Irvine, and by postdoctoral grant number F2MH07421A from the National Institute of Mental Health to Sally Ann Shumaker.

FOOTNOTES

1. Recent chapters by Barker (1979) and Proshansky, Nelson-Shulman, and Kaminoff (1979) are exceptions to this trend.
2. As examples of the polarity between objectivist and subjectivist viewpoints in psychological research, see Brunswik's (1943) "encapsulation" critique of Lewin's (1936) life-space concept ; Gibson's (1977) theory of environmental affordances vis-a-vis Neisser's (1976) constructivist view of perception, and Wohlwill's (1974) article, "The environment is not in the head !"
3. A glossary of the various terms introduced throughout our analysis is provided at the end of this chapter.
4. The dimensions of functional, motivational, and evaluative salience reflect the three factors of semantic meaning identified by Osgood, Suci, and Tannenbaum (1957) : activity, potency, and evaluation.
5. Considering the perceived social field as a whole (*i.e.*, as a composite of multiple meanings), an index of the social imageability of a place can be derived by weighting the diverse meanings of the social field (reflecting its content and complexity) by their relative clarity among setting occupants. An ambiguous social field would be characterized by low imageability—that is, by a lack or small number of vivid images and/or by a lack of agreement among occupants regarding place meanings. See also Jackson's (1965, 1966) analysis of the norm "crystallization" for an alternative approach to the assessment of collectively perceived social meanings, and Milgram and Jodelet's (1976) methods for analyzing collective images of Paris.
6. The distinction between particular and generic places was suggested by Stephan Kaplan in a personal communication.
7. This presentation of place dependence extends an earlier definition presented in Stokols (1981). In the original definition, place dependence referred to an *on-going setting*, and the degree to which the major functions and actual existence of the setting are linked to a specific physical environment. In addition, the definition was limited

to group members' collective perceptions of the connections between setting functions and places.

Our revised definition of place dependence is broader than the initial description, and differs in certain respects. These differences include: (1) an emphasis on the occupants' perceptions of the strength of association between *themselves* and places, as well as between their group and places; (2) the inclusion of individuals and aggregates, as well as groups, as possible setting occupants; (3) a detailed discussion of the processes underlying the development of place dependence and those factors that strengthen people's subjective attachments to places; (4) an extension of the concept by applying it to categorically, similar places, as well as to specific geographical areas; and (5) the inclusion of a temporal component of place dependence that extends the concept from present to past and idealized, future places.

8. This possibility was suggested by Allan Wicker in a personal communication.

REFERENCES

Altman, I. *The environment and social behavior*, Monterey, Calif.: Brooks/Cole, 1975.

Altman. I. Research on environment and behavior: A personal statement of strategy. In D. Stokols (Ed.), *Perspectives on environment and behavior*, New York: Plenum, 1977.

Argyle, M. Predictive and generative rules models of P×S interaction. In D. Magnusson and N.S. Endler (Eds.), *Personality at the crossroads: Current issues in interactional psychology*. Hillsdale, N.J.: Lawrence Erlbaum Associates, 1977.

Barker, R.G. Ecology and motivation. *Nebraska Symposium on Motivation*, 1960, 8, 1-48.

Barker, R.G. On the nature of the environment. *Journal of Social Issues*, 1963, 19, 17-34.

Barker, R.G. *Ecological Psychology: Concepts and methods for studying the environment of human behavior*. Stanford, Calif.: Stanford University Press, 1968.

Barker, R.G. The influence of frontier environments on behavior. In J.O. Steffen (Ed.), *The American west: New perspective, new dimensions*. Norman, Oklahoma: University of Oklahoma Press, 1979.

Barker, R.G. and Associates *Habitats, environments, and human behavior*. San Francisco: Jossey-Bass, 1978.

Barker, R.A., and Bell, P.A. Aggression and heat: The influence of ambient temperature, negative affect and cooling drink on physical aggression. *Journal of Personality and Social Psychology*, 1976, 33, 245-255.

Baum, A., and Valins, S. (Eds.). *The social psychology of crowding : Studies of the effects of residential group size.* Hillsdale, N.J. : Lawrence Erlbaum Associates, 1977.

Bechtel, R.B. *Enclosing behavior*. Stroudsburg, Pa. : Dowden, Hutchinson, and Ross, 1977.

Berger, P., and Luckmann, T. *The social construction of reality*. Garden City, N.Y. : Doubleday, 1966.

Berlyne, D.E. *Conflict, arousal, and curiosity*, New York : McGraw-Hill, 1960.

Bronfenbrenner, U. Toward an experimental ecology of human development. *American Psychologist*, 1977, 32, 513-531.

Bronfenbrenner, U. *The ecology of human development*. Cambridge, Mass. : Harvard University Press, 1979.

Brunswik, E. Organismic achievement and environmental probability. *Psychological Review*, 1943, 50, 255-272.

Burton, I., Kates, R.W., and White, G.F. *The environment as hazard.* New York : Oxford University Press, 1978.

Campbell, D.T., and Stanley, J.C. *Experimental and quasi-experimental designs for research*. Chicago : Rand McNally, 1963.

Cartwright, D., and Zander, A. (Eds.). *Group dynamics* (3rd Ed.). New York : Harper and Row, 1968.

Chein, I. The environment as a determinant of behavior. *Journal of Social Psychology*, 1954, 39, 115-127.

Cohen, S., Glass, D.C., and Singer, J.E. Apartment noise, auditory discrimination, and reading ability in children. *Journal of Experimental Social Psychology*, 1973, 9, 407-422.

Craik, K.H. Environmental psychology. *Annual Review of Psychology*, 1973, 24, 403-422.

Devereux, E.C. *Psychological ecology : A critical analysis and appraisal.* Unpublished manuscript, Department of Human Development and Family Studies, Cornell University, Ithaca, N.Y., 1977.

Durkheim, E. *The rules of sociological method.* New York : Free Press, 1964.

Emery, F.E., and Trist, E.L. The causal texture of organizational environments. *Human Relations*, 1965, 18, 21-32.

Evans, G.W., and Howard, R.B. Personal space. *Psychological Bulletin*, 1973, 80, 334-344.

Firey, W. Sentiment and symbolism as ecological variables. *American Sociological Review*, 1945, 10, 140-148.

French, J.R.P., and Raven, B.H. The bases of social power. In D. Cartwright (Ed.), *Studies in social power*. Ann Arbor, Mich. : University of Michigan Press, 1959.

Fried, M. Grieving for a lost home. In L.J. Duhl (Ed.), *The urban condition*. New York : Basic Books, 1963.

Garfinkel, H. *Studies in ethnomethodology*. Englewood Cliffs, N.J. : Prentice-Hall, 1967.

Gergen, K.J. Social psychology as history. *Journal of Personality and Social Psychology*, 1973, 26, 309-320.

Gerson, E.M., and Gerson, M.S. The social framework of place perspectives. In G.T. Moore and R.G. Golledge (Eds.), *Environmental knowing*. Stroudsburg, Pa. : Dowden, Hutchinson, and Ross, 1976.

Gibson, J.J. The concept of the stimulus in psychology. American Psychologist, 1960, 15, 694-703.

Gibson, J.J. The theory of affordances. In R. Shaw and J. Bransford (Eds.). *Perceiving, acting and knowing*, Hillsdale, N.J., Lawrence Erlbaum Associates, 1977.

Gove, W.R., Hughes, M., and Galle, O.R. Overcrowding in the home : An empirical investigation of its possible pathological consequences. *American Sociological Review*, 1979, 44, 59-80.

Hare, A.P., Borgatta, E.F., and Bales, R.F. (Eds.). *Small groups : Studies in social interaction*. New York : Knopf, 1965.

Harre, R. The ethogenic approach : Theory and practice. In L. Berkowitz (Ed.), *Advances in experimental social psychology* (*Vol. 10*). New York : Academic Press, 1977.

Harre, R., and Secord, P.F. *The explanation of social behavior*. Oxford : Blackwell, 1972.

Hull, C. The problem of intervening variables in molar behavior theory. *Psychological Review*, 1943, 50, 273-291.

Ittelson, W.H. (Ed.). *Environment and cognition*. New York : Seminar Press, 1973.

Jackson, J. Structural characteristics of norms. In I.D. Steiner and M. Fishbein (Eds.), *Current studies in social psychology*. New York : Holt, Rinehart, and Winston, 1965.

Jackson, J. A conceptual and measurement model for norms and roles. *Pacific Sociological Review*, 1966, 9, 35-47.

Jacobs, J. *Death and life of great American cities*. New York : Random House, 1961.

Kaplan, S. An informal model for the prediction of preference. In E.H. Zube, R.O. Brush, and J.G. Fabos (Eds.), *Landscape assessment : Values and perceptions, and resources*, Stroudsburg, Pa. ; Dowden, Hutchinson, and Ross, 1975.

Kaplan, S. Concerning the power of content-identifying methodologies. In E.H. Zube and T. Daniel (Eds.), *Environmental aesthetics*. Washington, D.C. : U.S. Forest Service, 1978.

Katz, D., and Kahn, R.L. *The social psychology of organizations*. New York : Wiley, 1966.

Kelley, H.H., and Thibaut, J.W. *Interpersonal relations : A theory of interdependence*. New York : Wiley, 1978.

Lewin, K. *Principles of topological psychology*. New York : McGraw-Hill, 1936.

Lozar, C.C. Application of behavior setting analysis and undermanning theory and supermarket design. In D. Carson (Ed.), *Man-environ-*

ment interactions : Evaluations and applications (Vol. 8). Washington, D.C. : Environmental Design Research Association, 1974.

Lynch, K. *The image of the city.* Cambridge, Mass. : M.I.T. Press, 1960.

Magnusson, D. (Ed.). *Toward a psychology of situations : An interactional perspective.* Hillsdale, N.J. : Lawrence Erlbaum Associates, 1981.

Maruyama, M. The second cybernetics : Deviation-amplifying mutual causal processes. *American Scientist*, 1963, 51, 164-179.

Maslow, A.H. *Toward a psychology of being.* Princetion, N.J. : Van Nostrand, 1968.

McGrath, J. *Social psychology : A brief introduction.* Holt, Rinehart, and Winston, 1964.

Mead, G.H. *Mind, self, and society.* Chicago : University of Chicago Press, 1934.

Michelson, W. *Man and his urban environment : A sociological opproach* (2nd ed.). Reading, Mass. : Addison-Wesley, 1976.

Michelson, W. *Environmental choice, human behavior, and residential satisfaction,* New York : Oxford University Press, 1977.

Milgram, S., and Jodelet, D. Psychological maps of Paris. In H. Proshansky, W. Ittelson, and L. Rivlin (Eds.), *Environmental psychology (2nd ed.).* New York : Holt, Rinehart, and Winston, 1976.

Moore, G.T., and Golledge, R.G. (Eds.). *Environmental knowing : Theories, research and methods.* Stroudsburg, Pa. : Dowden, Hutchinson, and Ross, 1976.

Moos, R.H. *The human context : Environmental determinants of behavior.* New York : Wiley, 1976.

Neisser, U. *Cognition and reality : Principles and implications of cognitive psychology.* San Francisco : Freeman, 1976.

Newman, O. *Defensible space.* New York : MacMillan, 1973.

Osgood, C.E., Suci, G.H., and Tannenbaum, P.H. *The measurement of meaning.* Urbana, Ill. : University of Illinois Press, 1957.

Pervin, L.A. Definitions, measurements, and classifications of stimuli, situations, and environments. *Human Ecology*, 1978, 6, 71-105.

Price, R., and Blashfield, R.K. Explorations in the taxonomies of behavior settings : An analysis of dimensions and classifications of settings. *American Journal of Community Psychology*, 1975, 3, 335-351.

Price, R., and Bouffard, D.L. Behavioral appropriateness and situational constraint as dimensions of social behavior. *Journal of Personality and Social Psychology*, 1974, 30, 579-586.

Proshansky, H.M., Nelson-Shulman, Y., and Kaminoff, R.D. The role of physical settings in life-crisis experiences. In I.G. Sarason & C.D. Spielberger (Eds.), *Stress and anxiety* (Vol. 6). Washington, D.C. : Hemisphere Press, 1979.

Ring, K. Experimental social psychology : Some sober questions about some frivolous values. *Journal of Experimental Social Psychology*, 1967, 3, 113-123.

Secord, P.F. Social psychology in search of a paradigm. *Personality and Social psychology Bulletin*, 1977, 3, 41-50.

Seligman, M.E.P. *Helplessness*. San Francisco : Freeman, 1975.

Shaw, M.E. *Group dynamics : The psychology of small group behavior*. New York : McGraw-Hill, 1976.

Skinner, B.F. *Science and human behavior*, New York : MacMillan, 1953.

Smith, M.B. Is experimental social psychology advancing ? *Journal of Experimental Social Psychology*, 1972, 8, 86-96.

Sommer, R. *Tight spaces : Hard architecture and how to humanize it*. Englewood Cliffs, N.J. : Prentice-Hall, 1974.

Srivastava, R.K. Undermanning theory in the context of mental health care environments. In D. Carson (Ed.), *Man-environment interactions : Evaluations and applications* (Vol. 8). Washington, D.C. : Environmental Design Research Association, 1974.

Steiner, I.D. *Group process and productivity*. New York : Academic Press, 1972.

Stokols, D. Environmental psychology. *Annual Review of Psychology*, 1978, 29, 253-295.

Stokols, D. A congruence analysis of human stress. In I.G. Sarason and C.D. Spielberger (Eds.), *Stress and anxiety* (Vol. 6). Washington, D.C. : Hemisphere Press, 1979, 27-53.

Stokols, D. Group x place transactions : Some neglected issues in psychological research on settings. In D. Magnusson (Ed.), *Toward a psychology of situations : An interactional perspective*. Hillsdale, N.J. : Lawrence Erlbaum Associates, 1981, 393-415.

Suttles, G.D. *The social order of the slum : Ethnicity and territory in the inner city*. Chicago : University of Chicago Press, 1968.

Taylor, S.E., and Fiske, S.T. Salience, attention and attribution : Top of the head phenomena. In L. Berkowitz (Ed.), *Advances in experimental social psychology* (Vol. 11). New York : Academic Press, 1978.

Terreberry, S. The evolution of organizational environments. *Administrative Science Quarterly*, 1968, 12, 590-613.

Thibaut, J., and Kelley, H. *The social psychology of groups*. New York : Wiley, 1959.

Tolman, E.C. The determiners of behavior at a choice point. *Psychological Review*, 1938, 45, 1-41.

Tyler, S.A. (Ed.). *Cognitive anthropology*. New York : Holt, Rinehart, and Winston, 1969.

Underwood, B. *Psychological research*. New York : Appleton-Century-Crofts, 1957.

von Bertalanffy, L. The theory of open systems in physics and biology. *Science*, 1950, 111, 23-29.

Weick, K. *The social psychology of organizing* (2nd ed.). Reading, Mass. : Addison-Wesley, 1979.

White, W.P. *Resources in environment and behavior*. Washington, D.C. : American Psychological Association, 1979.

Wicker, A.W. Ecological psychology : Some recent and prospective developments. *American Psychologist*, 1979, 34, 755-765. (a)

Wicker, A.W. *An introduction to ecological psychology*. Monterrey, Calif. : Brooks/Cole, 1979. (b)

Wicker, A.W., and Kauma, C.E. Effects of a merger of a small and a large organization on members' behaviors and experiences. *Journal of Applied Psychology*, 1974, 59, 24-30.

Wicker, A.W., McGrath, J.E., and Armstrong, G.E. Organization size and behavior setting capacity as determinants of member participation. *Behavioral Science*, 1972, 17, 499-513.

Willems, E.P., and Raush, H.L. (Eds.). *Naturalistic viewpoints in psychological research*. New York : Holt, Rinehart, and Winston, 1969.

Wohlwill, J.F. The emerging discipline of environmental psychology. *American Psychologist*, 1970, 25, 303-312.

Wohlwill, J.F. The environment is not in the head. In W.F.E. (Preiser (Ed.), *Environmental Design Research* : *Volume 2, Symposia and Workshops*, Stroudsburg, Pennsylvania : Dowden, Hutchinson, and Ross, 1974, 166-81.

Wohlwill, J.F. Environmental aesthetics. The environment as a source of affect. In I. Altman and J.F. Wohlwill (Eds.), *Human behavior and environment* : *Advances in theory and research* (Vol. 1). New York : Plenum, 1976.

Wortman, C.B. and Brehm, J.W. Responses to uncontrollable outcomes : An integration of reactance theory and the learned helplessness model. In L. Berkowitz (Ed.), *Advances in experimental social psychology* (Vol. 8). New York : Academic Press, 1975.

Zajonc, R.B. Social facilitation. *Science*, 1965, 149, 262-274.

Zeisel, J. *Stopping school property damage*. Boston : American Association of School Administrators and Educational Facilities Laboratories in collaboration with City of Boston Public Facilities Department, 1976.

PART TWO

COGNITIVE IMAGE OF THE CITY

FOUR

GARY W. EVANS

ENVIRONMENTAL COGNITION

Research is reviewed on human spatial cognition in real, everyday settings. The cognitive mapping literature is organized into five empirical categories : age, familiarity, gender, class and culture, and physical components of settings. Methodological and conceptual issues in the environmental cognition literature are discussed, emphasizing problems with hand-drawn sketch map methodologies and theoretical ambiguities about the cognitive-mapping process. In particular, the lack of integration of pertinent cognitive research with the environmental psychology literature on cognitive mapping is noted. Finally, the potential applications of environmental cognition work to architecture, planning, and education are discussed.

How human beings comprehend real-world environments is a major question within environmental psychology and has also recently been addressed by cognitive psychologists.[1] As early as 1913, however, Trowbridge studied how individuals oriented in geographic space. Scant human research ensued until the early 1960s (see I.P. Howard and Templeton 1966, for a review), but important animal work was initiated during this period by Tolman (1948) in his classic studies of place learning that challenged strict S-R learning theories. Although con-

Reprinted from *Psychological Bulletin*, vol. 88 (2), 1980, 259-87.

troversy still exists regarding place versus cue response theories of learning, the term *congitive map* has remained as a general descriptor of the cognitive processes involved in the acquisition, representation, and processing of information about actual physical settings (Downs and Stea, 1973 ; Moore, 1979 ; Moore and Golledge, 1976).

Real-world settings differ from stimulus arrays used in most experimental studies of cognition. In a real-world setting, the observer is an interactive part of the environment, not a passive observer of stimulus objects. The environment surrounds the observer and is viewed from multiple vantage points as it is explored. Further, information in real-world settings is not isolated, nonsensical material ; instead, the information has meaning within the context of the setting (Ittelson, 1973). Cognitive maps can also be distinguished from other cognitive representations of information. First, cognitive maps primarily represent spatial relationships among loci. Principles of commutativity and associativity are important criteria for map utility. Second, the representation, although not strictly cartographic, experientially contains some maplike qualities. A good cognitive map facilitates movement through the actual physical setting represented by the cognitive schemata of that space. Information about location and not simply content (*e.g.*, semantic meaning) is a central component of cognitive representations of physical space (Pick, Note 1).

This article addresses several salient issues in environmental cognition. First, problematic aspects of the empirical work pervade the literature, particularly poor methodology and theoretical difficulties. Specific criticisms of hand-drawn sketch map and small-scale model methodologies are presented, and alternative techniques for data acquisition and analysis are offered. Information-processing perspectives on how visual and spatial information in actual settings is mentally encoded and manipulated are discussed, emphasizing proposition and analog explanations of cognitive representation.

In addition, several empirical issues are examined. Research on both developmental and familiarity variables has emphasized qualitatively different stages of knowledge acquisition with increased age or environmental experience. Some theorists have also suggested that the developmental and familiarity trends parallel one another. Although there is some support for the similarity of the ontogenetic and familiarity trends in the literature, I conclude that it is difficult to distinguish qualitatively distinct stages of cognitive development or familiarity. A reasonable alternative is that quantitative improvements in accuracy occur. Another issue in the familiarity literature is how environmental experience has been operationalized. Although most investigators have made cross-sectional comparisons (*e.g.*, newcomers vs. long-term residents), recent research has analyzed more precisely where and how frequently people actually use settings.

The few gender or class/cultural differences found in environmental knowledge may be explained by individual's daily activity patterns. Individuals with the greatest extent of daily range have greater and more accurate knowledge of their environments. Clear evidence indicates that various physical features of settings such as landmark placement and street grid configurations affect setting knowledge. Yet few investigators have simultaneously examined both individual and physical variables in environmental cognition. Finally, practical applications of environmental cognition in planning, architecture, and education are discussed.

COGNITIVE REPRESENTATIONS OF THE PHYSICAL ENVIRONMENT

This section discusses prevailing models of the cognitive-mapping process in the environmental cognition literature and examines relevant information-processing research.

The seminal work on environmental cognition is *The Image of the City* by Lynch (1960), an urban planner. Lynch reasoned that cognitive maps of cities function primarily as orientation aids and reflect basic elements of the physical, city form. His own research plus that of several other planners (Appleyard, 1969, 1970 ; de Jonge, 1962 ; Francescato and Mebane, 1973 ; Gulick, 1963) suggest five key features that comprise cognitive maps of urban settings : paths, path intersections (nodes), landmarks, districts, and boundaries (edges). Landmarks are external points of reference from the observer that possess some distinct form that contrasts with background information. Districts are medium-sized subsections of the city that one may enter and feel "inside of" (Lynch, 1960). This taxonomy of urban elements of cognitive maps has been derived primarily from subjective analyses of hand-drawn, sketch maps. Magana (1978), however, has recently verified Lynch's five-part typology through cluster analysis of individual's free-pile sorts of verbal labels for physical city features. Cognitive maps also reflect information about the hierarchical arrangement of points in space, with respect to relative distance and size. They also contain information about the degree of interconnectedness among points in the geographic environment (Stea, 1969).

Until recently there have been two relatively distinct models in cognitive psychology on how information is cognitively represented. Propositional models of cognitive representation state that information is stored in lists or associated networks based on abstract representations of meaning (Anderson and Bower, 1973 ; Pylyshyn, 1973). Closely related to the propositional view is the concept of schemata. Cognitive maps have been viewed as a type of schematic structure that helps humans search for and comprehend environmental information critical to location and orientation decisions (Kaplan, 1973b ; Neisser, 1976 ; Stea, 1969). A second perspective on cognitive representations of information is the analogical view which states that mental representations maintain some rough, isomorphic correspondence to the actual physical structure of the information in the world (Kosslyn, 1975 ; Shepard, 1975). The correspondence between the internal, imaginal construct and the external object is considered functional, not literal. The reconstruction of the external array by the internal representation reexcites neural processes that are functionally equivalent to those mental processes elicited by the external array directly. These opposing views have been modified to the position that cognitive representations may code information in the form of propositions but can manipulate it analogically (Kosslyn and Pomerantz, 1977).

The view adopted here is that knowledge about the content and location of places in the geographic environment is stored in both propositional and anological form. Cognitive maps include abstract labelings of environmental elements (paths, landmarks, etc.) and cardinal directions and are affected by previous knowledge of settings in general. Some information, however, such as the relative spatial positions of objects in settings may be processed analogically.

Several studies have shown the influence of schemata on human spatial memory. Data indicate that schemata operate selectively, emphasizing the spatial arrangement of objects in complex visual arrays and not the descriptive detail of individual items (Mandler and Parker, 1976).

When individuals draw maps of familiar settings, certain systematic distortions occur, which suggests the influence of prototypic biases in the configuration of geographic settings. Among some of the more commonly noted distortions are the straightening of long, gradual curves, the squaring of nonperpendicular intersections, and the aligning of nonparallel streets (Appleyard, 1969, 1970 ; Byrne, 1979 ; Lynch, 1960). In another example of systematic drawing distortions, Norman and Rumelhart (1975) found that when residents drew their apartment floor plans in a particular housing complex, nearly half of them incorrectly extended their balcony beyond the flush, exterior plane of the apartment. An additional 20 per cent had to redraw the balcony several times. The author suggested that the resident's difficulty in drawing the balcony stemmed from its unusual construction. The balcony was recessed within the exterior plane of the building instead of overhanging as most balconies do.

The influence of higher order organizational structures on knowledge of spatial location has been demonstrated in a series of studies by Stevens and Coupe (1978). They found that the relative spatial position of geographic items was distorted in a predictable fashion by the relationship of an item with the superordinate unit in which it was situated. Thus in judging the relative position of Reno, Nevada, and San Diego, California, most people will incorrectly state that San Diego is west of Reno. This effect was found for real city locations as well as novel laboratory stimuli in which the predominant latitudinal or longitudinal relationship among superordinate units (U.S. states or novel counties) would strongly bias directional judgments of cities contained within the states or counties. Similarly, Wilton (1979) has recently shown that it takes subjects less time to verify if one town is north of another if the first town is in Scotland and the second in England, than if two towns are equidistant along the north south axis in the same country.

Finally, several studies have focused on the influence of higher order structure on distance judgments. Lea (1975) had people learn an array of objects located around a circle by visualizing the objects in space. Subjects were then asked to name the first, second, or nth target item in a given direction around the circle when given an initial starting point on the circle. Reaction time was a function of the number of intervening objects around the circle, not the actual distance to be traversed from the starting point to target. These data support a propositional model, since people were apparently searching through a listlike set of items and not scanning their visual image. Finally, in making interpoint distance estimates, adults were equally accurate when they had learned a novel route through random versus sequential presentation. Perceptual constancy was not necessary for the acquisition of route knowledge (Allen, Siegel, and Rosinski, 1978).

Summarizing, several cognitive studies suggest that aspects of spatial representations of geographic settings manifest propositional form. Spatial memory reflects higher order schematic structures partially derived from past geographic experiences. Further, distance estimation tasks under some circumstances rely on apparent list search strategies rather than scanning a visual image of the points in space.

Cognitive maps may also contain information in forms that have a more direct, albeit rough correspondence to actual setting structure. Evans and Pezdek (1980) asked students to judge which of two pairs of campus buildings or U.S. states was closer together in physical distance. They found that for either type of stimuli, decision time increased linearly as the ratio of the two intrapair distances approached one. Another investigator reported that subjects who had previously learned a novel map, took longer to scan their images of greater interpoint distances. Furthermore, scanning time was a direct linear function of actual interpoint distance on the original map (Kosslyn, Ball, and Reiser, 1978). Thus larger physical distances in memory take longer to scan, and physically closer distance discriminations take longer to make.

Evans and Pezdek (1980) also examined the ability of individuals to manipulate geographic information. They found that subjects' reaction time to determine the accuracy of the relative spatial position of triads of U.S. states was an increasing, linear function of the degree of triad rotation from the 0° Cartesian plan of a standard map of the United States. A similar rotation function was found for subjects who learned campus building loci from a campus map but not for residents of that campus. Together these data indicate that when settings are learned from multiple perspectives, as opposed to one perspective only, knowledge of spatial relationships in that setting may be flexible and not perspective bound. When information about the relative locations of geographic elements is learned from maps, knowledge is perspective bound and reflects some structural analogy to the physical relationships among the actual geographical elements in the setting.

Summary

It is evident that human beings have cognitive representations of various physical settings they have experienced. These representations may function as schemata that help facilitate and organize information extraction and storage of real-world scenes. Controversy exists over the nature of these representations, particularly whether they are imaginal, functional analogues of actual stimuli with second-order isomorphic structure or if they are propositional statements about real-world information.

METHODOLOGICAL ISSUES

The essential methodological problem faced by investigators of cognitive representations of the real-world environment is how to externalize the individual's mental map of the environment. Researchers in environmental cognition have depended largely on individual's hand-drawn sketch maps of their immediate surroundings as indicators of the cognitive processes invoked in the perception and comprehension of the everyday environment. Investigators have also used modeling techniques. and a few have probed cognitive representations of the real environment with picture recognition tasks. Unfortunately, there have been few psychometric investigations of the measurement techniques used in cognitive-mapping research. This section begins with an overview of some psychometric aspects of these techniques, followed by a critique of sketch maps, and then an overview of procedural and analysis issues.

Measurement issues

The use of models and photographs in environmental cognition research raises a fundamental issue—Are these techniques valid simulations of actual settings ? Data suggest that the degree of scale reduction in models and the use of photographs can have important effects on cognition. Dirks and Neisser (1977) compared children's and adults' memory for complex visual scenes presented as models and photographs and found no differences between the two media.

Small-scale models preclude motoric experience that, as shown later, is a critical component of learning to orient in a setting. Perception of a small model is also from an oblique visual perspective rather than on the same visual plane on which real-world settings are viewed. Acredolo (1977) found that significant developmental differences in the use of landmarks in a full-scale room were not replicated in a small-scale model of the same room. Furthermore, greater place responding (using objects in the room as frames of reference), as opposed to egocentric responding, occurred in the small-scale model. In addition, the relative influence of landmarks diminished substantially in the small-scale model. Herman and Siegel (1978) also found less developmental differences when children were tested on scale models placed within a smaller, bounded space (classroom) than in a larger, unbounded space (gymnasium). They also manipulated the scale of their model (300 square m vs. 80 square m) and found significantly greater accuracy, independent of grade level, in the larger model. On the other hand, Siegel, Herman, Allen, and Kirasic (1979) reported that children performed comparably in large- and small-scale models, provided that reconstruction tasks were required at the same scale. However, when children learned a setting on a small-scale model and then reconstructed it on a large-scale model, they had considerable difficulty. If children were first exposed to a large-scale model, the scale of the model for the reconstruction task did not matter. Thus the scale of models, their placement in rooms, and the extent of scale transition are important factors in research that uses models.

Two studies have examined psychometric properties of sketch maps (R.B. Howard, Chase, & Rothman, 1973 ; Rothwell, 1976). R.B. Howard and colleagues had adults perform one of the following tasks in a familiar, outdoor environment : (a) Draw a map of the environment, (b) place objects in scale models, (c) make magnitude estimation judgments of interobject distances, and (d) make ratio estimates of interobject distances by marking off a standardized line in proportion to the real distance. All four methods proved to be reliable, with reliability coefficients ranging from .987 to .995. Correlations among the subjective distance estimates and the actual distances were high, with a minimum correlation of .98 out of 25 correlations. Similar high levels of reliability were found in adults' drawings of their apartment floor plans (Rothwell, 1976).

These two studies suggest relatively good reliability and some validity for hand-drawn maps of macrospaces. Several cautions, however, are in order. First, both studies focused on interobject distance and did not examine the accuracy of relative object placement in space. Second, because each distance judgment was not independent from others, the predictive validity of the correlation data were limited. Furthermore, one cannot establish validity solely on the basis of high convergence among measures ; discriminant validation is also necessary.

Several studies have compared the accuracy of different methodologies used in environmental cognition research. Baird (1979) compared the nonmetric multidimensional scaling (MDS) solutions of magnitude estimates of interpoint distances among familiar buildings and a computer map technique in which subjects arranged buildings on a matrix display. Although both methods yielded comparable high accuracy, both the subjects and independent judges rated the computer maps as more accurate. MacKay (1976), however, found that MDS solutions of sketch maps were more accurate than were MDS outputs from the sorting of item pairs into similar distance categories. Finally, Magana, Evans, and Romney (in press) found comparable high accuracy among the MDS solutions of magnitude estimations of interpoint distances, triadic comparisons of interpoint distances, and hand-drawn maps. In all of these studies, accuracy has been operationalized as the degree of fit between the MDS solutions of the interpoint distance matrix from the actual setting and the interpoint distance matrix produced by the subject using the respective methodologies.

Different measurement techniques have also been compared in the amount of information remembered in verbal and drawing recall probes, picture recognition, and eye fixation data. Carr and Schissler (1969) found some discrepancies between subjects' eye movement data, free-recall data, and sketch maps of the same area collected on different individuals earlier by Appleyard, Lynch, and Myer (1964). There was high correlation between verbal free recall of elements and recall on sketch maps, but neither was highly related to eye fixation data. Some data indicate possible retrieval difficulties in sketch map reconstructions. Both Banerjee (1971) and Milgram and Jodelet (1976) found that accurate picture recognition was slightly greater for some objects than free recall on sketch maps. Furthermore, verbal free-recall descriptions of city elements exceeded the recall of elements on sketch maps for the same city, particularly for low-frequency items (Appleyard, 1976 ; Banerjee, 1971 ; Lynch, 1960 ; Magana, 1978 ; Milgram & Jodelet, 1976).

Summarizing, preliminary data suggest problems with the use of small-scale models to test individuals' cognitive representations of macroenvironments. Psychometric research on sketch map techniques indicates adequate reliability, but important questions about validity remain.

Problems with hand-drawn sketch map methodologies

The use of sketch maps as a source of data raises several questions. For example, do individual differences in drawing ability seriously confound sketch map output ? Golledge (1976) and Blaut and Stea (1974) have argued that sketch map data underrepresent a person's knowledge because of limitations in drawing ability. This may be particularly true for children. Kosslyn, Heldmeyer, and Locklear (1977), who systematically studied children's drawings of simple objects, concluded that cognitive representations of objects in school children cannot be inferred on the basis of their drawings. Little data are available on the effects of graphic ability on sketch maps of actual environments. Rothwell (1976) found a small but significant correlation (.14) between adults' graphic skills (Lurcat Test of Graphic Ability) and the accuracy of home floor plan drawings. For children, however, there was a substantial correlation (.62) between judges' ratings of the accuracy of children's floor plan sketches and the children's scores on the Goodenough-Harris Draw-A-Man-Test. Although this test may indicate graphic ability, it is highly correlated with standard intelligence measures. Rothwell's adult data indicate that graphic ability may have only slight effect on sketch map productions. His developmental findings, when coupled with Kosslyn et al.'s data, however, indicate that children's drawings are not a suitable measurement technique for probing their cognitive representations of large-scale environments.

Parameters of the drawing task itself may be problematic as well. The issue of scale is pertinent. Artifactual variables that could have an impact on scale include the size of the drawing surface and the order in which things are drawn. Initially drawn elements may have substantial effects on the relative size and/or position of subsequent elements. The more elements one has put down on a drawing, the fewer are the degrees of freedom that remain to maintain size and distance scale. Research on young children's drawings of simple objects (typically human figures) has shown that initial picture units impose restrictions on the size and relative position of subsequent picture components (Goodnow, 1977). The lack of independence among drawn elements also creates statistical problems.

Another point of concern is the tendency of some investigators to treat the temporal ordering of the recall of elements on a map as indicative of relative importance (Golledge, 1976). On the other hand, Milgram and Jodelet (1976) did find a high correspondence among first-drawn elements and those most frequently recognized in a picture recognition probe.

Finally, the potential influence of individual differences in map interpretation experience has not been systematically examined. Several studies provided suggestive evidence that map experience enhances the accuracy and complexity of hand-drawn sketch maps (Beck & Wood, 1976 ; Dart & Pradham, 1967 ; Magana, 1978). Furthermore, as discussed earlier, Evans and Pezdek (1980) concluded that the use of maps affected how environments were cognitively encoded.

General procedural issues

There are numerous procedural issues involved in cognitive mapping research that have not been adequately explored. Instructions to subjects in environmental cognition articles are frequently not described adequately. For example, what degree of information should one provide subjects in an orientation problem or sketch map task ? Some investigators have provided subjects with basic landmarks and/or boundaries, whereas others have measured free recall without cues. Another methodological difficulty is the level of linguistic competence assumed in instructions. For example, can a child comprehend what it means to imagine standing in front of his/her bathroom sink and describe what one could see on the other side if they were able to see through the wall (Pick, Acredolo, & Gronseth, Note 2) ? With young children in particular we need to carefully consider whether inferior performance indicates deficiencies in cognitive representation or inability to understand instructions.

Another set of problems concerns the confounding of age and experience. When older children represent an environment more accurately, is it because they have had more experience with it ? Developmental studies can avoid confounding experience with age by examining individuals at different age levels crossed with groups with different amounts of experience in a given setting.

Data analysis is also a concern. Golledge (1976, 1977) has noted that many cognition researchers have treated sketch map data at an internal or ratio level when they should be treated either descriptively or analyzed within ordinal restrictions. For example, when someone draws two landmarks 6 cm apart and two other landmarks 3 cm apart on a sketch map, it seems more valid to assume that the individual knows that the first pair of landmarks is farther apart than the second pair, rather than assuming she/he knows that the first pair is twice as far apart as the second pair of landmarks. Several studies have also been vague in describing the judges who scored the maps or models. Frequently the criteria used in judging accuracy, complexity, and so forth have not been clearly delineated. Furthermore, judgment criteria, when described adequately, have varied across studies. Thus basic methodological studies are sorely needed to compare different rating procedures of accuracy.

A final problem is how to best present aggregate descriptions of data. Few researchers have described how they have constructed modal or mean descriptions of sets of individuals' map or model data. Furthermore, the extent of individual variability often goes unreported or cannot be adequately determined. Two possible solutions are first, use of non-metric MDS techniques to aggregate data on an objective basis (Evans, Marrero, & Butler, in press ; Galledge, 1976, 1977 ; Kosslyn, Pick, & Fariello, 1974). A second approach is the use of computer mapping capabilities (Baird, 1979). Both of these techniques avoid constructions of aggregate or modal maps based on judges' or authors' subjective criteria. Instead, these techniques use scaling algorithms that compute aggregates on the basis of summated, interpoint distance matrices taken directly from map displays. More detailed descriptions are available in Golledge and Baird.

Alternatively, one can circumvent some of the problems raised here by using photographic probes as Milgram has recommended (Milgram, Greenwald, Kessler, McKenna, & Waters, 1972) whereby scoring and analysis difficulties are substantially reduced. Recognition paradigms, however, eliminate important data such as estimates of subjective distance and the relative locations of objects. Hardwick, McIntyre, and Pick's (1976) sighting tube methodology also provides an innovative approach to cognitive map research that is free of many of the procedural and analysis issues raised. Subjects sight several target places in space from three different viewing stations behind opaque barriers. The intersection of the three sighting lines (triangulation) provides a location estimate. Kozlowski and Bryant's (1977) simple sketching procedures using the basic outline shape of an area embellished with one or two existing landmarks also provides researchers with a less error-prone method for drawing than a freehand sketch map. Finally, orientation tasks in the actual environment can be experimentally examined, given sufficient ingenuity, as evidenced by the research programs of Acredolo and Pick and their colleagues (Acredolo, 1976, 1977 ; Acredolo, Pick, & Olsen, 1975).

COGNITIVE-MAPPING RESEARCH : EMPIRICAL FINDINGS

Research from the environmental cognition literature is reviewed and summarized below in five empirical categories : age, familiarity, gender, class and culture, and physical components of environments.

Age

Ontogenetic research on environmental cognition can be divided into two broad categories : frame of reference and representation research. Frame of reference work focuses on the types of information people use to spatially orient themselves in space. Representation research examines the degree of accuracy and complexity in an individual's memory for spatial relationships in the environment. The Piagetian perspective on spatial cognition has greatly influenced both lines of developmental research on environmental cognition. This perspective states that the ontogeny of spatial comprehension proceeds through a logical ordering of three kinds of spatial information : topological, projective, and metric (Euclidean) space (Piaget & Inhelder, 1967 ; Piaget, Inhelder, & Szeminska, 1960).

Topological information includes an object's proximity, separation, extent of continuity, and degree of enclosure. The ability to comprehend topological space that arises during the transition period from sensorimotor to preoperational cognition is strongly linked to direct tactile and motor experience. Projective spatial comprehension that emerges during the latter preoperational stage of cognitive development is based on the interrelationships among objects in space as perceived from various perspectives. Shape and form information (*e.g.*, rectilinearity) are comprehended with changes in projective spatial relationships involving shifts in viewing perspective. Initially, there is a strong egocentric bias in projective spatial comprehension. Finally, children comprehend Euclidean spatial properties (*e.g.*, angularity, distance) with respect to an abstract set or sets of coordinates.

Frames of reference research in children

Several investigators have suggested that younger children learn to orient in settings primarily through egocentric relationships. This is followed by place learning in which one orients to the fixed location of proximate elements such as landmarks. Finally, orientation occurs with respect to coordinated systems of reference. At this stage children do not orient in terms of the relationship of their body position in space or the spatial relationships among proximate landmarks. Instead, location is determined with respect to the broader area and is expressed in more abstract terms such as cardinal directions (Hart & Moore, 1973).

Empirical research on this topic is generally consistent with the views of Piaget and their extension to geographic settings by Hart and Moore. Several studies have examined the cues children use to describe others' perspectives in scale models. Piaget and his colleagues in an early study of perspective taking asked children to determine what a doll's view of three, distinctive modeled mountains would be when it was placed at various viewpoints. Preoperational children (4–6½ years) maintained primarily egocentric viewpoints, drawing, modeling, or selecting the picture that represented their own view. These younger children persisted in this egocentric representation, even when allowed to walk around the model and view it from the doll's perspective. With the onset of concrete operations (7—9 years), children coordinated perspectives, generally reflecting a correct sense of in front of/in back of, then followed by left and right. Not until the latter stages of concrete operations, however, did children correctly perform the task indicating that they could coordinate perspectives that were independent of their own egocentric viewpoint.

Subsequent research has replicated the major developmental trends found by Piaget and Inhelder but has raised two questions. First, to what extent do the developmental differences reflect qualitative shifts in spatial cognition as opposed to quantitative progress ? Flavell, Botkin, Fry, Wright, and Jarvis (1968) concluded that only egocentric and nonegocentric responses could be differentiated and that other changes were simply quantitative, whereas others have concluded that qualitative shifts occur, including the orderly comprehension of object interposition, object orientation, and left/right relationships (Coie, Costanzo, and Farnill, 1973 ; Laurendeau and Pinard, 1970 ; Nigl and Fishbein, 1974). Second, procedural variations can improve younger children's comprehension of another's perspective. The use of easily differentiated objects or requiring children to mentally rotate the model may reduce egocentric responding in preoperational children (Borke, 1975 ; Fishbein, Lewis, and Keiffer, 1972 ; Huttenlocher and Presson, 1973 ; Masangkay *et al.*, 1974).

Younger children can also adopt perspectives other than their own in interpreting aerial photographs (Blaut, McCleary, and Blaut, 1970 ; Blaut and Stea, 1974). Four-year-olds located their homes and traced routes between points on aerial photographs. An important difference between these studies and Piaget's is that subjects here could successfully perform the tasks required primarily by object identification (*i.e.*, "that is a road", etc.). In the previously described studies, comprehension of relative object *location*, not descriptive content, was required.

In a second study on frame of reference, Piaget and Inhelder (1967) asked children to place objects on a scale model. To locate a doll on the landscape model, the child was presented a model (Model A) on which the experimenter placed a doll. Separated from Model A by a screen was a second identical model (Model B), rotated 180°. To accurately locate the doll on Model B, children could not use their own reference position (egocentric orientation) but had to rely on either parts of the model itself (fixed location) or some abstract coordinate system of cardinal directions.

At ages 3-4, doll position was determined primarily by relative proximity of surroundings. Thus the doll was placed next to the same object or one in the same part of the model, with little or no apparent recognition of distance, before-behind, left-right, and so forth. Children at this age could not logically transpose more than one proximate relationship at a time. For example, if the doll was placed in a stream in Model A at the bottom of the model, nearly all children placed it in the stream in Model B but at many different locations. During

Stage II (4-6 years), two substages were reported. Children 4 and 5 years old located the doll relative to their own position and disregarded rotation but used more than one feature at a time to locate the doll. During the latter part of Stage II (5-6 years), representation gradually appeared that accounted for rotation. Left-right and before-after relationships, order, and distance emerged gradually as the result of a laborious trial-and -error process. At Stage III (6-7 years), model rotation no longer affected the child's judgment, and the doll was placed accurately.

Several investigators have replicated these findings, particularly initial egocentrism and inability to coordinate more than one spatial referent simultaneously. This is followed by rotation comprehension but continued difficulty with multiple referents coordination, with final emergence of multiple, referent coordination abilities (De Lisi, Locker, and Youniss, 1976 ; Laurendeau and Pinard, 1970 ; Pufall and Shaw, 1973). Controversy remains, however, about the specific ages for each stage. It is also unclear whether mental age (as distinguished from IQ) accounts for some of the age differences reported. Unfortunately, there are no data on this question. One important issue in many of the described developmental studies is the unknown influence of language comprehension on children's task performance. For example, younger children will behave less egocentrically in spatial modeling tasks when told to mentally rotate a model versus when told to adopt another's spatial perspective.

An additional limitation in all of the described studies is their reliance on small-scale models that, as discussed earlier, may affect results, particularly with children. Recently, researchers have examined the frames of reference children use to orient in larger scale models. In one study 3-, 4-, and 10-year-olds were led to a table on their right as they entered an otherwise empty room and were then blindfolded. Children were then led around the room, with half of them ending their walk at the opposite side of the room from the original entry and half returning to the original entry point. In addition, for half of them, the table was moved to the opposite side of the room. The blindfold was removed, and the child asked to return to the spot at which the blindfold had been fastened. Three-year-olds either responded egocentrically, turning to their right regardless of change in bodily position or table placement or depended on a fixed frame of reference provided by the table position. The 4-year-olds used table position predominantly to orient, whereas the 10-year-olds relied on a coordinated frame of reference (*e.g.*, the room itself), correctly locating the original blindfolding point irrespective of their relative body position or the location of the table (Acredolo, 1976). In subsequent research Acredolo (1977) has shown that egocentric responding in 3-, and 4-year-olds under similar conditions is reduced by providing landmark cues in the room.

A second developmental research program on orientation examined the abilities of first-grade, fifth-grade, and college students to sight target items through a sighting tube when the targets are in the same room but not visible (Hardwick *et al.*, 1976). The intersection of three different viewing sights on each target was used to measure accuracy. First graders performed significantly poorer on the task but still had relatively good knowledge of the familiar environment (school library). There were greater age differences in two variations of the task in which subjects sighted all the targets from one viewing station while imagining that they were sighting the targets from each other viewing station (perspective taking) or that the room had rotated relative to their fixed position in space (mental rotation). Only adults accurately performed these tasks, and qualitatively different errors were noticed among the first and fifth graders. The first graders made egocentric errors, frequently confusing target sightings as if no imagined location shifts had occurred. Fifth graders correctly determined ordinal distance relationships among targets but failed to accurately coordinate this information with specific angular data. Thus fifth graders made relatively accurate gross directional determinations but failed to fine tune their responses. First graders frequently did not discern basic directional information.

Summary of developmental frame of reference research

Research on frame of reference information used to orient in modeled and realistic settings generally supports the developmental sequence posited by Piaget and subsequently elaborated on by Hart and Moore. Initially, young children rely heavily on egocentric cues to orient in space. This is followed by the use of fixed objects in space, first singly and eventually coordinating multiple objects' interrelationships to the observer. Finally, comprehension of space as a coordinate system, independent of the object's or person's position within that space occurs. Controversy remains regarding the precise age ranges of these changes, the influence of differentiated landmarks on the process, and whether sequential, qualitative differences among nonegocentric errors can be discerned.

Frames of reference and orientation behavior in the elderly

Orientation abilities of the elderly have not been examined in great detail. Looft and Charles (1971) and Rubin, Attewell, Tierney, and Tumolo (1973) found the elderly less accurate than young adults in perspective-taking tasks like the Piagetian three-mountain problem but did not examine the types of errors made. Schultz and Hoyer (1976) found that the elderly made more nonegocentric errors than young adults but the same amount of egocentric errors in a perspective-taking task. They did not examine the kinds of nonegocentric mistakes made. More recently Ohta, Walsh, and Krauss (Note 3) examined error rates, reaction times, and types of errors made by elderly and young adults in a spatial memory task. Subjects examined a small-scale model of three buildings and then judged the accuracy of various slides that represented either the actual view of the model, an egocentric view, interposition shifts, 180° rotation of each building, or a right/left reversal. The elderly's correct slide judgments were slower, and overall error rates were higher than the younger adults' ; however, the elderly made the same proportion of error types at the young adults.

Representation research in children

A second line of inquiry on developmental aspects of environmental cognition has examined the properties of children's mental representations of spatial layouts. This research has focused on the accuracy and complexity of children's memory for spatial information in actual and modeled settings. Siegel and White (1975), drawing from the Piagetian perspective on spatial cognition, have posited a developmental model of spatial representation. First, the young child notices and remembers landmarks. Once landmarks are established, route learning occurs within their context in a point-to-point fashion. Third, landmarks and routes are organized into small clusters that have good internal organization but that are poorly coordinated with one another. Finally, survey representation is achieved wherein routes are coordinated within an overall frame of reference. A similar distinction was made earlier by Shemyakin (1962) between route and survey knowledge. He found that 6-8-year-olds' maps of familiar settings frequently reflected familiar routes of locomotion, whereas older children's were more holistic, accurately coordinating landmarks and paths in space.

Empirical research on the development of spatial representations has relied on models, sketch maps, and behavior in actual settings. Several early studies by Piaget *et al.* (1960) illustrate the use of small-scale models to study spatial representation abilities in children. In the first study children were presented diagrammatic layouts of a model landscape and asked to either draw pictures or duplicate it with another model. Children 4 years and under did not comprehend the spatial arrangement and frequently did not even choose the same components or the right number when duplicating the model. The 4-6-year-olds correctly identified the model objects but could not logically order more than one spatial relationship simultaneously. Children grouped objects together that were near one another in the model. Intergroup arrangement, as opposed to intragroup arrangement, appeared particularly distorted and uncoordinated. Finally, at 7-10 years a more complete coordination of projective and Euclidean spatial properties emerged. Left-right and behind-before positions and relative distance were conserved and accurately modeled, culminating in a final Stage IV in which proportional scale reduction was accomplished.

In another study Piaget *et al.*, (1960) had children model known routes in a sandbox with components provided to represent buildings, rivers, and so forth. Children under 4 years could not do the task but responded to questions as they were taken for an actual walk. There was a clear egocentric perspective in orientation ; direction reversals, for example created confusion. From 4-7 years there was a strong reliance on landmarks as they appeared in serial order in locomotion along the route. Position and distance were not accurately represented; instead, landmark position in sequence was a critical orientation cue. When children drew routes, Piaget noted a similar influence of actual motoric representation in recall. Each portion of the journey was constructed in seriation with various subsections joined only loosely and with considerable error. Thus the route was represented as a collection of links between landmark pairs or small groups. The influence of motoric experience in younger children's (4-7 years) spatial representations has also been demonstrated in distance judgment tasks. Preoperational children are strongly affected by functional distance, as opposed to actual visual distance. Younger children are more likely to distort their distance judgments between objects when barriers exist between the points (Kosslyn, Pick, and Fariello, 1974) or when the points are linked by indirect (looping) versus direct pathways (Anooshian and Wilson, 1977). Older children's and adults' distance judgments rely on direct visual estimates and less on the path one would have to take to get from one point to another.

Children 7-9 years old in Piaget's experiment grouped objects in terms of a fixed reference system of landmarks but not in terms of a whole, abstract coordinate system. Parts of the plan were organized correctly, but the relationships among parts or object clusters were not fully coordinated. Finally, older children assumed a more holistic coordinated referential system. Object groups were interconnected, with distance and relative position accurate both within and between element clusters. Caution in interpreting the developmental data in both of these studies by Piaget is warranted, given earlier discussion of difficulties with children's drawings and small-scale model building.

In an interesting extension of Piaget's route-modeling experiment, Herman and Siegel (1978) walked kindergartners, second graders, and fifth graders through a large model of a town that contained eight distinct buildings. Half of the children constructed the town from memory after each of three walks, whereas the other half of the children constructed the town only after their third walk through the model. After initial exposure to the model, fifth graders exhibited significantly greater building placement accuracy (both correct quadrant placement and exact location). The experience of walking through the model also significantly increased both types of accuracy. Furthermore, an interaction of age and construction experience suggested that with greater experience the age differences diminished significantly.

The high level of Euclidean accuracy obtained by the younger children with repeated experience in this study is contradictory to Piagetian theory and to much of the work discussed earlier. Herman and Siegel (1978) suspected that this high level of apparently Euclidean comprehension on the part of the younger children was due to a procedural artifact. In a second study the same layout was used in the middle of a large room (gymnasium) in which the walls of the space were far enough away so that it was unlikely that the room itself could function as a bounded space, providing topological cues external to the model itself. In the first study the model had been set up in the middle of a classroom in which the walls of the room were close to the edges of the model. The room change had a substantial effect on the Euclidean accuracy of the younger children. The kindergartners did not improve with practice over initially low levels of accuracy for the exact placement of buildings. Furthermore all of the children, although to a lesser extent than the kindergartners, performed more poorly in the unbounded space of the larger room. Again, we see reasons to be cautious in using models for measuring environmental cognition abilities in children.

Working at the interior scale, Day (1977) asked children (kindergarten and first, third, and fifth graders) to replace furniture in a model house they had walked through. Both the exact location of the furniture and the relative positioning of furniture in rooms was more accurate with increasing age, with the largest increments between third and fifth grade. Although the relatively low level of exact object placement accuracy for the younger children is consistent with the Piagetian perspective, the continued improvement in relative object location accuracy over the four grades is not in accord with the Piagetian position.

At least two model studies of children's spatial representation knowledge have found no age differences. Siegel and Schadler (1977) asked children 61-70 months old to build a model of their classroom in a sandbox. No age differences in either exact or relative object placement were found, Stea and colleagues (Blaut and Stea, 1974 ; Stea and Taphanel, 1974) in a series of studies instructed 3- and 4-year-olds to arrange toys on a large, novel landscapelike graphic on the floor. Both age groups were equally adept at building realistic models and navigating certain routes with "cars". Given the narrow age range in the Siegel and Schadler study, the lack of age differences therein is not surprising. The absence of age differences in Stea's research is difficult to interpret because of the dependent measures used. It is not clear if judges' ratings of landscape realism and route navigation performance reflect cognitive, developmental change.

Three studies have tested children's knowledge of actual settings with spatial problem solving tasks. Pick *et al.* (Note 2), asked 3-, 4-, and 5-year-olds to select a rectangular shape most like their bedroom and to indicate where the doors, closets, and windows were located by placing models of these components in the appropriate places. The same task was also completed for the kitchen. Children were also asked how they would go from their kitchen to their bedroom and to describe what they would see if they were able to see through their bathroom mirror. For the second phase of the experiment, the children were asked what was behind two walls of their own room and the kitchen while they were actually present in their own home.

Groups did equally well in identifying the shape of their own room and kitchen. The older group, however, averaged greater correct object placement across the two rooms and gave more accurate descriptions of what was beyond the walls of their room than the younger children. Both groups did poorly on the mirror imagination task with no age differences. In addition to some of the problems in using scale models, these age-related data may partially reflect differences in the younger and older children's ability to comprehend instructions.

In a second experiment 3-, 4-, and 8-year-old children were led on a walk through a hallway in their school (Acredolo *et al.*, 1975). During the walk, the experimenter "accidently" dropped her keys in a hallway that was either bare of furniture or had a few distinctive landmarks (different chairs). The landmarks were not near the key drop. The child's task was to return to the location of the key drop after walking through the hall. Pre-schoolers made greater errors than older children when no landmarks were present, but when landmarks were present, no age differences were found.

Finally, Hazen, Lockman, and Pick (1978) compared 3-6 year-old's ability to navigate in four or six interconnected rooms. Once they had learned a specified route and several landmarks in the rooms, the children retraced their original route in reverse. They also were required to anticipate in serial order each landmark as they approached it, infer the location of other landmarks not directly on the original route, and finally build a model of the rooms when the test walk was completed. All ages performed equally well on the route reversal task, but the 3-year-olds were less accurate in the landmark reversal testing. Only the 6-year-olds completed the landmark inference task accurately. The age differences in landmark reversal and inference tasks may reflect differences in language comprehension more than spatial cognition. The 6-year-olds were better than the 5-year-olds in model building only when a more complex route had originally been taken through the rooms (zigzag vs. a U), but otherwise 5 and 6-year-olds had equally accurate models that were better than the 3-year-olds' models.

Scant research has examined the spatial representation abilities of adolescents. Ladd (1970), Lynch (1977), Maurer and Baxter (1972), and Moore (1973) have reported no significant age effects in the neighborhood sketch maps of junior high adolescents. Andrews (1973), however, found that high school seniors were more accurate in locating down-town Toronto landmarks on a schematic map than were ninth graders. This age effect interacted with residential location, indicating that only students who lived within seven miles of Toronto exhibited these age trends. Thus a plausible explanation for these age differences is differential experience.

Two recent studies suggested deficiencies in the elderly's recall of the spatial layout of settings. Weber, Brown, and Weldon (1978) asked elderly residents of a nursing home whether they recognized various photographs of their residence and what section of the home the photo was from. In comparison with college students considerably less familiar with the nursing home, the elderly were less accurate on both tasks. The identification data may reflect response bias differences, however, since no scenes not from the nursing home were used. Although all of the elderly patients participating had been rated by nursing staff as alert and mobile, the college students had been given a tour of the entire building, whereas certain areas of the home may not have been frequented by the elderly patients. In a second study, the authors in fact found that the patients spent most of the day in their own rooms. Walsh, Krauss, and Regnier (in press) asked elderly and young adults to draw maps of their neighborhoods. Independent judges rated the elderly's maps as more disorganized, simple, and inaccurate. The elderly's maps were also smaller in size and moderately correlated with the use of facilities in the area and self-ratings of mobility. Elderly who were more mobile and who used a broader range of facilities in their neighborhood drew larger maps. No sex differences or educational level effects were found. In both of these studies with the elderly, mobility provides a partial explanation for age effects.

Summary of spatial representation research

Children's knowledge of spatial information generally fits the developmental sequence posited by Piaget and elaborated on by Siegel and White. Initially, route knowledge develops and involves at least two aspects : direction choice at landmarks and knowledge of landmark sequence. A strong, motoric experiential bias is present in preschoolers learning of geographic spatial information. Thus the dependence on model tasks in several studies is bothersome. At the next stage of development, knowledge of the relative location of objects within small proximate clusters is apparent, but intercluster, relative position is poor. Accurate intercluster representation gradually emerges with the development of an overall coordinate system of spatial referents that is independent of landmark locations or the observer's position in the setting. There is little difference in the accuracy of the oridinal relationships among objects in space for different aged children, but marked differences appear in the ability to exactly locate points in space. Although the converging lines of evidence for this developmental sequence are strong, a caveat is in order. All of the developmental, spatial representation studies except one have relied on scale models, and several included instructions that may be difficult for younger children to understand.

Little data are available on the cognitive mapping abilities of adolescents and the elderly. Adolescent trends suggest that few changes occur between the ages of approximately 12 and 17 years in mapping accuracy. The elderly may have some deficits in environmental cognition, but the influence of mobility needs to be considered more carefully.

Familiarity

Several researchers have examined the effects of setting familiarity on cognitive maps. This research has focused primarily on two issues : the kinds of elements individuals rely on to learn new environments and changes in accuracy that occur with increased environmental familiarity.

Physical elements

There are two competing models of how people learn a new setting. One position argues that individuals initially rely on paths and districts to orient in a novel environment. Later, when they are more familiar with the setting, they rely primarily on landmarks for orientation (Appleyard, 1970, 1976 ; Lynch, 1960). Conversely, both Hart and Moore (1973) and Siegel and White (1975) theorized that environmental learning is primarily landmark based, with path structures elaborated subsequently within original anchor, landmark points.

Appleyard (1970, 1976) compared the sketch maps of adults who had lived in an urban area for less than 6 months, for 6 months to 1 year, for 1 to 5 years, and for greater than 5 years. People who had lived in the city for 1 year or less produced maps characterized by greater path usage (sequential dominant map). More long-term residents drew maps emphasizing schematic boundaries and landmarks (spatial dominant map). In addition, Devlin (1976) found that newcomers to an area (2 weeks) used nearly the same pathways 6 weeks later in sketch maps but showed greater variability in landmarks. Early paths seemed to establish initial structures that were then elaborated on with continued setting experience. Thus both of these studies are consistent with Lynch's and Appleyard's hypothesis that path structure are most critical as early learning cues in the physical environment. Unfortunately, Appleyard's classification scheme of sequential or spatial dominant maps includes other criteria in addition to route or landmark predominance and does not directly isolate the two important features. Devlin's data clearly support the primacy of path structures in early learning but may not generalize well, since her setting was a small town with few distinct, easily visible landmarks.

Evans, Marrero, and Butler (in press) assessed changes in adults' sketch maps of their residential environment over a 1-year-period. Subjects from two independent samples recalled significantly more paths and nodes after 1 years residence but recalled the same number of landmarks. The landmarks recalled were nearly identical to those recalled during the first week. Furthermore, path systems were elaborated within the initial landmark structure with most of the increases in paths reflecting alternative routes between already established landmarks. In addition, Heft (1979) reported that adults relied more on landmarks to learn a route through a novel path network the first time they walked through it than when they had traversed the path system several times.

Accuracy

The environmental learning sequences posited by Hart and Moore (1973) and Siegel and White (1975) may be extended to shifts in accuracy with experience that resemble the ontogenesis of spatial cognition (Piaget & Inhelder, 1967). Preliminary contact with an environment provides comprehension of the relative positions of items in space with respect to the body. Thus the relative location of objects close in space can be correctly processed, provided no perspective shifts are demanded. Projective accuracy follows with items comprehended in terms of their relative positions with respect to various fixed points in space. Finally, Euclidean comprehension emerges wherein space is encoded as a unit in which items are located with respect to their position in two or three-dimensional space.

There are a few findings in the environmental cognition literature generally consistent with this Piagetian trend. Appleyard (1970, 1976) found that newcomers to a city (less than 6 months) were more apt to reverse the location of different city zone than were long-term residents. Both newcomers and long-term residents, however, placed roads and landmarks within zones equally accurately. Moore (1974) had independent judges sort students' maps of familiar and unfamiliar city areas. Area familiarity was determined by self-report. For unfamiliar map areas the relative positions of objects within small, proximate groups were correct, but the relative positions of the clusters were not correct. Familiar map areas appeared to be more abstractly coordinated, with both high intra and intercluster accuracy. Similar results were obtained by Banerjee (1971) and Tzamir (Note 4), who experimentally manipulated familiarity by exposure to a model.

Two studies directly measured changes in topological, projective, and Euclidean accuracy over time. Siegel and Schadler (1977) examined the effect of 6 months experience on 5 and 6-year olds' model reconstructions of their classroom. Independent of maturation, experience significantly enhanced Euclidean accuracy (exact object placement) but had no impact on topological or projective accuracy (relative object placement within an object cluster, relative cluster placement within the model). Evans, Marrero, and Butler (in press) also found that for adults, intracluster relative landmark placement and intercluster placement did not improve over a 1-year period but that exact landmark placement did. Euclidean accuracy was measured by comparing the nonmetric MDS solutions for individuals' maps at the beginning and end of the year, respectively, with the MDS solution for the real maps in each setting. Golledge, Rivizzigno, and Spector (1976) also used MDS techniques, comparing subjects' estimates of interpoint distances. They found that object location was better in old residents (6 months to 1 year) than in newcomers (less than a few weeks).

At least two studies, however, found no effects of environmental experience on accuracy. Ladd (1970) reported that the accuracy of adolescents' sketch maps of their neighborhood was unrelated to length of residence based on judge's rating of accuracy. Length of residence was grossly dichotomized, however, into less than or greater than 3 years residence, which may have been too broad a time period. The high levels of map accuracy found from 6 months to 1 years residence by several researchers (Appleyard, 1976 ; Evans, Marrero, and Butler, in press ; Golledge *et al.*, 1976) plus Ladd's data suggest that accuracy may improve and then reach asymptote within roughly a 1-year period. In the second study, Acredolo *et al.* (1975), found that children accurately recalled where a particular recent event had occurred equally well in familiar and unfamiliar school hallways. Accuracy was measured as the distance between where an object had previously been dropped by the experimenter and the child's relocation of that event.

A possible explanation for Acredolo *et al.*'s (1975) failure to find familiarity effects is that children in their study acquired less familiarity with the "farmiliar" setting, a known hallway, than the children in the Siegel and Schadler (1977) study, who were probed about their classroom, or Evans, Marrero, and Butler's (in press) subjects, who were asked about their residential neighborhood. The operationalization of familiarity in the Acredolo study as amount of exposure illuminates an interesting problem in the study of environmental familiarity. One could live in an area for several years but spend less time exploring it than a newcomer. Several recent studies suggest that environmental cognition is strongly affected by actual usage patterns.

Patterns of setting use

The relative locations of home, work schools, and shopping areas strongly affect, the extent of individual's knowledge of the immediate geographic environment (Horton & Reynolds, 1971). Similarly, cognitive representations of downtown urban areas differ in their overall distribution of detail as a roughly linear function of distance from where individuals work or live to the downtown (Lynch, 1977 ; Saarinan, Note 5). Finally, Holahan (1978) demonstrated that students draw more complete, detailed maps of campus areas they actually use more often. Displacement of the perceived center of campus was also skewed toward a student's usual entry point onto campus.

There is also evidence that recognition memory for components of settings is related to actual experience as well as to general residential history. Banerjee (1971) reported that the longer a person lived in Boston, the greater the number of photographs of the city they could correctly identify and locate. Milgram *et al.* (1972) asked residents of various boroughs of New York City to identify color slides of randomly chosen pictures of the various boroughs. Residents of each borough recognized substantially more photographs of their own borough than did nonresidents. An exception to this pattern was Manhattan, for which there were uniformly high recognition scores. Thus while subjects were familiar with their immediate home area, Manhattan is considerably well-known as well. This is probably because many people who live in surrounding boroughs work, shop, and enjoy recreational activities in Manhattan. In a second study, Milgram and Jodelet (1976) asked residents of Paris to draw maps of their city, identify photographs, and rate the 10 most familiar and 10 least familiar districts of the city. Recognition data matched the map data very well, particularly for frequently recalled items. The elements of Paris most frequently recalled and recognized were located in the heart of Paris (*e.g.*, l'Etoile, Notre Dame). Familiarity ratings also corresponded with these data, as the center districts of the city were rated as most familiar by all subjects. The latter finding is somewhat consistent with the explanation offered previously for the high recognition accuracy found for Manhattan scenes in the New York City study. City knowledge also varied as a function of residential location. Wealthier Parisians who lived in the western sector of Paris rated lower-class areas on the eastern sector as least familiar and knew less about the eastern sector. The opposite occurred for poorer Parisians' ratings and knowledge.

Therefore, the extent of actual setting contact as well as overall length of residence may affect human knowledge of settings. Future research on environmental learning should specifically examine the contributions of specific setting experience and overall length of residence. The two variables clearly correlate, but they are not necessarily synonymous. Furthermore, the effects of environmental contact may interact with other individual characteristics. Kozlowski and Bryant (1977) found that people who had a better sense of direction (self-ratings validated against actual orientation and map tasks) showed greater learning of a novel environment than did individuals with a poorer sense of direction. Subject were led through an unfamiliar tunnel five different times. After the initial incidental trial and Trials 2, 3, and 5, they were asked to draw an arrow on a small diagram of the tunnel entrance from the starting point to the end. The picture indicated only the first leg of the tunnel and did not include several remaining changes in direction. They also estimated the relative direction and distance from the tunnel entrance to the end point. Persons with better sense of direction significantly improved their performance with repeated exposures to the tunnel, whereas those with poorer sense of direction did not.

Summary

Research on environmental familiarity has focused on two major issues : the kinds of elements individuals rely on to learn new environments and changes in accuracy that occur with increased setting exposure. Competing hypotheses have proposed that landmarks or paths serve as primary, initial navigational cues in environmental learning. Whether people learn to orient in a new setting primarily by landmarks or by pathways may depend on the physical structure of the setting. Familiarity research should more carefully examine the interplay between physical structures and learning.

Several studies have consistently found that more changes occur in Euclidean accuracy over time than in the accuracy of relative object location or clusters of objects in space. Both the changes in accuracy and the kinds of elements used in learning environments resemble the developmental changes noted earlier in orientation cues and spatial representation. The importance of landmarks in initial environmental learning as fixed frames of reference and shifts in accuracy from good intracluster but poor intercluster accuracy to more precise Euclidean accuracy with experience are both similar to the developmental trends discussed in the prévious section.

Whether these age or experience trends reflect qualitative shifts in spaital cognition or quantitative, scalar changes is a point of controversy. Several studies suggest that memory for exact object location in the environment improves with experience but that the relative position of objects in space is accurately comprehended with little experience. The operational distinctions among these Piagetian stages may reflect scalar differences instead of distinct stages of spatial cognition. One could argue that as the number of paths between a given set of points in space increases, there is increased restriction on the possible locations of items in space. Given a large enough set of points, if the relative position of items is accurate, then each item can only exist in one particular locus in space.

Finally, two additional familiarity issues warrant research. First, the operationalization of environmental familiarity. Many researchers have equated familiarity with time periods (months, years), ignoring experiential differences in setting exposure across different persons. Second, most of the familiarity research to date has examined large, cross-sectional differences in time. There is need for more finegrained, longitudinal analysis that examines the same individual's environmental learning over smaller periods of time.

Gender

Most research on sex differences in spatial cognition has found few differences until adolescence, with a slight male advantage emerging (Maccoby and Jacklin, 1974). Nearly all of this research, however, has used two dimensional spatial tasks (paper-and-pencil tests) and has not investigated three-dimensional, spatial comprehension at real scale. Most cognitive mapping research has found no sex differences in environmental knowledge based on sketch maps (Francescato and Mebane, 1973 ; Maurer and Baxter, 1972 ; Orleans and Schmidt, 1972), recall of roadside information (Carr and Schissler, 1969), or in locating objects in real space with a sighting tube (Hardwick *et al.*, 1967). Furthermore, Kozlowski and Bryant (1977) have shown that sex is unrelated to self-ratings of sense of direction that were a potent predictor of performance in maze learning, locating the direction of familar buildings on a schematic diagram, and accuracy in map drawing.

Orleans and Schmidt (1972), however, found that males constructed sketch maps using base map coordinates that were provided, whereas women used their own home as a fixed referent system and largely ignored the abstract coordinates provided. Appleyard (1976) also found that men drew slightly more accurate and extensive city maps than did women, which he attributed to greater travel and exposure in the city. Similar differences among the sketch maps of adolescent girls and boys have been related to setting exposure. In cultures in which girls' home ranges were restricted (Argentina, Mexico), their neighborhood sketch maps were smaller and less accurate than the boys'. For cultures in which all adolecents were given similar home range privileges (Australia, Poland), no sex differences in mapping were apparent (Lynch, 1977). Hart (1979) also found a strong positive relationship between the accuracy and extent of children's sketch maps and the extent of their home range. In the New England town he studied, girls' ranges were more restricted and their map smaller and less accurate than those of boys.

Siegel and colleagues (Herman and Siegel, 1978 ; Siegel and Schadler, 1977) in their developmental research also found some sex differences in environmental cognition. In the model classroom study, kindergarten boys were more accurate than girls in both relative and exact object placement in the model. When children worked on models in a small, clearly bounded space, as opposed to a large, open space, sex differences were absent. Second and fifth-grade boys, however, performed better than girls in reconstructing a model in a large, unbounded space. The relatively low overall error rate in the simpler, model reconstruction task may have obscured sex differences in spatial cognition abilities.

Summary

Although there are some trends suggesting male superiority in spatial cognition for small-scale stimuli, the preponderance of evidence from real-scale spatial tasks indicates few sex differences in environmental cognition. Furthermore, when sex differences have been noted, they can often be explained by differences in the entext of neighborhood exposure.

Class and culture

Much of the research in this area has focused on class differences in environmetal cognition, although a few cross-cultural investigations have been conducted. Dart and Pradham (1967) asked 10-15-year-olds in Nepal and the United States to draw maps of their route from home to school. They found that the Nepalese maps were generally less functional and less cartographic in form, relying more on a pictorial mode that depicted line drawings of objects (house, child, school) without connecting routes. They suggested that these differences were because of differential experience with maps. Blaut *et al.* (1970), reported that 6-year-olds in the United States and Puerto Rico were equally adept at interpreting aerial photographs, including measures of object identification and navigational problem solving. Finally, Maurer and Baxter (1972) compared neighborhood maps of lower-class black, Chicano, and white children living in the same neighborhood. Several ethnic differences emerged, including greater neighborhood extent in white children's maps, use of more human-made structures by white and Chicano children and more natural features by black children. (The total number of elements used was similar.) Black children drew their home first more often and covered a larger percentage of their maps with it. Finally, significantly more white children drew a larger map of the entire city of Houston when asked to do so. The authors suggest that some of the unique aspects of the white children's data were due to the fact that they had significantly more friends farther from their home and more frequently attended school outside the immediate neighborhood.

In the described studies it is difficult to separate class from cultural variables. Several studies suggest class differences in environmental cognition that may result from differential setting exposure. Orleans (1973) discovered that an upper-class, professional group drew much broader, more accurate maps of Los Angeles than both middle- and lower-class respondents, whose maps were restricted and accurate only for their immediate environment. Orleans argued that these differences emanated from the greater breadth of social contacts that the upper class had. He found that the upper-class subjects were significantly more likely to have close friends outside of their immediate neighborhood than were subjects in the other groups. Appleyard (1976) found the opposite result in his research in Ciudad Guayana, Venezuela. Lower-class people had more complex maps that indicated more detailed knowledge of the city than did the upper class, although the latter group more accurately coordinated the interrelationships among distinct districts of the city. Appleyard suggested that the greater knowledge of the lower class was explained by their daily travel experiences. The wealthy lived near the major places of employment and rarely traveled to lower-class areas of the city. The poor traveled across town each day to the factories, offices, and homes of the wealthy in which they worked, thus gaining wider city exposure.

Francescato and Mebane (1973) reported that lower-class residents of Milan and Rome, Italy, drew maps that covered less area and had fewer elements (especially districts) than middle-class residents. They also found that a greater number of lower-class individuals refused to draw maps of their city. Magana (1978), who examined class differences in Guadalajara, Mexico, also found that lower-class people were less likely to draw maps of their city and a higher percentage of unscorable maps (less than four elements) than upper-class residents. Furthermore, those lower-class maps that were scorable were less accurate and had fewer elements than did the maps of the upper class. A free-listing technique, however, yielded no class differences in number of elements or willingness to do the task. Cultural differences in environmental cognition may be due to fundamental differences in cognitive style. Appleyard (1976) suggests that analytical styles are more common in developed societies, whereas people in underdeveloped societies use more relational modes of thinking. The analytic mode abstracts bits of information from settings and is stimulus centered, whereas the relational mode operates more concretely, focusing on general impressions of the global setting, without appreciation of the abstract relationships among various parts. Unfortunately, no data are currently available on this issue.

In addition to the amount of experience, the type of experience in the setting may be important. Appleyard (1976) found significant travel mode effects comparing bus and automobile users, which in turn was correlated to class. Bus riders generally saw more of the city, especially off-the-road features, but had a poorer sense of the overall configuration of the city. Similar data have been reported by Beck and Wood (1976).

Summary

Class and cultural differences in environmental cognition may reflect different cognitive styles. Alternatively, they may simply be explained by environmental experience, particularly as affected by extent of setting exposure and travel mode. Furthermore, individuals in some cultures and/or classes have had little map exposure, which appears to affect sketch map production. Thus at present it is difficult to demonstrate cultural or class differences per se in environmental cognition. Research in this area must pay closer attention to variables such as map experience, travel mode, and extent of home range.

Physical setting components

Unfortunately, insufficient attention has been given to the impact of physical components of settings on environmental cognition (Wohlwill, 1976). Furthermore, the interaction of the components of physical settings and personal variables has been neglected. Existing research has focused primarily on two variables : environmental structure and landmarks.

Environmental structure : Urban planners have stressed the importance of city structure in environmental cognition (Appleyard, 1976 ; Lynch, 1960), with particular emphasis on regular, well-defined path systems. Some empirical data support these concerns. de Jonge (1962) found that residents of cities with more regular (*i.e.*, linear, parallel, and perpendicular configuration) street grid patterns drew more complete, accurate city maps. Tzamir (Note 4) has extended this earlier work by varying the similarity of pathway distance and pathway angles of intersect in a scale model. Subjects viewed videotapes made by a camera that moved through the model, simulating a drive around the city, and were then asked to draw the model from memory. For this task they were provided lists of path and node names that had been on the model. Incorrect or absent path linkages or basic topological distortions of path configurations were scored as structural distortions. Consistent with Lynch's hypothesis, models with the least variability in path distances and angles of intersect had the fewest structural errors. One problem with de Jonge's research is that other variables such as complexity may have covaried with street grid pattern regularity in cities. Tzamir's study, however, carefully controlled for other structural parameters, systematically varying grid structure regularity only.

Zannaras (1976) also explored the effects of city structure on cognitive representations of the environment. She asked subjects to trace routes from the outskirts to the central core of three cities on either models or maps. Each city represented one of the three major urban organization patterns : concentric zone, sector zone, and mixed concentric/ sector zone. The major dependent variable was ratings of the relative importance of environmental features in way finding. Traffic features (railroad crossings, traffic lights) were most important in the concentric zone city structure, and land-use cues (institutional use, buildings) were most predominant for the other zonal organizations.

Thus both the configuration of street grid patterns and overall city zonal structure can affect cognitive mapping. Regular street grid patterns apparently facilitate environmental clarity. Furthermore, people may use different orientation cues to navigate in concentrically arranged cities than in cities with sector structure.

Landmarks

Recent empirical work verifies the importance of landmarks in cognitive mapping of the physical environment. Siegel and Schadler (1977) asked young children (5-6 years) to construct three-dimensional models of their classrooms. For half of the subjects, accurately placed landmarks had been placed in the model. This manipulation significantly enhanced the accuracy of the model construction.

Acredolo *et al.* (1975) asked children to recall where a particular event had occurred in an interior space that the child had previously walked through. They found that the addition of landmarks to the environment significantly improved the recall of 3- and 4-year-olds but not of 8-year-olds. Acredolo (1977) also examined the effect of landmarks on children's frames of reference in making orientation judgments. In this study, 3-, 4-, and 5-year-olds were tested in a room that had either no landmarks or a few landmarks. Without landmarks, 3- and 4-year-olds used place responding (object frame of reference) significantly less than did the 5-year-old. Landmarks did not affect the behavior of the 5-year-olds. Landmarks decreased egocentrism and increased place responding, however, in the younger children. Landmarks may have facilitated orientation by (a) denoting changes in bodily position in the room or (b) differentiating the targets. To investigate these possibilities, Acredolo replicated the no-landmark condition of the experiment with 3- and 4-year-olds. In addition, she reminded the children as they changed position in the room, that they were now in fact standing in a different place. This reminder significantly helped the 4-year-old children but not the 3 year olds.

Thus for younger children, at least, there is evidence that landmarks facilitate cognitive representation of the physical environment. Older children may not gain as much advantage from landmarks because they no longer depend primarily on topological relationships for self-location and orientation in space. Younger children, however, appear to rely more heavily on topological relationships (*e.g.*, relative position) and are thus helped more by accurately placed landmarks. Nevertheless, familiarity research with adults, as previously discussed, indicates the importance of landmarks in learning new settings (Evans, Marrero, and Butler, in press).

Approaching the problem of cognitive mapping from a planner's perspective, Appleyard (1969) asked the question, What attributes of buildings enhance their recall? Buildings of high use and/or important symbolic significance, buildings with high size contrast to surroundings, and buildings with sharp, singular contours and bright surfaces were recalled more frequently than others. These findings were replicated by Pezdek and Evans (1979) in a model reconstruction task for both building recall and recognition memory, provided that no semantic labels were on the model buildings. When written labels were provided (*e.g.*, *library*), there was no relationship between the physical features of the buildings and memory. Additional experiments demonstrated that the effects of semantic labeling on the relationship between building features and memory were due to the different coding strategies that were used when labels were provided. Pezdek and Evans also found that when these labels were available, relocation memory for buildings was significantly better than when no labels were provided.

Building location may also affect recall. Buildings proximate to important road inter-sections or visible from primary traffic arterials in the real world (Appleyard, 1970, 1976 ; Heft, 1979) or positioned close to a road in a scale model (Herman and Siegel, 1978) are more frequently recalled or more accurately relocated, respectively.

Other efforts have focused on what aspects of settings are remembered or used when traveling. Appleyard, Lynch, and Myer (1964) asked subjects to make rapid sketches depicting what they perceived as they traveled over designated road sectors. Subjects also recalled features along the route. Of the respondents, 20 per cent-25 per cent drew the road ahead, 10 per cent-15 per cent drew objects overhead and large objects at the edge of the road, 5 per cent-10 per cent drew distant landmarks, guide rails and other road edge details, and 2½ per cent-5 per cent drew signs, layouts, traffic and hills. Carr and Schissler (1969) extended this work by examining travelers eye movements and free recall over the same route. In comparison with Appleyard *et al.* sketch data, Carr and Schissler reported considerably less attention to the road itself. In addition, the amount of time an object was looked at was highly correlated (0.61) to item recall. Furthermore, the degree of correlation among what different subjects actually looked at was relatively high (0.41).

In another stduy subjects viewed sequential slides that depicted a drive down a novel but typical urban street in Los

Angeles (Jones, 1972). At appropriate intervals five cross streets were shown on a screen 90° to the left. At each intersection subjects had to choose whether to continue straight ahead or make a left turn and proceed down the side street that was then simulated. The subject's task was to reach and enter a freeway entrance. The correct solution of the problem entailed continued travel on the main road, that is, no branching off to the left. Thus the correct solution was unfortunately confounded with continued progress on the road and no exploratory behavior. Subjects behavior was monitored in three conditions : no cues removed from slides, high-rise buildings removed, high-rise buildings and freeway structures removed (ramps, bridges, abutments). Analyses revealed no differences for the first two conditions, but in the third condition (both cues removed) subjects made substantially more incorrect branching off decisions. Based on these findings, the author tentatively concluded that proximate cues were more important than distant high-rise buildings in making path choice decisions in a novel environment. In direct support for this claim was evident in the type of cues subjects mentioned in a free-response format, as they were "traveling" along the road. For Conditions 1 and 2, the most frequently mentioned cues included concrete freeway structures, freeway ramps, changes in road grade, and signs. Both Carr and Schissler's (1969) fixation data and Appleyard et al.'s (1964) sketch data also suggest that distant landmarks are not important in adults roadside cognition. On the other hand, Allen *et al.* (1978) found, like Jones, that proximate landmarks facilitate environmental cognition in route travel.

In conclusion, some data suggest that landmarks are most likely to facilitate environmental comprehension in preschool children. Furthermore, proximate landmarks facilitate adult learning in novel settings. The memorability of landmarks may be enhanced by certain physical features such as size, shape, and functional uniqueness.

Summary

More regularly structured settings with ordered pathways that meet at perpendicular angles are more readily comprehended. The importance of landmarks, particularly for younger children in environmental cognition, has been shown in several studies. Individuals more than 6 years of age are helped by proximate landmarks when learning a new setting. More empirical research is needed on how specific aspects of the configuration, composition, and location of elements contribute to environmental legibility. Insufficient attention has also been given to other setting variables, including boundary clarity and complexity. Finally, researchers have generally ignored the potential influence of social meaning and symbolism in environmental cognition. How we feel about a place and its historical and cultural significance may influence cognitive processing (Appleyard, 1979 ; Moore, 1979).

PRACTICAL APPLICATIONS

Architecture and planning

Lynch's (1960) concept of legibility has had a profound influence on the fields of planning and architecture. Appleyard and his colleagues, for example, planned the major new city of Ciudad Guyana, Venezuela, based on legibility principles (Appleyard, 1976), *Legibility* is "the case with which its [the city's] parts can be recognized and can be organized into a coherent pattern" (Lynch, 1960, pp. 2-3). Lynch proposed various systematic changes in physical city structure that would enhance urban form, particularly the development of regular city street patterns. As previously discussed, several studies have found that path structures with parallel streets and perpendicular intersections are more readily comprehended (de Jonge, 1962 ; Tzamir, Note 4). Lynch also hypothesized that distinct, easily visible landmarks and clearly bounded city districts would enhance legibility. Two limitations of improving urban legibility are first, the danger of making environments so routine or boring that prediction and exploration become trivial (S. Kaplan, 1973a, 1973b). Second, an overemphasis on physical aspects of settings per se may ignore the symbolic meaning of spaces to various people. Both Appleyard (1979) and Moore (1979) have noted the paucity of research on how individuals' interpretive, symbolic labeling of geographic places might affect their cognitive representations of settings.

At the urban scale, landmarks that are distinctive in size, color, or form, are functionally unique, or are frequently used are more easily remembered (Appleyard, 1970, 1976). Landmarks are also important in learning novel environments (Evans, Marrero, and Butler, in press; Heft, 1979). Landmarks in interior spaces help orientation, particularly for preschool children (Acredolo, 1977; Acredolo *et al.*, 1975). Furthermore, building designs with greater visual differentiation among various subsections and with more regular floor plans (*e.g.*, interior hallways and stairs parallel on all floors) are more easily remembered by adults (Weisman, 1979). Color coding of building interiors also enhances legibility. Individuals who learned the interior of an unfamiliar building that had been color coded performed better on actual wayfinding tasks in the building, floor plan recall and recognition tasks, and target sighting tasks using a surveyors transit than did persons who learned the building interior without the color coding (Evans, Fellows, Zorn, and Doty, in press).

Planners and other design professionals have implicitly assumed that physical settings that facilitate the formation of good cognitive maps are preferable (Appleyard, 1976; Lynch, 1960). Unfortunately, few investigators have examined the relationship between environmental legibility and preference or feelings of personal satisfaction, competence, and so forth. A notable exception is research by S. Kaplan (1973a, 1975). He found that setting features that enhance map formation also increase preference. Two key concepts are *coherence* and *moderate uncertainty.* Structural features that provide coherence include continuous texture gradients, thematic color or graphic patterns, and variable but identifiable physical forms; moderate uncertainty is provided by variety, moderate complexity, moderate spaciousness, and occasional structural irregularities.

Education

Two researchers have developed preliminary educational programs to enhance children's cognitive-mapping abilities. Pick (Note 1) found that preschoolers who received a short, map-training curriculum performed slightly better than controls in an unrelated task in which they had to locate where a particular event had occurred in interior hallways near their classroom (Acredolo *et al.*, 1975) and made fewer errors in locating objects on maps. Training consisted of asking children to indicate where and in what order various objects were located on models or photographic and map representations of the models. R. Kaplan, and colleagues (Devlin, 1973 ; R. Kaplan, 1976) used picture maps, contour maps, and aerial photography, integrated with game formats, to prepare junior high school students for subsequent exploration of a novel, natural area. Games included finding a hidden location through a series of questions with a partner, determining which paths were absent from one's own map by verbal exchange with a game partner who had complementary missing paths, and general probes about the location of specific elements and features of the setting. In general, children playing these games exhibited more confidence exploring actual settings and found the experience more positive and less frightening than did controls. Finally, computer-assisted map displays may provide important techniques for enhancing geographic knowledge. Collins, Adams, and Pew (1978) developed an interactive, computer map display technique that significantly increased high school students' knowledge of world geography.

Cartographers have also become interested in the implications of environmental cognition research for map design (Robinson & Petchenik, 1976). Bronzaft, Dobrow, and O'Hanlon (1976), for example, examined the effectiveness of New York City subway maps by assigning recent city residents actual trip segments of varying difficulty on the subways. Almost all subjects felt insecure traveling and made numerous navigational errors including choosing a nonoperative train, transferring at incorrect stations, and confusing similarly named subway stops. The data strongly indicated that present subway maps and other graphic aids are inadequate. Thorndyke and Stasz (1980) have recently investigated the strategies people use to acquire knowledge from maps. Significant individual difference in map-reading performance and geographic knowledge revealed that better map readers use more active learning strategies. Good map readers more accurately determine what information they already know, focusing attention on unlearned information.

With the exception of a few studies (R. Kaplan, 1976; Kozlowski and Bryant, 1977; Thorndyke and Stasz, 1980), cognitive mapping has been treated exclusively as a dependent variable. Researchers need to examine cognitive mapping abilities as an independent variable. Does greater knowledge of a place make a difference in self-esteem, competence, or the likelihood that one will explore a setting? Furthermore, are people with orientation problems adversely affected by their deficiency? Both the visually handicapped and recently de-institutionalized groups such as psychiatric patients may have reduced self-confidence and may avoid exploring their environs because of fear of getting lost. Mobility training for the blind, for example, explicitly trains mapping techniques to enhance both self-confidence and orientation skills (U.S. Department of the Interior, Note 6).

CONCLUSIONS

Human beings know a considerable amount about the content and location of information in real-world settings they experience. Yet we know little about how this information is processed. Environmental psychologists studying this question have relied primarily on questionable methodologies such as hand drawings and small-scale models. In addition, theoretical development has been minimal, with largely descriptive taxonomies of the geographic features contained in cognitive maps. Cognitive psychologists, on the other hand, have ignored the study of real-world spatial memory. They have developed more rigorous methodologies and sophisticated models of cognitive representation but used simplistic, out-of-context stimuli. Very recently these two approaches have begun to merge with more rigorous studies of how information in actual geographic settings is processed. More thorough psychometric examination of predominant cognitive-mapping methodologies is critical. High-priority issues include comparisons among different accuracy rating scales, analysis of model and drawing procedures, with particular attention given to comparisons among processing in actual settings and in modeled or photographic simulations of the same settings. We also need to more carefully consider procedural issues that may influence data production. Recent applications of chronometric paradigms, scaling algorithms, and quantifiable orientation tasks in situ are preliminary steps in the right direction.

Many conceptual questions remain unresolved. First, we cannot determine at this time whether cognitive representations of realistic, large-scale settings consist primarily of propositional, analogical, or some combination of information. Cognitive maps seem to function as schemata on at least two levels. Generically we approach settings with general, prototypic expectations about the location and relative spatial positioning of certain parts of settings. We assume, for example, that streets are parallel and intersect at right angles. We also selectively represent particular, familiar settings. Our general knowledge of even highly familiar settings is incomplete and uneven. Once we form an initial, highly schematic model of a place, subsequent geographic knowledge is largely assimilated within the framework of that initial structure. On the other hand, comparative judgments about relative distance or spatial interposition of well-known loci may operate in a manner largely analogous to how that information is actually configured in real space.

Developmental research on environmental cognition provides some support for Piaget's analysis of an orderly stage acquisition of knowledge about topological, projective, and Euclidean spatial properties. Frame of reference data show that young children use egocentric cues to orient in space, followed by reliance on relative position to one and then to multiple fixed points in space. Finally, comprehension of space as a coordinate system emerges. Spatial representation research suggests the following related sequence : Initial learning is strongly tied to direct motoric experience ; knowledge of the relative location of objects within small, proximate clusters follows but without good intercluster accuracy. Next, children can comprehend both intra- and intercluster spatial relationships, and then they acquire knowledge of the exact location of objects in space. There is insufficient data on the elderly to draw conclusions about their environmental cognition abilities. Two important limitations of these conclusions are (a) are these stages actually qualitatively distinct, or do they simply reflect quantitative refinements in precision, and (b) to what extent do the developmental differences reflect procedural artifacts ? Comprehension of instructions, and reliance on drawings or small-scale models may obscure developmental differences in environmental cognition. These procedural cautions apply especially to the spatial representation studies. Several actual way-finding studies replicate the developmental frames of reference sequence posited by Piaget. More research is needed on the effects of procedural variables in developmental studies of cognitive mapping.

Amount of experience in a setting is an important variable in environmental cognition research. Many of the gender and cross-cultural differences found in environmental cognition research can be more parsimoniously explained by the extent of actual setting exploration permitted to various subgroups of populations. Although it is clear that we gain knowledge of a place with continued exposure, we cannot precisely describe these increments in knowledge. Conflicting data suggest two hypotheses on the physical cues people use to learn to orient in a new setting. Some studies suggest initial reliance on landmarks as orientation aids with subsequent path learning embedded within the initial landmark network. Other researchers have found the opposite sequence. At least two logical possibilities for resolving the contradictory data are apparent. First, the type of orientation cues used to learn a setting may depend on the physical configuration of the physical environment itself. Certain physical cues in a setting may direct our spatial learning strategies by the opportunities they provide. For example, visually distinctive buildings placed near major path intersections may lend themselves to a landmark-dominant learning strategy. A second logical possibility for resolving the competing learning hypotheses is that perhaps some people are landmark dependent in their learning strategies, whereas others are path dependent. Previously successful orientation experiences in unfamiliar settings could selectively reinforce an individualized orientation strategy for learning to orient in new settings.

Several researchers have concluded that systematic changes in accuracy occur with increasing environmental familiarity. More changes occur in Euclidean accuracy over time than in the accuracy of relative object location. Although these accuracy trends in environmental learning seem stable, these Piagetian-like distinctions may reflect quantitative, scalar differences in spatial accuracy. Better exact location accuracy of objects in space with increasing familiarity may be due to greater restrictions on the possible locations of items in space with more knowledge of alternative path linkages in a given set of points in space.

A final familiarity issue worthy of further investigation is the issue of how familiarity is operationalized. We need to examine more carefully the relationships between actual setting contact and the acquisition of knowledge. It is the actual amount and kind of setting exploration that really matters and not simply how long we have lived in a place.

We know little about how physical variables affect environmental cognition. Landmarks appear to be important in learning new environments and as aids for young children's orientation in large-scale spaces. There is some evidence that more regularly structured path networks (90° intersects) are more easily comprehended. Several issues remain unexplored. How does the symbolic meaning of places affect our knowledge of them, and does historical or cultural significance affect our knowledge of a setting ? Although it is intuitively reasonable to suspect that emotion affects cognition, with few exceptions psychologists have largely compartmentalized thinking and feeling into separate topics of inquiry. What is the relationship between legibility and preference ? If a setting is too simple, too easily comprehended, it may be boring, if too complex, confusing. Further, how do other physical elements like boundaries and districts affect knowledge of real-world settings ?

As psychologists, our focus has largely been on information processing within the head, forgetting that variables related to the physical structure of stimuli affect cognitive processing. The study of environmental cognition is a relatively new area of psychology that provides potentially important conceptual links among environmental psychology, cognitive psychology, urban planning, and geography. Research on environmental cognition should provide further impetus for the study of information processing under more realistic, ecologically valid conditions.

FOOTNOTES

*This article does not discuss research on environmental assessment or preference that has been called environmental perception (Gould and White, 1974 ; Lowenthal, 1967).

1. Pick, H.L., *Mapping children-mapping space*. Paper presented at the meeting of the American Psychological Association, Honolulu, Hawaii, September 1972.
2. Pick, H.L., Acredolo, L., and Gronseth, M., *Children's knowledge of the spatial layout of their homes*. Paper presented at the meeting of the Society for Research in Child Development, Philadelphia, Pa., March 1973.
3. Ohta, R., Walsh, D., and Krauss, I., *Spatial perspective-taking ability in young and elderly adults*. Paper presented at the American Psychological Association, San Francisco, September 1977.
4. Tzamir, Y., *The impact of spatial regularity and irregularity on cognitive mapping* (Tech. Rep.) Haifa, Israel : Technion-Israel Institute of Technology, Center for Urban and Regional Studies, December 1975.
5. Saarinan, T., *Perception of environment* (Commission on College Geography, Resource Paper No. 5). Washington, D.C. : Association of American Geographers, 1969.
6. U.S. Department of the Interior. *Experimental maps of D.C. area for visually handicapped*. News release, Washington, D.C., January 26, 1979.

REFERENCES

Acredolo, L.P., Frames of reference used by children for orientation in unfamiliar spaces. In G. Moore and R. Golledge (Eds.), *Environmental knowing*. Stroudsburg, Pa. : Dowden, Hutchinson and Ross, 1976.

Acredolo, L.P., Developmental changes, in the ability to coordinate perspective of a large-scale environment. *Developmental Psychology*, 1977, 13, 1-8.

Acredolo, L.P., Pick, H.L., and Olsen, M., Environmental differentiation and familiarity as determinants of children's memory for spatial location. *Developmental Psychology*, 1975, 11, 495-501.

Allen, G., Siegel, A., and Rosinski, R., The role of perceptual context in structuring spatial knowledge. *Journal of Experimental Psychology : Human Learning and Memory*, 1978, 4, 617-630.

Anderson, J.R., and Bower, G.F., *Human associative memory*. New York : V.H. Winston, 1973.

Andrews, H.F., Home range and urban knowledge of school-age children. *Environment and Behavior*, 1973, 5, 73-86.

Anooshian, L.J., and Wilson, K.L., Distance distortion in memory for spatial locations. *Child Development*, 1977, 48, 1704-1707.

Appleyard, D.A., Why buildings are known. *Environment and Behavior*, 1969, 1, 131-156.

Appleyard, D.A., Styles and methods of structuring a city. *Environment and Behavior*, 1970, 2, 100-116.

Appleyard, D., *Planning a pluralistic city*. Cambridge, Mass. : MIT Press, 1976.

Appleyard, D., The environment as a social symbol. *Journal of the American Planning Association*, 1979, 45, 143-153.

Appleyard, D., Lynch, K., and Myer, J.R., *The view from the road*. Cambridge, Mass. : MIT Press, 1964.

Baird, J., Studies of the cognitive representation of spatial relations. *Journal of Experimental Psychology : General*, 1979, 108, 90-106.

Banerji, T.K., Urban experience and the development of city image : A study in environmental perception and learning (Doctoral dissertation, Massachusetts Institute of Technology, 1971), *Dissertation Abstracts International*, 1971, 32, 335.

Beck, R.J., and Wood, D., Cognitive transformation of information from urban geographic fields to mental maps. *Environment and Behavior*, 1976, 8, 199-238.

Blaut, J.M., McCleary, G., and Blaut, A., Environmental mapping in young children. *Environment and Behavior*, 1970, 2, 335-349.

Blaut, J.M., and Stea, D., Mapping at the age of three. *Journal of Geography*, 1974, 73, 5-9.

Borke, H., Piaget's mountains revisited : Changes in the egocentric landscape. *Developmental Psychology*, 1975, 11, 240-243.

Bronzaft, A., Dobrow, S., and O'Hanion, T., Spatial orientation in a subway system. *Environment and Behavior*, 1976, 8, 575-594.

Byrne, R., Memory for urban geography. *Quarterly Journal of Experimental Psychology*, 1979, 31, 147-154.

Carr, S., and Schissler, D., The city as a trip : Perceptual selection and memory in the view from the road. *Environment and Behavior*, 1969, 1, 7-36.

Coie, J.D., Costanzo, P.R., and Farnill, D., Specific transitions in the development of spatial perspective-taking ability. *Developmental Psychology*, 1973, 9, 167-177.

Collins, A., Adams, M.J., and Pew, R.W., Effectiveness of an interactive map display in tutoring geography. *Journal of Educational Psychology*, 1978, 70, 1-7.

Dart, F.E., and Pradham, P.L., The cross-cultural teaching of science. *Science*, 1967, 155, 649-656.

Day, J.D., *Veridical and inferential memory for the spatial layout of a small house*. Unpublished master's thesis, University of Illinois at Urban-Champaign, 1977.

de Jonge, D., Images of urban areas : Their structure and psychological foundations. *Journal of the American Institute of Planners*, 1962, 28, 266-276.

De Lisi, R., Locker, R., and Youniss, J., Anticipatory imagery and spatial operations. *Developmental Psychology*, 1976, 12, 298-310.

Devlin, A.S., Some factors in enhancing knowledge of a natural area. In W. Preiser (Ed.), *Environmental design research* (Vol. 2), Stroudsburg, Pa. : Dowden, Hutchinson and Ross, 1973.

Devlin, A.S., The small town cognitive map : Adjusting to a new environment. In G.T. Moore and R.G. Golledge (Eds.), *Environmental knowing*. Stroudsburg, Pa. : Dowden, Hutchinson and Ross, 1976.

Dirks, J., and Neisser, U., Memory for objects in real scenes : The development of recognition and recall. *Journal of Experimental Child Psychology*, 1977, 23, 315-328.

Downs, R., and Stea, D., *Image and environment*. Chicago : Aldine, 1973.

Evans, G.W., Fellows, J., Zorn, M., and Doty, K., Cognitive mapping and architecture. *Journal of Applied Psychology*, in Press.

Evans, G.W., Marrero, D., and Butler, P., Environmental learning and cognitive mapping. *Environment and Behavior*, in Press.

Evans, G.W., and Pezdek, K., Cognitive mapping : Knowledge of real-world distance and location information. *Journal of Experimental Psychology : Human Learning and Memory*, 1980, 6, 13-24.

Fishbein, H.D., Lewis, S., and Keiffer, K., Children's understanding of spatial relations. *Developmental Psychology*, 1972, 7, 21-33.

Flavell, J., Botkin, P., Fry, C., Wright, J., and Jarvis, P., *The development of role-taking and communication skills in children*. New York : Wiley, 1968.

Francescato, D., and Mebane, W., How citizens view two great cities : Milan and Rome. In R. Downs and D. Stea (Eds.), *Image and environment*. Chicago : Aldine, 1973.

Golledge, R.G., Methods and methodological issues in environmental cognition research. In G. Moore and R. Golledge (Eds.), *Environmental knowing*. Stroudsburg, Pa. : Dowden, Hutchinson and Ross, 1976.

Golledge, R.G., Multidimensional analysis in the study of environmental behaviour and environmental design. In I. Altman and J. Wohlwill (Eds.), *Human behavior and environment* (Vol. 2). New York : Plenum Press, 1977.

Golledge, R.G., Rivizzigno, V.L., and Spector, A., Learning about a city : Analysis by multidimensional scaling. In R.G. Golledge and G. Rushton (Eds).), *Spatial choice and spatial behavior*. Columbus : Ohio State Press, 1976.

Goodnow, J., *Children drawing*. Cambridge, Mass. : Harvard University Press, 1977.

Gould, P., and White, H., *Mental maps*. Baltimore, Md. : Penguin, 1974.

Gulick, J., Images of an Arab city. *Journal of the American Institute of Planners*, 1963, 29, 179-197.

Hardwick, D.A., McIntyre, C.W., and Pick, H.L., The content and manipulation of cognitive maps in children and adults. *Monographs of the Society for Research in Child Development*, 1976, 41 (3, Serial No. 166).

Hart, R., *Children's experience of place*. New York : Irvington, 1979.

Hart, R.A., and Moore, G.T., The development of spatial cognition : A review. In R. Downs and D. Stea (Eds.), *Image and environment*. Chicago : Aldine, 1973.

Hazen, N., Lockman, J., and Pick, H., The development of children's representations of large-scale environment. *Child Development*, 1978, 49, 623-636.

Heft, H., The role of environmental features in routelearning : Two exploratory studies of way-finding. *Environmental Psychology and Nonverbal Behavior*, 1979, 3, 172-185.

Herman, J., and Siegel, A., The development of spatial representations of large-scale environments. *Journal of Experimental Child Psychology*, 1978, 26, 389-406.

Holahan, C., *Environment and behavior*. New York : Plenum Press, 1978.

Horton, F., and Reynolds, D., Effects of urban spatial structure on individual behavior. *Economic Geography*, 1971, 47, 36-48.

Howard, I.P., and Templeton, W.B., *Human spatial orientation*. New York : Wiley, 1966.

Howard, R.B., Chase, S.D., and Rothman, M., An analysis of four measures of cognitive maps. In W. Preiser (Ed.), *Environmental design research* (Vol. 1). Stroudsburg, Pa. : Dowden, Hutchinson and Ross, 1973.

Huttenlocher, J., and Presson, C., Mental rotation and the perspective problem. *Cognitive Psychology*, 1973, 4, 277-299.

Ittelson, W., Environmental perception and contemporary perceptual theory. In W. Ittelson (Ed.), *Environment and cognition*. New York : Seminar, 1973.

Jones, M.M., Urban path-choosing behavior : A study of environmental cues. In W. Mitchell (Ed.), *Environmental design : Research and practice*. Los Angeles : University of California Press, 1972.

Kaplan, R., Way-finding in the natural environment. In G.T. Moore and R.G. Golledge (Eds.), *Environmental knowing*. Stroudsburg, Pa. : Dowden, Hutchinson and Ross, 1976.

Kaplan, S., Cognitive maps, human needs, and the designed environment. In W. Preiser (Ed.), *Environmental design research* (Vol. 1). Stroudsburg, Pa. : Dowden, Hutchinson and Ross, 1973. (a)

Kaplan, S., Cognitive maps in perception and thought. In R. Downs and D. Stea (Eds.), *Image and environment*. Chicago : Aldine, 1973. (b)

Kaplan, S., An informal model for the prediction of preference. In E.H. Zube, R. Brush, and J. Fabos (Eds.), *Landscape assessment : Values, perceptions and resources*. Stroudsburg, Pa. : Dowden, Hutchinson and Ross, 1975.

Kaplan, S., Adaptation, structure, and knowledge. In G. Moore and R. Golledge (Eds.), *Environmental knowing*. Stroudsburg, Pa. : Dowden, Hutchinson and Ross, 1976.

Kosslyn, S.M., Information representation in visual images. *Cognitive Psychology*, 1975, 7, 341-370.

Kosslyn, S.M., Ball, T.M., and Reiser, B.J., Visual images preserve metric spatial information : Evidence from studies of image scanning. *Journal of Experimental Psychology : Human Perception and Performance*, 1978, 4, 47-60.

Kosslyn, S.M., Heldmeyer, K.H., and Locklear, E.P., Children's drawings as data about internal representations. *Journal of Experimental Child Psychology*, 1977, 23, 191-211.

Kosslyn, S.M., Pick, H., and Fariello, G., Cognitive maps in children and men. *Child Development*, 1974, 45, 707-716.

Kosslyn, S.M., and Pomerantz, J.P., Imagery, propositions, and the form of internal representations. *Cognitive Psychology*, 1977, 9, 52-76.

Kozlowski, L.T., and Bryant, K.J., Sense of direction, spatial orientation and cognitive maps. *Journal of Experimental Psychology : Human Perception and Performance*, 1977, 3, 590-598.

Ladd, F., Black youths view their environment : Neighborhood maps. *Environment and Behavior*, 1970, 2, 74-99.

Laurendeau, M., and Pinard, A., *The development of the concept of space in the child*. New York : International Universities Press, 1970.

Lea, G., Chronometric analysis of the method of loci. *Journal of Experimental Psychology : Human Perception and Performance*, 1975, 1, 95-104.

Looft, W., and Charles, D., Egocentrism and social interaction in young and old adults. *Aging and Human Development*, 1971, 2, 21-28.

Lowenthal, D. (Ed.), *Environmental perception and behavior*. Chicago : University of Chicago Press, 1967.

Lynch, K., *The image of the city*. Cambridge, Mass. : MIT Press, 1960.

Lynch, K. (Ed.), *Growing up in cities*. Cambridge, Mass. : MIT Press, 1977.

Maccoby, E., and Jacklin, C., *The psychology of sex differences*. Stanford : Stanford University Press, 1974.

MacKay, D.B., The effect of spatial stimuli on the estimation of cognitive maps. *Geographical Analysis*, 1976, 8, 439-452.

Magana, J.R., An empirical and interdisciplinary test of a theory of urban perception (Doctoral dissertation, University of California, Irvine, 1978). *Dissertation Abstracts International*, 1978, 39, 1460B (University Microfilms No. 78-15, 840).

Magana, J.R., Evans, G.W., and Romney, A.K., Scaling techniques in the analysis of environmental cognition data. *Professional Geographer*, in press.

Mandler, J.M., and Parker, R.E., Memory for descriptive and spatial information in complex pictures. *Journal of Experimental Psychology : Human Learning and Memory*, 1976, 2, 38-48.

Masangkay, Z. et al., The early development of inferences about the visual percepts of others. *Child Development*, 1974, 45, 357-366.

Maurer, R., and Baxter, J.C., Images of the neighborhood and city among black, anglo, and Mexican-American children. *Environment and Behavior*, 1972, 4, 351-388.

Milgram, S., Greenwald, J., Kessler, S., McKenna, W., and Waters, J., A psychological map of New York City. *American Scientist*, 1972, 60, 194-200.

Milgram, S., and Jodelet, D., Psychological maps of Paris, In H. Proshansky, W. Ittelson, and L. Rivlin (Eds.), *Environmental psychology*, (2nd ed.). New York : Holt, Rinehart and Winston, 1976.

Moore, G.T., Developmental differences in environmental cognition. In W. Preiser (Ed.), *Environmental design research*. Stroudsburg, Pa. : Dowden, Hutchinson and Ross, 1973.

Moore, G.T., The development of environmental knowing : An overview of an interactional-constructivist theory and some data on within-individual development variations. In D. Canter and T. Lee (Eds.), *Psychology and the built environment*. New York : Halstead Press, 1974.

Moore, G.T., Knowing about environmental knowing : The current state of theory and research on environmental cognition. *Environment and Behavior*, 1979, 11, 33-70.

Moore, G.T., and Golledge, R.G. (Eds.), *Environmental knowing*. Stroudsburg, Pa. : Dowden, Hutchinson and Ross, 1976.

Neisser, U., *Cognition and reality*. San Francisco : Freeman, 1976.

Nigl, A.J., and Fishbein, H.D., Perception and conception in coordination of perspectives. *Developmental Psychology*, 1974, 10, 858-866.

Norman, D., and Rumelhart, D., *Explorations in cognition*, San Francisco : Freeman, 1975.

Orleans, P., Differential cognition of urban residents : Effects of social scale on mapping. In R. Downs and D. Stea (Eds.), *Image and environment*. Chicago : Aldine, 1973.

Orleans, P., and Schmidt, S., Mapping the city : Environmental cognition of urban residents. In W. Mitchell (Ed.), *Environmental design : Research and practice*. Los Angeles : University of California Press, 1972.

Pezdek, K., and Evans, G.W., Visual and verbal memory for objects and their spatial location. *Journal of Experimental Psychology . Human Learning and Memory*, 1979, 5, 360-373.

Piaget, J., and Inhelder, B., *The child's conception of space*. New York : Norton, 1967.

Piaget, J., Inhelder, B., and Szeminska, A., *The child's conception of geometry.* New York : Basic Books, 1960.

Pufall, P., and Shaw, R., Analysis of the development of children's spatial reference systems. *Cognitive Psychology*, 1973, 5, 151-175.

Pylyshyn, Z.W., What the mind's eye tells the mind's brain : A critique of mental imagery. *Psychological Bulletin*, 1973, 80, 1-24.

Robinson, A.H., and Petchenik, B.B., *The nature of maps.* Chicago : University of Chicago Press, 1976.

Rothwell, D., Cognitive mapping of the home environment (Doctoral dissertation, University of British Columbia, Canada, 1974). *Dissertation Abstracts International*, 1976, 36, 4758A (Available on microfiche from the National Library of Canada, Ottawa, Ontario).

Rubin, K., Attewell, P., Tierney, M., and Tumolo, P., Development of spatial egocentrism and conservation across the life span. *Developmental Psychology*, 1973, 9, 432.

Schultz, N., and Hoyer, W., Feedback effects on spatial egocentrism in old age. *Journal of Gerontology*, 1976, 31, 72-75.

Shemyakin, F.N., General problems of orientation in space and space representations. In B.G. Ananyev (Ed.), *Psychological science in the USSR* (Vol. 1 ; Tech. Rep. No. 11466). U.S. Office of Technical Reports, Arlington, Va. : 1962 (NTIS No. TT 62-11083).

Shepard, R.N., Form, formation and transformation of internal representation. In R.L. Solso (Ed.), *Information processing and cognition : The Loyola Symposium.* Hillsdale, N.J. : Erlbaum, 1975.

Siegel, A.W., Herman, J., Allen, G., and Kirasic, K., The development of cognitive maps of large and small scale spaces. *Child Development*, 1979, 50, 582-585.

Siegel, A.W., and Schadler, M., Young children's cognitive maps of their classroom. *Child Development*, 1977, 48, 388-394.

Siegel, A.W., and White, S.H., The development of spatial representations of large-scale environments. In H.W. Reese (Ed.), *Advances in child development and behavior* (Vol. 10). New York : Academic Press, 1975.

Stea, D., Environmental perception and cognition : Toward a model for mental maps. In G. Coates and K. Moffett (Eds.), *Response to environment.* Raleigh : North Carolina State University Press, 1969.

Stea, D., and Taphanel, S., Theory and experiment on the relation between environmental modeling (toy play) and environmental cognition. In D. Canter and T. Lee (Eds.), *Psychology and the built environment.* New York : Halstead Press, 1974.

Stevens, A., and Coupe, P., Distortions in judged spatial relations. *Cognitive Psychology*, 1978, 10, 422-437.

Thorndyke, P., and Stasz, C., Individual differences in procedures for knowledge acquisition from maps. *Cognitive Psychology*, 1980, 12, 137-175.

Tolman, E.C., Cognitive maps in rats and men. *Psychological Review*, 1948, 55, 189-208.

Trowbridge, C.C., On fundamental methods of orientation and imagery maps. *Science*, 1913, 38, 888-897.

Walsh, D., Krauss, I., and Regnier, V., Spatial ability, environmental knowledge, and environmental use : The elderly. In L. Liben, A. Patterson, and N. Newcombe (Eds.), *Spatial representation and behavior across the life span*. New York : Academic Press, in press.

Weber, R., Brown, L., and Weldon, J., Cognitive maps of environmental knowledge and preference in nursing home patients. *Experimental Aging Research*, 1978, 4, 157-174.

Weisman, J., Way-finding in the built environment : A study in architectural legibility (Doctoral dissertation, University of Michigan, 1979). *Dissertation Abstracts International*, 1979, 40, 505A (University Microfilms No. 79-16,843).

Wilton, R., Knowledge of spatial relations : The specification of the information used in making inferences. *Quarterly Journal of Experimental Psychology*, 1979, 31, 133-146.

Wohlwill, J.F., Searching for the environment in environmental cognition research : A commentary on research strategy. In G.T. Moore and R.G. Golledge (Eds.), *Environmental knowing*. Stroudsburg, Pa. : Dowden, Hutchinson and Ross, 1976.

Zannaras, G., The relation between cognitive structure and urban form. In. GT. Moore and R.G. Golledge (Eds.), *Environmental knowing*. Stroudsburg, Pa. : Dowden, Hutchinson aud Ross, 1976.

FIVE

REGINALD G. GOLLEDGE, G. DONALD RICHARDSON, AND
NATHAN GALE

COGNITIVE IMAGES OF THE CITY

MUCH has been written over the last two decades about people's images of cities. Apart from references to the development of some key concepts, definitions, and methodologies, we will not survey this literature. Conducting such a review would inevitably involve us in further argument concerning the quality and appropriateness of the literature and we believe these arguments have been adequately summarized elsewhere (Golledge, 1981). Instead we first offer a brief introduction on early research on the images of cities, then in an urban context we develop a theory of spatial cognition. Thereafter we summarize the current state of the art in terms of recovering and representing city images. This latter task is achieved by constructing cognitive mappings of a sample city from a variety of subject populations. Errors in the matching of subjective and objectvie configurations are examined by referring to notions of distortion and fuzziness in the maps so produced. In the summary, we focus on new directions for research in this area and the types of problems that face the practitioner interested in obtaining and using cognitive images of the city.

INTRODUCTION

The process of cognitive mapping has been defined by Downs and Stea (1973, p. 9) as " . . . a process composed of a series of psychological transformations by which an individual acquires, codes, stores, recalls, and decodes information about the relative locations and attributes of phenomena in his everyday spatial environment." In other words, cognitive mapping is a means of structuring, making sense of, and coping with, the complexities of the environment. Thus, the subjective definition of places, paths and areas is an individual categorization of spatial variation resulting from cognitive taxonomic processes. The result is the construction of a cognitive map. Cognitive maps are internal representations of segments of the environment resulting from the sensory transformation of information emitted by elements of that external environment. A cognitive map, therefore, is an individual's model of the world.

At this stage, the reader should be aware that the "map" portion of the term cognitive map is used more as a metaphor than as a strict analogy (Downs, 1981). It should not be inferred that people carry information in their mind in terms of little maps of the environment, or even that they store information in terms of locational coordinates, Cartesian co-ordinate systems, or any other pseudo-cartographic representational form. The question of whether cognitive information is represented and stored as holistic images, propositional strings, analogs, or other storage media is currently a topic of hotly contested debate (*e.g.*, Anderson, 1978 ; Hayes-Roth, 1979).

City images can be recovered and represented in a variety of ways. Perhaps the seminal work in this area is that by Lynch (1960) who proposed a five element classification system for examining cognitive maps. Regardless of how information about the environment is stored in the mind, Lynch pointed out that, via a series of parallel experimental procedures, one can obtain an external representation of stored knowledge about a place (such as a city). By examining several representative modes such as sketch mappings, verbal descriptions, and information lists, he inferred that there were five elements that could be considered fundamental components of cognitive imagery and which, if recovered with a suitable level of rigor, could be used to construct a map summary of that stored knowledge. The five elements were defined as paths, edges, districts, nodes, and landmarks. The paths were basically channels along which an observer would customarily, occasionally, or potentially move as he conducted a set of spatial activities in the urban area. Edges were conceived more as barriers that could be either permeable or impenetrable, and which tend to mark off or differentiate one segment of space from another. Districts were the areas delineated by the edges, and were seen as having some common identifying characteristics. Nodes were strategic spots acting as intensive foci that anchored the behavioral patterns of each individual. Landmarks were easily identified elements of the physical landscape and could be drawn from the entire range of urban functions or structures.

Following Lynch's innovative work, planners such as Appleyard (1970), de Jonge (1962), and Gulick (1963) conducted research in Venezuela, the Netherlands, and Lebanon (respectively), identifying reasons why certain nodes or landmarks may be expected to be incorporated into cognitive images, defining more clearly the point, line and areal component of the basic Lynch structure, and investigating the connective and relational properties of these fundamental components. Other work by Lee (1965), Carr and Schissler (1969), Downs (1970), Golledge, Briggs and Demko (1969), Ladd (1970), Golledge and Zannaras (1973), and Orlean (1973) all further investigated possible components of city images and helped develop the belief that cognitive mapping could be viewed as an essential component of human adaptation and use of particular environments. The argument was made that the success of everyday behaviors (such as journey to work, trips to a grocery store, giving directions to a lost stranger, or undertaking any of the complex interactions that are part of the periodic activities that an individual undertakes with their external environment), are all at least in part dependent on the cognitive transformation of that environment and the type and quality of stored information that can be accessed once a given task situation is faced. These various researchers clearly indicated that, as the completeness and accuracy of this stored information varied, so too did individual behaviors depart from what one might objectively consider to be optimal—in the spatial, economic, social, psychological, political, or other sense. Thus it was argued that in order to understand relations between man and environment one needed to discover the information base on which activities are overlain. It has been on this conceptual and empirical base that the surge of interdisciplinary literature on cognitive images and cognitive mappings has been rapidly building for the last two decades.

Given that such a background exists, we now present a conceptualization of the process of environmental cognition from a particular perspective—the anchor point theory of spatial cognition (Golledge, 1976).

Developing cognitive images of a city

The conceptualization we put forward here is based on the idea that learning about an external environment results primarily from interacting with it and that more complex cognitive representations of those environments are built up over time.

The anchor point theory of the environmental learning process (Golledge, 1978 (b)) relies on the notion that individuals develop a hierarchical ordering of places, paths and areas in the spatial environment (called "environmental cues"). The position of a cue within this hierarchy is based on its significance to the individual. The theory is further based on an interactional component that argues that individuals first learn where key nodes are in the environment, than develop a variety of ways to get to, from and between these places. In other words, environmental information is anchored by the initial establishment of primary nodes (including places such as home, work, or critical landmarks) and that as experience with the environment continues, a path structure emerges so as to link these nodes. As ways are explored for linking primary nodes, other places and other route segments become known. As more places become known and their interactive value to the individual becomes formalized, there is a spread effect or spillover in the vicinity of some of those places that results in the development of knowledge about areas. This knowledge about places and their perceived significance can accrue from continued interaction (as with a place of work or residence) or because of social, historical, economic, ethnic, aesthetic or other criteria of importance. Consequently, any individual's cognitive image of say, a city, should consist of points, lines and areas which are connected to a greater or lesser extent, depending on experience with the environment. Obtaining information about which environmental elements are tapped for the points, lines and areas, enables us to construct a cartographic representation of the information contained in long term memory storage. Obviously, as people accumulate more information about the environment, their maps become more complex. To show how this occurs, let us follow the case of a neophyte first entering a new urban environment.

We assume that we have an individual who is completely new to a given urban environment. We shall further assume that this individual is an adult, capable of logical reasoning, and has an understanding of concepts such as location, proximity or closeness, distance apart, and other general spatial relationships. We shall also assume at this point that the individual has a specific employment opportunity available to him in the city. The question is a simple one : How would such an individual learn to use, and to survive in, this new urban environment ?

The most immediate needs faced by our urban immigrant would be those relating to shelter, food and employment. With no home base prepared for him/her, our urban immigrant must take up a temporary residence or begin an immediate active search for a place to live. Depending on the length and nature of this search, he or she may also have to undertake a simultaneous exploration for places at which the need for food could be satisfied. Since a job opportunity is available, there is also the urgent need to locate the given place of employment and to develop a means of accessing it. Let us assume, therefore, that a place of residence has been found and that the individual has acquired knowledge, either through a space search process or through external information sources, concerning the exact location of the work place.

Under these conditions, the home and work place immediately established themselves as identifiable and important places in the individual's emerging process of understanding the city. Paths that connect these primary nodes become key elements in developing an understanding of the urban environment (Golledge and Zannaras, 1973). Simultaneously our urban immigrant develops an understanding of the location of various food sources and an awareness of the paths that he/she may have to follow in order to access them. While home and work place become fixed relatively quickly as primary nodes, it may take a somewhat longer period of time for other primary nodes to develop. For example, shopping may involve a trial and error process itself with continued experimentation associated with adding and deleting possible sources of food supply as assessments of their relative worth are made. Obviously some less rewarding centers may be visited and may consequently be eliminated from a feasible set of shopping alternatives.

While a search for other critical anchor points (or primary nodes) is being undertaken, information is also accumulating about secondary and lower order nodes. Associated with the home and the work place and the paths connecting them, one would expect to find a set of secondary nodes which may include the locations of friends or neighbors, urban functions that are visited only on an infrequent basis (*e.g.*, parks and recreation areas, certain types of shopping facilities, professional services, government activities, financial and business functions), and so on. Also simultaneously there is a spillover effect or spread effect in the areas surrounding the primary nodes and the emergence of the first concepts of neighborhood. The search patterns for high order retail, recreational and other socio-economic cultural, and political requirements of the individual, also produce local areal knowledge. The coalescing of neighborhoods in an area provides the basis for the identification of a community, and the coalescence of these communities define for an individual the concept of a "region" within the total city structure. Over time, as more paths and more places become more familiar to the individual, they too are consolidated into the skeletal structure of knowledge, and information about them may be generalized such that they also have local areal effects.

Carr and Schissler (1970) have shown that regular travelers over a given route tend to recognize and remember more details along the route (and details off to the side of it) than do intermittent or new users of the route. This suggests that as places become well known, their environs become better known also. The extent of knowing apparently is related to the level of interaction, which allows us to hypothesize that a subject's cognitive representation of an urban environment will be a constantly evolving one with the most significant places acting as primary nodes and anchoring the representation at specific points. At different time periods, different elements of the environment will have different meanings, interaction potentials, and consequent levels of significance as far as individual subjects are concerned. As the significance of a place, a route, or an area changes, then it will proceed up or down (or stay at the same level) in the hierarchy of informational components. The result should be an incomplete schematized and perhaps augmented representation of selected segments of the urban environment placed in long term memory storage which, through the recall process, can be accessed and used at a moment's notice for a particular task situation.

The information stored in the mind may consist of analogs, holograms, propositional links and sequences, and so on. It is extremely unlikely that the spatial information stored in memory is in the form of Cartesian coordinates and Euclidean linkages or any similar type of recording mechanism (Tobler, 1976; Golledge and Hubert, 1982). However, the information has to be stored such that as individuals develop understandings of *spatial concepts* such as location, configuration, proximity, closeness, dispersion, clustering, orientation and so on, the stored environmental information can be manipulated according to specific sets of these relations, and judgements made about the nature of the interaction that takes place between an individual and the environment. In other words, it is assumed the spatial relations are understood if only implicitly, and cognitive representations of an external environment can be interpreted in terms of spatial relations. The precise interpretation of each of these concepts may vary among individuals and it becomes a task to find those individuals who interpret spatial data in approximately the same way. What should be obvious, however, is that judged relations between primary nodes should be better represented than judged relations between pairs (or sets) of lower ordered nodes, or connections between lower and higher order nodes. In turn, this translates into an expectation that any cognitive image will have elements that closely reflect sets of real world environmental characteristics together with poorly represented spatial data, knowledge voids, and may include connections between cognized bits of data that may be difficult to substantiate in an objective reality.

Given this conceptualization, one can easily see how disturbances and/or distortions might occur in an individual's spatial knowledge structure. For example, in the early periods of developing such a knowledge structure about a given external environment even the spatial relations among the primary nodes may not be well understood and consequently each of these may be misplaced or misconnected in some way. Such a result would distort an experimenter's attempt to reconstruct a traditional cartographic representation of the knowledge structure. Over time, however, as the knowledge structure is anchored by a stable set of points, paths, and areas that closely correspond to specific elements of the external environment, it should be correspondingly be easier for an experimenter to represent spatial knowledge in a meaningful manner. It should also be possible to speculate about the nature of the transition that has taken place as the environment is learned.

To briefly summarize this section, therefore, we postulate that learning about an environment in essence becomes the process of compiling information sets that include all the spatial relations among environmental elements as well as their socio-economic, cultural, political, or other meanings and significances. Over time, we suggest that a cognitive representation will become more stable in terms of a basic set of primary and secondary structures, and that continued interaction with the environment will produce a constant situation of evaluating and re-evaluating the nature of stored information and the spatial structure of knowledge deduced from this stored information. We would further postulate that after a given period of time, continued interaction with the same environment will produce only minor perturbations of the information already retained in the cognitive map. Obviously once some type of stable representation has evolved, and a method has been developed for externally representing critical elements of that representation, attempts can be made to compare recovered information with appropriate spatial structurings of the same data in objective reality (*e.g.*, through constructing cartographic configurations). In later sections, we will show how such evaluations and matchings can take place.

Cognitive mapping of a city

Empirical work by Golledge, *et al.* (1978(a), 1978(b), 1981), Evans, *et al.* (1981), Garling, *et al.* (1981), and Richardson (1982) supports the contention that learning about urban environments conforms to an anchor point hypothesis. Let us now examine a selection of cognitive mappings of a given city to see how its image could be represented in a cartographic form such that we can deduce information about the common structure underlying sets of city images.

Many examples of well known cognitive maps appear in the book by Downs and Stea, *Maps in Minds : Reflections of Cognitive Mapping.* These include classics such as "The New Yorkers View of the United States" and residents' views of Paris, as well as a host of others reflecting the images that children and adults have of cities both in their own cultural context and in the world at large. Rather than repeat that information in this paper, we simply refer the reader to the above book for multiple examples and we concentrate instead on a particular city in the United States urban environment—Columbus, Ohio. Columbus represents a moderately large SMSA (approximately 1 million people) with a distinct downtown, a comprehensive freeway system, and sets of cues that are well known to its inhabitants.

It has been a common practice since Lynch's pioneer work to attempt to recover the critical cue structure of cities by the process of simply asking people for a list of best known places and compiling composite scores based on the frequency with which particular places are mentioned. An example of the use

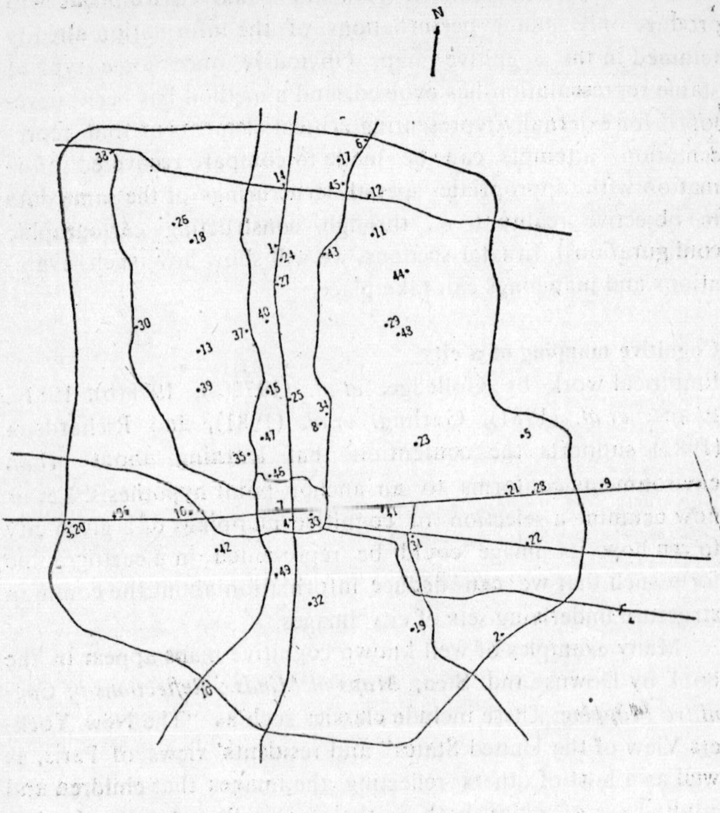

FIG. 5.1 : *Location of Cues in Columbus*

of this procedure for Columbus, Ohio is shown in Fig. 5.1. Associated with each of the cue names located on this map is an average familiarity score (Table 5.1). This average familiarity score is obtained from sets of respondents who undertook detailed testing to determine the nature of their spatial knowledge about the city (see Golledge and Rayner, 1977), and reflects the hierarchical ordering of the cues used in the experiment. In this section we will discuss some of the ways of representing spatial information about the city (such as the cues recovered by the above (procedure), illustrate how this information can be represented both in terms of simple warped grids and as modified street maps, and comment on some of

TABLE 5.1 : **Average familiarity score for each test location**

	Location	Score
1.	Graceland Shopping Center	7.36
2.	Eastland Shopping Center	5.65
3.	Westland Shopping Center	5.80
4.	Lazarus, Downtown	7.98
5.	Port Columbus	7.85
6.	I-71 N and I-270 Intersection	7.84
7.	Veterans Memorial Auditorium	6.98
8.	Ohio State Fair Coliseum	6.66
9.	Western Electric Industrial Plant	3.21
10.	I-71 S and I-270 Intersection	5.13
11.	Northland Shopping Center	8.14
12.	Karl Rd. and I-161 Intersection	7.45
13.	Kingsdale Shopping Center	6.02
14.	High St. and I-161 Intersection	7.93
15.	OSU Football Stadium	7.18
16.	Ohio State Hospital	4.34
17.	Anheuser Busch Brewery	6.67
18.	Henderson Rd. and Reed Rd. Intersection	6.98
19.	Refugee Rd. and Alum Creek Dr. Intersection	3.04
20.	W. Broad St. and Georgesville Rd. Intersection	4.08
21.	Town and Country Shopping Center	4.36
22.	Hamilton Rd. and E. Main St. Intersection	4.49
23.	Ohio Dominican College	4.18
24.	Morse Rd. and N. High St. Intersection	7.84
25.	Lane Ave. and N. High St. Intersection	6.97
26.	Don Scott Air Field	5.84
27-	Henderson Rd. and N. High St. Intersection	6.80
28.	E. Broad St. and Hamilton Rd. Intersection	4.76
29.	Northern Lights Shopping Center	5.16
30.	Golden Bear Shopping Center	5.23
31.	Capital University	4.81
32.	Shottensteins, South	3.47
33.	Grant Hospital	5.07
34.	Ohio Historical Society	7.14
35.	Jai Lai Restaurant	7.16
36.	Great Western Shopping Center	5.70
37.	Riverside Hospital	7.83
38.	Dublin Rd. and I-161 Intersection	7.00
39.	Lane Ave. Shoping Center	6.23
40.	Whetstone Park	5.77
41.	Franklin Park	3.59
42.	Central Point Shopping Center	3.39

TABLE 5.1 (*Contd.*)

43. I-71 N and Morse Rd. Intersection	8.03
44. Cleveland Ave. and Morse Rd. Intersection	7.18
45. French Market	7.16
46. Thurber Club Apartments	4.11
47. Battelle Memorial Institute	5.84
48. Shottensteins, North	5.36
49. Southview Park	2.10

Note : These averages reflect the scores given at the end of the experiment. As a result of data loss, only 116 subjects are represented here.

the classes of distortions that can be easily identified in sets of such map phenomena. To be consistent with our earlier arguments on the nature of recovering stored information, we construct these configurations from responses individuals give us about the relative proximity of pairs of places in the city : they do not represent actual hand drawn maps of the individuals themselves.

To explain this point a little further, we briefly summarize the type of experiment that was used to collect data from individuals and that subsequently allowed us to construct the city configurations. First, subjects were obtained from a wide variety of social, religious, political, sporting, and other organizations within Columbus. Over a period of nine months, the subjects responded to a series of paired comparison experiments in which pairs of cues were scaled according to their distances apart. The scale scores obtained from each subject were then analyzed by a non-metric multidimensional scaling algorithm (KYST, Kruskal, Young and Seery, 1973), with the output being constrained to a two dimensional solution. The starting configuration for the scaling algorithm in each case was the actual locational configuration of cues in the city : in this way, the scaled configuration represented a distortion of the actual pattern based on the proximity scores developed by each individual.

Each two dimensional output configuration was then matched with the original objective configuration *via* a process of standardizing, centralizing and rotating the two configurations

TABLE 5.2 : **Examples of correlation between subjects' configurations and actual test location**

Subject	Bidimensional Correlation
6	.62
7	.30
8	.54
9	.48
11	.71
12	.73
32	.72
37	.71
38	.87
42	.73
43	.77
47	.69
51	.71
53	.79
55	.88
57	.91
60	.80
61	.84
62	.64
63	.84
64	.84

until the closest possible match had been achieved. The degree of coincidence associated with this procedure was recorded in the form of a bidimensional correlation coefficient (Olivier, 1970; Tobler, 1965, 1977). Thus, individual configurations that closely matched a two dimensional Euclidean map of the objective configurations would score high bidimensional correlation coefficients (*e.g.*, over .80). As the fit between the subjective and the objective configuration decreased, so too did the correlation drop. Examples of the degree of fit between objective and subjective configurations for selected Columbus subjects are shown in Table 5.2.

To highlight the type of discrepancies found between subjective and objective configurations, the subjective configurations were generalized by warping a standard grid to fit the subjective

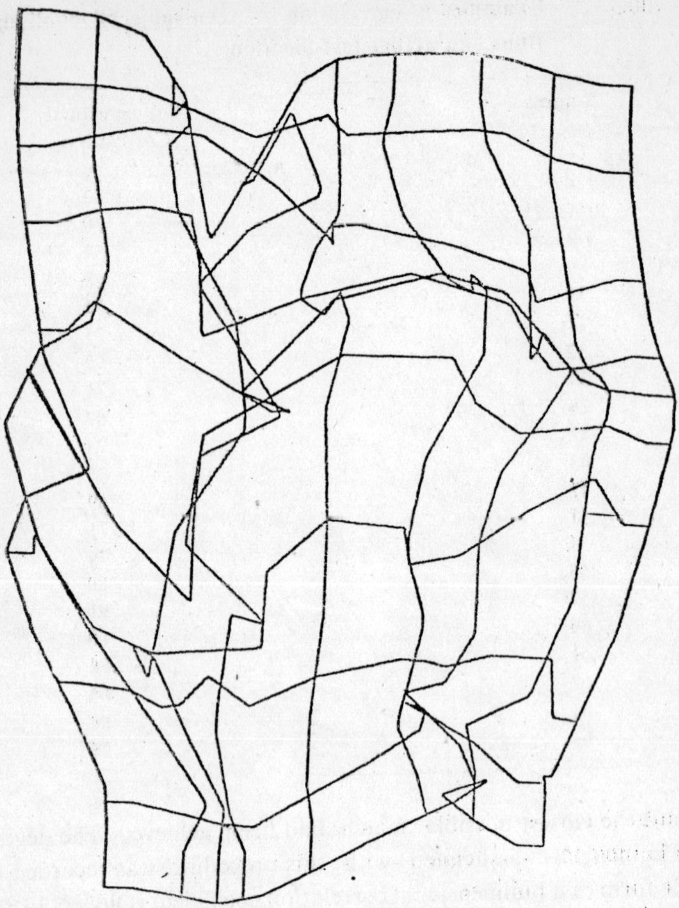

FIG. 5.2 : *Distorted grid—Subject 131*

locations of points. These grids are generalizations or summaries of the main types of variations found in each configuration. They are compiled by interpolating grid lines between points in each configuration in a manner similar to that used in interpolating contour lines on a map of discrete elevations. Obviously, some of the finer displacements and distortions cannot be shown on the relatively course grids we use here for illustrative purposes. Although each simplified grid has its own distinctive pattern of distortion (*e.g.*, Figs. 5.2 and 5.3), there are several striking similarities that are repeated among many

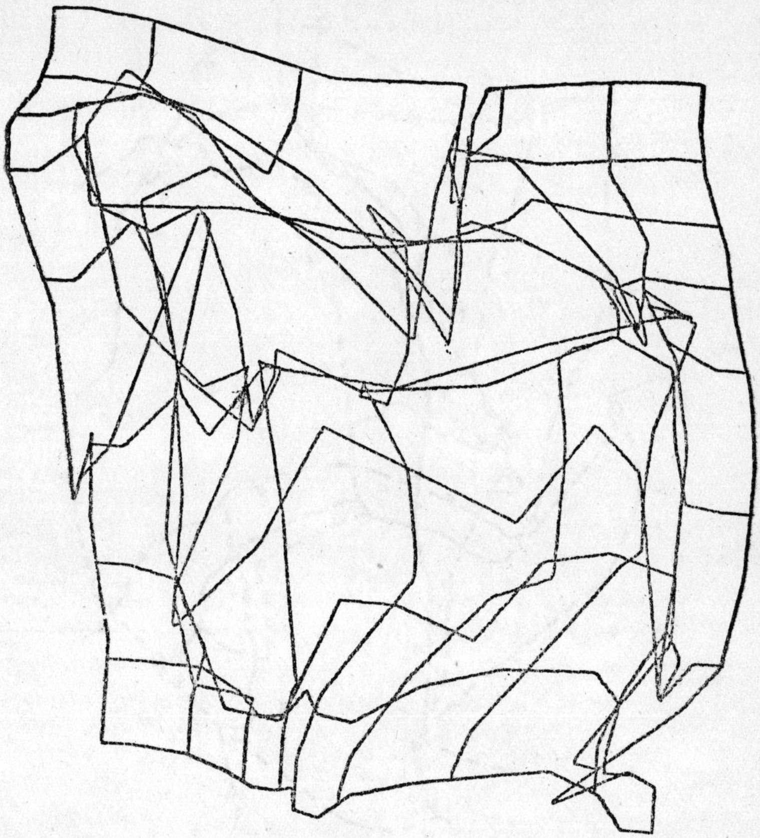

FIG. 5.3 : *Distorted grid—Subject 175*

group members. For example, many grids indicated a pronounced exaggeration of shorter distances ; for many others, there was a pronounced exaggeration of interpoint distances in the northeastern segment of the city of Columbus ; on others there was a northward pull of downtown and Southern locations. These distortions are a product of the representational mode we have chosen for eliciting information from individuals and of course may be immediately repudiated by most subjects if they were faced with such a map and told "this is what your city image really looks like" ! Figs. 5.4 and 5.5 show distortions

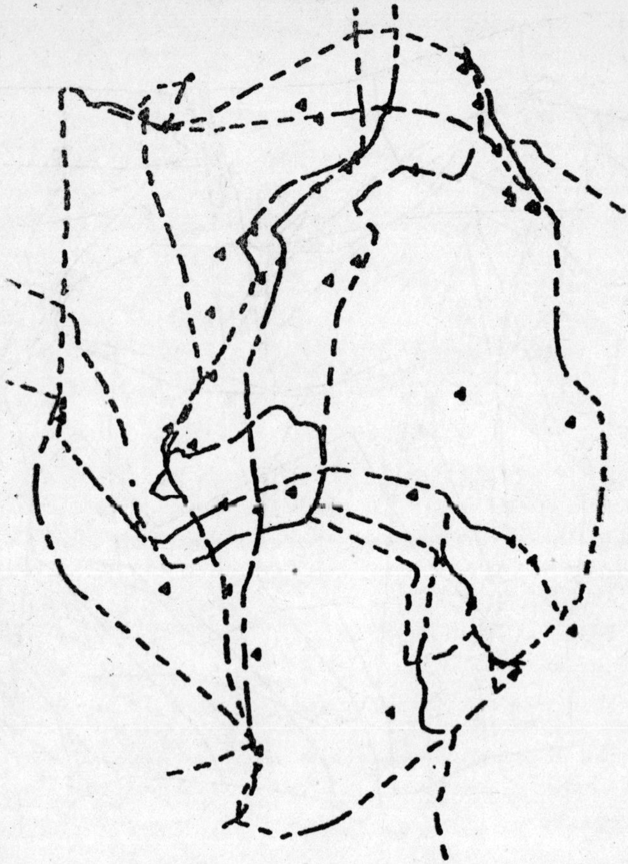

FIG. 5.4 : *Distorted street system—Subject 131*

of the basic street system of Columbus for the same subjects whose grids were given in earlier figures.

Like other studies of city images, the results above provide evidence that people's knowledge structure of cities is much as we expected—incomplete, schematized, having holes representing places of little or no knowledge, and with places of greatest interaction being represented most confidently and most faithfully. Most of the maps reflect some common characteristics of spatial cognitions such as over-estimating of close or well known distances and under-estimation of the distances

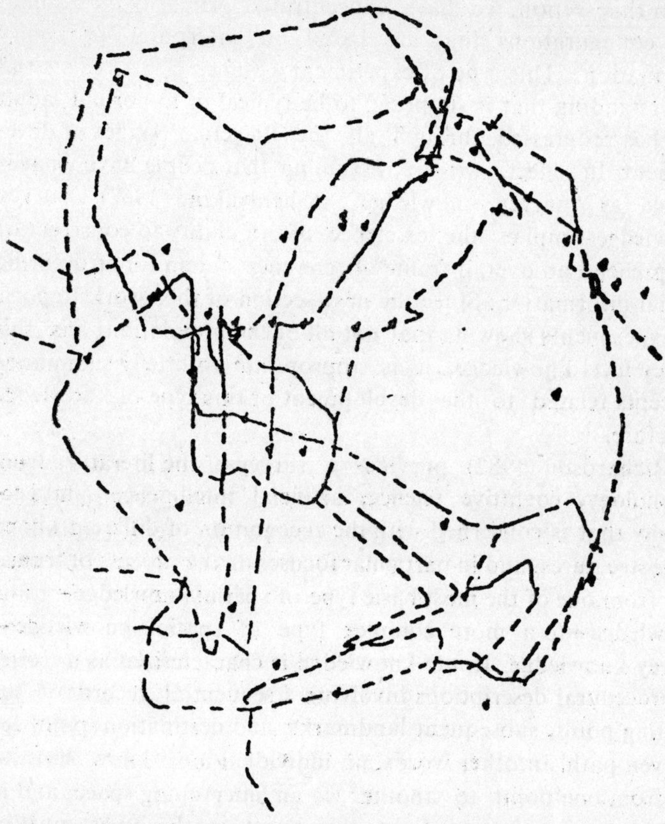

FIG. 5.5 : *Distorted street system—Subject 175*

apart of places that are further away or less well known. The information contained in the maps also indicates that there are pronounced local effects (in that knowledge peaks exist around well known places), and that the "knowledge surface" declines exponentially away from these places—but not equally in all directions. Obviously, there are more precise measures of distortion, disturbance, or error than can be encompassed by these simple grid distortions and street map transformations. We will examine some of these error characteristics in a later section.

In this section, we have concentrated primarily on examining configurations that are based on interpoint proximity information. This type of experiment assumes a level of spatial understanding that is supposed to be typical of a normal adult who has progressed through all the Piagetian stages of development. In effect, we are assuming that people have what is known as "survey knowledge" (Shemvakin, 1962). Survey knowledge implies the existence of an ability to construct or comprehend an overall frame of reference system for structuring spatial information. Since the next section of this work reports on experiments showing that not all of the population has this survey level knowledge, it is appropriate to briefly summarize concepts related to the development of this type of knowledge structure.

Richardson (1982) provides a survey of the literature from psychology, cognitive science, artificial intelligence, and geography that is concerned with the recognition of different knowledge structures, and in particular focuses on the process of transition from one of the most basic type of spatial knowledge—route knowledge—to a more complex type of spatial knowledge—survey knowledge. Route knowledge is characterized as a series of procedural descriptions involving a sequential record of the starting point, subsequent landmarks, and destination point for a given path. In other words, an individual must know how to get from one point to another *via* an intervening space, and in the process of getting from one point to the other, must be able to use cues from the environment to tell him whether or not he is proceeding in such a manner as to solve his way finding task. The individual must, therefore, be able to identify decision points where changes of orientation or direction are required, or must be able to identify transition points between different transport modes that are necessarily used in order to achieve his ultimate goal. He must also be able to identify whether particular cues are "on" or "off" a given route. This simple type of way finding knowledge in complex environments appears to emerge in preschool age children. Prior to this, most spatial knowledge is posited to be egocentric, rotating around the individual or around the principal anchorpoint of their objective spatial existence—the home base. Route knowledge is generally typified as being topological in character rather than strictly metric.

As information about environments mount and as the ability of individuals to make connections between scattered places within an environment improves, information about orientation, direction, and distance between landmarks emerges along with the prior information relating to angularity, location, and cue sequence. Thus route knowledge becomes the fundamental component of survey knowledge because the procedural descriptions of paths are eventually structured into an overall spatial frame of reference. Our initial conceptualization of the environmental learning process suggests that such spatial reference systems develop around a set of anchorpoints and that point, line, and areal knowledge accumulates as a greater degree of interaction takes place with the general environment.

Progression from one dimensional route knowledge to two dimensional survey knowledge incorporates concepts such as angle or direction, orientation, location, and distance apart. It also implies a qualitative difference in the nature of the spatial information represented in long-term memory (Chase and Chi, 1980). The hierarchical nature of survey knowledge allows for more efficient coding, storage, and recall of spatial information as opposed to the rather cumbersome, cognitively inefficient procedural descriptions of route knowledge. Each of the spatial components has a configurational component, and information can be recovered about these and used as the basis for a cartographic summary of an individual's knowledge structure. The distorted grids and street maps used in this section, therefore, necessarily assume that survey type knowledge exists in the sample populations and that it has been recovered via the experimental method chosen. Examination of the full range of distorted grids and street maps, however, indicates that some of the sample subjects may not have achieved survey level information about the city in which they lived. There are a large number of hypotheses that could be advanced to account for this lack of achievement. These include recency of location in the urban environment ; restricted daily activity patterns ; lack of access to transportation modes that would allow one to explore the total environment ; lack of access to information dispensed by media such as radio, television, or printed materials that would help fix a given cue in the knowledge structure of an individual ; lack of economic ability to explore ; existence of ethnic, religious, societal, administrative or other barriers that inhibit the gaining of knowledge about a place ; and so on. Most of these hypotheses to this day remain untested and precise knowledge of why specific "disturbances" occur in mental maps is unavailable.

Let us now turn to an examination of the cognitive images of non-normal adults, and at the same time change the scale of analysis from the city as a whole to a much smaller spatial unit—the urban neighborhood.

THE CITY THROUGH THE SENSES OF THE DISADVANTAGED : CASE OF THE MENTALLY HANDICAPPED

The problem of investigating the cognitive representations of the environment held by the mentally retarded is a particularly important one. With government cutbacks in mental health budgets and with an emergent programing stressing the retardeds right to live among the rest of society, the process of deinstitutionalizing the mentally retarded raises several questions about their ability to comprehend the spatial environment and navigate within it. Some of these questions include : what aspects of existing adaptive behavior scales are related to retarded individuals cognitive mapping abilities ? Since spatial and navigational concepts are markedly absent from current behavior (or competency) scales, what fundamental concepts and principles about spatial cognition might be incorporated into such assessment scales ? Can knowledge about the cognitive mapping process be used to develop more sophisticated programs for training the mentally retarded to navigate within the environment ? Do the current theories of spatial cognition generalize to individuals at levels of subnormal cognitive abilities (*i.e.*, the mentally retarded) ?

Although these questions have yet to be fully answered, considerable research efforts at the University of California at Santa Barbara, and The Ohio State University have focused on the cognitive mapping abilities of the mentally retarded. A capsule summary of the research will be presented here. The reader is referred to Golledge, Parnicky, and Rayner (1979a,

1979b, 1979c, 1980), Golledge, Richardson, Rayner, and Parnicky (1982), and Richardson (1982) for complete details of this research.

Subjects and experiments

An experimental group and a contrast group of subjects from Columbus, Ohio (study area 1) or Santa Barbara, California (study area 2) participated in a series of experiments aimed at assessing the spatial knowledge about the neighborhood in which the subject resided. The experimental group consisted of young adults who were classified as either severely mentally retarded, moderately mentally retarded, mildly mentally retarded, or borderline retarded. The mean IQ score for the experimental group was 56.6. Each member of the experimental group was living in the community either in a group home or in an individual apartment for a period of at least six months before the start of the experiment. Additionally, each experimental subject was physically able to travel throughout the environment. The contrast subjects were normal adults with lengths of residence in the same two neighborhoods roughly equivalent to those of the experimental group.

Two experiments were used to assess the level of spatial knowledge held by each subject. First, a map model methodology was used to assess survey knowledge. This consisted of each subject placing 2″ × 3″ kodachrome pictures of nineteen neighborhood landmarks on a plywood board. The sides of the map board were marked with tape to depict the bordering streets of the defined neighborhood. Also, the two major crossroads of the neighborhood were depicted as strips of tape on the map board. Extensive pretesting was done to insure that each subject completely understood that the plywood board represented a map of the neighborhood.

The second experiment, aimed at representing route knowledge, was a route-sequencing task. Each subject was told to consider a yard-long stick as a route to a particular destination (*e.g.*, neighborhood grocery store, local theatre, downtown department store, local shopping mall). The researcher placed a picture of the subject's residence at one end of the stick and a picture of a particular destination was located at the other end of the stick. Each subject was then given pictures of six landmarks occurring along the route and was asked to locate the pictures at the appropriate places along the stick.

Results

For the map board experiment, the location of landmarks as placed by each subject (the so-called cognitive configuration) can be related to the landmark locations as they should actually appear on the map board (the objective configuration). The congruence between cognitive and objective configurations of each subject (Table 5.3) was measured using a bidimensional correlation coefficient (Tobler, 1965, 1977). Clearly, the contrast subjects from Columbus and Santa Barbara performed much better on the map model task than did the experimental subjects. Figures 5.6 and 5.7, showing the displacement between cognized locations ('A', 'B', etc.) and objective locations ('*') for two of the subjects, typify the performance on the map board task by the experimental subjects and contrast subjects, respectively. The vast majority of experimental subjects randomly located each landmark on the map board on what appeared to be a random manner.

Similarly, for the route-sequencing task, the contrast subjects' estimates of landmark locations along each route were far superior to the locational estimates of the experimental subjects. The average rank correlation between cognitive and objective landmark locations was 0.525 for the experimental subjects and was 0.900 for the contrast subjects. The experimental subjects, however, did not locate landmarks along all routes in a random fashion.

Survey versus route knowledge

The level of cognitive development reached by a person can be evaluated via a selection of IQ, Adaptive Behavior, Motivational, Personal Independence, and other performance tasks. For our subjects, the level of development was found to be related to whether or not the experimental subjects had progressed to the stage of two-dimensional, survey-level, spatial knowledge. For example, significant positive correlation was found between the performance on the map board task and the following variables : IQ scores ; the cognitive portion (but not

TABLE 5.3 a : **Bidimensional correlation between each subject's cognitive configuration and the objective configuration**

Columbus Experimental Group

Subject ID#	Bidimensional Correlation Coefficient
002	0.27
003	0.40
004	0.39
005	0.27
006	0.14
007	0.41
008	0.26
009	0.24
010	0.72
011	0.07
012	0.32
013	0.16
014	0.46
015	0.33
016	0.29

Columbus Contrast Group

Subject ID#	Bidimensional Correlation Coefficient
102	0.88
103	0.58
104	0.74
105	0.44
106	0.79
107	0.46
109	0.44
110	0.86
112	0.55
113	0.83
114	0.92
115	0.42
116	0.79
117	0.76
118	0.60
119	0.38
120	0.67

121	0.82
122	0.51
123	0.55
124	0.83
125	0.94
126	0.87
127	0.52
128	0.79
129	0.24
130	0.59
131	0.34
132	0.24

TABLE 5.3 b : **Bidimensional correlation between map board configuration and objective configuration**

Santa Barbara Experimental Group

Subject ID#	Bidimensional Correlation Coefficient
901	0.18
902	0.71
903	0.92
904	0.76
905	0.71
906	0.29

Santa Barbara Contrast Group

Subject ID#	Bidimensional Correlation Coefficient
701	0.91
702	0.58
703	0.96
704	0.93
705	0.91
706	0.71
707	0.99
708	0.65
709	0.98
710	0.79
711	0.99
712	0.99
713	0.91
714	0.95

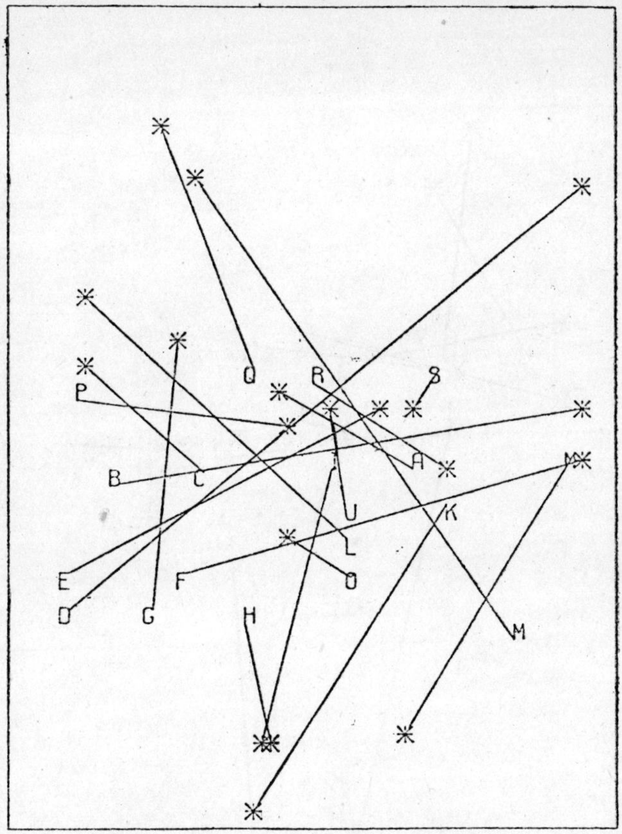

FIG. 5.6 : *Displacements—Subject 002*

personal and social motivational domain, personal independence domain, or physical development domain) of the Adaptive Behavior Scale ; and Wide Range Achievement tests (see Richardson, 1982). These results suggest that individuals in the upper level of mild mental retardation, or in the borderline category of retardation (or higher), *had* the pre-existing mental capacity to cognitively construct survey knowledge from experiencing and interacting with the environment. The severely and moderately retarded subjects did not appear to have the ability to cognitively code, construst, and represent spatial

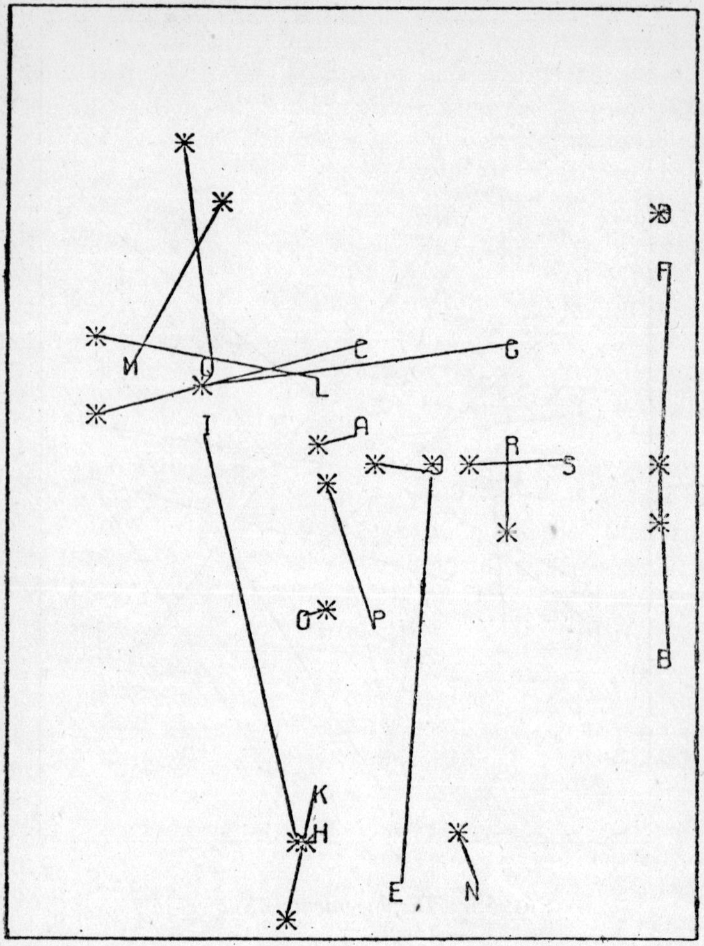

FIG. 5.7 : *Displacements—Subject 104*

experiences as survey knowledge. None of the severely or moderately retarded had map board cognitive configurations that were significantly congruent with objective reality, despite the fact that some of these subjects had lived in the neighborhood for up to 2-1/2 years. On the other hand, 37 of the 43 contrast subjects had a survey-level knowledge of their neighborhood—as reflected in their ability to produce configurations of the cues on the map board that correlated highly with a 2-dimensional map of cue locations. The six normal adult subjects not progressing to survey knowledge had limited experience in the neighborhood ; that is, an average length of residence in the neighborhood of around 2 months.

In contrast to the above results, no apparant relationship between route knowledge and cognitive developmental level was found in these experiments. The research suggests that individuals with cognitive abilities as low as severe mental retardation do have the mental capacity to represent experiences as route knowledge, and can thus competently navigate environments, even those as complex as the inner suburbs of large cities.

Having discussed the nature and composition of city images from a variety of viewpoints, let us now examine the problem of evaluating the spatial character of the mapped configurations that have been produced.

MATCHING COGNITIVE AND OBJECTIVE CONFIGURATIONS : ELEMENTS OF DISTORTION AND FUZZINESS

Given that it is possible to obtain an externalized configuration that is assumed to reflect an internal subjective representation of the location of certain cues in the environment, it then becomes of interest to ask how such a configuration relates to an objective, or 'real' configuration. In other words, is there any correspondence between what is out there as measured and portrayed by conventional cartographic techniques, and what can be reconstructed from the image of the world inside the mind ?

To answer this question one may take several approaches and use a variety of analytical techniques ; here we will discuss very briefly just a few of the ways in which the problem may be dealt with. Our focus will be on three basic aspects of the problem : 1) overall correspondence, or structural agreement ; 2) distortion or the amount of displacement from objective to subjective locations ; and 3) fuzziness, or the degree of variability of subjective estimates.

Overall correspondence

If we have an objective configuration Z, defined by a set of x, y coordinates, and a subjective configuration W, defined by a set of u, v coordinates, then the problem becomes one of finding a function $\hat{W}=f(Z)$ relating the two sets such that the mapping $Z \rightarrow \hat{W}$, (or $(x, y) \rightarrow (u, v)$), is as close as possible to the observed association between the two configurations. In the simple Euclidean case the transformation between these two sets can be written :

$$\begin{bmatrix} \hat{u} \\ \hat{v} \end{bmatrix} = \begin{bmatrix} \alpha_1 \\ \alpha_2 \end{bmatrix} + \begin{bmatrix} \beta_{11} & -\beta_{12} \\ \beta_{12} & \beta_{11} \end{bmatrix} \begin{bmatrix} X \\ Y \end{bmatrix}$$

Verbally, we could express the same relationship as follows :

$$\begin{vmatrix} \hat{u} \\ \hat{v} \end{vmatrix} = \text{(Translation)} + \text{(Scale) (Rotation)} \begin{vmatrix} X \\ Y \end{vmatrix}$$

This transformation brings the two configurations into best coincidence by 1) a translation to bring the mean location into coincidence ; 2) a rotation about this location ; and 3) a uniform change of scale.

We may estimate the parameters that describe such a mapping by treating the problem in a least squares fashion and finding α_1, α_2, β_{11}, and β_{12} so as to minimize the residual variance, or

$$1/n \, \Sigma \, [(u_i - \hat{u}_i)^2 + (v_i - \hat{v}_i)^2]$$

One convenient measure of the degree of coincidence is the root mean square error obtained by taking the square root of the residual variance. Alternatively, one may define a bidimensional correlation coefficient and also an r-squared value, analogous to regular regression, by taking the ratio of 'explained' variance to total variance (see Tobler, 1965, 1977 ; Olivier, 1970).

A different approach to overall structural correspondence is to consider the problem in a matrix matching framework.

Here one begins by defining the objective and subjective configuration by $n \times n$ proximity matrices (where n is the number of locations) such that the entries in the matrices are some measure of distance between pairs of points. The question is then one of assessing the degree to which the structure in one matrix reflects that of the other. Quite versatile non-parametric techniques developed by Hubert and Shultz (1976) and Hubert and Golledge (1981) are available for use in this context. An illustration of how they may be applied to cognitive configurations can be found in Halperin and Gale (forthcoming).

Distortion

In a seminal discussion of the geometry of mental maps, Tobler (1976) suggested that when analyzing cognitive configurations one should look at both distortion and fuzziness. Distortion has to do with the accuracy, or average displacement, of a cue from its objective location. It refers to the amount of bias or noncompensating systematic error ; by definition it involves a relation to some 'actual' value that has been measured by another means or is in some way 'given'. Thus, one way to represent distortion is by means of a displacement vector from the objective to subjective location (Figs. 5.8 and 5.9).

Given a set of displacement vectors it is possible by interpolation to obtain a vector field. The distortion at each point can then be described by a set of local derivatives :

$$\frac{\hat{\partial u}}{\partial x}, \quad \frac{\hat{\partial u}}{\partial y}, \quad \frac{\hat{\partial v}}{\partial x}, \quad \frac{\hat{\partial v}}{\partial y}$$

Tissot's (1881) theorems may also be applied, and thus one may represent the stretching at each point by an ellipse, or tensor (a, b, θ), where a and b are the semi-major and semi-minor axes respectively, and θ is the angle of inclination (Fig. 5.10). A computer program, DARCY (Tobler, 1977) has been written to perform this type of distortion analysis.

Preliminary aggregate studies of normal adults in the Columbus, Ohio experiment discussed earlier, showed that distortion generally increased in amount with distance from the center of the city. In addition, the distortion close to the center was

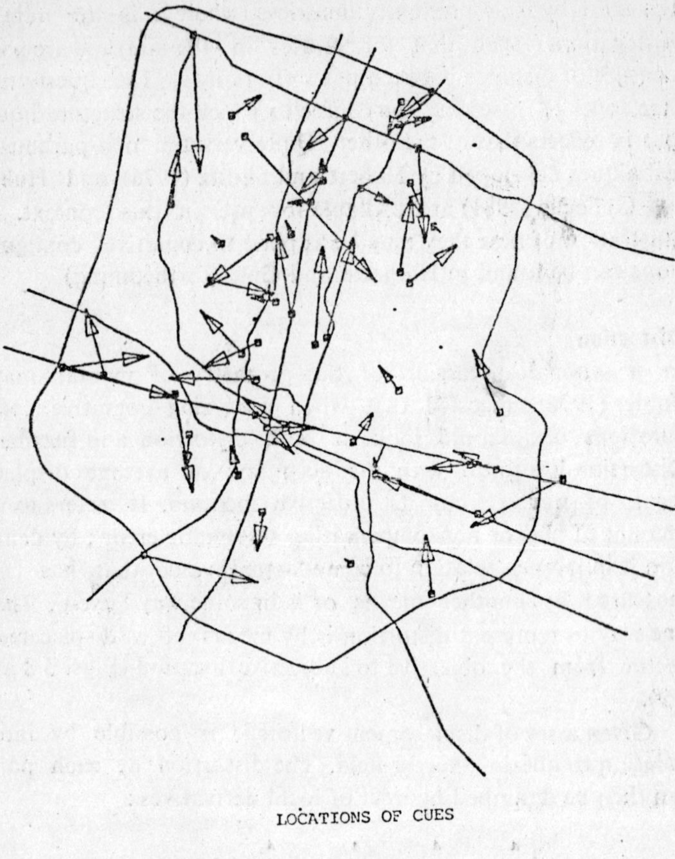

FIG. 5.8 : *Displacements—Subject 131*

primarily outward along radial axes, while at the periphery the distortion was mostly inward. Furthermore, in this context, distortion did not appear to be significantly related to the familiarity of places ; in the absence of such a relationship one might hypothesize that it may be more related to physical aspects of the city (Gale, 1980, 1982).

Fuzziness

Fuzziness refers to the variability, or imprecision, of estimated locations. It should not be confused with distortion as it has

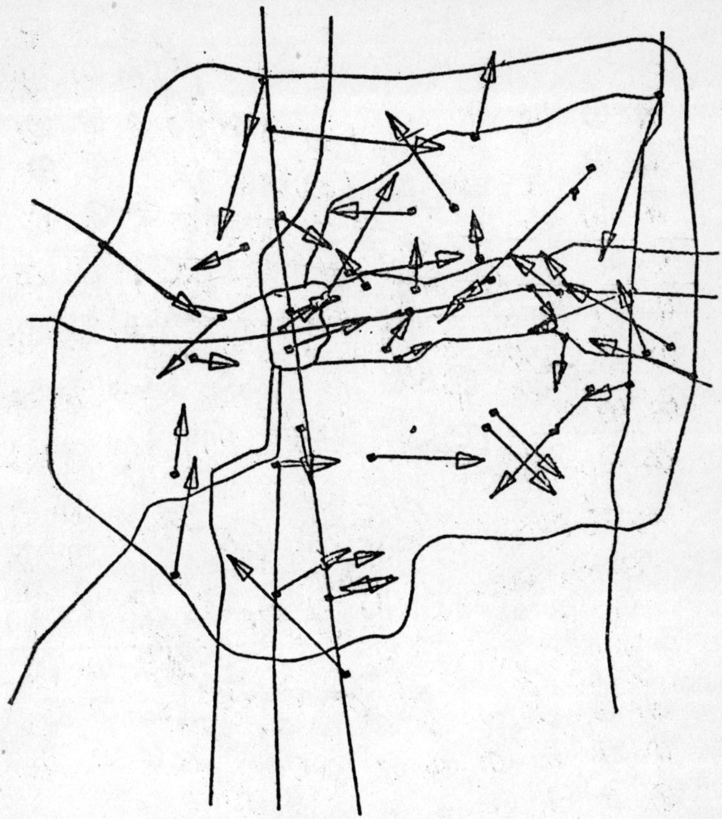

FIG. 5.9 : *Displacement—Subject 175*

nothing to do with deviance from an 'actual' or objective model ; rather, it describes the relationships within a set of estimates themselves without outside reference. One, therefore, needs redundant information to measure fuzziness. This can be obtained in several ways : 1) aggregating individual estimates by location ; 2) acquiring estimates between each point and several others ; and 3) multiple estimates of configurations.

One convenient way to describe and measure a distribution of spatial estimates is by a standard deviational ellipse. The characteristic roots of the covariance matrix of estimates define the axes of such an ellipse that can be used to characterize the

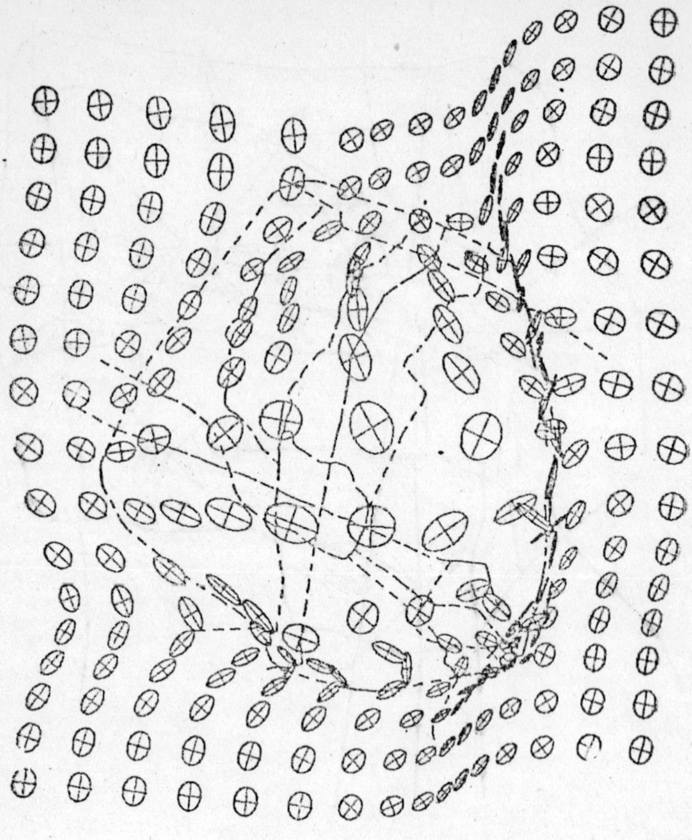

FIG. 5.10 : *Tissot's ellipses—Mean configuration*

amount and direction of spatial dispersion (Bjerhammer, 1973). Fig. 5.11 illustrates the use of these ellipses (at 1/4 size) to portray the aggregate fuzziness of location cues.

With regard to empirical study of the Columbus, it was found that there was not a strong relationship between the amount of fuzziness associated with each location cue and the amount of distortion. Neither were the directions of these two components of error significantly related. Fuzziness, however, was found to have a very significant negative relationship ($r = -.69$) with familiarity. In other words, for this study, how

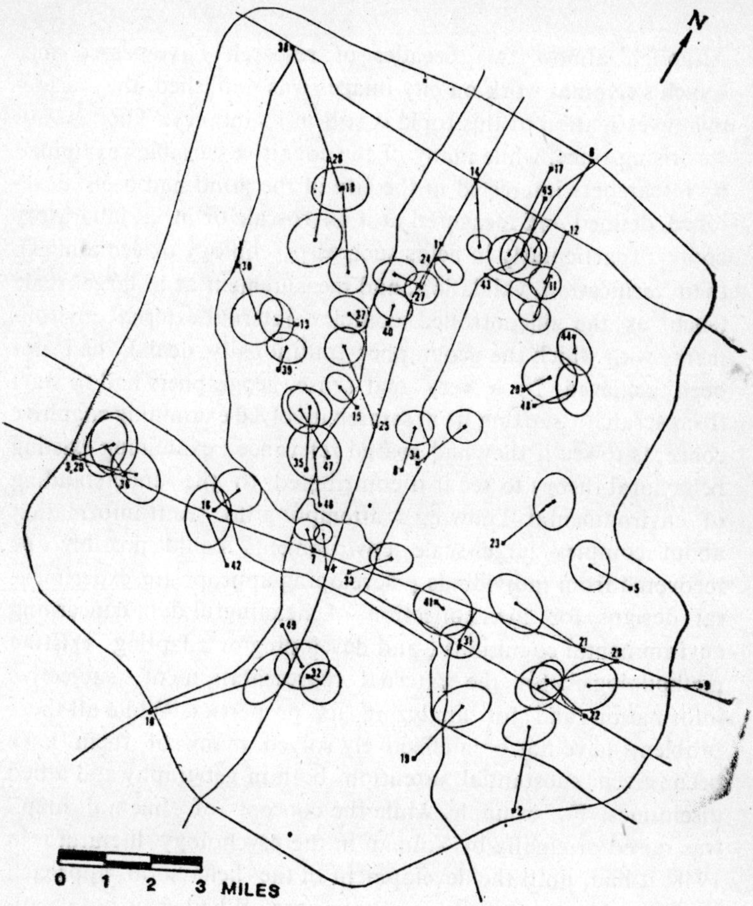

* *Map location*
+ *Mean center of estimates*

FIG. 5.11 : *Composite cognitive configuration—Average distortion and fuzziness* (*at 1/4 S.D.*)

well a place was known seemed to have little bearing on how accurately (with respect to objective reality) it was located, but much more to do with how precisely its position was defined in relation to other places.

PROBLEMS AND PROSPECTS

Although almost two decades of research have passed since Lynch's seminal work on city images was published, the academic investigation of this topic is still in its infancy. This is not surprising since, while many of the cognitive variables examined by researchers interested in the city of the mind had been developed, defined and measured at a microscale or in a laboratory context (particularly in fields such as psychology or economics), their verification, validation, and measurement at a large scale (such as the uncontrolled complex internal-external environments with which the geographer traditionally deals), had not been achieved. In a very real sense, geographers had to start from scratch. Starting from scratch involved examining cognitive concepts to see if they had spatial relevance ; examining existing behavioral theory to see if it contributed to the understanding of environmental knowing ; attempting to see if information about complex large scale environments could possibly be recovered from individuals ; developing appropriate experimental designs for the collection of meaningful data concerning environmental cognitions ; and developing or adapting existing methodologies for the external representation of subjective information and for analyzing its properties. While all these problems have not been effectively solved, many of them have been given substantial attention both in geography and allied disciplines. For example, while the concept of "mental map" was raised originally by Tolman in the psychology literature in 1948, it had, until the development of the behavioral approach in geography, no geographic counterpart. Whether or not cognitive images were map-like in form or propositional in content, and whether people could externalize cognitive information in schematic map-like form, was completely unknown.

It has taken a substantial number of isolated, individual studies of these phenomena to get to the point where some general conclusions can be drawn about the external representation of cognitive information and some degree of confidence can be given to the nature of the information so represented (Downs and Stea, 1973-1977 ; Kuypers, 1978 ; Evans, 1980). For example, focusing on "image" is a part of the process of explaining spatial behavior. If one cannot define, measure, or represent an image, one cannot include it in any way in an explanatory schema. Therefore, before one can accept a premise that image is a relevant concept, one has to have confidence in the attempts to obtain data on it, measure it, and/or represent it. The last decade, in particular, has seen numerous attempts to measure and represent such images via means such as sketch mapping, verbal descriptions, model manipulation, interpoint distance judgements, and so on. There appears at this stage to be no consensus as to the most appropriate way of externally representing image information.

While this chapter has concentrated to a large extent on showing that it appears possible to represent cognitive information cartographically, it is also apparant that we may not have reached the stage of being able to recover the full geometry of such a cognitive representation. Many of the problems associated with representing cognitive information in cartographic form are the same problems that surfaced in interpreting the original sketch maps suggested by early researchers as an appropriate way of obtaining information on city images. Just as those sketches were incomplete, had holes, folds, cracks, and tears, and in some parts incorporated ordinal information whereas in other parts they were may be fully metric, so also may the attempt to cartographically represent cognitive information suffer from the same problems. While some recent investigations of cognitive images have focused on questions such as the suitability of using Euclidean distance measures (Tobler, 1976 ; Richardson, 1979 ; Golledge and Hubert, 1982), the question of how best to represent cognitive information has not yet been solved. Recent experiments in cognitive science and artificial intelligence are even now suggesting alternate ways for representing such information (Haves-Roth, 1978). Other problems that occur with considerable frequency in analyzing cognitive images are things such as : asymmetry of distance relations ; incompleteness of information sets ; lack of metricity ; a mixture of topological and fully metric information within the same broad area ; unreliability of data obtained from subjects ; validation of methods for extracting data ; and selection of the most appropriate experimental designs and analytic methods for working with subjective data.

The problems mentioned above are primarily oriented to the extraction and/or representation of image data. There are many other unsolved problems associated with work in this area and these unsolved problems should provide exciting prospects for future work. For example, the nature of the relationship between cognitive images and actual spatial behavior still remains a vastly under-researched area. A growing mass work in psychology and some work in geography has indicated that the two appear to be quite strongly connected. But more evidence needs to be collected before we have sufficient faith that this type of premise is suitable as a base for explanations and understandings of spatial phenomena. A second problem that again details an exciting area for future research concerns the process of acquiring spatial knowledge. At this stage there is considerable speculation concerning how information is selected, attended to, coded, constructed, stored and represented in the mind. Relevant questions concern the role of experience, familiarity and environmental interaction in the construction and maintenance of this basic knowledge structure.

Perhaps the fundamental question that all geographers would raise and which has barely been touched is : how do variations in the environment itself influence the nature of cue selection and the storage of environmental information ? Are some environments more imagable than others ? How complex need an environment be before it becomes overwhelming ? And how do variations in the physical landscape or changing land use patterns effect cognitive images ? Along with such questions is the fact that we have not adequately researched the problem of how variations of personal, social and cultural characteristics of individuals effect cognitive images. We have had some evidence on the nature and role of historical, social, and cultural features on the selection of environmental information, but the general problem of determining the role of values and beliefs in forming environmental images has not been examined in great detail. Given the above summary of problems and prospects, one can see that there is a mass of work still to be done on city images. This should make the area one of the more exciting research arenas of future geographic research.

To conclude, however, a word of caution is in order. Work on the cognitive images of cities should not be undertaken lightly. Most of the work requires a very careful experimental design, the careful collection and monitoring of data sets, the selection of appropriate representational modes, and the development and use of appropriate ways of representing cognitive information. Research efforts in this area will take a lot of time, and the researcher must be dedicated.

REFERENCES

Anderson, J.R. (1978). "Arguments Concerning Representations for Mental Imagery", *Psychological Review*, 85, 249-277.

Appleyard, D. (1970). "Styles and Methods of Structuring a City", *Environment and Behavior*, 2, 100-117.

Bjerhammer, A. (1973). *Theory of Errors and Generalized Matrix Inverses*, New York : Elsivier.

Carr, S. and D. Schissler (1969). "The City as a Trip : Perceptual Selection and Memory in the View from the Road", *Environment and Behavior*, 1, 7-35.

Chase, W.C. and Chi, M.T.H. (1980). "Cognitive Skill : Implications for Spatial Skill in Large Skill Environments" in J. Harvey (Ed.), *Cognition, Social Behavior, aud the Environment*. Potomac, MD : Lawrence Earlbaum, Assoc.

de Jonge, Derk (1962). "Images of Urban Areas : Their Structure and Psychological Foundations", *A.I.P. Journal*, 28, 266-276.

Downs, R.M. (1970). "The Cognitive Structure of a Shopping Center", *Environment and Behavior*, 2, 13-39.

Downs, R.M. (1981). "Maps and Metaphors", 33, 287-293.

Downs, R.M. and D. Stea (Eds.) 1973, *Image and Environment*. Aldine : Chicago, IL.

Downs, R. and D. Stea (Eds.) 1977, *Maps in Minds*. Harper and Row : New York.

Evans, G. (1980). "Environmental Cognition", *Psychological Bulletin*, 88, 259-287.

Evans, T.W., Marrero, D., and Butler, P. (1981). "Environmental Learning and Cognitive Mapping", *Environment and Behavior*, 13, 83-104.

Gale, N. (1980). *Analysis of the Distortion and Fuzziness of Cognitive Maps by Location*, M.A. Thesis, Department of Geography, U.C.S.B., Santa Barbara.

Gale, N. (1982). "Some Applications of Computer Cartography to the Study of Cognitive Configurations". *The Professional Geographer*, 34, in press.

Gale, N. and R.G. Golledge (1982). "On the Subjective Partitioning of Space", *Annals of the Association of American Geographers*, 72, 60-67.

Garling, T., Book, A., Ergezen, N., and Lindberg, E. (1981). "Memory for the Spatial Layout of the Everyday Physical Environment : Empirical Findings and their Theoretical Implications" in A.E. Osterberg, C.P. Teirman, and R.A. Findlay (Eds.), *Design Research Interactions*, Ames, IO : Proceedings of the EDRA 12 Conference, 69-76.

Golledge, R.G. (1976). *Cognitive Configurations of a City* : Vol. I, Department of Geography, Ohio State University.

Golledge, R.G. (1977). "Multidimensional Methods in the Analysis of Environmental Behavior and Design" in I. Altman and J. Wohlwill (Eds.), *Human Behavior and Environment* : Vol. II, Plenum Press, 1-42.

Golledge, R.G. (1978a). "Representing, Interpreting, and Using Cognized Environments", *Papers of the Regional Science Association*, 41, 169-204.

Golledge, R.G. (1979b). "Learning About Urban Environments" in T. Carlstein, *et al.* (Eds.), *Making Sense of Time*, London : Edward Arnold, 76-98.

Golledge, R.G. (1981). "Misconceptions, Misinterpretations, and Misrepresentations of Behavioral Approaches in Human Geography", *Environment and Planning A*, 13, 1325-1344.

Golledge, R.G., Briggs, R., and Demko, D. (1969). "The Configuration of Distances in Intra-Urban Space", *Proceedings of the Association of American Geographers*, 1, 60-65.

Golledge, R.G. and L.J. Hubert (1982). "Some Comments on Non-Euclidean Mental Maps", *Environment and Planning A*, 14, 107-118.

Golledge, R.G., Parnicky, J.J., and Rayner, J.N. (1980). "The Spatial Competence of Selected Populations", Department of Geography and Ohio State University Research Foundation, November.

Golledge, R.G., Parnicky, J.J., and Rayner, J.N. (1979a). *The Spatial Competence of Selected Populations* : *Vol. I.* Columbus, Ohio : Department of Geography and Ohio State University Research Foundation.

Golledge, R.G., Parnicky, J.J., and Rayner, J.N. (1979b). *The Spatial Competence of Selected Populations* : Vol. II. Columbus, Ohio : Department of Geography and Ohio State University Research Foundation.

Golledge, R.G., Parnicky, J.J., and Rayner, J.N. (1979c). "An Experimental Design for Assessing the Spatial Competence of Mildly Retarded Populations", *Social Science and Medicine*, 13d, 291-295.

Golledge, R.G., Parnicky, J.J., and Rayner, J.N. (1980). *The Spatial Competence of Selected Populations*. Final N.S.F. Report, Columbus, Ohio : The Ohio State University Research Foundation.

Golledge, R.G., and Rayner, R.N. (1977). *Cognitive Configurations of a City* : Vol. II, Department of Geography, Ohio State University.

Golledge, R.G., Rayner, J.N., and Parnicky, J.J. (1980). "Teaching Spatial Concepts to Mentally Retarded Persons : An N.S.F. Progress Report" in Golledge, *et al.* (Eds.), *The Spatial Competence of Selected Populations,* 59-86.

Golledge, R.G., Richardson, G.D., Rayner, J.N., and Parnicky, J.J. (1980). "Procedures for Defining and Analyzing Cognitive Maps of the Mildly and Moderately Mentally Retarded" in Golledge, *et al.* (Eds.), *The Spatial Competence of Selected Populations*, Department of Geography, Ohio State University Foundation, 87-114.

Golledge, R.G., Richardson, G.D., Rayner, J.N., and Parnicky, J.J. (1981). "The Spatial Competence of Selected Mentally Retarded Populations" in H.L. Pick and L. Acredolo (Eds.), *Spatial Orientation and Spatial Representation.* Potomac, MD : Lawrence Earlbaum.

Golledge, R.G. and A. Spector (1978). "Comprehending the Urban Environment : Theory and Practice", *Geographical Analysis,* 10, 403-426.

Golledge, R.G. and Zannaras, G. (1973). "Cognitive Approaches to the Analysis of Human Spatial Behavior" in *Environment and Cognition*, William A. Ittleson (Ed)., New York : Seminar Press, 59-94.

Gulick, J. (1963). "Images of An Arab City", *A.I.P. Journal,* 29, 179-198.

Halperin, W.C. and Gale, N. (1982). "Matrix Matching as a Means of Map Comparison : The Drake's Landing Controversy and other Applications", Unpublished Manuscript, Department of Geography, U.C.S.B., Santa Barbara.

Hayes-Roth, F. (1978). "The Role of Partial and Best Matches" in D.A. Waterman and F. Hayes-Roth (Eds.), *Knowledge System in Pattern Directed Inference Systems,* New York, NY : Academic Press, 557-576.

Hubert, L.J. and Golledge, R.G. (1981). "A Heuristic Method for the Comparison of Related Structures", *Journal of Mathematical Psycology*, 23, 214-226.

Hubert, L.J. and Schultz, J.V. (1976). "Quadratic Assignment as a General Data Analysis Strategy", *British Journal of Mathematical and Statistical Psychology*, 29, 190-241.

Kruskal, J.B., Young, F.W., and Seery, J.B. (1973). *How to Use KYST II : A Very Flexible Program to do Multidimensional Scaling and Unfolding*, Bell Labs : New Jersey.

Kuypers, B. (1978). "Modelling Spacial Knowledge", *Cognitive Science*, 2, 129-153.

Ladd, F.C. (1970). "Black Users View their Environment : Neighborhood Maps", *Environment and Behavior*, 2, 74-99.

Lee, T.R. (1964). "Psychology and Living Space", *Transactions of the Bartlet Society*, 2, 1136.

Lee, T. (1968). "Urban Neighborhood as a Socio-Spatial Schema", *Human Relations*, 21, 53-61.

Lynch, K. (1960). *The Image of the City*, Cambridge, MA. : The M.I.T. Press.

Olivier, D. (1970). *Metrics for the Comparison of Multidimensional Scaling*, Unpublished Manuscript.

Orleans, P. (1973). "Differential Cognition of Urban Residents : The Effects of Social Scale on Mapping" in *Image and Environment : Cognitive Mapping and Spatial Behavior*, R.M. Downs and D. Stea (Eds.), Aldine : Chicago, IL, 115-130.

Parnicky, J.J., Golledge, R.G., and Rayner, J.N. (1980). "Mental Maps of Mentally Retarded Adults of Their Neighborhood" in Golledge, *et al.* (Eds.), *Spatial Competence of Selected Populations*", *Department of Geography, Ohio State University Research Foundation*, 115-140.

Richardson, G.D. (1979). *The Appropriateness of Using Various Minkowskian Metrics for Representing Cognitive Maps Produced by Non-Metric Multidimensional Scaling*, M.A. Thesis, Department of Geography, University of California, Santa Barbara, CA.

Richardson, G.D. (1982). *Spatial Cognition*, Ph.D. Dissertation, Department of Geography, University of California, Santa Barbara, CA.

Shemyakin, F.N. (1962). "General Problems of Orientation in Space and Space Representations" in B.G. Ananyev (Ed.), *Psychological Science in the U.S.S.R.* US. Office of Technical Reports, NTIS #TT62-11083.

Tissot, M. (1881). *Memoire sur la representation des surfaces*. Paris : Gauthier.

Tobler, W.R. (1965). "Computation of the Correspondence of Geographical Patterns", *Papers and Proceedings of the Regional Science Association*, 131-139.

Tobler, W.R. (1976). "The Geometry of Mental Maps" in R.G. Golledge and G. Rushton (Eds.) *Spatial Choice and Spatial Behavior*, Ohio State University Press : Columbus, Ohio, 69-82.

Tobler, W.R. (1977). "Bidimensional Regression : A Computer Program", Department of Geography, University of California, Santa Barbara.

Tobler, W.R. (1978). "Comparison of Plane Forms", *Geographical Analysis*, 10, 154-162.

Tolman, E. (1948). "On Cognitive Maps in Rats and Men", *The Psychological Review*, 55, 189-208.

SIX

NATHAN GALE AND REGINALD G. GOLLEDGE

ON THE SUBJECTIVE PARTITIONING OF SPACE

FOR many years a major concern of the discipline of geography has been the partitioning of space. The main purpose of this paper is to discuss an approach to the problem from the subjective perspective associated with environmental cognition research.

In the 1960's there was a major trend in geography toward considering the partitioning of space as a procedure analogous to scientific classification. Emphasis was given to the classical set-theoretic and logical foundations of numerical taxonomy. Instead of an attempt to discover "natural" divisions, classification was seen as a research tool, or device, that could be used to impose order on complex distributions. The hope underlying continued research of this type is that the results of such categorizations will yield patterns helpful in the construction of hypotheses that attempt to expain the spatial variability of phenomena.

In contrast to examinations of the objective spatial form of the environment, an emphasis on spatial processes emerged in the late 1950's and has continued through the 1970's. The focus of this approach is on the human actors of a system and, more specifically, human behavioral processes such as perception, learning, attitude formation, and decision making. Along with this development has been an increasing interest in subjective environments. An important aspect of this research field is that section devoted to environmental cognition.

A broad formal definition of environmental cognition has been given by Moore and Golledge (1976, p. 5) :

> Environmental cognition refers to the awareness, images, information, impressions, and beliefs that individuals and groups have about the elemental, structural, functional, and symbolic aspects of real and imagined physical, social, cultural, economic, and political environments.

The more specific term, cognitive mapping, refers to the means of structuring, making sense of, and coping with the complexities of the environment. It has been defined by Downs and Stea (1970, p. 9) :

> Cognitive mapping is a process composed of a series of psychological transformations by which an individual acquires, codes, stores, recalls, and decodes information about the relative locations and attributes of phenomena in his everyday spatial environment.

Within this context the geographer can examine the partitioning of space from the inside looking out rather than on the basis of some arbitrarily chosen objective variables. We therefore define the subjective partitioning of space as a conceptual categorization of spatial variance resulting from cognitive taxonomic processes. In more practical everyday geographic terms, it refers primarily to the mental definition and delineation of places, paths, areas, and interactions.

Though a considerable amount of work has been carried out in this area over the past two decades, the roots of the research are rarely adequately described. Our purpose is in part to state some of these and to show how they relate to different strands of research. This paper, therefore, will be an overview of (1) some basic assumptions and epistemological positions, (2) the significance of variations in the scale of inquiry, and (3) some of the current major research questions. This overview will be supplemented with a summary of a selection of major hypotheses that have been or are now under investigation in geography and related disciplines.

Assumptions and epistemology

Fundamental to an inquiry into the subjective partitioning of space is a set of basic assumptions. Upon these assumptions is built the model of the world that implicitly, if not explicitly, underlies much current research. In the general context of human geography, a very common paradigm (in its simplest form) is that the interaction between people and environment is a two-way process, with each affecting the other in a myriad of ways. In the more specific context of environmental cognition, the individual becomes the knower while the environment is that which is known. We feel that, because such paradigms play an important role in guiding research, it is useful and indeed necessary to examine, however briefly, some of the relevant assumptions and related epistemological positions on which these paradigms are based (Golledge, 1981).

The first assumption is that things or objects can have a physical existence ; that is, things or objects have substance and are in this sense real. The world is composed of many such objects existing simultaneously in the two fundamental contexts of space and time. Reflection on space and time brings one immediately face to face with the enigmo of philosophical limit questions, and thus these two contexts may be intuitively accepted as "given" (Kant, 1966, pp. 24, 30). If it is said, therefore, that the world is made up of objects that exist in space and time, it is possible to assume that phenomena are both discrete and relatively permanent. In other words, objects can be distinguished from one another by the unique property of location, and objects have an unbroken continuous existence over some substantial period of time. Simply put, then, it can be said that something is "there".

The second basic assumption is that a distinction can be made between the object world and the subject mind (K. Cox, in Cox and Golledge, 1981 ; Olsson, 1980). In this framework it is possible to consider the fundamental elements of existence in terms of mind and not-mind. Thus, what may be called a state of consciousness, or "the internal sense" (Kant, 1966, p. xliv), exists in juxtaposition to what is there.

This leads to the third essential assumption, that the mind is capable of knowing what is not-mind. Knowledge has to do inextricably with the relation between subject and object. It can be broadly described as a condition involving experience, perception, awareness, conceptualization, and cognition.

The epistomological question of how knowledge is obtained has been approached from a variety of philosophical positions ; because this subject is discussed exhaustively in numerous philosophical works, it needs to be treated only selectively here. By and large, the position held by the majority of scholars in the field of environmental cognition recently and at present is one of constructivism (Moore, 1979). Perhaps one of the major reasons that geographers, among others, have adopted this view is that it is considered an attempt to synthesize other theories of knowledge. For those unfamiliar with this approach it will be helpful to review some of the major positions represented in this synthesis, but in general we suggest a thorough reading of Moore (1979) and Moore and Golledge (1976). Very broadly speaking, treatments of knowledge can be categorized into two dominant approaches, and for the sake of simplicity these can be generally characterized by empiricism and positivism on the one hand, and rationalism and idealism on the other (Moore and Golledge, 1976, p. 12).

Empiricism begins with the stuff of the external environment (Berkley, 1952). This view holds that it is the environment that controls and determines knowledge. The reality of the object world is known solely through the acquisition of sensory data. The mind, therefore, is seen as a receptor of sensations. Knowledge is the result of the accumulation of repetitive inputs of unique facts and generalizations or empirical laws relate data concerning these facts a posteriori by association.

Positivism, like empiricism, considers sensory experience the only source of knowledge (Entrikin 1976). Once again, matter determines mind. The mind is seen to be somewhat like a mirror, and thus the information contained therein is little more than an internal reflection of the external reality. A principal difference between empiricism and positivism is that the latter considers laws to be a priori rather than a posteriori. Such independently given laws, however, are merely tautological rules for handling sensations (Moore and Golledge, 1976).

From the opposite perspective, the rationalist point of view is one of mind over matter (Descartes, 1911-12). Knowledge, which is the essential form of reality, is given a priori before any experience of sensory perception. External reality exists, but only as a passive environment to be acted upon by the mind (Bochenski, 1966, p. 3).

The pure idealist rejects even this admittance of an external world and claims that innate knowledge is the source of all that is (Croce, 1956). Anything beyond knowledge is unknowable and therefore amounts to nothing. The object has no truly independent existence apart from the subject (Bochenski, 1966, p. 84).

These epistemological positions are reflected in associated behavioral theories. On the empiricist-positivist side there are the behaviorist theories of environmental determinism (Huntington, 1945 ; Skinner, 1938). Not only is the mind a passive state, but human beings are passive organisms and their behavior is governed by the stimulus sensations generated by the external world, which elicit response patterns both among groups and at the individual level (Jung, 1959). On the other hand, associated with rationalism and idealism is nativism. Nativist theories assume that behavior is controlled by hereditary and biological factors. A person's actions in, or perhaps more precisely on, the world are the result of given knowledge predetermined by the mind rather than the senses.

A third major epistemological position is that identified by the aforementioned term, constructivism (Moore, 1979). Following Kant, knowledge, in this view, can be divided into the two main elements of matter and form. The matter of knowledge is that derived from sensation, whereas the form of knowledge is that which gives order to the content (Kant, 1966, p. 21). The sense in which this position synthesizes the extremes of empiricism and rationalism is that it holds that the matter of knowledge is given experientially, while the form of knowledge is given a priori. Thus knowledge is built or constructed through the integration of sensory experiences and the intuitive forms of space and time.

The constructivist epistemological position is also reflected in behavioral theories, which can be classed as interactional and transactional (Tibbetts, 1972). Whereas in the case of environmental determinism people were passive, and in the case of nativism the environment was passive, the interactional/transactional positions take the view that behavior can be understood only in terms of the ongoing relationship between the two, in which both are, in some sense, actors. This view does not go as far as the phenomenological position, where human beings are in environment and, simultaneously, environment is in them. Neither does it assume a strict dualist dichotomy between people and environment. Rather, it holds that what is taken to be the "real" environment cannot fully be defined independently of the sensory perceptions and mental conceptualizations of the individual. Thus knowledge in general, knowledge of the spatial environment in particular and behavior are linked to cognitive constructions that are influenced by the individual, the environment, and the interactions and transactions between the two.

If the constructivist position is accepted as a working basis from which to approach the problem of the subjective partitioning of space (a position that is of course open to debate), a few more assumptions must be made. First, it is assumed that the capability of sensory perception is essentially universal across the nonhandicapped human race. It is also assumed, however, that each individual forms his or her own constructions from this perceptual input. Hence, it follows that no two individuals construct things in exactly the same way. This means that there are as many different cognitions of the world as there are people. If, in the extreme case, each of these cognitions were fully independent, it is hard to imagine the result as being anything less than utter chaos. Furthermore, the same situation would result from the assumption that each bit of experiential data is completely unique. Therefore, it must be assumed that there is a significant degree of congruence among different cognitions of reality, and that some kind of structure can be given to sensed information (Golledge, 1979).

The structuring of reality is possible only if events in the world can be cognitively connected (Wapner, 1977). In other words, facts must be categorized in some way. In order to manage the continuously battering mass of perceptual data, the mind groups objects together on the basis of observed or assumed properties or relationships they have in common.

Thus cognitive taxonomic processes are essential to knowledge. It follows, then, that knowledge of the environment involves the use of conceptual categorization, and one convenient categorizing process for spatial data involves partitioning space into recognizable and acceptable units such as country, region, community, neighborhood, and so on. If each individual considered the infinite number of points on the earth's surface to be unique, there would be no such thing as environmental knowing. Only when the individual begins to join points together into groups that we identify by terms such as clusters, paths, and areas, and that we can link together by the concepts of interaction, can we say that any real knowledge of the environment exists. Because spatial information is so abundant, it is particularly important to be able to categorize (and generalize from) bits of spatial data. Thus the subjective partitioning of space can be seen as part of the general categorization process that contributes to knowledge and understanding. And clearly, without at least a minimal knowledge of environment, directed spatial behavior is impossible.

If we are to speak of anything beyond unique knowledge and unique behavior, if in fact we are to speak at all, it is imperative that there be a sufficient degree of communal agreement among categories. That such is the case is ensured by culture, where this term is taken to refer to a combination of transmitted structuring systems (or more simply, the shared habits of human groups). Probably the most fundamental of such systems is language, because it forms the basic interpretive framework for constructions of the world. Numerous other institutions, however, also constrain individual life experiences to various degrees. Examples of such are political, legal, social, economic, psychological, and religious systems. These systems are learned formally and informally in the normal development from birth to adulthood and enable communication, social interaction, and the giving of meaning to the known environment. With respect to spatial knowledge, categories of space differ with the objective experience and the subjective constructions of each individual, but are at the same time conditioned to a lesser or greater degree, by culture-specific structuring systems.

The significance of scale in the partitioning of space

An important aspect of categorization is that it involves many different levels of generalization. At one extreme, each individual object is in its own unique class, and at the other the universe is an undifferentiated whole. Obviously, levels of generalization somewhere between these two extremes are necessary for meaning to exist. In the geographical context it is possible to identify a hierarchy of scales that people use to partition space. Today these form a focus for a considerable volume of research on environmental cognition.

At the most fundamental level, each individual has an area around him or her that can be directly perceived by the senses. Within this perceptual space, several subspaces can be recognized (Hoyt, 1978 ; Saarinen, 1976). There is first of all an immediate body zone, which is the space necessary for an organism to exist and which is violated only in situations of intimate physical contact. A bit larger than this is normal personal space, which is the minimum "bubble" of portable territory surrounding the individual. At the next level is a slightly broader social space, which defines distances for more impersonal business-like interactions. Finally, stretching the boundaries of perceptually sensed areas out yet further is public space. Hall (1966) claims that the perception and use of all these four basic levels of spatial partitioning are conditioned to a large degree by the structuring systems of culture.

Beyond the limits of the space that can be immediately sensed lie the much vaster areas of cognitive space. This is space that is known through more than the presence of directly experienced stimulus objects. Knowledge of space beyond the perceptual horizon involves the retention, organization, and structuring of spatial information in the mind, that is, the cognitive mapping process as defined above. This transition from personal to cognitive space has not always been oppreciated by geographic researchers, who have at times confused not only the concepts relevant for the study of different scales of cognitive spatial organization (*e.g.*, perception for the immediate sensory experiences, cognition for the vaster areas beyond immediate experience), but also have confused the epistemologies that have been accepted as suited for study at each scale (*e.g.*, empiricism at the immediate sensory level, constructivism at the cognitive level).

Current problems and hypotheses

Whereas the preceding sections of this paper have presented some assumptions necessarily underlying research on spatial cognition and briefly discussed the confusing question of scale in the subjective partitioning of space, the next section will focus on questions of current concern. This is felt to be necessary because of considerable divergence of opinion as to what are the most critical problems in this area, and what appears to be the nature of findings from research on the subject.[1] To help define some general problems in this type of research, several fundamental questions can be delineated :

(1) How is space subjectively partitioned ?

(2) What is the relation between these subjective categorizations and others determined objectively ?

(3) What are the important physical, social, and cultural variables of the environment and of human beings that relate to the subjective partitioning of space ?

(4) What is the relation between cognized space and spatial behavior ?

The first of these questions is inextricably tied up with the development of methodologies designed to recover and represent information held in the mind. In order to study subjective space, it is necessary to externalize internal conceptions. Clearly, as a recent review effectively points out (Evans, 1980), it involves what Downs and Stea (1973) succinctly call "looking in from the outside at the inside looking out".

Once some form of external configuration is obtained, it can be compared to "objective reality" and to other subjective realities (however defined). This involves the analysis of externalized cognitive information in terms of content and structure. Such comparisons yield measures of differences and similarities between individuals that can be used to examine the significance of numerous environmental and personal variables (*e.g.*, Rivizzigno, 1975 ; Spector, 1978). Finally, if such research is coupled with an investigation of behavioral patterns, it may be possible to make some valid statements about the relationship between the world inside the mind and actions in the external world (*e.g.*, Thorndyke and Stasz, 1979).

Over the past two decades, research into subjective partitioning of space has led to the investigation of a number of hypotheses. Some of the more significant of these and their principal investigators are summarized below. As there have been several recent reviews of the psychology literature (Evans, 1980), and a recent overview by Thrift (1981) covers the contributions of English and Swedish geographers, emphasis will be placed here primarily on contributions from geographers in the United States. Where widely referenced material from other disciplines is deemed important, it will also be mentioned.

A. People do differentiate and categorize space in their minds. Of primary importance in this activity is the initial identification of points and paths, which are then built up with additional information into conceptualizations of areas (Golledge, 1978a, 1978b, 1981 ; Thorndyke and Stasz, 1979 ; Wapner, 1977). Much of this work is based on constructivist positions, and relates to Problem Number 1, identified previously.

B. It is possible by various means to recover meaningful configurations of internally held cognitive constructions of the world. Hypotheses such as this have been generated from research into Problem Number 2. Many different methodologies have been employed in this pursuit. For example, Lynch's procedures using sketch maps and verbal descriptions of urban areas have been followed by many (Appleyard, 1970 ; Carr and Schissler, 1969 ; de Jonge, 1962 ; Gulick, 1963 ; Lee 1968). Direct mapping has also been done interactively on a computer screen (Baird, 1979). Others have asked subjects to draw lines on maps (Golledge and Zannaras, 1973 ; Hoyt, 1978 ; Lee, 1968), or sort photographs, cards, or place names by association (Cox and Zannaras, 1973 ; Klein, 1967). Many psychological methods have proved quite useful. Some of these are environmental toy play (Blaut and Stea, 1969 ; Piaget *et al.*, 1960), semantic differentials and repertory grid tests (Downs, 1970 ; Harrison and Sarre, 1976 ; Silzer, 1972), and pairwise judgments in conjunction with multidimensional scaling (Golledge, 1978b). Research in this area is often based on empiricist or positivist positions.

C. Place specific characteristics of the environment help to define areas. Especially significant in this respect are changes in land-use homogeneity and specific distinguishable landmarks or cues (Appleyard, 1970 ; Lynch, 1960 ; Rivizzigno, 1975 ; Spector, 1978). This hypothesis is broadly based on positivist principles and derives from research on Problem Number 3.

D. Some of the individual characteristics that may affect how space is partitioned subjectively are age, income, education, place and length of residence, and work location (Klein, 1967 ; Lee, 1968 ; Rivizzigno, 1975 ; Spector, 1978 ; Zannaras, 1973). Although this research is based on different epistemologies, it appears to be dominated by rationalist principles ; it also derives from work on Problem Number 3.

E. Interactions, information flows, levels of familiarity, and responses such as stress and fear are crucial determinants of area image and definition. At different scales, different types of interactions and information gathering take place (Cadwallader, 1975 ; Ley, 1974 ; Spector, 1978). Again this research has a varied base, with idealist and constructivist principles dominant, and derives from research on Problem Number 3.

F. Culture is a significant component of spatial knowledge because it determines both the linguistic framework for conceptualization, and a set of constraining structuring systems for experience. In this sense, culture cannot be fully isolated from the preceding hypotheses, for it is simultaneously part of the environment, part of the individual, and a conditioner of reactions (Ley, 1974 ; Ley and Samuels, 1978 ; Lowenthal, 1968 ; Lowenthal and Prince, 1964 ; Rapoport, 1976). Much of this research is based on idealism or phenomenological principles ; it also derives from Problem Number 3.

G. People make decisions regarding such things as location, shopping, recreation, travel, migration, resource allocation, and domestic and foreign policy, at least in part, on the basis of the subjective definition of areas. In other words, behavior is more directly related to the way the world is thought to be, rather than objective measurements of it (Cox and Golledge, 1969 ; Cox and Golledge, 1981 ; Golledge and Spector, 1978 ; Rushton, 1969 ; Spector, 1978). Constructivist thought dominates much of this work, which is directly related to Problem Number 4. The evidence in support of these hypotheses varies in strength and degree of acceptance, and continued investigations of their epistemological and empirical bases represent many of the major lines of current research activity.

Other hypotheses may be distilled from the ever-increasing literature covering the subjective partitioning of space. Although this paper is but the start of what could be a long process of examination of research results, it does indicate that there are identifiable epistemologies associated with much of the research in this area, that it is possible to identify problems that are common to widely different research papers, and that identifiable hypotheses are being produced from this research. It remains for more ambitious researchers to document thoroughly other key problems, other major hypotheses, and to test those hypotheses before positive or negative evolutions of the generalizability and worth of research in this area can be adequately assessed.

FOOTNOTE

1. For example, see the Bunting and Guelke statements reported in Golledge (1981) as opposed to those in Cox and Golledge (1969, 1981).

REFERENCES

Appleyard, D., 1970, Styles and methods of structuring a city, *Environment and Behavior* 2 : 100-17.

Baird, John C., 1979, Studies of the cognitive representation of spatial relations : I, overview, *Journal of Experimental Psychology*, 108 : 90-91.

Berkley, G.T., 1952, *The principles of human knowledge* (*reproduced*), Chicago : Benton.

Blaut, J.M., and Stea, David, 1969, *Place learning*, Place Perception Report No. 1, Graduate School of Geography, Clark University, Worcester, Mass.

Bochenski, I.M., 1966, *Contemporary European Philosophy*, Berkeley : University of California Press.

Codwallader, M.T., 1975, A behavioral model of consumer spatial decision making, *Economic Geography*, 51 : 339-49.

Carr, S., and Schissler, D., 1969, The city as a trip : perceptual selection and memory in the view from the road, *Environment and Behavior*, 1 : 7-35.

Cox, K.R., and Golledge, R.G., eds., 1969, *Behavioral problems in geography : a symposium*, Studies in Geography No. 17, Evanston, Ill. : Northwestern University Press.

Cox, K.R., and Golledge, R.G., eds., 1981, *Behavioral problems in geography revisited*, Boston : Methuen.

Cox, K.R., and Zannaras, Georgia, 1973, Designative perceptions of macro-spaces : concepts, a methodology, and applications, In *Image and environment*, eds., R.M. Downs and D. Stea, pp. 162-78, Chicago: Aldine.

Croce, B., 1956, *Aesthetic as a science of expression : general linguistic* (translated by D. Ainslie), New York : Noonday Press.

de Jonge, Derk, 1962, Images of urban areas : their structure and psychological foundations, *A.I.P. Journal* 28 : 266-76.

Descartes, R., 1911-1912, *The philosophical works of Descartes*, London : Cambridge University Press.

Downs, Roger M., 1970, The cognitive structure of a shopping center, *Environment and Behavior* 2 : 13-39.

Downs, Roger M., and Stea, David, 1970, From the outside looking in at the inside looking out. *Environment and Behavior* 2 : 3-12.

Downs, Roger M., and Stea, David, 1973, *Image and environment*, Chicago : Aldine.

Entrikin, N., 1976, Contemporary humanism in geography, *Annals of the Association of American Geographers* 66 : 615-32.

Evans, G., 1980, Environmental cognition, *Psychological Bulletin*, 88 : 259-87.

Golledge, R.G., 1978a, Representing, interpreting, and using cognized environments, *Papers of the Regional Science Association* 41 : 169-204.

Golledge, R.G., 1978b, Learning about urban environments, in *Making sense of time, eds.*, T. Carlsten et al., pp. 76-98, London : Edward Arnold.

Golledge, R.G., 1979, Reality, process, and the dialectical relation between man and environment, In *Philosophy in geography*, eds., S. Gale and G. Olsson, pp. 109-20, Dordrecht : D. Reidel.

Golledge, R.G., 1981, Misconceptions, misinterpretations and misrepresentations of behavioral approaches in human geography, *Environment and Planning A*.

Golledge, R.G., and Spector, Aron, 1978, Comprehending the urban environment : theory and practice, *Geographical Analysis*, 10 : 403-26.

Golledge, R.G., and Zannaras, Georgia, 1973, Cognitive approaches to the analysis of human spatial behavior, In *Environment and cognition*, ed., William A., Ittleson, pp. 59-94, New York : Seminar Press.

Gulick, John, 1963, Images of an Arab city, *A.I.P. Journal* 29 : 179-98.

Hall, Edward T., 1966, *The hidden dimension*, Garden City, N.Y. : Doubleday.

Harrison, John, and Sorre, Philip, 1976, Personal construct theory, the repertory grid, and environmental cognition, In *Environmental knowing*, eds., G.T. Moore and R.G. Golledge, pp. 375-84, Stroudsburg, Pa. : Dowden, Hutchinson and Ross.

Hoyt, Frederick W., 1978, Neighborhood images : an investigation of the cognitive and behavioral dimensions of neighborhood space. Unpublished manuscript, Department of Geography, Ohio State University, Columbus, Ohio.

Huntington, E., 1945, *Mainsprings of civilization*, New York : New American Library.

Jung, C.G., 1959, *The archetypes and the collective unconscious*, Princeton, N.J. : Princeton University Press.

Kant, Immanuel, 1966, *Critique of pure reason*, Trans, F. Max Muller, Garden City, N.Y. : Doubleday.

Klein, Hans-Joachim, 1967, The determination of the town center in the image of its citizens. In *Urban core and inner city*, pp. 286-306, Leiden : Brill.

Ladd, Florence C., 1970, Black youths view their environments : neighborhood maps, *Environment and Behavior* 2 : 74-99.

Lee, H.N., 1973, *Percepts, concepts and theoretic knowledge*, Memphis : Memphis State University Press.

Lee, Terence, 1968, Urban neighborhood as socio-spatial schema, *Human Relations* 21 : 53-61.

Ley, David, 1974, *The black inner city as frontier outpost*. Washington : The Association of American Geographers.

Ley, D., and Samuels, M.S., eds., 1978, *Humanistic geography : prospects and problems*, Chicago : Maaroufa Press.

Lowenthal, D., 1968, The American scene, *Geographical Review*, 58 : 61-88.

Lowenthal, D., and Prince, H.C., 1964, The English landscape. *Geographical Review*, 54 : 309-46.

Lynch, Kevin, 1960, *The image of the city*, Cambrige, Mass. : M.I.T. Press.

Moore, G.T., and Golledge, R.G., eds., 1976, *Environmental knowing*, Stroudsburg, Pa. : Dowden, Hutchinson and Ross.

Olsson, Gunnar, 1980, *Birds in egg : eggs in bird*, London : Pion Press.

Piaget, J., et al., 1960, *The child's conception of geometry*, New York : Basic Books.

Rapoport, Amos, 1976, Environmental cognition in cross-cultural perspective, In *Environmental knowing*, eds., G.T. Moore and R.G. Golledge, pp. 220-34, Stroudsburg, Pa. : Dowden, Hutchinson and Ross.

Rivizzigno, V.L., 1975, Individual differences in cognitive structuring of an urban area, In *On determining cognitive configuration of a city*,

Vol. 1, pp. 471-87, Edited by R.G. Golledge, Columbus : Department of Geography, Ohio State University Research Foundation.

Rushton, Gerard, 1969, Temporal changes in space preference structures, *Proceedings of the Association of American Geographers* 1 : 129-33.

Saarinen, Thomas F., 1976, *Environmental planning : perception and behavior*, Boston : Houghton-Mifflin.

Silzer, V.J., 1972, *Personal construct elicitation in space preference research*, Deparment of Geography Discussion Paper No. 1, York University, Toronto.

Skinner, D.F., 1938, *The behavior of organisms*, New York : Appleton, Century Crafts.

Spector, Aron, 1978, An analysis of variations of representations of cognitive images in an urban environment, Ph.D. dissertation, Department of Geography, Ohio State University, Columbus, Ohio.

Thorndyke, P., and Stasz, C., 1979, Individual differences in knowledge acquisition from maps, Rand Corp. Report R-2375-ONR, Santa Monica, Calif.

Thrift, N., 1981, Behavioral geography : paradigm in search of a paradigm, in *Quantitative geography in Britain : retrospect and prospect*, eds., R.J. Bennett and N. Wrigley, London : Kegan Paul.

Tibbetts, P., 1972, The transactional theory of human knowledge and action : notes towards a "behavioral ecology." *Man-Environment Systems* 2 : 37-59.

Wapner, S., 1977, Environmental transition : a research paradigm deriving from the organismic developmental systems approach. In *Behavior environment research methods*, eds., D. Burke, et al., pp. 1-9, Institute for Environmental Studies, University of Wisconsin-Madison, Oct. 2-4, 1977.

Whitehead, Alfred North, 1933, *Adventures of ideas*, New York : Macmillan.

Zannaras, G., 1973, An analysis of cognitive and objective characteristics of the city : their influence on movements to the city center, Ph.D. dissertation, Department of Geography, Ohio State University, Columbus, Ohio.

[illegible] 1973. [illegible] Geography [illegible] University [illegible] dissertation.

[illegible] 1969. [illegible]

[illegible]

[illegible] 1975. An analysis of origin [illegible] urban [illegible] Department of Geography, Ohio State University, Columbus, Ohio.

[illegible] and [illegible], C., 1952. Individual [illegible]

[illegible] 1974. Behavioural geography [illegible]

[illegible]

[illegible] 1973. Environmental [illegible] decision-making [illegible] approach [illegible] Institute for Environmental Studies, University of [illegible]

[illegible] Alfred North [illegible]

Zannaras, G. 1973. An analysis of cognitive and objective characteristics of the city: Their influence on movements to the city centre. PhD dissertation, Department of Geography, Ohio State University, Columbus, Ohio.

PART THREE

IMAGES AND RESIDENTIAL ENVIRONMENT

SEVEN

TRIDIB BANERJEE AND WILLIAM BAER

VARIABLE CONSTRUCTS AND IMAGES OF THE RESIDENTIAL ENVIRONMENT
Findings from Los Angeles

CITY planners and designers have always had strong convictions about what constitutes a residential environment, how it should be defined, or how big it should be. These are implicit in the principles and standards expounded by the planning and design profession.[1] What has not been fully explored is how the residential environment is actually perceived by the public and whether the public's perception matches that of the profession. Nor for that matter has it been known whether different segments of the public uniformly share the same perceptions of the residential environment. These questions have largely been begged in past practices of residential planning and design.

The profession, for instance, has strong views on the "need" for sharply delineated boundaries in the physical environment so as readily demarcate areas or neighborhoods in the minds of the inhabitants, but do people really search for these demarcations in their everyday existence? Planners have typically believed that facilities—and public ones at that—such as schools or parks were the most salient facilities in peoples images of their residential area, and that paths and private places or nodes were of substantially lesser account, but do residential dwellers share these planning beliefs? Most physical design solutions assume a uniformity of imaging the urban environment among different clusters of people, but do the poor "image" and thereby "use" or "interact" with their environment differently than do the well-to-do ? Planners have tended to act as if sociological differences have little to do with environmental perceptions, but do the facts support such a supposition ? Moreover, it is commonly assumed that human territories or "home ranges" of people are invariant across social groups, as defined by income or ethnic differences, but is this known with assurance, or merely conjectured ?

This paper will report on our empirical investigation into these questions, how we approached these kinds of issues, and the results that we uncovered. While the specific results cannot be generalized, and may indeed be a strong reflection of the metropolitan culture and physical form in which we conducted our study (the Los Angeles region), the results are sufficiently different from the planner's design norms as to call into question their premises and foundations and the planning standards that are frequently adopted. The method used is sufficiently straightforward and easy to employ that taking these two points together, we are prompted to encourage others to undertake similar investigations in their own urban areas so as to better inform their design solutions.

Our premise here is that an understanding of how people perceive their residential environments could give us important guides about how they use and value their residential settings, and could assist us in critically examining existing lores and practices of neighborhood design. We further propose that research on perceptions and images of the residential environment must begin by considering such questions as : How do people individually or collectively construct the sense of a residential area ? What aspects cognitively differentiate the residential area from the larger urban space ? Are there significant differences in such representations ? To what extent can such differences, if any, be attributed to social characteristics of the observers ? Finally, to what extent, if any, do such representations of the residential area correspond to the planners' ideal ?

THEORETICAL BACKGROUND

In a general sense, images are representations of reality: of space, time, relations, persons, roles and organizations (Boulding, 1956). They help us interpret information, they guide our actions, and they serve as a frame of reference within which we organize our activities, beliefs and knowledge (Lynch, 1960). The "image", as Miller, Galanter and Pribam (1960) have argued, "is all the accumulated, organized knowledge that the organism has about itself and its world". They suggest it as the basis for our day to day plans and the structure of our behavior.

Our interests lie in environmental images—in particular, images of the residential environment. It is generally believed that these images of our everyday world evolve from the way we use, value and interact with the environment. As our images guide our actions in the environment, our experiences of acting in the environment in turn modify our images. This interactive relationship between the image and behavior is the essence of the underlying cognitive processes (Boulding, 1956; Lynch, 1960; Carr, 1967; Stea and Downs, 1973). According to Lynch (1960):

> "Environmental images are the result of a two-way process between the observer and his environment. The environment suggests distinctions and relations, and the observer—with great adaptability and in the light of his own purpose—selects, organizes, and endows with meaning what he sees. The images so developed now limits what is seen, while the image itself is being tested against the filtered perceptual input in a constant interacting process" (p. 6).

We believe that the residential image grows out of a similar interactive processes, that it mirrors not only how the environment is used but also how it is valued.

Despite these theoretical links between image and behavior, psychological concepts of the neighborhood or the residential area have not received serious attention in the past debate over whether a neighborhood is a social or a physical phenomenon (Keller, 1968 ; Webber, 1964 ; Issacs, 1948). Only in recent years has attention been given to how the neighborhood is construed and represented in the mind. Sociologist Terrance Lee (1968) for example, examined such constructs to test his hypothesis that a neighborhood is essentially conceived as a "socio-spatial schema". Others have utilized the psychological constructs of neighborhoods for the more practical purposes of defining an operational community or a service area (Sims, 1973 ; Wilmott, 1967 ; Walsh, Krauss and Regnier, 1980). Nevertheless major conceptual gaps concerning psychological constructs of the neighborhood still remain in the literature on residential preferences and behavior. Indeed both the theoretical and empirical underpinnings of the existing literature on this subject have been seriously vitiated by such gaps.

A study of the images of residential environments

Our inquiry about how the public perceive their residential environment is a part of a large study of user values and preferences which was conducted in the Los Angeles area in the mid-seventies. The study was based on a survey of twenty-two selected residential areas representing seven different social groups (see Fig. 7.1).[2] The respondents were asked to draw a map of their residential area on a standard 8½" by 11" sheet of paper, showing as much details as possible. Once the maps were drawn the respondents were asked if they could identify their "neighborhood" on that map. If the answer was affirmative the respondents were requested to mark the "neighborhood" area on the map.

The residential area maps were coded and analyzed in three different ways. First, a simple tally of various items (both labeled and unlabeled) shown in the maps was kept for each location. The items shown in the map were coded under the following categories : streets, highways and freeways ; public facilities (*i.e.*, police stations, fire stations, post offices, etc.) ; private facilities (*i.e.*, drug stores, super markets, gas stations, etc.) ; natural amenities (*i.e.*, beaches, mountains, rivers, etc.) and districts (*i.e.*, place names, campuses, "residential", "business district", etc.). This information was useful to compare the density, richness and diversity of the residential area representations of various localities. It was hoped that this information might give us some hints about the discriminating features of the residential area. These tallies were also used to develop the "composite" residential area maps for each locality, by transfering items mentioned in the maps drawn by the respondents on to an overlay of standard street map, and graphically differentiating the frequencies with which they are mentioned.

We also measured the area encompassed by the residential area maps. This was accomplished by transfering the essential features (mostly streets) of a residential area map to a standard street map of a known scale. The distance between the two farthest points on each map was measured, and divided by two. We called this measure the "ascribed radius" of the residential area, since the distance between the two farthest points is the diameter of the smallest circle that can circumscribe the area shown in Fig. 7.1.

Finally, a third type of analysis involved the territorial definition of the maps. If a map reflected a clear sense of boundary on three or more sides, it was coded as "closed"; maps lacking such clear definition were coded as "open". While most maps can be clearly differentiated in terms of one or the other type, others were less clear, primarily because of quality to drawing, etc. They were categorized as an intermediate group.

Elements of the residential image

The distribution of elements that characterize residential area maps vary from setting to setting as shown in Table 7.1. This is to be expected, as the physical characteristics of these settings are not the same. But what is interesting to note is the consistency with which certain types of physical-spatial elements dominate these maps, and how certain patterns of variability occur in the distribution of elements across social groups. Streets, highways and freeways comprise by far the most dominant category of elements shown in individual residential area maps. The represent one-third to one-half of all the different types of elements collectively mentioned by the respondents from each setting. The collective "images" of these areas, as shown in Fig. 7.2 through 7.8, are a vivid

TABLE 7.1 : **Distribution of items shown in the residential area maps broken down by the interview areas**

Sample Groups and Interview Locations	Category of Items and Elements Shown (*Percentages*)						
	Streets, highways, freeways	Public facilities	Private facilities	Natural amenities	District	Mean number of elements	N
Upper white							80
Pacific Palisades	29.2%	20.2%	26.9%	12.2%	10.9%	24.1	17
Palos Verdes	32.2	22.1	23.7	10.3	10.8	13.1	22
Bel Air	38.9	31.6	10.8	2.8	14.2	16.1	22
San Marino	41.2	19.4	24.2		14.1	20.7	19
Middle white							76
Westchester	38.4	20.9	30.3	3.4	6.5	10.2	19
East Long Beach	43.9	21.6	22.6	5.2	5.2	16.4	20
Van Nuys	42.1	12.3	40.7	0.5	3.6	20.7	18
Temple City	40.5	19.3	35.7		4.5	22.1	19
Middle black							76
Carson	53.0	34.0	10.9		1.4	12.5	31
Crenshaw	51.8	28.0	16.4		0.3	13.5	45
Middle Hispanic							53
Whittier	37.5	35.0	22.0	0.4	2.0	16.6	15
Monterey Park	39.0	35.0	20.0	1.0	3.0	18.9	21
Montebello	39,0	30,6	20.7	0,7		14,8	17

Lower white							82
Long Beach	42.0	36.0	21.0		1.5	9.5	20
Bell Gardens	59.0	22.5	15.0	3.0		17.3	19
Baldwin Park	55.0	20.0	16.0		1.0	9.4	23
Venice	60.0	17.0	18.0	1.0	3.0	8.8	20
Lower black							16
Watts	45.0	10.0	41.0			4.25	7
Slauson	50.0	33.0	17.0			8.44	9
Lower Hispanic							55
East Los Angeles	82.0	10.5	4.0	0.5	1.5	10.47	17
Boyle Heights	80.0	5.0	0.5		7.0	7.86	15
City Terrace	62.0	13.0	12.0			8.29	23

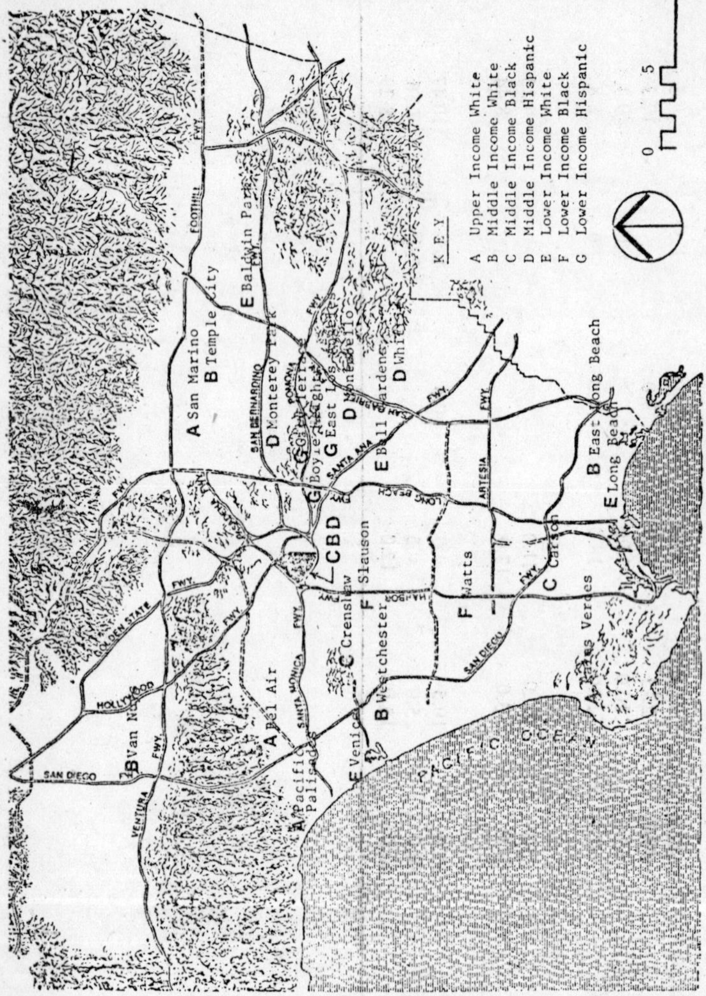

FIG. 7.1 : *Location of study areas in Los Angeles. The letters A through G represent seven different population groups, as shown in the key* (Source of the base map : *Figure 2-41A, p. 2.40, Final Environmental Impact Statement, The Los Angeles Downtown People Mover Program, UMTA, U.S. Department of Transportation, June 1980*)

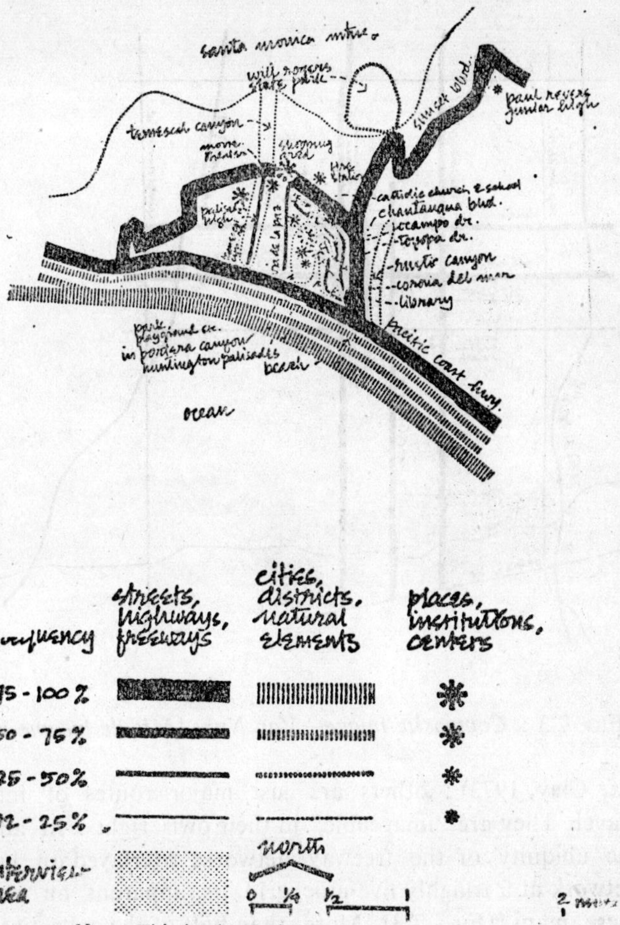

Note : This is also Index Ref. of Figs. 7.6 to 7.8

FIG. 7.2 : *Composite image-Pacific palisades (Upper income white)*

testimony to this pattern. Perhaps this is the inescapable signature of the automobile which has shaped so much of the Los Angeles metropolitan form. Shaped by the Jeffersonian grid system, and built according to contemporary traffic engineering standards, many seemingly endless arterials lace the Los Angeles metropolitan area in quarter or half-mile intervals. Many of them are automobile oriented "commercial strips"

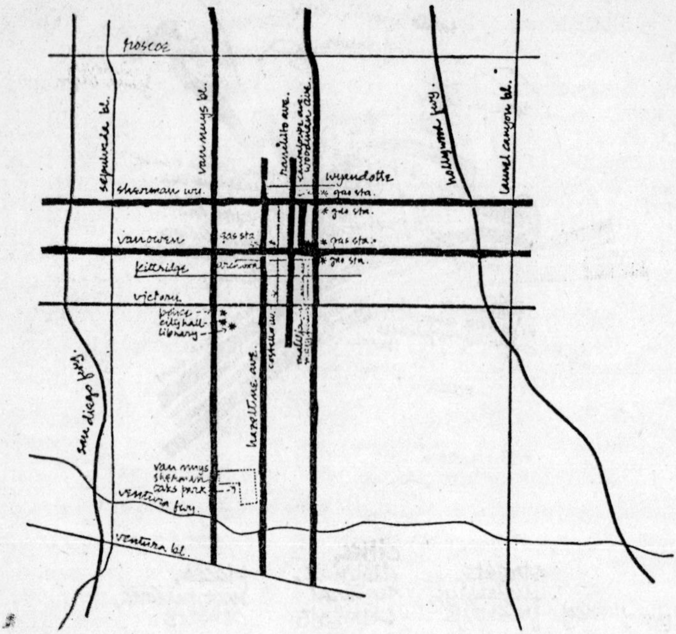

FIG. 7.3 : *Composite image—Van Nuys (Middle income white)*

(cf. Clay, 1973) ; others are just major routes of intra-city travel. They are "imageable" in their own rights. In addition, the ubiquity of the freeway network, overlayed on the street network at a roughly five-mile grid, is apparent on many of these maps (Fig. 7.3). More than half of the collective image maps include references to at least one freeway. Indeed some of these collective maps show that freeway on-ramps and off-ramps can become minor landmarks for many residents who live near a freeway.

The next two categories of more commonly mentioned elements are public and private facilities, which together, account for about half of all elements shown in the residential area maps. Public facilities refer to such elements of the residential setting as parks, playgrounds, schools, fire stations, post offices, and the like which are provided and maintained by the public sector. The amount and location of such public facilities have always been used in organizing the physical design of residential environments. But the collective image maps suggest that such public facilities, while appearing as important landmarks, do not necessarily act as a focal point in these cognitive maps, contrary to planners' expectations. Private facilities refer to mainly the privately owned institutional or business establishments such as the corner drug store, the gas stations, food markets, shopping centers, doctor's or dentist's office, and the like. Often these are important destinations in the daily activity cycle, and therefore equally as important a node or landmark as some of the public facilities. Indeed, in some areas, these private facilities visually dominate the residential landscape not only because of their size and bulk—such as in a shopping center—but also because of their heraldic accoutrements of signs and symbols.

The natural features of the setting are sparsely mentioned. Most commonly the ocean is used as a referent in coastal neighborhoods, and the mountains for the neighborhoods located in their slopes (see Figs. 7.2 and 7.4). One also finds occasional mentions of rivers. But, by and large, natural features are conspicuous by their absence in most of these collective residential area maps, reflecting the built-up environs of these localities. Similarly mentions of large physically identifiable districts are quite infrequent. Only occasionally one finds mentions of adjoining political entities as identifiable, if symbolic, frames of reference in these maps (Fig. 7.5).

In many ways these collective images of residential areas share the characteristics of public images of urban areas as reported in various other studies (Lynch, 1960; Appleyard, 1976; de Jonge, 1962; Gulick, 1963). Thus, to draw on the nomenclature suggested by Lynch (1960),[4] these maps too can be interpreted in terms of *paths*, *edges*, *landmarks*, *nodes* and *districts*. However unlike other public image maps, the Los Angeles residential area maps are dominated by *paths*, which are streets, highways and freeways. *Edges* (also largely defined by these elements), *landmarks* and *nodes* play only a minor role in these maps; *districts* are even less significant. Contrary to what physi-

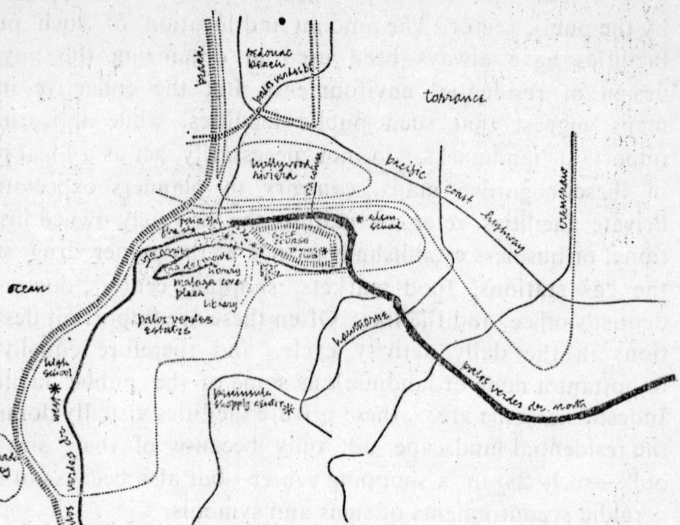

FIG. 7.4 : *Composite image—Palos Verdes (Upper income white)*

cal planners might expect, these maps do *not* give any special clues as to how the respondents' residential area is distinguished from the rest of the urban fabric. Indeed very few of them suggest anything like a focal point consisting of community facilities, shopping and open spaces or for that matter, a strong sense of boundary as envisaged in the neighborhood unit formula. Indeed these collective representations, in most cases, are a far cry from the textbook physical-spatial configuration of the neighborhood unit concept.

Inter and intra-group differences in residential area maps

The collective images of the residential area vary from location to location not only in terms of the elements included in the maps (see Table 7.1, for example), but also in terms of the amount of detail and areal extent. In general the middle and

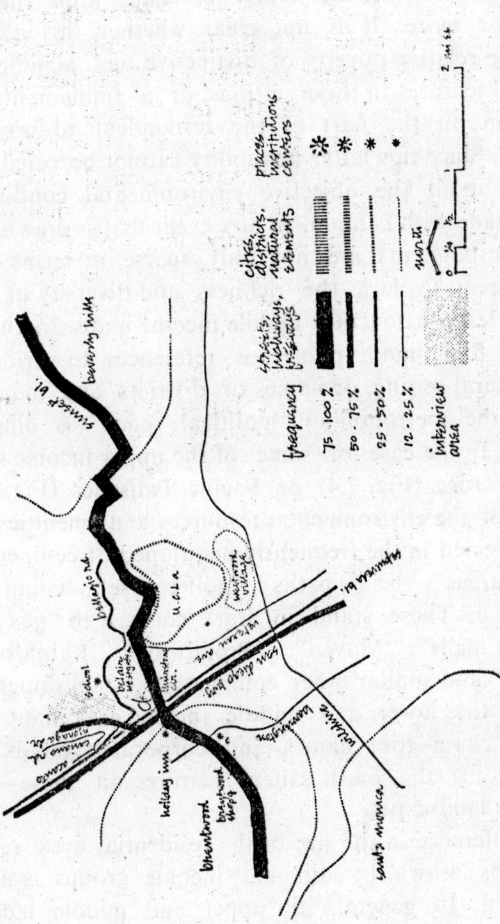

FIG. 7.5 : *Composite image—Bel Air (Upper income white)*

upper income maps tend to have a greater density of details than those of the lower income respondents. With the exception of Long Beach, all other low income area maps have, on the average, less than eleven items per map, while the rest have thirteen or more. It is not clear whether this lack of detail reflects the relative poverty of distinctive and significant environmental features in these settings, or a fundamental lack of enthusiasm on the part of the respondents to draw maps of their area. Since this latter possibility cannot be ruled out[5] any inference about the objective environmental conditions can only be made with caution. In any event maps drawn by lower income respondents are not only sparse in terms of details, but also seem to lack the richness and diversity of the upper and (to a lesser extent) the middle income maps. In these latter cases one finds more numerous references to various aspects of the natural setting, or names of districts and municipalities by which the metropolitan "political space" is differentiated (Fig. 7.5). In the case of some of the upper income settings as in Palos Verdes (Fig. 7.4) or Pacific Palisades (Fig. 7.2), the opulence of the environmental resources and amenities is abundantly reflected in the frequently mentioned "tree-lined streets", "wooded areas", "bridle paths", "golf course", "country clubs", and the like. These stand in stark contrast to "gas stations", "shopping malls", "Mayco", "Broadway", "Ralph's Market" "Safeway" and similar other commercial establishments which dominate the lower and middle income area maps. National and local chain-store names and corporate symbols (cf. Clay, 1973) become the most salient features in these otherwise featureless landscapes.

The difference in the size of the residential area represented in the maps drawn by different income groups is also rather pronounced. In general, all upper and middle income area maps (with the exception of Pacific Palisades and Whittier) cover larger territories than those drawn by the lower income respondents. Indeed the contrast between the collective map of the Palos Verdes residents and that of the Watts residents is dramatic (see Figures 7.4 and 7.8).[6] The mean radius of the Palos Verdes maps is over two miles, that of the maps drawn by the Watts residents is only one-eighth of a mile.[7] While these are extreme cases of expanded and shrunken concepts of residential space (the average for all groups being a little over three-fourths of a mile), the difference between the upper or middle income area maps and that of the lower income areas is quite consistent.

To be sure, physical form, density, and land use configurations are important factors in forming concepts of the residential environment (Sims, 1973). The inter-locality differences within a particular social group can be attributed to such differences in the site and its development. Consider, for example, the difference between the maps drawn by the residents of Palos Verdes and Pacific Palisades, both upper income areas (see Figures 7.2 and 7.4). The average radius of the Pacific Palisades maps is one-third of that of the Palos Verdes maps. Yet the locus of activities and distance to various facilities do not appear to be significantly different in these locations ; both have strong community oriented and conveniently located shopping and business districts. Thus it is highly likely that the difference in the areal coverage stems from a fundamental difference in the physical form and appearance of these two settings. The immediate setting of the Pacific Palisades residents is well delineated by a system of highways, streets, canyons and Palisades. Most respondents drew those boundaries and the relative smallness of the collective map seemed to be determined by the unique properties of the site. On the other hand, the immediate boundaries of the Palos Verdes interview area is less well-defined ; but the area shares the uniformity and exclusivity of appearance of most of the peninsula that grew out of strict land use, density and architectural controls applied to this unique topographical setting. It comes as no surprise to see the Palos Verdeans project a highly expanded concept of their residential area that includes almost the entire peninsula.

It can also be argued that the size of the residential area may reflect the objective density of the area. For, to the extent cognitive maps are shaped by the locus of various neighborhood scale activities (*i.e.*, doing food shopping, taking a walk, visiting a friend, etc.), and density dictates spatial concentration of public or private services and facilities, some association can be expected between density and the size of the residential

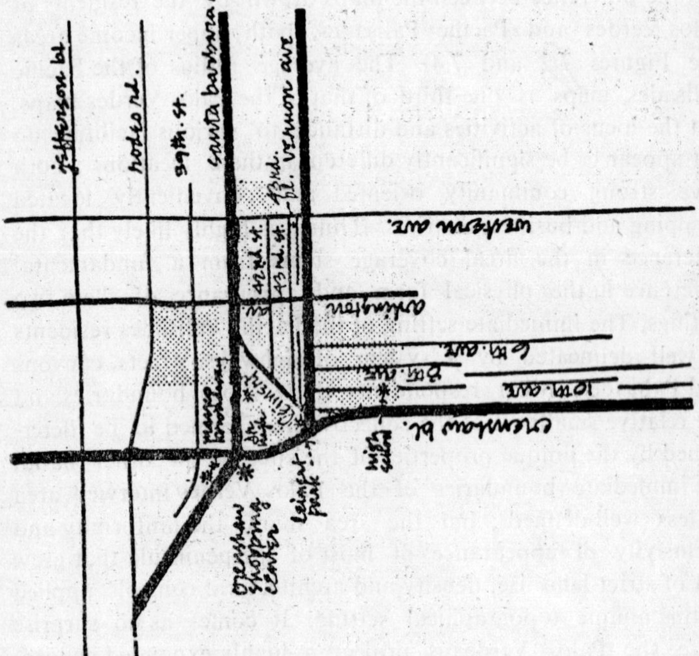

FIG. 7.6: *Composite image—Crenshaw (Middle income black)*

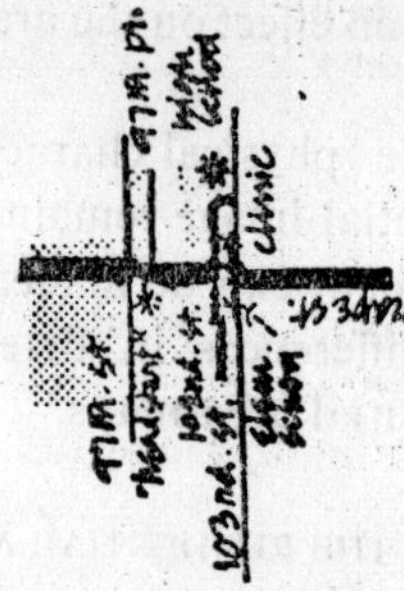

FIG. 7.8 : *Composite image—Watts (Low income black)*

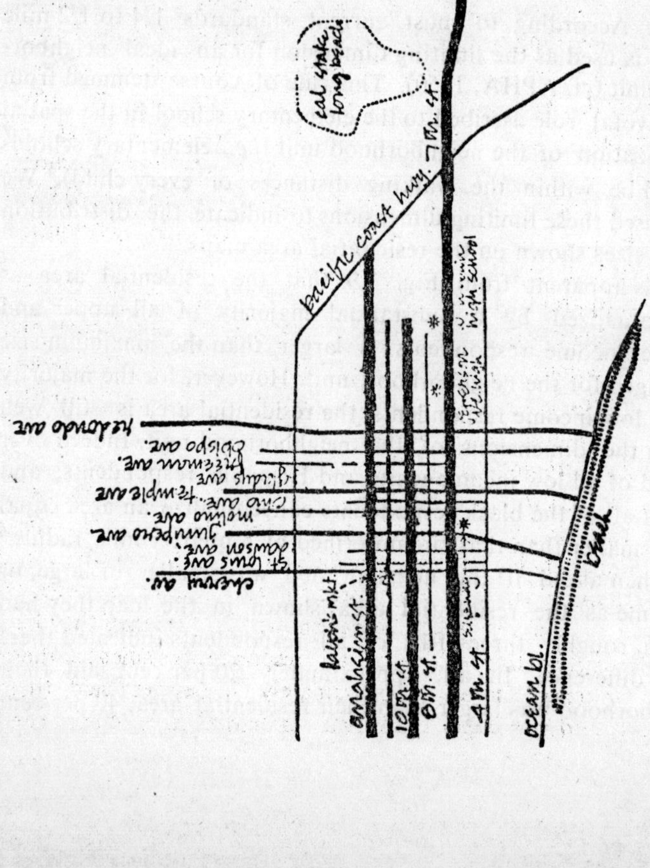

FIG. 7.7 : *Composite image-Long Beach (Low income white)*

area maps. This tends to support Terrance Lee's (1968) finding that housing density has no effect on the area of "neighborhood" schematics.

While the role of the physical characteristics of the setting in influencing the residential image remain less than conclusive, a more compelling argument can be made, in light of our data, for the role of social differences in determining at least the areal size of these residential area maps.

SIZE OF THE RESIDENTIAL AREA

The average radius of the residential area maps for different sample groups by location has been presented. The relationship between size and income is quite evident—perceived size increases with income. In Fig. 7.9 the data on the residential area maps are presented in slightly different form, to give a sense of the distribution of the radii within each population group. According to most current standards 1/4 to 1/2 mile radius is used as the limiting dimension for an ideal neighborhood unit (cf. APHA, 1950). This rule of course stemmed from the pivotal role ascribed to the elementary school in the spatial organization of the neighborhood unit (*i.e.*, elementary schools should be within the walking distances of every child).[8] We have used these limiting dimensions to indicate the distribution of the sizes shown on the residential area maps.

It is apparent from Fig. 7.9 that the residential area as conceptualized by a substantial majority of all upper and middle income respondents is larger than the maximum size envisaged for the neighborhood unit. However, for the majority of the low income respondents, the residential area is still well within the dimensions of the neighborhood unit. Indeed over a third of all low income white and Hispanic respondents, and almost all of the black respondents conceptualize an area equal to or smaller than that circumscribed by a quarter mile radius.[9]

When asked if the neighborhood was smaller, or large, or the same as the residential area shown in the map they had drawn, roughly three-fifths of all respondents indicated there was a difference. In all, approximately 20 per cent said their neighborhood was larger than their residential area, 40 per cent

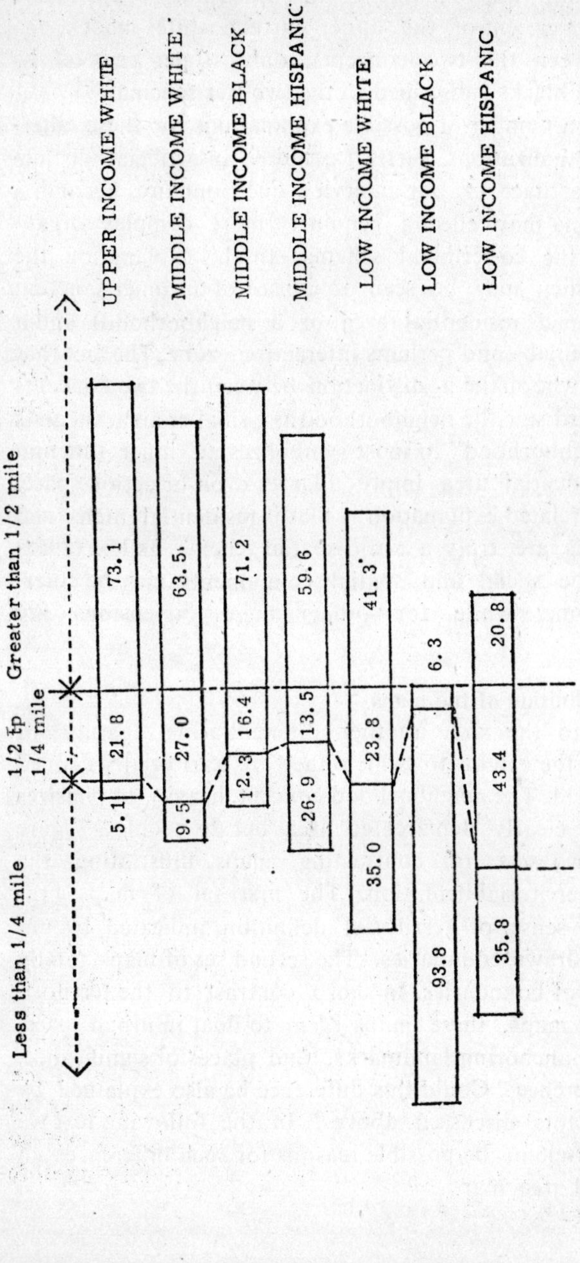

FIG. 7.9 : *Percentage distribution of the radius of the residential area maps by population groups*

said it was the same size, and 40 per cent said it was smaller. This distribution was similar for all population groups except that while 70 per cent of the upper income whites made a distinction between the two concepts, only 10 per cent of the lower income blacks subscribed to the two-tier schema.

There are a number of possible explanations for these alternative conceptualizations. First, it could be an artificial distinction, and an artifact of our interview questionnaire. Second, a two-tier schema may reflect a genuinely more complex organization than the co-terminal schema. In this explanation the residential milieu mey be seen to consist of an inner sanctum (whether termed residential area or a neighborhood) and a larger transitional—and perhaps interactive—zone. The fact that among those who make a distinction between the two concepts about two-third saw the neighborhood as a smaller area, suggests that the "neighborhood" to most symbolizes an inner sanctum while the residential area imply a larger orbit or action space. A third, and related explanation is that if residential areas and neighborhoods are truly a socio-spatial schema, as Lee (1968) has argued, the social and spatial components may be coterminal for some, while for others these dimensions are inseparable.

Territorial definition of the maps

In addition to the size, another differentiating feature of these maps is the extent to which they are territorially defined and demarcated. The neighborhood concept heavily emphasizes the bounded, clearly demarcated area but do people ? Figure 7.10 show two sets of contrasting maps illustrating the difference in territorial definition. The first set of maps project a strong sense of territorial definition indicated by unambiguously drawn boundaries. The second set of maps totally lack any hint of boundaries. In sharp contrast to the territorially bounded maps, these maps seem to float in urban space, save for some anchoring landmarks, and places of significance. Why this difference ? Could this difference be also explained by the social factors discussed above ? In the following text we will explore some of the possible reasons for such differences in the residential area maps.

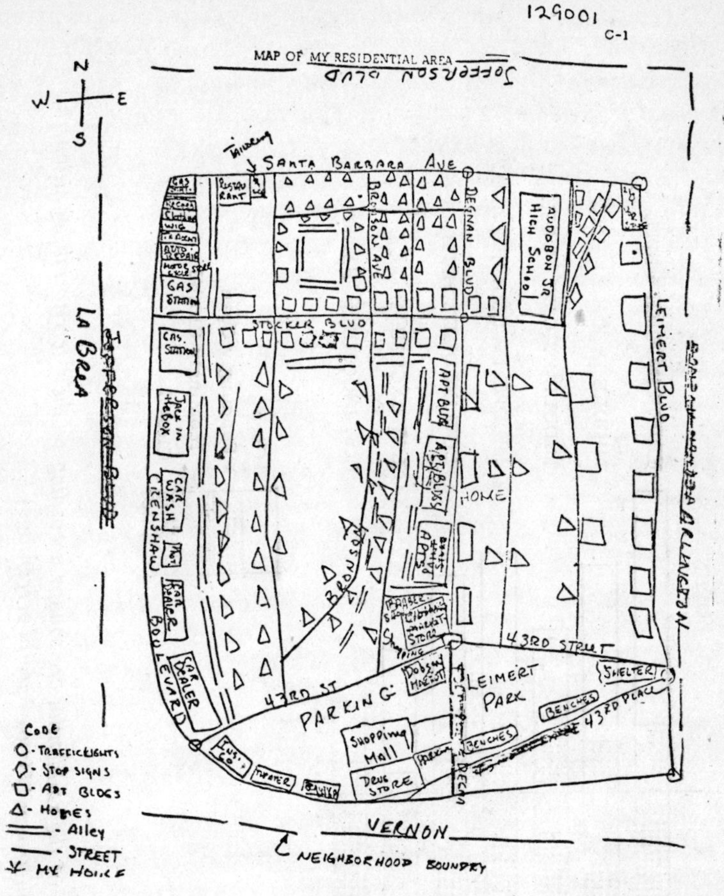

FIG. 7.10 : *An example of a "closed" map*

Of the 400 maps available for coding, a little over three-fourth could be easily categorized as either "open" or "closed" maps, and were almost equally divided between these two groups. The remaining one-fourth of the maps were more ambiguous, and were categorized in two intermediate levels of spatial definition, depending on their degree of boundedness. The distribution of the residential area maps according to their

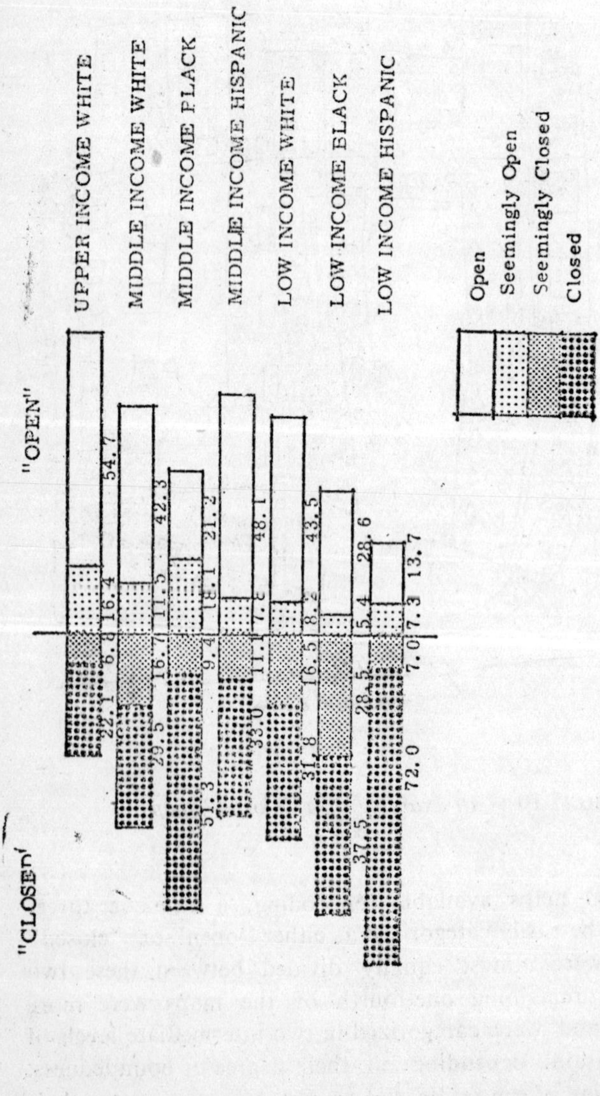

FIG. 7.11 : *Distribution of the residential area maps according to their territorial definition by population groups (Figures are in percentage)*

territorial definition is shown in Fig. 7.11 broken down by population groups.

The distribution shows some interesting differences. Overall, it seems that with the exception of the middle income Hispanic group, all other non-white respondents show a greater propensity to draw territorially closed maps than their white counterparts. This pattern holds even if we ignore the less un-ambiguous ("seemingly closed" and "seemingly open") categories. It is also apparent that the upper income group shows the highest propensity to draw territorially open maps. The difference between the middle income whites, Hispanics and lower income whites is much less pronounced.

It seems that the need for territorial definition may be more a factor of race than income. It is interesting to note that the only non-white respondents who have drawn a slightly higher portion of "open" maps—the middle income Hispanics—are residents of settings (Monterey Park, Whittier and Montebello) that are socially well-integrated with the white population.[10] All other non-white respondents were interviewed in settings that are essentially ethnic "ghettoes" ; this is true even for the middle income black respondents. Thus the greater propensity among the non-white groups to show their residential area as territorially bounded may reflect a sense of ethnic solidarity, if not a sense of isolation *vis a vis* the rest of the city.

Alternative constructs of the residential environment

The size and territorial definition are but only two of the many characteristics along which these maps can be classified and analyzed. Indeed they represent an overwhelming variety of styles and modes of representation. Some of them are cartographically accurate, others are, as Rand (1969) puts it, "pre-Copernican" in style. While most are schematic, a few are pictorial in style, resembling maps drawn by children (Ladd, 1970 ; Maurer and Baxter, 1972 ; Banerjee and Lynch, 1977 ; Lynch, 1977). Some are drawn in a "topological" manner, while others can be called "positional", as discussed by Appleyard (1970). No two maps—even of the same physical setting—are the same, in their content, scope or complexity. Each is a reflection of a personally relevant environment, endowed with individualized meanings and values (Lynch, 1960).

While the subject matter of style and mode of representation is fascinating, its link to policy application may be somewhat remote. Besides the limits of space would not allow us to undertake a thorough analysis of these characteristics. Nevertheless we believe that the way maps are drawn can give poignant hints about the ways people construct the residential area. Thus the Venice resident who showed just the intersection of Lincoln Boulevard and Superba Avenue (Fig. 7.12) must conceptualize the residential area very differently, than the Palos Verdean who shows the entire peninsula, or the Bel Air resident who draws the entire section of the city stretching from West Los Angeles to the Civic Center in downtown Los Angeles (see Fig. 7.13). It is not just a matter of size and territorial definition—which we have already reported—but also the content and configuration. In the following text we will present some of the basic categories of constructs of the residential environment as apparent in these maps. These categories are interpretive, and to some extent, speculative.

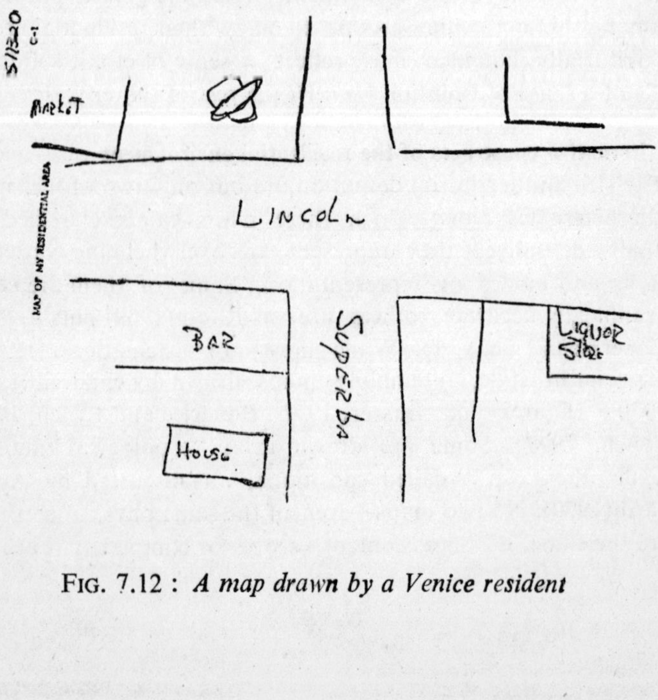

FIG. 7.12 : *A map drawn by a Venice resident*

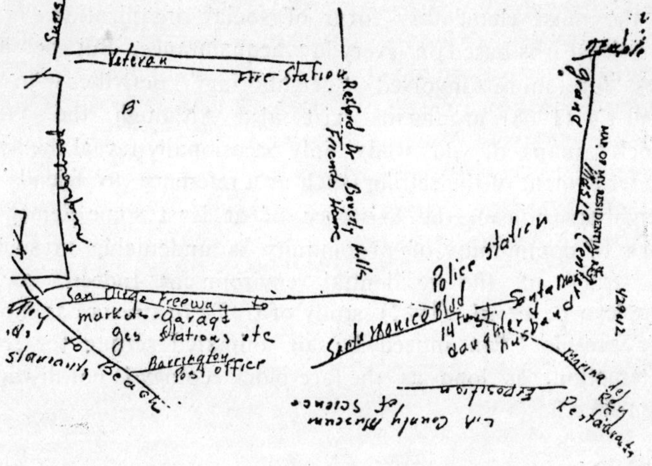

FIG. 7.13 : *A map drawn by a Bel Air resident*

Residential areas as the physical settings

A great many maps are simply carefully drawn replicas of the objective environmental settings. Main street network, topographical features, man-made adaptations, generalized land use political jurisdiction and the like are all carefully noted in these maps. How the setting is actually used may not be immediately apparent. Environmental affects may not be readily transmitted. Indeed the physical setting for these people may just be a passive backdrop, a neutral background which is largely inconsequential in their daily acts. It is entirely possible that the "place" realm is not relevant nor significant, even though they are aware of the physical setting itself (cf. Webber, 1964).

The face-block community

This category is taken from Suttles' (1973) schema of socially constructed communities. Many of the residential area maps in our study are essentially representations of the "face-block" environment. Typically maps of this nature encompass an area no larger than a block or two, or an intersection. Some of these maps are full of intimate physical details—traffic lights, bus stop and benches, trees, houses, street lights and the like. According to Suttles (1973) a face-block community is the most elementary form of social organization ; in the very least it is based on everyday acquaintance. But possibilities for more involved "neighboring" activities,—to use Keller's (1968) argument—exist also. Although the "face-block" maps of our study only occasionally reveal the social underlayment of the setting (such as a reference to friends' or neighbors house), the existence of at least some elementary form of community of propinquity is undeniable in such a construct of the residential environment. Indeed, as the Appleyard, *et al.* (1981) study of traffic in streets has shown, the face-block can indeed be an animated setting for social interaction, as long as the face-block ecology is not disrupted by traffic flow.

The orbit

A great many of the residential area maps simply suggest what Anslem Strauss (1961) has described as the "orbit" of activities of urban residents. Most of these orbits are local, and part of the "home range". A few are more extensive and seemingly cover the entire range of activity settings that comprise one's larger city- or region-wide action space. The map drawn by the Bel Air resident (see Fig. 7.14) falls in this latter category. Typically the "orbit" maps are open and not framed by territorial boundaries. Dominant features of these maps are networks of streets linking various physical settings and places. Indeed these maps can be seen as a constellation of the most significant, and overlapping "behavior circuits", as discussed by Perin (1972).[11]

In Grady Clay's (1973) language these maps can be seen as a collection of "beats"—the familiar travel routes, or the locus of everyday activities in time and space.

The enclave

Finally, the last model of residential constructs can be best described as an "enclave". Perhaps the most distinctive feature of these maps is that all of them have a very strict sense of boundary. The authors of these maps seem to know precisely where his or her residential area ends and begins. These maps seem to convey a clear sense of what is inside and what is outside. It would appear that the authors have a very clear sense of when he is entering or leaving their residential area. In these cases pervasive fear, anxious alienation and rampant xenophobia may heighten the perceived need or territorial enclosure and boundedness, and may be particularly true for the residents of the minority "ghetto". But when this sense of boundedness appears also in some of the maps in the upper and middle income area, it may suggest still another reason for these enclosures. In this case it may stem from the "need of belongingness" as suggested by Maslow (1954). Here the search for a spatial identification may merge with the need for social and group identity.

SUMMARY AND CONCLUSIONS

In this paper we have attempted to explore how people perceive and image their residential environment ; and if variabilities in these images can be explained by social and physical factors. In seeking answers to these questions we have primarily focused on the mental representations or "cognitive maps" of the physical place. Image, we have argued, is part and parcel of the system of facts and values that mediate our preferences and satisfactions related to places where we live. It has also been our premise that how one images the environment is an important documentation of how one uses the environment.

Initially we have concentrated largely on the collective images of various localities to interpret what physical form features constitute the residential environment. And these maps have suggested that the elements of the movement system—streets, freeways – are the key reference systems people use in identifying their residential area. Other elements of the environment—natural site features, buildings, etc.—only play a secondary role in these cognitive maps.

There are however some invariant features in the collective residential area images. Schools, fire stations, police stations, parks and playgrounds are mentioned commonly enough to make them a legitimate component of the residential environment. These public facilities are generally considered as important service functions of a neighborhood (APHA, 1950). However, outside of a cursory acknowledgement of the need for a neighborhood shopping area or center, commercial land uses have largely been ignored in the idealized model of a neighborhood unit. Yet, our maps show that such commercial establishments—super markets, gas stations, drug stores, quick-order restaurants, drive-in snack shop, etc. are all part of the essential "life-line" that supports a residential area, and as a result appear as important components of the residential area.

We have also seen that the personal constructs of the residential area vary greatly among individual to individual and between social groups. We have attempted to show such difference by concentrating on two attributes of the residential area map—size and territorial definition. It also appears that in terms of size, only low income residents are more likely to show an area of less than ½ mile radius, which is considered optimal according to the neighborhood unit formula. The territorial identity—another criterion recommended in the neighborhood unit formula—is more prevalent in the non-white (with the exception of middle income Hispanics) maps than the white ones. It would thus seem that some of the formula prescribed in the neighborhood unit formula may still have some validity for the low income, and minority groups, even though the model population for the neighborhood unit formula was presumed to be middle income white families with children. On the other hand, the prescriptions for the size and possible territorial boundaries may not be all that relevant for many middle and upper income respondents.

It is also apparent that there is no single definition or construct of the residential environment. The maps reflected a wide variety demonstrating the many different ways it can be conceptualized. We have been able to extract four most obvious and basic types of these maps. These suggest that the residential area may just mean a physical setting to some ; to others it may amount to a setting characterized by propinquity at the scale of the face-block ; still others may consider the residential area essentially comprising of the relevant behavior settings and familiar routes of travel ; and finally, it may mean just a well-delineated spatial enclave that symbolizes security and socio-spatial affiliation.

All these reflect the variety of perception, image, and use, that residents can hold. Taken collectively, they caution against attempts by designers and standard setters to mold this perception, image, and use to fit some preconceived image of the designer or standard setter. This is not to say, however, that many of the features in the physical residential environment are not also salient to the inhabitants. They are. Time and again, the respondents identified the very aspects of their residential area that planners and designers also think are important. But the way the respondents put these separate aspects together into a coherent image—the variety of these images—suggest that the designer should include these aspects in their design, but not necessarily attempt to dictate the way the parts will be put together by the inhabitants. The "package" that each of us puts together is based on a complexity, upon a sufficient variety of personal experience and behavior, on the stage in the family cycle and ethnic background, on the income and other aspects, many of which the designer can never know. It is futile, therefore to try to impose the packaged product. It is very important, however, to provide a variety of items in the "kit" so that the inhabitants themselves can construct a rich and rewarding package.

FOOTNOTES

1. Six physical attributes of the neighborhood were specified in detail : (Perry, 1929) :

   (a) *Size* : It should be sufficient to support an elementary school. Although actual area might vary according to population density, 1/4 to 1/2 mile radius was seen as the optimal dimension based on maximum walking distance for elementary school children.

   (b) *Boundaries* : To be defined by arterial streets to reduce penetration by through-traffic.

   (c) *Open Spaces* : Adequate parks and recreation areas to serve the residents.

   (d) *Local Shops* : Shopping areas to serve the area should be placed on arterial boundary streets.

(e) *Institution Sites* : Schools, community centers, churches should be centrally placed around a commons or a core.

(f) *Internal Street System* : The internal street network should be designed to discourage through traffic.

2. A stratified sampling design was developed to interview seven different population groups : upper income white ; middle income white ; middle income black ; middle income Hispanics ; lower income white ; lower income black ; and lower income Hispanics. This sampling scheme allowed us to test effects of income and race/ethnicity. Within each of the population groups quota was established for three stages of family cycle : households with children ; households without children ; the elderly. For each of the seven population groups, a minimum of two or a maximum of four different, widely separated geographic areas were chosen within the Los Angeles county.

   Tentative survey areas were picked after first determining relatively homogeneous areas from the preliminary returns of 1970 census, and where necessary, after discussions with persons knowledgeable about the County. Following this tentative identification, a field check was made and the final survey areas were more determined.

   Potential households in the areas were picked at random from street address lists and screened as to eligibility. If determined as eligible, the member of the household to be interviewed (those members over 16 years old) was selected using a set of randomly generated numbers.

   The interviews were done in two phases—in the Spring of 1972, and again in the Spring of 1974. Interviews were conducted in twenty-two different neighborhoods.

   The sampling rigor was violated repeatedly for the two low income minority groups, because of practical difficulty of obtaining willing respondents. It is for this reason the results from the last two groups will have to be treated with some caution.

   The survey instrument covered many substantive areas of inquiry—perception and evaluation, cognitive mapping, satisfaction, trade-off preferences, time budget and activity patterns. Here we are only reporting on the perception aspect.

3. These represent a selected set of maps from seven different locations. Space would not permit us to present all twenty-two residential area maps.

4. Lynch (1960), has proposed five basic elements of the city image : paths ; edges ; districts ; nodes : and landmarks. *Paths* are usually channels of movement, familiar routes of travel. *Edges* are lateral references that define, frame or "close off" an area. *Districts* are "medium to large sections" of the city with some common, identifying features. *Nodes* are points in space, a concentration of activities, or a convergence of paths. *Landmarks* are reference points of identity in the city.

5. The low income residents have been consistently less articulate, communicative and responsive to most of our questions. This is not unusual. Other researchers have spoken of this type of response variability among different social and cultural groups. See Karan, Bladen and Singh (1980), and Evans (1980).
6. This contrast is reminiscent of similar contrasting public images of the city of Los Angeles as elicited from residents of different neighborhoods in a survey conducted by the staff of the Los Angeles City Planning Department (See Orleans, 1973).
7. The fact that all Watts respondents were drawn from a public housing project may have something to do with this highly shrunken concept of the residential space. However, the average size of the Slauson (the other low income black neighborhood) area maps was also quite small, only three-sixteenth of a mile in radius.
8. Cf. end note 1, and also APHA (1960) for details of these standards.
9. Admittedly, we are not quite comparing the same things. *Planning the Neighborhood* (APHA, 1960), spoke of the neighborhood unit while we measured the size of the respondents' residential area. It is entirely possible that "neighborhood" may imply a different level of conceptualization, involving a different spatial configuration than "residential area". For example, it is possible that spatial boundaries of a neighborhood are dictated by the location of friends' or relatives' homes, or spatial correlates of one's relevant social milieu, whereas the residential area may essentially reflect ones residential action space.
10. While our sampling aim was to select respondents from socially homogeneous settings, it was difficult to meet in the case of middle income Hispanic groups. The locations from where they were chosen, while containing the most significant concentration of this population in the region, were not as homogeneous as other sample locations. In a way, it reflects the fact that with rising income Hispanics have been able to assimilate more easily into integrated neighborhoods than the blacks.
11. Perin (1972) defines "behavior circuit" as follows : "The things, that people do at the widest compass are *behavior streams* or *activities*, such as recreation or work. These in turn are separable into units which I call *behavior circuits*, differentiated by specific purpose . . . . By behavior circuit I mean to denote both the movement and the completion integral to tasks, errands, recreation, work, visiting, and so on . . . what behavior circuit implies is an anthropological ergonomics, tracking people's behavior through the fulfillment of their everyday purposes at the scale of the room, the house, the block, the neighborhood, the city, in order to learn what resources—physical and human—are needed to support, facilitate or enable them" (pp. 77-78).

REFERENCES

American Public Health Association, Committee on the Hygiene of Housing, 1960, *Planning the Neighborhood*, Chicago : Public Administration Service.

Appleyard, D., 1970, "Styles and Methods of Structuring a City", *Environment and Behavior*, 2 : 100-116.

Appleyard, D. 1976, *Planning a Pluralistic City*, Cambridge, MA : MIT Press.

Appleyard, D., et al., 1981, *Liveable Streets*, Berkeley : The University of California Press.

Banerjee, T., and Lynch, K., 1977, "On People and Places : A Comparative Study of the Spatial Environment of Adolescence", *Town Planning Review*, 48 : 105-115.

Boulding, Kenneth, 1956, *The Image : Knowledge in Life and Society*, Ann Arbor : The University of Michigan Press.

Carr, S., 1967, "The City of the Mind" in W.R. Ewald (ed.) *Environment for the Man*, Bloomington : Indiana University Press.

Clay, G., 1973, *Close-Up : How to Read American Cities*, New York, Praeger.

de Jonge, D., 1962, "Images of Urban Areas : Their Structure and Psychological Foundations", *Journal of the American Institute of Planners*, 28 : 268-276.

Downs, R.M., and Stea, D., 1973, *Image and Environment : Cognitive Mapping and Spatial Behavior*, Chicago : Aldine.

Evans, G., 1980, "Environmental Cognition", *Psychology Bulletin*, 88 : 259-287.

Gulick, J., 1963, "Images of an Arab City", *Journal of the American Institute of Planners*, 29 : 179-197.

Isaacs, R., 1948, "The Neighborhood Theory", *Journal of the American Institute of Planners*, 14.

Karan, P.P., Bladen, W.A., and Sing, G., 1980, "Slum Dwellers' and Squatters' Images of the City", *Environment and Behavior*, 12 : 81-100.

Keller, S., 1967, *The Urban Neighborhood*, New York : Random House.

Ladd, F., 1970, "Black Youths View Their Environment : Neighborhood Maps", *Environment and Behavior*, 2 : 74-99.

Lee, T., 1968, "Urban Neighborhood as a Socio-Spatial Schema", *Human Relations*, 21 : 241-288.

Lynch, Kevin, 1960, *The Image of the City*, Cambridge : The M.I.T. Press.

Lynch, K., (ed.) 1977, *Growing Up in Cities*, Cambridge, MA : M.I.T. Press.

Maslow, A.H., 1954, *Motivation and Personality*, New York : Harper Bros.

Maurer, R., and Baxter, J.C., 1972, "Images of the Neighborhood and City among Black, Anglo and Mexican-American Children", *Environment and Behavior*, 4 : 351-388.

Miller, G.A., Galenter, E., and Pribam, K.A., 1960, *Plans and the Structure of the Behavior*, New York : Holt & Co.

Orleans, P., 1973, "Differential Cognition of Urban Residence : Effects of Social Scale on Mapping" in R. Downs and D. Stea (eds.) *Image and Environment*, Chicago : Aldine.

Perin, C., 1972, *With Man in Mind*, Cambridge, MA : M.I.T. Press.

Perry, C., 1929, "The Neighborhood Unit, a Schema for Arrangement for the Family-Life Community" in *Neighborhood and Community Planning*, Regional Plan of New York and Its Environs, New York, pp. 22-140.

Rand, G., 1969, "Pre-Copernican Views of the City", *Architectural Forum*, Vol. 131.

Sims, W., 1973, *Neighborhoods : Columbus Neighborhood Definition Study*, Columbus, Ohio.

Strauss, A., 1961, *The Images of the American City*, New York : The Free Press of Glencoe.

Suttles, G., 1973, *The Social Construction of Communities*, Chicago : The University of Chicago Press.

Walsh, D., Krauss, I., and Regnier, V., 1981, "Spatial Ability, Environmental Knowledge, and Environmental Use : The Elderly" in L. Liben, A. Patterson and N. Newcombe (eds.) *Spatial Representation and Behavior Across the Life Span*. New York : Academic Press.

Webber, M., 1964, "The Urban Place and the Nonplace Urban Realm" in M. Webber et al. (eds.), *Exploration into Urban Structure*, Philadelphia : University of Pennsylvania Press.

Wilmott, P., 1967, "Social Research and New Communities", *Journal of the American Institute of Planners*, 32 : 387-397.

EIGHT

HERMANN ZINN

INTERRELATIONSHIPS BETWEEN HOUSING ENVIRONMENT AND SOCIAL BEHAVIOUR

DURING the last 20 years research on the interrelationships between the built environment and social behaviour has gradually emerged as a new field of scientific study. There are primarily two motivations behind this development : the first derives from the criticism which is being generally levelled at urbanism as a way of life, and is in fact the desire to test the frequently expressed supposition that there is a causal relationship between certain characteristics of urban living patterns and certain social phenomena such as crime rates, and suicide, for example. The second motivation arises from the necessity to gain some insight into the future needs of different social groups and what requirements urban development and housing will have to fulfil.

Thus far, man-environment research has been mainly fundamental research, however recent years have seen considerable efforts to obtain scientifically based data for practical planning purposes. With this in view, methods were developed to observe and classify the reactions of the users to different types of housing environment, and mathematical models designed to simulate future behaviour patterns and housing needs, the basic idea of researchers and sponsors alike being that such a procedure ought to enable them to arrive at housing environments tailored to the needs of the inhabitants in which the latter would show the desired reactions of evident satisfaction, and there would be no deviant behaviour patterns due to the housing environment.

Have these expectations in fact been fulfilled ? There is no simple answer to this question for we are facing a rather paradoxical situation : on the one hand the modern mass housing projects which have come into being in recent decades (with increasing scientific participation) are being devastatingly criticized by some experts and in mass media, while on the other the construction companies can point to the results of numerous user surveys which reflect a high degree of need satisfaction among the occupants. Again, the findings of such surveys are now often dismissed by social scientists on the grounds that they are irrelevant or misleading. Man-environment research is still quite incapable of resolving this state of affairs, while recently doubts have increased as to whether the approaches and methodology it has employed thus far are really adequate. It is our own impression that so far research and practical planning alike have had only an inadequate understanding of the problems involved, a too one-sided notion of the user and his interrelationship with his physical environment. Our misgivings have grown in the course of our analysis of a large volume of research material on the interrelationships between the built environment and social behaviour.

We found that in most of the research work undertaken to date the relationship between man and his environment has been regarded as being merely equivalent to a straightforward stimulus-response type of system. Man is depicted as an organism with relatively invariable behaviour patterns which are either biologically determined or else acquired in the process of socialization, and largely static needs. It is assumed that man is by no means an autonomous being with the freedom of choice to determine his relationship with his environment, but rather that he behaves largely reactively in response to the stimuli of his social and physical environment to which he is more or less passively subjected. According to this approach therefore, man learns by positive and negative sanctions to adapt to environmental constraints. The main object of this research which – intentionally or unintentionally follows the tradition of behaviourism—is consequently to determine by means of observation, standardized interviews or experiments, what rules there may be in the interplay of ecological variables and behavioural variables. Now we are not going to dispute the fact that a large part of human behaviour is actually ruled by fixed sets of social norms and apparently runs "automatically" along fairly well-defined lines—and it is also clear that a knowledge of these processes is of very great importance for any kind of environmental planning. In our view, however, any research which only deals with this one aspect of social action does not cover the whole picture and therefore cannot be expected to supply a full basis for planning.

This is particularly true of research work which—as is often the case—does not explicitly indicate the author's own understanding of man-environment relationships. This category includes for example the many system-theory-oriented, often very complex methodological studies in which procedures to determine the activities, wishes, and needs of the users of the built environment are developed or tested. What has been found in the case of standardized sociological opinion surveys and the more recent experimental psychology also applies to very many of these pieces of research, viz. that usual interview or experimental set-up forces the interviewed or tested person into a role excluding any open dialogue with the researcher about motives for certain verbal or non-verbal expressions of behaviour. The experimental set-up in fact tends to filter out as irrational any deviant behaviour, subjective comments or perhaps counter-questions on the part of the subject or interviewee. Largely as a result, therefore, of the research methods currently in vogue, the potentially large spectrum of everyday human action in the empirical findings appears reduced to the types of uni-dimensional responses found among animals.

It seems that there are some fundamental barriers which prevent the "behaviour-theory-oriented" approach from regarding the observed behaviour as subjectively motivated and subjectively meaningful social action since it considers subjectivity to be unscientific. We consider one implication of this particularly doubtful, namely that this theory disregards the fact that man need by no means accept his social and physical environment as he finds it, but instead can criticize, question, and change that environment. And indeed reality is full of examples of how users of the built environment utilize the scope allowed them, in order to manipulate their environment to suit their spontaneous needs, and in doing so to look for new forms of self-expression. And fortunately they also succeed again and again, even where they do not appear to have any scope, in acting in a way which is contrary to the expected trends, much to the vexation of the planners.

And this kind of experience emphasizes the importance of another kind of approach (we call it "action theory" approach) which stresses the active function of human behaviour. As against the determinist model of a stimulus-response system, it comes up with the idea of a dialectic relationship, *i.e.* of an active interrelationship between man and his environment. Here man is considered to acquire a repertoire of more or less differentiated cognitive, moral and linguistic abilities which in principle put him in a position to act autonomously and influence his environment in a constructive manner. These capabilities enable him to adapt to his physical and social environment and to social constraints, not blindly, but in full possession of his critical faculties and, furthermore, to set himself apart from his environment and confer upon it a certain individuality. The "action theory" approach therefore presupposes in principle, if perhaps only in an "Ideal-Typus" the existence of a fundamental human inclination to interact with the environment, both social and physical, to gain control over it and change it, and to find some self-expression in the fruits of this activity.

To what extent this basic impulse is actually detectable in the everyday behaviour of contemporary people of different social groups, is of course a second question which is largely dependent on the particular societal conditions. The "action theory" approach is therefore at least in this field of research more a postulate which is derived from a certain socio-political position. Nor do we know whether the basic impulse which it postulates, *i.e.* an active interchange with the environment, necessarily refers equally to the physical and the social environment. We might however suppose that the chance to find identity and satisfaction in the products of one's own work, which varies very widely among different social groups, also has some influence on the relationship between these groups and their physical environment in general and their housing environment in particular.

However, since the term "alienation" has largely been employed exclusively in connection with the relationship between man and his working environment, there are only very vague hypotheses in existence today regarding the problem of man's alienation from his housing environment, and the interrelationships between the housing and working environments.

The contrast between the two approaches we have just discussed and which we consider to be the crux of the matter, could be dismissed as merely a quarrel between two rival ideologies, if it did not have immediate practical consequences for the planning of the built environment. Any planner oriented toward the "behaviour theory" model will be looking primarily for an environment which is tailored as closely as possible to certain need and behaviour patterns, and the necessarily inflexible programmes for using the dwelling space developed from such patterns. The main problem is then how to cater for the empirically determined needs in a space utilization programme which is feasible from the constructional point of view, taking financial and legal restrictions into consideration. The "action theory" model, on the other hand, rejects inflexible building programmes of that kind which only permit certain use patterns. It is oriented towards the principle of the maximum freedom of choice for the user, which means that the latter's ability and willingness to choose between alternative types of behaviour and action in the built environment should as little restricted as possible. It aims at constructional and organizational forms which give the user the opportunity to manipulate his environment gradually to suit his own needs, in a manner which has not thus far been ascertainable in concrete terms, and in the course of the utilization process, to develop new needs—in short, at letting him be as completely in control of his environment as possible. It must be added here that direct participation of residents-to-be in the planning processes, which is so often advocated nowadays, is not only very difficult to achieve in reality as the future dwellers are often still largely unknown, but is also not in itself sufficient for the "action theory" requirements to be met, if the actual planning is not at the same time directed at achieving freedom of utilization and a product which can be constantly changed.

The practical consequences from the point of view of the built environment can perhaps be illustrated, in a somewhat simplified manner, by comparing different types of settlement. In our opinion it can be demonstrated that the inhabitants of settlements which consist mainly of terrace houses, or other forms of high density, low-rise housing, have, also as tenants, considerable scope for action and decision-making, and thereby for shaving and modifying their housing environment as an expression of their individual identity. In striking contrast to this appear to us to be the bureaucratic constraints, regulations and behavioural restrictions which are imposed upon many of the occupants of just as "densely" built dwellings in high-rise mass housing projects.

Whether or not advantage is actually taken of any scope which exists for action and decision-making is—as we were able to show in our study—dependent on a whole series of other factors, only some of which are known. One factor of particular importance here is obviously the legal status of the user. Someone who owns his dwelling, or is an occupier with a long-term lease, and who can be sure that he will never be forced to leave his housing environment against his will, is much more prepared to develop his own initiative in shaping his environment and put this into effect, than someone else who only regards his dwelling as a temporary residence or must bear in mind that he may have to change his environment one day without having any say in the matter.

We have made these and other, similar findings in our study, mentioned above, of the interrelationships between the built environment and social behaviour. In it we have treated recent research on territorial behaviour, man's perception of his physical environment, development of abilities for action in the built environment, historical changes in living habits, socio-spatial behaviour patterns and forced relocations, as well as with the results of housing experiments in which the residents were given more scope for action. In what follows we will touch upon two sets of questions taken more or less at random from this study.

In analogy to the term used in animal ethology, "territorial behaviour" refers to a general claim to the possession and use of a certain spatial territory made by human individuals or groups. Here we are using the concept of territoriality in a wider sense however, to include too the research into "personal space", "distancing", and privacy, as well as into the effects of limited privacy under crowded conditions. Like most animal species, man too likes to stake out certain physical domains which others may not enter without the owner's permission. The most familiar example of this is the inviolability of man's home and of his "private sphere" in general. Over and above this, every individual has a series of specially protected territories of his own, including his own "body territory". If the control over, and autonomy in, this territory becomes limited, as can be the case in rooms occupied by too many people, the individual may experience a sense of being "crowded", which is frequently accompanied by stress reactions, and in the extreme case can lead to emotional disorders. Human being, moreover, maintain characteristic minimum distances to others of their own kind, as animals do, which vary from one culture to another, but which are generally speaking greater between strangers meeting in public than they are in a group of people who know each other, and which are least of all in the case of personal and intimate relationships. Numerous empirical studies have already been made concerning all these questions.

But what is the function of human territorial behaviour ? We cannot concern ourselves here with the very simplified interpretations which have been formulated from an observation of animal behaviour and assumed without further ado to apply to human relationships as well. Instead we want to refer back to the drive in man, already described, to interact with his environment, to his efforts to integrate himself with his environment on the one hand, and on the other to assert his individuality and seek ways of self-expression. These interactions between the individual and society always involve the risk that either the individual autonomy perishes and the relationship ends in subjugation and oppression, or conversely, that society suffers from a lack of consent, sense of responsibility and participation among its member. This is where the personal territories in the built environment seem to have a stabilizing influence. The security of having a territory of his own may make it easier for the individual to develop the autonomy and critical distance which is necessary if the socialization process is to be successful, *i.e.* allow both individual aptitudes and abilities, and society as a whole, to develop freely.

This means that the private "free space" of an individual territory would not be primarily a place of fearful retreat from society, but rather a base which would give the individual more scope for interactions of all kinds, increase his freedom to take up any contacts he chooses, intensify or again possibly reduce them, and allow him more control over how he will appear to others, and whom he will permit to come closer to himself. The feeling of being crowded in densely populated places would be a warning signal that the individual was threatening to lose his ability to control his own interactions with his environment and his freedom to behave in an alternative manner. We feel that this "territorial" need in man to have autonomous control over a piece of living space of his own has probably increased rather than decreased in the course of human history, as social relationships became more complex and more difficult for the individual to comprehend, and the number of real possibilities open to him to express himself through his work decreased. Our analysis of the change in living habits in the course of history has therefore led us to be skeptical rather than anything else of the chances of experimental living patterns which aim at having the small family unit give way to "communal" or other "communicative" forms of living.

In another section of our study, which we can also only touch upon briefly here, we dealt with the development of abilities to act, *i.e.* with the problem of whether and how a certain physical environment can help the individual to develop an active rather than a reactive relationship with his environment, both physical and social. To date this question has been studied from a very specific angle viz. the case of the development of logical, spatial thinking and perception, and "spatial intelligence", *i.e.* the ability to orientate oneself actively in one's environment. Piaget in his psychology of child development has found out that the development of spatial thinking in the child takes place in several stages.[2] Each stage builds upon the achievements of the preceding one, and the ability to interpret, apply and process what is perceived increases from one stage to the next. At all these stages of development, the possibility of direct interaction with concrete objects and forms of its spatial environment is enormously important for the child. According to Piaget, the perception of the spatial environment is never simply an inference of the properties of the objects, but instead always action directed at the objects.

The more abundant, complex and contradictory the experiences of early childhood in the interaction with the immediate surroundings, which have been amassed and processed to rules, the more finely differentiated and effective the "programme" of control functions can develop in the nervous system. If, on the other hand, the child has been prevented from interacting freely with its surroundings, this whole development process is thrown out of gear, since according to Piaget, perception fails if there is no action. It is only once the different stages of development have been successfully completed that the "adult" concept of space gradually comes into being, which finally allows the individual to orient himself abstractly (*i.e.* without the need for real manipulative interaction with objects and spaces) in his environment, to form an image or model of reality in his mind, and grasp the world mentally without still having to grasp it physically, as a child would have to.

These findings lead to a number of interesting conclusions and questions which have important implications for practical building. It looks, for example, as if children are dependent in their first few years not only – as is known—on close and stable relationships with their social environment ; but also on similar relationships with their physical environment.

On the basis of the studies carried out thus far, we may assume that not only is the development of intelligence and logical thinking directly dependent on the conditions in the physical environment – in fact the entire process of the child's socialization, *i.e.* of its training to fulfil and accept as its own the expectations, values, and standards of adult society is affected by its living conditions. Initial conclusions have already been drawn for the practical planning and building of houses and dwellings suitable for families with children.[3]

It is an open question what the consequence is, from this point of view, of the generally weak position of the user in rental housing today, who has scarcely any influence on how his physical environment is built, designed or modified. To what extent does this situation prevent adolescents from acquiring a fully developed, abstract concept of space ? Can it also perhaps cause the spatial intelligence of adults, too, to atrophy to some extent ? We do know, after all, that adults from socially under-privileged groups in many cases never achieve adequate mastery of the highest level of spatial intelligence, viz. formal operational thinking. Can we conclude from this that in such groups the need for an environment which can be physically manipulated is particularly marked, and of greater importance than in the case of adults from other social groups with a completely developed spatial intelligence ?

We cannot go into a detailed discussion of these very topical questions in this paper. Summing up, we can however say that both the research work into space-related, "territorial" interaction processes, and the insight gained into the part played by the physical environment by the development of abilities to act, seem to confirm what we said above about there being a fundamental need for the individual to develop an active, autonomous user-relationship with his built environment. Where such autonomy exists—and this depends on economic and social conditions and on personal attitudes and interests—the spatial environment is in fact used in the most diverse ways for the fulfilment of needs of all kinds. It would seem to us therefore to be justifiable to infer that it would be not only impossible, but quite undesirable too, to look for an immutable, "ideal" dwelling or "ideal" environment tailored closely to supposedly static, fixed "basic needs", for an environment of that kind would be more likely to limit, rather than widen, the scope of the inhabitants.

For this reason we cannot be persistent enough in emphasizing the importance of planning principles such as variability, flexibility and individualization, the purpose of which is to offer the widest possible range of alternatives to the user, to ensure that the physical environment is constantly adaptable to changing needs and interests, and to give the individual scope for personal shaping of his physical environment. Our experience goes to show however that these principles are by no means fulfilled if for example a builder creates "flexibility" by virtue of the presence of movable partitions inside individual apartments. We would attach greater importance to experiments which involve the immediate vicinity of the housing environment—above and beyond the apartment itself—as a whole, and try to provide for greater scope for the individual within this more "semi-private" domain. There are many older settlements, which were built, without any claim to originality, generally in the form of high density, low-rise housing, and which can be looked upon today as outstanding examples of an interaction between inhabitants and their built environment which "works", even if they may, in other respects, fall short of modern urban standards. If research aims at finding out what physical and social, economic and legal criteria can lie behind the "functioning" of such older settlements, and which therefore ought to be applied in the planning of new settlements, it will not be able to avoid becoming involved more directly in planning and building processes than it has generally done so far. Without first-hand experience of experimental projects, it will scarcely be possible to check the relevance of "desk research" theories, methods and proposals.

FOOTNOTES

1. The paper presented here is based on the following publication: Institute Wohnen und Umwelt (E. Muhlich, H. Zinn, W. Kroning, I. Muhlich-Klinger): Expertise on interrelationships between housing environment and social behaviour, Darmstadt, 1976.
2. Piaget, J., and Inhelder, B.: *La representation de l'espace chez l' enfant*, Paris, 1947.
3. Baumann, R. and Zinn, H.: *Kindergerechte Wohnungen fur Familien*, Bern, 1973.

[illegible]

[illegible]

NINE

VINCENT B. ROBINSON AND LINDA C. ROBINSON

DIMENSIONS OF RESIDENTIAL DEVELOPER DECISION-MAKING IN A RAPIDLY URBANIZING REGION

INTRODUCTION

THE process of converting vacant land to residential use is the result of a chain of decisions made by various individuals or groups guided by their own incentives. Pre-development landowners impelled by pecuniary and personal motives to sell ; developers influenced by profit motives ; and household consumers seeking their own housing need and preferences are at the core of the process while realtors, financiers, public officials and other related professionals act as supporting agents (Kaiser and Weiss, 1969).

The lead role in the residential land development process is taken by the developer whose land purchase decision constitutes the locational commitment to develop residential housing units on a specific plot of land. Not only is the developer making an investment in the land, he is also the principal agent who will decide the type of development to build on the site, its size, density, and the rate at which his property will be converted from vacant parcels to residential packages (Kaiser and Weiss, 1969). Therefore it is the developer, who through his land purchase decision, is the primesculptor of spatial structure through the residential land development process.

THE PROBLEM

Although many studies have focused upon the importance of various locational factors in the developers lccational decision, few have studied developer attitudes in areas undergoing rapid land use change. The focus of this study is on residential land developer attitudes towards locational information in his operational environment. Although this focus is not unique in studies of developer decisionmaking, this study is undertaken in an area undergoing rapid urban development while anti-development pressures from public officials are escalating. The objective of this study is to identify and evaluate the major independent dimensions of the locational decision of residential developers in a rapidly urbanizing region.

METHODOLOGY

The study area

Geauga County in northeast Ohio is an area currently undergoing the pressures of urbanization. Located within the Cleveland S.M.S.A., Geauga County experienced a 32.4% rate of population growth between 1960 and 1970 which was the second largest growth rate in Ohio (Planning Associates, 1971). During 1977, Geauga County experienced a boom in proposed residential subdivisions totalling 2293 sublots on 6019 acres (Geauga County Planning Commission, 1977). Seventy-two major residential subdivisions were proposed to the Geauga County Planning Commission during this period compared with an average 5 to 10 proposals in previous years. The majority of the proposed subdivision activity is occurring in the western townships bordering the Cleveland suburbs ; however this activity is rapidly moving eastward.

Definitions

A residential developer is defined as an entrepreneur or member of a land development firm who issues the final approval to purchase land for a major residential subdivision. There is no distinction made between entrepreneurs or members of firms who engage in both subdividing are excluded.

A major subdivision is defined as any subdivision containing more than five lots fronting upon an existing street, or involving any new street easement of access or extension of public facilities. A major subdivision also requires that the landowner prepare a plat prior to Geauga County Planning Commission approval (Geauga County Planning Commission, 1977).

Data

Data for this study were obtained from a questionnaire distributed to residential land developers operating in Geauga County during 1977. The developers were identified from a list of proposed subdivisions compiled by the Geauga County Planning Commission and from the sketch plans and legal plats required by the subdivision review process. Of the 55 developers contacted, three were disqualified from the survey because they did not meet the criteria established in the definition of a residential land developer. Twenty-four questionnaires were returned establishing a return rate of 43 per cent.

The questionnaire instructed the developers to rank 21 physical, locational, socio-economic, political and financial variables according to their importance in the developer's decision to purchase a tract of land for residential development. The variables selected for the questionnaire were based upon those factors identified as important by developers in the investigations of Bourne (1976), Goldberg and Ullinder (1976), Rolph (1973), Kaiser and Weiss (1969) and upon knowledge of the study are's political, social and physical characteristics.

RESULTS

The major independent dimensions of the locational decision were identified by performing a principal axis factor analysis with varimax rotation. The technique is especially suited to this type of investigation for the following reasons :

1. It enables the researcher to untangle linear relationships of questionnaire data into distinct patterns.
2. It allows the researcher to make generalizations concerning the underlying influences on those relationships.
3. It can be used to uncover the basic underlying dimensions

of variation in group characteristics and behavior (Rummel, 1967).

The basic premise underlying the factor analytic model is that the correlation among the variables is a function of the influence of common factors. These common factors may be viewed as descriptive concepts summarizing the behavior of a set of interacting variables.

The outcome of the varimax rotation is that five factors were found, accounting for approximately 60 per cent of the variation in the data. Examination of the factor loadings provides the following factors (Table 9.1)

Cost

This most important factor reflects developer concern with various physical and institutional variables with influence cost (Table 9.1). Kaiser and Weiss (1971) note that zoning and topography may impact cost by influencing the number of lots derivable from a tract of land and the provision of streets, utilities, and dwelling units. Similarly, existing road accessibility and site amenities are considered in order to estimate, respectively, the layout of the subdivision and the costs necessary to enhance the amenity value of the site. The search for suitable land is costly in time and expense (Kenney, 1972). The availability of raw land suitable to the developer's needs may be viewed as a reflection of this concern since the availability of land influences its price.

Market location

The market location factor accounts for 16.5 per cent of the variation in the data. The variables loading heavily on this factor reflect developers' concern with finding an attractive location near a residential market where local authorities are receptive to the needs of the developer (Table 9.1).

The importance of cooperation in obtaining zoning variances is viewed as a measure of market entrance constraint. Market information from local businessmen and public officials is a self-explanatory variable. Importance of the proximity of land to employment, urban and shopping centers indicates that developers seek to delineate spatial housing markets which depend not only upon population and employment but also upon

TABLE 9.1 : **Results of the principal axis factor analysis**

Factor	Loading	Variable	Percentage Variance Explained	
			Ea. Factor	Cumulative
Cost	.83	Zoning at time of 1st consideration	19.12	19.12
	.79	Topographic char.		
	.73	Cost of raw land		
	.68	Site amenities		
	.61	Avail. of raw land		
	.50	Existing road access.		
Market Location	.77	Local auth. & zoning	16.46	35.58
	.76	Market info. from busi. men & public officials		
	.73	Prox. to employment		
	.64	Prox. to urban centers		
	.51	Prox. to shopping ctra		
	−.50	Social location & prestige		
	.45	Anticipated property taxes		
Public Utilities	.86	OEPA policy regarding central sewage collection & facilities	10.12	45.70
	.72	Avail. of public sewer & water service		
	.53	Local auth. & public utilities		
Marketability	.63	Rural character of	8.67	54.37
	.55	Improvement costs		
	−.54	Local auth. & public utilities		
	.50	Prox. to shopping		
	.45	Social location & prestige		
Land Suitability	−.61	Soil characteristics	6.06	60.43
	.61	Avail. of raw land		

Source : Authors' calculations.

income. Proximity to urban centers indicates size of market potential in terms of population. Proximity to employment centers indicates concern with the employment potential of an area. Concern with proximity to shopping centers is viewed as serving a dual role. In one sense it reveals a concern for the shopping behavior of potential residents, yet also indicates that developers use proximity to shopping centers as a rough measure of the income potential of an area.

Public utilities

The variables loading heavily on this factor are indicative of the developers' concern with infrastructure provided according to public policies (Table 9.1). Of interest is that none of the variables loading on this factor load highly on the cost factor. This suggests that developers operating in Geauga County are aware that public policies regarding public utilities may act as constraints which indirectly influence costs. The variables noted in the cost factor may influence the course of action that a developer can take subject to a public utilities constraint. For example, developers in Geauga County are aware that a sewer moratorium exists. They have a choice of providing some form of home waste disposal system, applying to the Ohio Environmental Protection Agency for a permit to install a private sewer and treatment plant or invest considerable time and expense to challenge the policy. Thus, the cost implications of the policy are indirect and may be evaluated independent of the direct cost therefore variably.

Marketability

This factor is labeled the marketability factor of the locational decision because the variables loading on this factor reflect those attributes which enhance the attractiveness of the site of the consumer (Table 9.1).

This cluster of variables is indicative of what developers consider important in marketing the site to the residential consumer. Rural character and proximity to shopping centers are exogenous factors beyond the developer's control whereas improvement costs reflect the endogenous factors of marketability which the developer controls.

Local authority cooperation in the extension of public utilities was found to load negatively on this factor. This inverse relationship suggests that public utilities are not an unimportant consideration in the developer's estimation of marketability. Kenney (1972) has noted that utilities appear important to the developer because they are recognized to be a prerequisite for development, yet they perceive consumers assuming utilities are provided and therefore are not important in consumer purchase-decisions.

Land suitability

The last factor, a bipolar factor, has been labeled the land suitability factor (Table 9.1). The factor is bipolar because of the large positive loading (.61) of the availability of raw land variable and the large negative loading (—.61) of the soil characteristics variable. Both of these variables relate to the physical characteristics of a site.

It appears that developers operating in Geauga County are concerned with the suitability of the raw land in terms of soil constraints and land availability. Therefore, land availability is viewed as an asset while soils are viewed as a constraint in estimating land suitability.

SIGNIFICANCE OF THE FINDINGS

In most studies of developer decision making, discussions of the importance of locational variables are conducted on the basis of independent variables. The findings of this study indicate that five major patterns of interrelationships exist among such variables.

The most important is the cost factor. The importance of this factor contradicts Kaiser and Weiss (1971) assertion that the effects of contextual, property, and developer characteristics on marketability and revenue serve to make cost considerations secondary. However, it supports Goldberg and Ullinder's (1976) conclusion that developers are primarily concerned with factors influencing costs, thus placing less emphasis on variables influencing revenue.

The structure of the market location factor suggests that market information is derived through assessment of the urban spatial structure and interaction with various decision makers. It supports Kenney's (1972) contention that the fact component in market analysis is weak and that developers rely upon information from local decision makers and the spatial structure to decrease their uncertainty. In addition, this study found that proximity to urban activities is important in the developer's locational decision. This substantiates the importance of locational characteristics noted in the works of Bourne (1976), Kaiser and Weiss (1971) and Rolph (1973). The social location and prestige variable loads negatively on this factor implying that it is not as important as the relative distance variable since it is a characteristic whose attributes can be assigned directly to site by the developer.

The public utilities factor is the only factor identified which relates directly to public policy. A possible explanation for this is that the provision of utilities is a prerequisite for development and may influence development costs. The results suggest that in the developer's preference space such variables cluster together to form an independent dimension of the locational decision.

The marketability factor is composed of variables which can enhance the attractiveness of the site to consumers. Although rural character is addressed in this factor, only one urban service variable (*i.e.* proximity to shopping) was identified. The presence of proximity to shopping centers on this factor suggests that developers view it as the sole urban service which aids them in estimating both marketability and market location. Other variables which load on this factor reflect those locational qualities which can be given to the site by the developer. The reliance on personal judgement as to what improvements are needed to enhance the social location and prestige of the site or the attractiveness of the site in general may increase the uncertainty of this investment decision.

The last factor reflects developer concern with the suitability of undeveloped land in terms of quality and quantity. It supports Bourne's (1976) findings that the availability of land is important in site selection and Kaiser and Weiss' (1971) observations that soils may act as a constraint. With particular reference to Geauga County where a sewer moratorium exists, soils are of importance since they must be suitable for waste disposal systems such as septic tanks. If sufficient land is available, developers may substitute land area to avoid soil constraints ; however, if land is scarce, developers may spend considerable time and expense providing waste-disposal systems to overcome this constraint.

Although there are similarities in the results of this study with those conducted in the Southern U.S. (Kaiser and Weiss, 1971 ; Kenney, 1972), Western U.S. (Rolph, 1973), and Western Canada (Goldberg and Ullinder, 1976), differences in the importance of some factors and variables are evident. Of particular interest is the general lack of importance exhibited by the variables (1) proximity to schools and (2) availability of equity capital. Equity capital may be considered a prerequisite for beginning the land search. Thus, equity capital would not be an important variable in the location decision per se. Previous studies have stressed the importance of proximity to schools as a locational criterion (Kaiser and Weiss, 1971 ; Kenney, 1972), however it is not of importance in any dimension of the locational decision of developers operating in Geauga County, Ohio.

Contrary to the findings of Kaiser and Weiss (1971), the cost factor proved more important than the marketability factor. The importance of shopping center location in both the market location and marketability factors contrasts with the unimportance of proximity to schools. Such a result is not suggested by other studies in the U.S. As suggested by Rolph (1973), the divergence of these results from other studies in the U.S. may be a function of the type of areas previously studied. Results of this study serve to emphasize the need for conducting developer behavior studies in a variety of geographical areas and the hazards of formulating generalizations based on the study of developer behavior in only a few geographic settings.

REFERENCES

Bourne, Larry S. "Urban Structure and Land Use Decisions". *Annals of the Association of American Geographers* 66 (1976) : 531-47.

Clawson, Marion. *Suburban Land Conversion in the United States : An Economic and Governmental Process.* Baltimore : Johns Hopkins Press, 1971.

Cleveland Plain Dealer 30 March 1977.

Geauga County Planning Commission. *Housing Analysis : A Study of Needs and Supplies in Geauga County.* Chardon : Geauga County Planning Commission, 1974.

Geauga County Planning Commission. "Major Subdivision Review". Chardon, Ohio : Geauga County Planning Commission, 1977 (mimeographed).

Goldberg, Michael A. and Ullinder, Daniel D. "Residential Developer Behavior 1975 : Additional Empirical Findings". *Land Economics* 52 (1976) : 363-69.

Kaiser, Edward J. "Locational Factors in a Producer Model of Residential Development." *Land Economics* 44 (1968) : 351-62.

Kaiser, Edward J. and Weiss, Shirley F. "Local Public Policy and the Residential Land Development Process". *Law and Contemporary Problems* 32 (1962) : 232-49.

Kaiser, Edward J., and Weiss, Shirley F. "Decision Agent Models of the Residential Development Process : A Review of Recent Research". *Traffic Quarterly* 23 (1969) : 597-630.

Kaiser, Edward J. and Weiss, Shirley F. "Public Policy and the Residential Land Development Process". *In Internal Structure of the City : Readings on Space and Environment.* Edited by Larry S. Bourne. New York : Oxford University Press, 1971.

Kenney, Kenneth B. "The Residential Developer and His Land Purchase Decision". Ph.D. dissertation, University of North Carolina, 1972.

Northeast Ohio Areawide Coordinating Agency, *Housing Element.* Cleveland : Northeast Ohio Areawide Coordinating Agency, 1978.

Planning Associates. *Comprehensive Plan : Housing Element, Geauga County.* Cleveland : Urban Research and Planning, Inc., 1971.

Rolph, E.S. *Decisionmaking by Residential Developers in Santa Clara County.* Santa Monica, California : Rand Corporation, 1973.

Rummel, R.J. "Understanding Factor Analysis", *Journal of Conflict Resolution.* Vol. 11 (1967), 448-51.

TEN

WILMER M. HARPER AND JOEL A. DIEMER

QUALITY OF LIFE ASSESSMENT
A Methodology for Intraregional Comparisons

INTRODUCTION

THE realization and maintenance of some minimum standard of living or quality of life (Q of L) is integral to the social welfare goals of virtually all contemporary societies. This is amply manifest in the actions of national, sub-national and local governments as they propose and initiate programs to reduce unemployment, improve public services, etc. However, with few exceptions the measurement of the efficiency of such programs in achieving improvements in perceived well-being and Q of L has been particularly difficult. Understandably this is often a particularly distressing situation for target groups and program administrators, not to mention responsible politicians. This is, of course, particularly true during periods of economic downturn when demands are highest and resources most scarce.

Most developed societies are entering what Angus Campbell has called the era of "psychological man". When researchers at the Institute for Social Research asked individuals "What does quality of life mean to you—that is, what would you say the overall quality of life depends on?", the following areas in order of frequency were reported : (1) economic security, (2) family life, (3) personal strengths, (4) friendships, (5) attractiveness of the physical environment [11, p. 4]. As society becomes more affluent and the general standard of living rises, economic values are not disappearing nor are they likely to do so. What is important, however, is the growing number of additional concerns, the number of people voicing these additional values, and their preparedness to make monetary and/or other economic sacrifices to achieve these values or changes.

It is conceivable that the problems encountered in the process of attempting effective resource allocations would be more easily dealt with if a measure which reflected differences in individual local and regional perceptions of well-being and Q of L were available. While methods for estimating the marginal contribution to quality of life from specific variables may be too imprecise for interpersonal comparison, the methodology appears sufficiently advanced to allow intergroup comparison of quality of life for the formulation of public policy that will impact unevenly on different groups.[1] The discussion that follows presents a methodology for integrating existing approaches to Q of L assessment to facilitate such comparisons.

MEASURES OF SOCIAL WELL-BEING

Economics, sociology, and psychology all point to potential and significant sources of variation in perceived quality of life. The issue then becomes, how may existing, but insufficiently robust measures be aggregated into a more comprehensive measure.

From the literature, four approaches were identified as appropriate for use in an attempt to build an operational QLI ; each approach has certain features which contribute to its attractiveness. These alternative approaches are discussed in order of their relationship to the individual's perception of his well-being and his environment.

Individual social well-being

The approach is utilized by Harper and Tweeten.[9] The approach uses established social indicator scales to derive an individual quality of life index (QLI). Derived from measures of individual social well-being, QLI is a relative measure of how the individual perceives his interaction with his socio-economic environment and thus his Q of L. QLI is then taken as the dependent variable in the development of a regression model. Model development is directed toward a theoretically acceptable model which will explain the variation observed in QLI. *A priori* relevant variables were taken to be: income, education, age, number of individuals in the family unit, geographical location of residence, race, sex, ratio of farm income to total family income, net worth, and a time trend variable. The procedure used to develop the QLI, the variables which were found to have significant coefficients, and the functional form derived are shown in Appendix A.

The social well-being approach has the intrinsic attractiveness of measuring the individual's perception of himself in his socio-economic environment and thus his perceived Q of L; however, as put forth, the model measures environmental impact on QLI only through the indirect influence of environment upon individual perception. The QLI model allows the evaluation of personal variables such as income, education, etc., but it does not have the capacity to directly evaluate environmental impacts on Q of L. Quality of school, public services, etc., may be critical to individual perception of Q of L in an area, but only to the extent that they alter perception of the self do they enter the QLI model. To serve adequately as a flexible, broad range policy tool, the QLI must be expanded to allow environment to directly enter the model.

Community preference function (CPF)

This approach was developed and tested by Diemer and McKean.[5] Individuals are assumed to derive an amount or level of satisfaction from their perception of and their interaction with the physical, social, and economic environment in which they live. The CPF approach measures the individual's satisfaction with his Q of L and then identifies those variables which account for a rating of satisfaction less than the maximum possible on a scale of 1 to 100 where 100 represents total satisfaction. The CPF score is then subtracted from 100 and used as the dependent variable in a regression model where the factors influencing dissatisfaction are taken as the independent variables.

The CPF approach provides a method, whereby, the rankings may be used to establish weights and priorities for those items which contribute to dissatisfaction, *i.e.*, lower Q of L. This prevents a common response from individuals who are relativcly satisfied with their Q of L from being considered equally with those of respondents who are relatively dissatisfied with their

Q of L. The theoretical framework for the CPF approach is presented in Appendix B.

Just as the QLI approach lacks environmental sensitivity, the CPF approach lacks self-perception considerations. The individual's perception of self and personal relationship to the socio-economic environment will directly influence the evaluation of those physical and socio-political factors which contribute to or lower perceived Q of L. An index which deals only with this issue may lead to policy measures which attack symptoms, not causes. This, in turn, may lead to short run solutions where one dissatisfaction is replaced by another.

Regional index (RI)

Two approaches may be identified which utilize a regional approach to the Q of L issue. The first approach relies upon secondary data to arrive at a regional ranking of counties or areas.[17] Weights are derived for counties based upon level of income, number of schools, medical doctors, etc. This approach is appealing in that the index or weighting scale may be generated at a relatively low cost, but it results in potential research bias in the selection of index components and has a tendency to include only those indicators which are readily available. A respondent oriented approach allows the individuals actually living in the areas under study to rank the various regions. Two alternatives may be used to develop a respondent oriented regional ranking. The method of paired comparisons[3, 6] in which respondents choose their preference from each possible pair of regions may be used. A ranking of the regions may then be determined and a scale value derived for each region. This scale value may then be used to determine a weighting for the regions. A second, respondent oriented approach, was developed by Coelen[4] and is based upon revealed preference analysis.[10, 15] The basic method of this approach is to assume that an index of community preference does, in fact, exist, that it is defined over the complete system, and that it may be interpreted with log normally distributed random errors. Individuals are to make paired comparisons of communities to determine best liked and least liked among alternatives available. These comparisons are aggregated to determine an implicit regional ranking.

A theoretical framework of the Coelen approach is presented in Appendix C.

CONCEPTUAL INTEGRATION

The three conceptual frameworks discussed above have certain similarities, but they also have certain aspects which are respectively unique. Combination of the concepts into an integrated system offers the potential for a more comprehensive and conceptually robust measure of perceived Q of L.

Social welfare functions and the concept of lexicographic ordering[7] are relevant to the construction of a quality of life index (QLI). Within a Q of L (utility) context, lexicographic ordering has the following meaning. Consider two sets of personal conditions, community services, *etc.* : $x^0 = (x_1^0,\ x_2^0, \ldots, x_n^0)$ and $x^1 = (x_1^1, x_2^1, \ldots, x_n^1)$. If QLI is the preference index function, then a regular ordering ranks QLI $(x^0) >$ QLI (x^1) if $x_1^0 \geq x_1^1$ for all i with the strict inequality holding for at least one of the x_i's. Lexicographic ordering, however, recognizes a hierarchy within the x_i's, *i.e.*, the components of the theoretical QLI are not taken to be equally important. If it is assumed that the subscripts indicate the order of importance for the components of QLI, then QLI $(x^0) >$ QLI (x^1) if $x_1^0 > x_1^1$ regardless of the relationship among the other x_i's, and if $x_1^0 = x_1^1$ then the evaluation must be based upon x_2. Viewed in this manner, lower components of the hierarchy are relevant only after the higher order components are satisfied.

The social well-being which the individual experiences is not, however, made up entirely of components which can be subjected to interval evaluation, comparison, and maximization. This is intuitively obvious for such things as age, education, sex, occupation, etc. It seems desirable, therefore, to develop a measure (QLI) which accommodates individual perceptions as determined by interaction with the socio-economic environment and to integrate this measure into a community wide measure which will allow policymakers to examine options. When a constrained situation within which the policymakers must operate is assumed, the application of the principles of lexicographic ordering come into play.

If the measure is to be more than a novelty to be relegated to academic exercises, it must be able to reflect weights within the context of the theory of economic welfare. Thus, if a measure's importance is comparable for all areas, a weighting measure must be available which will distinguish relative importance among areas or subsets of areas. Without this important characteristic, any QLI developed would have limited applicability for policymakers and planners at any level.

Simultaneous determinations : Within areas

The QLI and the CPF contain sufficient variables in common to suggest their ready integration into a comprehensive framework. The quantitative value of QLI is derived from measures of social well-being and these responses are assumed to be determined and/or be influenced by the individuals socio-economic environment and various personal characteristics. The value of CPF is derived from the individual's perception of the quality of his community and personal environment which are also influenced by various personal characteristics. In addition, it is hypothesized that the individual's perceived social well-being, which is measured directly by the QLI, will interact directly with how the individual perceives the environmental features of the CPF.

The following formulation is suggested as a possible conceptual integration :

$$C_j = F(X_1, X_2, \ldots, X_n) \qquad \text{(Step 1)}$$

$$CPF = \delta_1 + \delta_2 OCC + \delta_3 HOME + \sum_{j=1}^{n} \beta_j C_j + U_c \qquad \text{(Step 2)}$$

$$\begin{aligned} QLI = {} & \alpha_1 + \alpha_2 Y^* + \alpha_3 Y^{*2} + \alpha_4 ED^2 \\ & + \alpha_5 AGE + \alpha_6 AGE^2 + \alpha_7 AGEED \\ & + \alpha_8 N + \alpha_9 L + \alpha_{10} PERFARMY \\ & + \alpha_{11} CPF + U_q. \end{aligned} \qquad \text{(Step 3)}$$

where

C_j = community factors
X = concerns or community characteristics
OCC = occupation (seven of binary variables)
$HOME$ = homeowner (binary variable)
U_c = error for the CPF
Y^* and Y^{*2} = expected quarterly income and expected quarterly income squared, respectively
ED^2 = respondents years of education squared
AGE and AGE^2 = age of respondent and age of respondent squared, respectively
$AGEED$ = age education interaction term
N = number of individuals in the family unit
L = location of residence (binary variable)
$PERFARMY$ = ratio of farm to non-farm income
U_q = error term for the QLI

Conceptually, in step 1 the respondent would be allowed to indicate as many X_n's (concerns) as perceived to be significant. The responses for all respondents would then be aggregated into a number of somewhat homogeneous community factors (C_j's) which would be entered into the CPF. This aggregation would be accomplished through the use of factor analysis and a weighting of C_j components based upon the eigenvalues resulting from the factor analysis.

In step 2, the conceptual C_j's are incorporated into the model which estimates CPF. In the final step, the CPF is incorporated into the QLI. While somewhat involved, the three step procedure allows the estimation of QLI to take place with a minimum loss of underlying structural information.

Regional determinations

QLI, CPF, and their structural determinants provide information regarding those factors which appear to measurably affect Q of L within the individual community and those variables which are most likely to produce measurable changes for the individual. There is not, however, any information included in this development which allows the comparison of regions or zones within a region. It seems reasonable to assume, that once an individual accommodates within his value system the fact that he lives and will continue to live in a given area, certain of the potentially negative features of that area may no longer be considered. Thus, it would follow that an individual who would prefer to live in region A, but who lives in region B, may still score high on both QLI and CPF. For this reason, a feature must be incorporated into the overall system which allows a weighting or ranking of alternatives as perceived by all regional subsets of the total population. It is at this point that the RI concept enters consideration. Two methods appear to hold promise for this procedure. The RI conceptualization of Coelen has been identified in Appendix C. An alternative approach is to develop a ranking for regions (*e.g.*, planning districts) and another ranking for regional subsets (*e.g.*, urban areas) through the method of paired comparisons.[3, 6] Either of the scales could then be used to weight the QLI and/or CPF values from a region when policy decisions require that inter-regional or intra-regional comparisons be made.

Application of the QLI concept : An example

The potential applicability of an integrated quality of life framework to policy and planning decisions can be illustrated by example. The hypothetical data used relates to seven substate planning districts for the state of New Mexico in the south-western United States. The state itself is a relatively large geographical entity of approximately 31,524,696 hectares with three district scicio-ethnic groups : American, Indian, Hispanic and Anglo-American. As a result of the region's varied physiography, the population is distributed rather unevenly throughout the state with a number of district cultural concentrations evident. The QLI concept allows intraregional and intraurban comparisons which are relevant to such situations.

Assume that a mean QLI and CPF of 135 and 75, respectively, have been found for all of the sub-regional planning districts. If state planners are faced with the need to make comparative evaluations of projects or expenditures between any of the districts, additional information will be required. Assuming that a RI approach has been used to derive scale values for the districts, the respective QLI-CPF values may be weighted to compare the regions. If the scales accurately measure the perceived differences which the average individual experien-

TABLE 10.1 : **Hypothetical regional index (RI), mean quality of life index (QLI) values, mean community preference function (CPF) values, weighted me n quality of life index (QLI′) values and weighted mean community preference function (CPF′) values for the seven sub regional planning districts, 1979**

District	RI Scale Value	QLI	CPF	QLI'	CPF'
1	2.235	135	75	301.725	167.625
2	5.447	135	75	735.345	408.525
3	3.011	135	75	406.485	225.825
4	4.200	135	75	567.000	315.000
5	5.111	135	75	689.985	383.325
6	1.237	135	75	166.995	92.775
7	0.000	135	75	135.000	75.000

ces in each district, the weighted values QLI′ and CPF′ (see Table 10.1) should reflect the differences which would be found with movement from one district to another.

Given the values in Table 10.1, the following conclusion might be reached. Within each district, the mean QLI and CPF experienced are the same, but based upon the scale values for each district which are derived from the preferences of the respondents, the values of QLI and CPF from one district relative to another are not qualitatively equal. Consider three potential results of the expenditure of public funds in any of the seven districts : increased income, increased population, and increased pollution. On a statewide basis the contribution of income to QLI can be measured and assigned weights. The influence of population and pollution could be considered in CPF. If the planning districts have been constructed such that each is comparable for planning purposes, then it is possible to determine where to allocate expenditures so as to maximize (or minimize) the various outcomes in terms of QLI and CPF, or stated alternatively, to determine whether gross, measured regional welfare has increased or decreased.

This type of comparison is particularly relevant to the growing metropolitan areas around the world. These areas become, in many ways, entities within themselves but rural to urban migration trends force them to deal with the population and cultural differences which are mirrored in the example presented for New Mexico.

There is an additional advantage to be gained from consideration of both the weighted and unweighted values. It is conceivable that individuals may feel that their quality of life is quite satisfactory, and that they may resent social engineering by outsiders. A comparison of the unweighted values would allow the degree to which this might be true to be ascertained. The integrated concepts of the RI, QLI, and CPF should allow planners to develop more reliable information as they search for methods to deal with the intraregional and intraurban comparison required for public policy decisions.

FOOTNOTE

1. Since $\bar{X}$ is the unbiased, consistent, and efficient estimator for in any population (Freund, 1971, pp. 254-264), group or regional means allow reliable estimates to be made about QLI comparisons for formulation public policies that impact unevenly on different groups.

REFERENCES

1. Bradburn, Norman M., *The Structure of Psychological Well-Being*, Chicago : Aldine, 1969.
2. Bradburn, Norman M., and David Caplovitz, *Reports on Happiness*, Chicago : Aldine, 1965.
3. Bradley, Ralph A., "Science, Statistics, and Paired Comparisons", *Biometrics*, Vol. 32, No. 2, June 1976.
4. Coelen, Stephen P., "Regression Analysis of Regional Quality of Life", Staff Paper, Department of Economics and Regional Analysis Center, The Pennsylvania State University, 1977.
5. Diemer, Joel A. and John R. McKean, "The Assessment of Community Preference : A Methodology and Case Study", *Land Economics*, Vol. 54, No. 2, May 1978.
6. Edwards, Allen L., *Techniques of Attitude Scale Construction*, New York : Appleton-Century-Crofts, Inc., 1957.
7. Ferguson, C.E., "The Theory of Multidimensional Utility Analysis in Relation to Multiple-Goal Business Behavior : A Synthesis", *Southern Economic Journal*, Vol. 32, No. 2, 1965.

8. Freund, John E., *Mathematical Statistics*, Second Edition, Englewood Cliffs, New Jersey : Prentice-Hall, Inc., 1971, pp. 254-264.
9. Harper, Wilmer, M. and Luther G. Tweeten, "Socio-psychological Measures of Quality of Rural Life : A Proxy for Measuring the Marginal Utility of Income", *American Journal of Agricultural Economics*, Vol. 59, No. 5, December 1977.
10. Houthakker, H.S., "Revealed Preference and the Utility Function", *Economics*, Vol. 17, No. 66, May 1950.
11. Institute for Social Research, "The Paradox of Well-Being", *ISR Newsletter*, The University of Michigan, Spring 1981.
12. McClosky, Hubert and John H. Schaar, "Psychological Dimensions of Anomy", *American Sociological Review*, Vol. 30, No. 1, February 1965.
13. Rosenbury, Morris, *Society and the Adolescent Self-Image*, Princeton : Princeton University Press, 1965.
14. Rotter, J.B., "Generalized Expectancies for Internal Versus External Control of Reinforcement", *Psychological Monograph*, Vol. 80, No. 609, 1966.
15. Samuelson, Paul A., *Foundations of Economic Analysis*, Cambridge, Mass. : Harvard, 1945.
16. Samuelson, Paul A., *Economics*, Ninth Edition, New York : McGraw-Hill Book Company, 1973, p. 3.
17. Shabman, Leonard A., "Some Considerations in Social Indicator Analysis : Reflections of a Case Study", Staff Paper SP-76-2, Department of Agricultural Economics, Virginia Polytechnic Institute and State University, April 1976.
18. Srole, Leo, "Social Integration and Certain Corollaries : An Exploratory Study", *American Sociological Review*, Vol. 21, No. 6, December 1956.
19. Torgerson, Warren S., *Theory and Methods of Scaling*, New York : John Wiley and Sons, 1958.
20. U.S. Department of Agriculture, *Rural and Small Town Population Change, 1970-80*, ESS-5, ESS-USDA, Washington, D.C., February 1981.

APPENDIX A

Established social indicator scales, [1, 2, 13, 14, 15] were *a priori* grouped into three subindices—Alienation (A), Worry (W), and Self-Esteem (SE)—and the grouping was verified by principal axis factor analysis. Individual values for the i-th individual were calculated on each scale as :

$$M_i = \sum_{k=1}^{m} E_k \left(\sum_{j=1}^{m} f_{kj} R_{ij} \right)$$

where M_i = scale value for the *i-th* individual
m = number of factors extracted for the scale
n = number of item in the *j-th* scale
E_k = the eigenvalue for the *k-th* factor
f_{kj} = factor loading for the *j-th* item on the *k-th* factor
R_{ij} = standardized response of the *i-th* individual to the *j-th* item of the scale

Subindices were then calculated as :

$$A_i = An_i + P_i + NA_i$$

and

$$SE_i = SS_i + LS_i + PA_i$$

where An_i = anomie scale value for the *i-th* individual (m=1)
P_i = powerlessness scale value for the *i-th* individual (m=2)
NA_i = negative affect scale value for the *i-th* individual (m=2)
SS_i = self-satisfaction scale value for the *i-th* individual (m=2)
LS_i = life satisfaction scale value for the *i-th* individual (m=2)
PA_i = positive affect scale value for the *i-th* individual (m=1)

The worry subindex consisted of only one scale

$$W_i = W_i \; (m=1)$$

The QLI was then calculated as the weighted summation of the three indices

$$QLI_i = E_a A_i + E_w W_i + E_{se} SE_i$$

where E_a, E_w, E_{se} are the respective eigenvalues obtained from the analysis that verified the grouping of the scales into subindices.

Based upon an evaluation criteria of R^2, coefficient signs, and size of t-ratios, various functional forms of an OLS regression model were considered, and a model of the general form

$$QLI_i = f(Y^*, Y^{*2}, ED^2, PERFARMY, AGE, AGE^2, AGEED, QTR)$$

where

Y and Y^{*2} = expected quarterly income and expected quarterly income squared respectively

ED^2 = years of education squared

$PERFARMY$ = total farm income/total family income

AGE and AGE^2 = age and age squared respectively

$AGEED$ = interaction term for age and education

QTR = time trend variable

was selected.

APPENDIX B

Based upon psychometric findings that individuals are capable of making consistent and reliable estimates of relative magnitudes,[21] each individual is asked that at the onset to rate his own Q of L on a scale of 0-100 where 100 implies maximum satisfaction.

The individual is then asked to rate in order of decreasing significance up to ten of those concerns (variables) which account for the amount by which the Q of L rating falls below 100. This indicates individual ranking for sources of dissatisfaction and allows interpersonal comparison. Interpersonal comparisons are replaced, however, by an OLS regression model which partials out the average expected effects of the intensity of each type of complaint on overall dissatisfaction.

Individual dissatisfaction may be represented by

$$D = a_0 + a_1x_1 + \ldots + a_mx_m + b_1y_1 + \ldots + b_ny_n + U$$

where D = dissatisfaction rating

$x_1, \ldots, x_m$ = socio-economic characteristics of the individual

$a_1, \ldots, a_m$ = coefficients for the respective socio-economic variables

$y_1, \ldots, y_n$ = environmental factors producing the reduced quality of life

$b_1, \ldots, b_n$ = coefficients for the respective environmental factors.

Since 100 is assumed to be the maximum CPF value, estimating the equation, substituting 100 − CPF for D, and rearranging terms, one has

$$CPF = 100 - \hat{a}_0 + \hat{a}_1x_1 + \ldots + \hat{a}_mx_m + \hat{b}_1y_1 + \ldots + \hat{b}_ny_n + e$$

APPENDIX C

The model assumes a preference ranking, R, exists over a grouping of N communities. A revealed preference approach involving paired comparisons of preference relationship between the group's N members is employed to implicitly define a regional ranking of relative Q of L states. For example, if F is chosen as best and D is chosen as worst of six communities, then directly, F } D, but also, implicitly, F P A, F P B, F P C, F P E, A P D, B P D, C P D, and E P D, where } indicates "is preferred over".

A community chosen at random to be the *numeraire*, for convenience is assigned the value of 100. The *numeraire* is the standard which is chosen and all other values are then stated in terms of their value relative to the *numeraire*. An implicit, but undefined ralationship (the object of the study being to determine the relationship) exists between each pair of communities within the group, as follows :

$$R(1) = 100$$

$$R(2) = R(1) . r_{1,2}$$

where $r_{1,2}$ defines the preference relationship between 1 and 2,

and

$$R(k) = R(i) . r_{i,k}$$

where i and k are in ascending order.

The generalized relationship is :

$$R(i) = 100 \prod_{\alpha=2}^{k} r_{\alpha-1},$$

where i=2, . . . , N.

The ratio of two index elements, i and k is :

$$R(k) / R(i) = \prod_{\alpha=i+1}^{k} r_{\alpha-1},$$

where α=2, . . . , N.

Aggregate judgements of a number of individuals comparing communities i and k were used to test the functional form :

$$P(k \} i) = \psi \, [\log (R(k) \, / \, (R(i)) \, (\varepsilon_{i,})]$$

where $P(k \} i) = (n_{ki} - n_{ik}) \, / \, (n_{ki} + n_{ik})$

and n_{ki} = the number of people preferring k to i

n_{ik} = the number of people preferring i to k

ψ = a proportionality constant

$\varepsilon_{i,k}$ = a log-normally distributed random error.

The functional form relates the expected preferences, $(P(k \} i)$ to the implicit index values symmetric around $(R(k) \, / \, R(i) = 1$.

Substituting for $R(k) \, / \, R(i)$ in the equation we obtain :

$$P(k) \} i) = \psi \, [\, \log (\prod_{\alpha=i+1}^{k} (r_{\alpha-1,\alpha}) \, . \, \varepsilon_{i}, k) \,].$$

To obtain a form suitable for regression estimation of r coefficients, two series of terms (from $\alpha=2, \ldots, i$ and $\alpha=k+1, \ldots, N$) each raised to the power 0 (thus leaving the value unaffected) are added to the equation. Then taking the required log, the following is obtained :

$$P(k \} i) = \psi \, [\, \sum_{\alpha=2} 0 \, . \log r_{\alpha-1,\alpha} + \sum_{\alpha=i+1} 1 \, . \log r_{\alpha-1,}$$

$$+_{\alpha} \sum_{\alpha=k+1}^{N} 0 \, . \log r_{\alpha-1,\alpha} + \log \varepsilon_{i,k} \,]$$

The coefficients estimated are, as noted, the various log $r_{\alpha-1,\alpha}$. The independent variables are specified as 0 or 1 depending upon whether or not alphabetically neighboring communities, p and $p-1$ are between communities i and k, being compared. The significance of elements of the index equation is obviously invariant to ψ by virtue of the equation's functional form.

PART FOUR

RURAL-URBAN MIGRATION

ELEVEN

EMMA HOOPER

BEHAVIOUR AND PERCEPTION
The Decision to Migrate

THE DECISION TO MIGRATE

MIGRATION patterns can be broadly classified into four main categories : urban-urban ; urban-rural ; rural-rural ; and rural-urban. It is primarily with the latter that this paper will be concerned. However, whilst broad categories of classification of types of migration can be made, the nature of migration and the identity of those who migrate will vary according to the socio-cultural context, as will the reasons for which they leave their areas of origin. Indeed, "the nature of the hinterland from which a city draws its population is one source of variation in the social structure of cities in underdeveloped countries" (Roberts, 1978 : 89).

There are numerous studies of migrants, and migration movements, whose findings are complex, and frequently contradictory. This is a result of generalisation between migrants of different socio-economic backgrounds, and different urban and rural contexts. As Roberts points out, migration is influenced by the particular stage and intensity of the industrial development through which a country is passing. This will affect both the rural and urban population structure, in terms of age/sex distribution ; and educational and occupational qualifications. The nature of future migration will be influenced, thus, by the type of in-migration that a city or region has previously experienced.

Migration may be of a temporary or of a permanent nature, voluntary or forced. In recent years, migration in developing countries has both increased in volume, and become increasingly urban-bound (Roberts, 1978). The move to the urban areas may be directly to a large urban centre ; or to a smaller city or town ; or may occur in stages, with migrants moving from rural areas to a small town and then to a larger one (Gilbert, 1974). Despite the complexities of precisely defining "urban" and "rural"—as outlined by Castells (1977) and others—an increasing number of people are moving to the large urban centres of the developing countries, with the result that between one-third and two-thirds of the population of such centres are migrants (Nelson, 1976). The reasons for this movement are conflicting, as will be shown.

The decision to migrate can similarly be classified under two typologies : "push" factors, involving a passive response to socio-economic variables which combine to make a migrant leave his/her home location ; and "pull" factors, involving the perceived attractions of urban living, which may be purely economic, purely social, or a combination of the two.

PROFILE OF MIGRANTS

The gradual inclusion of more remote and poorer regions in migration to the major urban centres suggests that contemporary migrations are selective processes (Gilbert, 1974 : 111/114). Browning, using Latin American and African data, shows that, in the early stages of migration, out-migrants are disproportionately concentrated in the young-adult age-groups ; are usually single ; relatively well-educated ; and are more likely to have non-agricultural occupations than the population of origin (Browning, 1971). In Latin America, migration to cities is predominantly female (Nelson, 1976), whereas, in Africa, it is predominantly male (Caldwell, 1969). The distance a migrant must travel, and the nature of his educational and occupational skills are all factors influencing the nature of migration and the identity of the migrant.

A migrant's choice of location is influenced also by the presence of friends and relatives, who offer more than just companionship. They reduce the cost of moving ; provide information about job opportunities ; and provide temporary support in the form of food and lodging. Migrants usually arrive in cities, therefore, with prior contacts and/or information. Many may well have jobs and lodgings assured for them before arrival, as a result of using kinship or friendship networks as support systems (Cornelius, 1975 ; Perlman, 1976). Married men will arrive before their families, if either employment or accommodation is unsure, and exploratory visits to the city before finally settling there are not uncommon—made feasible by the fact that most migration is short-distance (see Roberts, 1973a ; Roberts, 1978).

Economic reasons for migration

Economists and sociologists studying internal migration have stressed the dominance of the economic motive in the decision to migrate. Differences in economic opportunities within a country (and between countries) are seen as prompting individuals to change their place of residence.

Perhaps the most important single variable behind the decision to migrate, in this context, is the influence of land-tenure patterns. Lack of adequate access to land for, say, the younger sons of a family (because of inheritance patterns) ; or the inequalities of the class structure in villages, are among the primary reasons for leaving the rural hinterland to look for economic opportunities in the city. The search for employment, higher wages, and income security all combine to push migrants out of their rural areas of origin.

High rates of natural increase of population growth also combine with inheritance patterns and class inequality to augment the lack of access to productive employment experienced in rural areas. Unemployment and underemployment force a prospective migrant to look for better chances of subsistence elsewhere. A dualist perception of Third World economics regards the natural equilibrium existing in the capitalist system between the supply of, and the demand for, labour, as having been upset by the rapidity of population growth, resulting in large numbers of migrants living in cities either being unemployed, or working in the tertiary sector.

In contrast to this view of the causes of migration, historico-structuralists increasingly see rural-urban migration as a measure of the increasing and progressive integration of underdeveloped countries into the capitalist economy, with concomitant rural and urban change. The introduction of Western-style, capital-intensive technology has resulted in the replacement and displacement of labour in agriculture. Taken in conjunction with the fragmentation of land holdings through changes in tenure systems, the result has been a depression in rural incomes. The introduction of cash crops ; new farming techniques which reduce the number of jobs, and require changes in land distribution ; result in the release of a supply of labour for industrial expansion. Consequently, agricultural labour may migrate to urban areas to look for jobs during off-peak seasons ; or move to an urban area on a temporary basis for, say, a few years, which may reflect a need to enter the cash economy in order to accumulate savings, which would then be followed by a return to the rural hinterland.

It has been observed that job opportunities in agriculture do not grow at the same rate as population increases. "The most important consequence of rapid population growth is rural under-employment" (Koenigsberger, 1977). The only places where employment has visibly and rapidly increased are in big cities, as a result of concentrations of industries locating there. As Todaro points out, perceived job opportunities in urban areas are a source of attraction for the rural poor : a reflection too of income differentials between rural and urban areas (Todaro, 1969). The income that an individual can expect to earn with his occupation and training will influence his choice of location. In rural areas, an improvement in transportation facilities, and a reduction in mortality rates also results in an increase in out-migration (cf. the Latin American case, as cited by Balan, 1969).

What Lipton has termed the "urban bias" in development policies (Lipton, 1977) is a result of the development theories of the 1950's and 1960's, which stressed economic growth at the expense of holistic development. This "urban bias" is seen by Lipton as a major component of urban in-migration, resulting from the skewed distribution of resource allocation, with insufficient investment in rural areas and, hence, rural out-migration.

Large cities have remained a source of attraction for rural migrants ever since, reflecting rural inhabitants' perception of the city as a source of hope for the realisation of their economic and social aspirations, despite evidence to show that this perception is possibly misplaced—as will be elaborated on further. In the 1960's, developing countries experienced relatively high rates of economic growth, particularly in (urban-based) industry (World Bank, 1978—Table 2). This combined with the removal of restrictions on urban growth, and an increase in the number of jobs available to indigenous inhabitants in their newly-independent administrations, to perpetuate this impression of the economic opportunities offered to urban dwellers. From the 1970's, however, industrial investment and development lessened, in comparison with that of the previous decade, following the 1973 oil crisis, and world-wide recession (World Bank, 1978—Table 2). Agricultural investment and development lessened even further, resulting in people being pushed off the land, and migrating to urban areas in search of employment opportunities—which, upon examination of World Bank data, are less quantitatively than in the earlier decade.

Average annual growth rates (%)

	GDP		Agriculture		Industry	
	1960/70	1970/76	1960/70	1970/76	1960/70	1970/76
Low-income countries	3.6	2.9	2.3	1.6	6.7	4.5
Middle-income countries	5.7	6.0	3.6	3.2	7.6	7.2

From : World Development Report 1978, World Bank, August 1978, Table 2, Growth of Production, pp. 78/79.

Average annual growth rates (%)

	Total Population		Urban Population	
	1960/70	1970/75	1960/70	1970/75
Low-income countries	2.4	2.4	5.4	5.5
Middle-income countries	2.7	2.7	4.8	4.5

From : World Development Report 1978, World Bank, August 1978, Table 13, Population and Labour Force Growth, pp. 100/101.

In addition to the economic "pull" of cities in terms of their being (perceived as) a source of higher pay ; having better chances of upward socio-economic mobility ; better work conditions ; and offering a change in occupation ; the social "pull" factors of better opportunities for education, health care, entertainment, marriage, and public services also should be taken into consideration. Lee assesses the decision to migrate as being consistent with the "pushes" and "pulls" of poverty at the place of origin, and of higher expected income at the destination, together with personal factors and intervening obstacles (Lee, 1966 : 47/57). Because of the difficulty of quantifying the non-economic "pushes" and "pulls" of migration, the wholly economic hypothesis of urban migration being a function of expected rural-urban income differences is selected frequently as an explanation (for example, see Friedlander, 1965 ; Harris and Todaro, 1970 ; Todaro, 1969).

Non-economic reasons for migration

The decision to migrate is not always made by the migrant alone (or indeed, at all) : he or she may be "pushed" to migrate to an urban area as a result of a decision taken by the head of a household. For example, access to educational opportunities above that of primary level frequently do not exist in rural areas ; or, where they do, may be overcrowded or of poor quality.

The provision of health facilities can also be a "pull" for city-wards migration. Recently-settled Beduin living on the outskirts of Kuwait city were found by the author to cite access to health and educational services as a primary reason for abandoning a nomadic lifestyle for urban residence (Hooper, 1976).

The attraction of an "urban lifestyle" is one often cited in the literature as a cause of migration. Urban life may be perceived by young would-be migrants as qualitatively better, or more exciting than that available to them in rural areas. Not merely better entertainment facilities, but the attraction of an escape from a tradition-bound, hierarchical and conservative rural social structure can be powerful elements in a migrant's decision to move to an urban area. Barriers of caste and class may not disappear altogether, but can certainly be mitigated and frequently transgressed, with little or no fear of social sanctions in the anonymity of city life.

For some societies (West Africa for example) a period of urban residence is a much-valued, almost compulsory, "rite of passage" into adult-hood, and can significantly enhance the marriage prospects of the young, male migrant. Urban-orientated values are enhanced by education in the majority of developing countries, and result in the imposition of the social values of the metropolis on the village by many returned migrants.

Migrants may also be "pushed" to urban areas through political or environmental upheavals : (for example, civil strife was a major component of city-wards migration during the Nigerian Civil War). Forced to migrate unintentionally, as a result of flood, war or famine, having once moved to an urban area, migrants may then see its advantages, and so prefer to remain there ; or force of circumstances may be such that they are physically unable to return home : as, for example, the occupation of Palestinian territory by Israeli forces.

The decision to migrate : Conclusions

Education for the migrant or his/her family ; marriage (particularly for women) ; joining the family already living at the destination ; military service ; attraction of the city in general, or specifically for entertainment, adventure, or novelty value ; more and better educational, cultural, and welfare services—

such as schools, libraries, hospitals ; natural disaster ; the death of a family member (particularly the main income-earner) ; expressions of manliness ; freedom from elders and strict social controls of a traditional, rural life style ; prestige and greater opportunities for consumption ; are all non-economic factors which combine in the decision to migrate. The latter, consequently, is the result of many collective forces. In some instances, economic reasons may predominate over social ones, in the least developed areas within a country, while, in the more developed areas, other reasons may take precedence (Caldwell, 1969 : 106).

A distinction also can be made frequently between independent migrants, who voluntarily decide to move to the cities, and dependent migrants, who move to accompany an independent migrant (the forms usually being wives and children). Obviously, the reasons of dependent or "secondary" migrants for moving will differ from those of independent or "primary" migrants.

Despite a multiplicity of factors being involved in a decision whether to migrate or not, people are not always consciously aware of all the variables influencing their decision. Migration reasons that are not job-related seem influenced by the age of the migrant : younger migrants (15-24 years) often migrate for access to education ; while older migrants (40-60 years) may migrate primarily for housing and health reasons. The majority of cases of female Asian migration are for family or marriage reasons. Evidence from Latin America points towards economic or job-related reasons having been the most important influences on migration, and Asian data supports this (IBRD, 1973).

REFERENCES

Balan, Jorge, "Migrant-Native Socio-Economic Differences in Latin American Cities : A Structural Analysis", in *Latin American Research Review*, Vol. 4, No. 1, Spring 1969.

Browning, Harley L. and Feindt, W., "The Social and Economic Context of Migration to Monterrey, Mexico", in Rabinovitz, F.F. and Trueblood, F., (eds.), *Latin American Urban Research*, Vol. 1, Beverly Hills : Sage Publications, 1971.

Caldwell, John C., African Rural-Urban Migration, New York : Colombia University Press, 1969.

Castells, Manuel, The Urban Question, London : Edward Arnold, 1977.

Cornelius, Wayne (ed.), *Latin American Urban Research*, Vol. 5, Beverly Hills : Sage Publications, 1975.

Gilbert, Alan, Latin American Development, Harmondsworth, Mdlx. : Penguin, 1974.

Harris, John R. and Todaro, M.P., "Migration, Unemployment and Development : a Two-Sector Analysis", in *American Economic Review*, March 1970, pp. 126-142.

Hooper, Emma, Socio-Economic Survey of Low-Income-Group Housing in Kuwait, Report to the National Housing Authority of Kuwait, Colin Buchanan and Partners, London : 1976.

IBRD, Some Economic Interpretations of Case Studies of Urban Migration in Developing Countries, Working Paper, No. 151, Washington, D.C. : 1973.

Koenigsberger, Otto H., The Absorption of New-Comers in the Cities of the Third World, Paper for U.N. Habitat Preparatory Conference, June 1977.

Lee, Everett S., "A Theory of Migration", in *Demography*, Vol. 3, No. 1, 19.6, pp. 47-57.

Lipton, Michael, Why Poor People Stay Poor, London : Maurice Temple Smith, 1977.

Nelson, Joan M., "Sojourners vs. New Urbanites : Causes and Consequences of City-Migration in Developing Countries", in *Economic Development and Cultural Change*, 24 : 4, July 1976.

Perlman, Janice E., The Myth of Marginality, Berkeley : University of California Press, 1976.

Quijano Obregon, Anibal, "The Marginal Role of the Economy and the Marginalised Labour Force", in *Economy and Society*, Vol. 3, No. 9, 1972, pp. 393-428.

Roberts, Byran R., Organising Strangers, Austin : University of Texas Press, 1973.

Roberts, Bryan R., Cities of Peasants, London : Edward Arnold, 1978.

Todaro, Michael P., "A Model of Labour Migration and Urban Unemployment in Less Developed Countries", in *American Economic Review*, Vol. 59, No. 1, March 1969, pp. 138-148.

World Bank, World Development Report 1978, Washington, D.C. : IBRD 1978.

TWELVE

JAMES A. KING, WILLIAM A. MURACO AND KARL O. VEZNER

PSYCHOLOGICAL AND ENVIRONMENTAL IMPLICATIONS OF INTRA-URBAN MIGRATION

Community Adjustment and the Mental Patient

INTRODUCTION

THE dynamics of inter and intra urban migration have long been of major interest to the urban geographer. It is through the nature of these population adjustments that the morphological character of the urban system is formed and transformed. Migration models have suggested that the decision to move and its subsequent behaviors are a result of multiple spatial "push" and "pull" factors. In the case of interregional moves, the models suggest that the rationale of the move is generally motivated by employment, educational, residential and social/recreational spatial differentials (Long and Hansen, 1979; Lowry, 1966; Melnnis, 1971; Roseman, 1977). Movements within urban space, on the other hand, are generally more constrained and appear to be the result of different forces of attraction and repulsion. For the majority of intra-urban moves, migration is limited more to micro spatial differentials. For example, many moves are reflective of changes in life cycle, socio-economic status and general searches for improved housing conditions and location accessibility (McCarthy, 1976; Berry and Horton, 1970; Simmons, 1974; Butler, 1969).

The models of spatial migration are generally based on the objective of maximizing the place utility of the residential environment. Behavioral approaches to migration envision that residential stresses are exerted on individuals when the differential between residential aspirations widen relative to the place utility. Brown and Moore, for example, suggest that stress and its resultant strains are the factors which initiate the decision to move and lead to search behavior for a new dwelling (Brown and Moore, 1970).

The dynamics of the behavioral migration model suggest that the decision to move represents an environmental adjustment which resolves the strain between unattained residential needs and the failure of the present residence to meet that need. The implications of migration as a mechanism for reducing individual spatial inequities in residential utilities have far reaching implications to medical and urban geography. The actual impact that the act of migration has on the individual's psychological functioning and well being is not fully understood. The behavioral geographic model suggests that migration represents a spatially manifested stress coping mechanism (Wolpert, 1966). The change in a residential environment may be supportive and therapeutic to an individual. On the other hand, this change in location may create a new milieu of stresses resulting from a lack of familiarity with the new environment.

The objective of this study is to investigate the impact that migration has on the psychological status of the migrant. Rather than focusing the research on the public in general, the study concentrates on mental patients who were recently released from a state mental hospital. The rationale for the focus on mental patients is two-fold : (1) this group represents a population which is characterized by high mobility and one that may be more sensitive to changes in residential environments than other groups, and (2) recent treatment philosophies have stressed the value of deinstitutionalization in which the community environment is perceived to be more therapeutic. In other words, current treatment trends perceive the move to the community environment as more conducive to a positive outcome. Unfortunately, the decision to place patients in the community setting has occurred without the benefit of understanding the implications of this environment in meeting their residential needs. Current high migration rates characterize these patients and the intensive frequency of hospital recidivism suggest that the stabilization in the community setting may actually be problematic (Smith, 1975, 1976, 1978).

THE STUDY SETTING

The data for this research are taken from a longitudinal analysis of 472 chronic patients with a broad spectrum of psychiatric diagnoses.* These patients were studied for a one year period following their release from an urban state mental hospital in Ohio (King, Muraco, Vezner, 1981). The patients were selected randomly and were assessed at the point of discharge in terms of their psychiatric status, psychological and social functioning capabilities, and in respect to general demographic, residential, diagnostic and medical histories. These patients were subsequently monitored over a one year period as they experienced the community adjustment process. During the community phase the patients were monitored in terms of their social adjustment, psychological status, behavioral symptoms, physical symptoms, stress levels, treatments received and migration behavior. At the end of the one year community experience the patients were reassessed in terms of their post hospitalization history, psychiatric status, behavioral and physical symptoms, social adjustments and stress levels. Patients were monitored throughout the study for hospital recidivism, inpatient and outpatient facility usage.

The major instrument used to assess patient psychiatric status and function was Spitzer and Endicott's Psychiatric Status Schedule (1975). This instrument permits the construction of twenty-three individual scales which measure specific psychological symptomatology and functioning. The twenty-three scales used in the research are presented in Table 12.1.

SPATIAL CHARACTERISTICS OF AGGREGATE PATIENT MIGRATION PATTERNS

In order to evaluate the migration behavior from a geographic perspective, the patients were subdivided into two groups: those who were rehospitilized within a year, and those who remained in the community setting for the entire year. Evaluation of the movement patterns of the two groups was accomp-

TABLE 12.1 : **Psychiatric status symptom scales**

Scale	*Assesses*
1. Appearance	Physical behavior or acts which would be considered odd or inappropriate by untrained persons
2. Negativisim	Overt negativism, sarcasm, argumentativeness, shouting
3. Agitation	Overt agitation, e.g., handwringing, hyperactivity
4. Lack of Emotion	Visible signs of retardation in speech and movement, flat effect
5. Speech Disorganization	Impairment in the form or organization of speech
6. Grandiosity	Inflated appraisal of worth, contacts, power or knowledge, dillusions of power
7. Hallucinations	Distrustful, various paranoid delusions, ideas of reference
8. Overt Anger	Reports of overt anger, temper tantrums, threats or acts of violence
9. Anxiety/Depression	Feelings and concerns associated with depressions, anxious, phobic or obsessive-compulsive syndromes
10. Suicide/Self Mutilation	Suicidal thoughts, preoccupation, threats, gestures or attempts
11. Somatic Concerns	Preoccupation with physical complaint, e.g., somatic delusions
12. Social Isolation	Lack of friends, avoidance of contact or involvement, feelings of rejection, etc.
13. Time Impairment	Impact of pathology on daily routine on leisure time or activities
14. Antisocial	Lying, commission of or impulses to commit minor or serious illegal acts, stealing
15. Alcohol Abuse	Degree to which use of alcohol is excessive, compulsive, etc.

16.	Drug Abuse	Excessive self medication or addiction to barcituates, etc.
17.	Disorientation/Memory	Visible signs of disorientation as to time, place, persons
18.	Denial of Illness	Extent to which patient denies illness despite symptom evidence
19.	Subjective Distress	Summary of 5 subjective distress measures includes scales 9, 10, 11, 12, 13
20.	Behavioral Disturbances	Summary of 6 disturbance scales, includes scales 1 2, 3, 4, 5, 17
21.	Impulse Control	Summary of 3 impulse scales, includes scales 8, 14, 16
22.	Reality Testing	Summary of 2 reality measures, includes scales 6, 7
23.	Total Scale	Summary of all 18 scales

lished through the use of a nearest neighbor analysis focused on the initial hospital discharge address and the final terminal address location at the end of the monitoring period (Dacey, 1960). The findings of the nearest neighbor analysis are reported in Table 12.2. The data in the table show that migration, with respect to the discharge and to the final address, results in a highly concentrated distribution regardless of the study group. The high degree of spatial concentration strongly supports the notion that residential alternatives are extremely limited for this population. This finding is consistent with past research that suggests inner urban ghettos of mental patients are being created in cities. The data in the table show that the greatest distributional changes, with respect to locational clustering, are evident for the non-recidivist groups. The final addresses for both groups, however, indicate general comparability in the level of geographic concentration.

The nearest neighbor analysis provides a gross measure of migrational changes during the study year. Table 12.3 provides a more qualitative perspective of the character of the environments these patients are located in at the time of discharge and for their final address locations. The table reports weighted census tract means for a series of socio-economic, demographic and housing indicators that have been demonstrated to be important ecological indicators of high risk mental health problem areas (Redick and Goldsmith, 1971). The data reported

TABLE 12.2 : **Nearest neighbor analysis**

	Recidivists		Non-Recidivists	
	Grid*	Km's	Grid*	Km's
X Nearest neighbor Distance				
Discharge	1966	0.58	2761	0.81
Final	1891	0.55	2085	0.61
Expected Distance if Random				
Discharge	4411	1.29	3679	1.08
Final	4178	1.23	3589	1.05
Nearest Neighbor Statistic				
Discharge	.446		.751	
Final	.453		.581	

* State Plane Grid System Coordinate Distances

TABLE 12.3 : **Origin and destination migration neighborhood profiles (weighted means)**

Tract Characteristics	Total		Movers		Non-Movers	Urban-Total
	Discharge	Final	Discharge	Final		
	1	2	3	4	5	6
Recidivists						
Per cent overcrowded	6.7	6.2%	7.0%	6.1%	6.2%	5.3%
Md. housing value	$12957	$12922	$13092	$13076	$12648	$17623
Md. contract rent	$82	$85	$82	$87	$80	$100
Md. family income	$8992	$8945	$8995	$8905	$8985	$11013
Persons/household	2.9	2.9	2.9	2.8	2.9	3.1
Household/wife hsd.	78.9%	80.2%	79.1%	80.7%	78.4%	85.8%
Vacancy rate	5.4%	4.8%	5.9%	5.0%	4.2%	3.4%
Sex ratio	93.9	95.7	95.7	98.4	89.8	93.1
(Males/Females) % Owner occupied D.U.s	48.5%	51.1%	47.2%	50.7%	51.6%	67.4%
% Child. norm. family	77.9%	79.0%	77.4%	78.4%	79.3%	87.2%
% One person hsds.	27.1%	27.9%	28.0%	29.4%	25.0%	18.2%

TABLE 12.3 (*Contd.*)

	1	2	3	4	5	6
Non-Recidivists						
Per cent overcrowded	6.1%	6.1%	6.0%	6.0%	6.2%	5.3%
Md. housing value	$13435	$13780	$12260	$13182	$14097	$17623
Md. contract rent	$85	$87	$79	$83	$89	$100
Md. family income	$9145	%9393	$8544	$9066	$9618	$11013
Persons/household	2.9	3.0	2.8	2.9	3.1	3.1
Husband/wife hsd.	80.6%	81.8%	79.3%	81.6%	81.9%	85.8%
Vacancy rate	5.2%	4.8%	6.0%	5.2%	4.4%	3.4%
Sex ratio	94.9%	94.3%	97.3%	95.8%	92.8%	93.1%
(Males/Females) % Owner occupied D.U.s	52.6%	56.5%	44.0%	51.9%	60.9%	67.4%
% Child. norm. family	79.6%	81.4%	76.8%	80.2%	82.2%	87.2%
% One person Hsd.	25.4%	24.1%	29.9%	27.2%	21.4%	18.2%

Based on 1970 Population Census—Tract Characteristics.

in the table show that both groups are located in residential environments in which housing quality is below the urban average and where social environments are composed of above average proportions of small households. The data in the table illustrate that aggregate changes in neighborhood quality associated with migration behavior are minimal. In general, both the discharge and final address census tracts have relatively comparable socio-economic characteristics.

In summary, the preceding descriptive analysis shows that aggregate migration patterns appear to be constrained and generally limited to relatively homogeneous environments. Individual migrations in which changes in neighborhood quality and character may have occurred are not adequately isolated at the aggregate level of analysis. These dynamics are explored through a correlation analysis in the following section.

CORRELATES OF INDIVIDUAL MIGRATION CHANGES IN NEIGHBORHOOD CHARACTER AND CHANGES IN PSYCHOLOGICAL OUTCOME

A dynamic perspective of the association between changes in psychiatric status and individual changes in neighborhood character are presented in the significant Pearson Correlation Coefficients noted in Table 12.4. The analysis in this portion of the article is limited to only those non-recidivists who moved during the one year period. The rationale for restricting the sample to this group is based on the objective of defining the association between psychiatric outcomes and patients who remained in the urban community environment during the entire year.

The correlations presented in Table 12.4 provide two perspectives on the relationship between psychiatric adjustment and migration. In the first viewpoint, a pattern of psychiatric status scales that are associated with ecological characteristics of census tracts are defined. Included in the group of spatially sensitive measures are changes in the belligerence scale, agitation and excitement levels, lack of emotion, the behavioral disturbance scale and in the impulse control scales. The preceding are symptomatic dimensions which are suggestive of survival or defensive behavioral patterns within the control of the

TABLE 12.4 : **Significant correlations between psychiatric status scale changes and address change characteristics of movers in the nonrecidivists sample**

	Census Tract Characteristics :				
	Changes in per cent D.U. overcrowded	Changes in medium house value	Changes in medium rent	Changes in medium family income	Changes in $\bar{X}$ persons per household
	1	2	3	4	5
Psychiatric Status Scale Changes:					
Inappropriate Effect					
Belligerence					
Agitation/Excitement	−.301($p<.011$)		+.261($p<.024$)	+.280($p<.017$)	
Lack of Emotion					+.335($p<.005$)
Speech Disorganization					
Grandiosity					
Hallucinations					
Overt Anger					
Depression/Anxiety					
Suicide/Self Mutilation					

Somatic Concerns		−.228(p<.043)				
Social Isolation						
Time Impairment						
Anti-Social Impulses						
Alcohol Abuse						
Drug Abuse					+.226(p<.044)	
Disorientation						
Denial of Illness						
Subjective Distress						
Behavioral Disturbances						+.311(p<.009)
Impulse Control Disturbances						+.254(p<.027)
Reality Testing Disturbances						
Total Macro Scale						
Inappropriate Effect						

TABLE 12.4 (*Contd.*)

	Census Tract Characteristics					
	Changes in per cent husband wife households	Changes in per cent D.U. vacant	Changes in sex ratio males to 100 females	Changes in per cent owner occupied D.U.	Changes in per cent children both parents	Changes in per cent one person households
P ychiatric Status Scale Changes :						
Belligerence		−.278(p<.017)		+.223(p<.046)		
Agitation/Excitement	+.315(p<.008)	−.360(p<.003)		+.334(p<.005)	+.253(p<.028)	
Lack of Emotion		−.331(p<.006)	−.325(p<.006)	+.318(p<.007)	+.284(p<.015)	−.390(p<.001)
Speech Disorganization						
Grandiosity						
Hallucinations			−.228(p<.043)			
Overt Anger						
Depression/Anxiety						
Suicide/Self Mutilation						
Somatic Concerns						
Social Isolation						
Time Impairment						
Anti-Social Impulses		−.354(p<.003)		+.220(p<.049)		

Alcohol Abuse	+.264(p<.023)				
Drug Abuse		−.258(p<.025)			
Disorientation					
Denial of Illness					−.271(p<.020)
Subjective Distress		−.254(p<.027)			
Behavioral Disturbances		−.319(p<.007)	−.254(p<.027)	+.321(p<.007)	−.361(p<.003)
Impulse Control Disturbance		−.288(p<.014)	−.241(p.<.034)		−.234(p<.039)
Reality Testing Disturbance			−.227(p.<.044)		
Total Macro Scale		−.273(p<.019)		+.257(p<.026)	−.249(p<.030)

*Changes in the psychiatric scale scores have been computed so that positive increases in the scores indicate improved psychiatric status.

**Probabilities noted in the table are based on a one tailed T-test.

patient. These negative behavioral changes may represent defenses associated with placement of the patient in a hostile, nontherapeutic residential environment. The absence of relationships for psychiatric scales which appear to be unrelated to spatial variations in the residential tracts is supportive of this interpretation. These non-spatially associated scales are reflective of symptomatic behaviors which tend to be more autonomically controlled. For example, scales which measure speech disorganization, grandiosity, depression and anxiety, time impairment, reality testing disturbances and hallucinations are tapping the more autonomic aspects of behavior.

A second perspective evident in Table 12.4 is reflected in the cluster of significant correlations associated with specific ecological variables and changes in the psychiatric scales. Ecological dimensions which demonstrate multiple associations with the symptomatic scales are changes in vacancy rates, sex ratio, percentage of one person households and the mean number of person per house variables. These findings are not surprising, for the preceding set of variables are reflective of neighborhood environments that are likely to show considerable variability in social support systems. These same variables have been found to be important predictors for identifying neighborhoods where high risk levels of mental disorders may be found (King, Muraco, Vezner, 1974). In summary, Table 12.4 confirms that selective relationships exist between neighborhood characteristics and specific psychiatric pathologies. It must be emphasized, however, that these associations are selective and are oriented to dimensions of psychiatric status that define overt behavioral symptomatology.

SUMMARY AND CONCLUSIONS

The results of this examination suggest several urban policy implications relevant to mental patients and to the general population.

From the perspective of health care service delivery the findings portray a major planning dilemma. That is, do you create more housing for patients and disperse it throughout better residential environments or force patients to provide housing for themselves and move programming in closer proximity to the larger concentrations of former patients.

Both choices provide benefits and costs. Creation and dispersal of housing provides patients with better environments but is much more expensive. Additionally, former patients and support programs will have to contend with the hostility of residents in these residential areas. It is also highly likely that when patients leave such housing, they will migrate to these less desirable areas due to their inability to maintain themselves in the more desirable and expensive housing areas. On the other hand, services can be moved closer to the major concentrations of former patients which would be far less expensive though the patients are then confronted with environments that are highly stressful and non-supportive.

The nature of mental illness, including the fact that it is very often a chronic condition, when coupled with living in such non-supportive isolating environments demands the development of specific adjustment skills. Compensation for physical and psychological inadequacies, dealing with economic frustrations, pacing oneself, dealing with increased dependency status and the frustration of illness, etc , are all skills formerly hospitalized patients must acquire and maintain to remain healthy in the community.

The nature of the treatment effort, therefore, should be tailored to include these concerns. Such programming should include aggressive outreach and case finding activity, social living skills enhancement, social support, and case management activity oriented toward meaningful social involvement of the patient in the larger society.

The study findings may also have implications to the general urban population. The data suggest that migration behavior associated with moves to improved residential environments may be associated with a spatial stress coping mechanism. This observation is, of course, limited to the sample population. The finding, however, is consistent with the view that migration as hypothesized in the behavioral model may be viewed as a method of augmenting place utility. The augmentation of utility appears to favorably impact on psychological status and functioning. This research is obviously exploratory and faced with aggregate ecological inferential limitations. Nevertheless, it provides an initial research extension and linkage between the assumptions of behavioral migration models and the migrants psychological well being. Exploratory research into the psychological implications of migration behavior among the population in general is essential in the validation of behavioral migration theory.

REFERENCES

Berry, Brian J.L. and Frank Horton, *Geographic Perspectives on Urban Systems*, Englewood, Cliffs : Prentice-Hall, 1970.

Brown, L.A. and E. Moore, *The intra-urban migration process : A perspective*, Geografiske Annzler, Series B, Vol. 52B : 1970, 1-13.

Butler, E., *et al.*, Moving Behaviors and Residential Choice : A National Survey, Report 81, Highway Research Board, Washington, D.C., 1969.

Dacey, M.F., A note on the derivation of nearest neighbor distances, *Journal of Regional Science*, 2 : 1960, 81-87.

King, J.A., W.A. Muraco and K.O. Vezner, Transitional Services : The Community Adjustment Experience, Office of Program Evaluation and Research, Ohio Department of Mental Health, Columbus, Ohio, 1981.

King, J.A., W.A. Muraco and K.O. Vezner, Planning of future mental health care delivery systems : Toward a predictive model, Paper presented at the National Meeting of the Association of American Geographers, Special Session for Health Care Delivery Systems, Seattle, Washington, 1974.

Long, L.H., and K.A. Hansen, Reasons for Inner State Migration : Jobs, Retirement, Climate and Other Influences, Washington, D.C., Current Pub. Reports (Series P-23, No. 81), U.S. Department of Commerce (March), 1979.

Lowry, Ira, *Migration Theory and Metropolitan Growth : Two Analytical Models*, San Francisco : Chandler Publishing Co, 1966.

McCarthy, Kevin, The household life cycle and housing choices, Papers and Proceedings, *Regional Science Association*, 1976, 37 : 73.

McInnis, Marvin, *Age, Education and Occupation Differentials in Interregional Migration : Some Evidence for Canada, Demography* (May) : 1971, 195-204.

Redick, R.W. and Goldsmith, 1970 Census Data used to Indicate Access with Different Potentials for Mental Health and Related Problems, National Institute of Mental Health Statistics Series C, No. 3, DHEW Publication No. (HSM), 1971, 73-9058.

Roseman, Curtis C., Changing Migration Patterns Within the U.S., Washington, D.C., *Association of American Geographers*, 1977.

Simons, J.M., *Patterns of Residential Movement in Metropolitan Toronto*, University of Toronto, Department of Geography, Research Publication 13, Toronto, 1974.

Smith, C.J., *The Residential Neighborhood as a Therapeutic Community*, unpublished doctoral dissertation, Department of Geography, The University of Michigan, Ann Arbor, 1975.

Smith, C.J., Residential neighborhoods as humane environments, *Environment and Planning* 8 : 1976, 311-326.

Smith, C.J., Geography and Mental Health, Association of American Geographers Resource Paper (No. 76-4), Washington, D.C., 1977.

Spitzer, Robert L. and Jean Endicott, Manual of Instructions : Psychiatric Status Schedule, see also : Spitzer, R.L. and J. Endicott, 1975, Psychiatric rating scales, Comprehensive Textbook of Psychiatry-11, Vol. 2, 2nd ed. (edited by Freeman, *et al.*, The Williams and Willsins Co., Baltimore, Md., 1968, pp. 2015-2031.

Wolpert, J., Migration as an adjustment to environmental stress, *Journal of Social Issues*, 22 : 1966, 92-102.

THIRTEEN

C.S. YADAV

PSYCHOLOGICAL IMPLICATIONS OF RURAL-URBAN MIGRATION
A Case Study of Delhi

INTRODUCTION

THE magnitude, causes and significance of urban population growth in developing nations have envolved as topics of major interest among social scientist during the last three decades. The growth of urban population is assigned to three factors : The natural increase ; rural urban migration and the reclassification of urban boundaries into rural hinterland. It was reported in an U.N. report (1980) that approximately 61 per cent of the urban population growth in developing countries was due to natural increase and 39 per cent due to rural urban migration.[1] Thus rural urban migration has been one of the most dramatic occurrence of recent decades which has fostered the urbanization of large segments of peasants. The growth of literature in rural urban migration over last two decades has significantly improved our understanding of the behaviour of human movements. A Review of contributions such as those by Wolpart (1965),[2] Brown and Longbrake,[3] Ceballa and Vedder (1973),[4] Lee (1970),[5] Pack (1973),[6] Liu (1977),[7] Sajastad (1962),[8] Bowels (1970),[9] R.A. Fabricant (1970),[10] Nelson (1959),[11] Parrish (1973),[12] Trott (1972),[13] Warriner (1970),[14] Zelinsky (1977)[15] and Ravenstein (1885),[16] have demonstrated the complexity of rural urban population shift and challenges associated with interpreting them. These discussions have indicated, differing perspectives on urbanization and migration processes, and led to diverse interpretations of rural urban migration. These studies have highlighted that rural urban migration is a complex phenomena and its incidence and consequences are multidimentional. Bogue and Zachariah (1962)[17] have rightly asserted that rural urban migration is by far the most important component of urbanization and is the chief mechanism by which all the world's great urbanization trends have been accomplished. However it is not merely a mechanical process but governed by economic, social and political factors. The rural urban migration does not merely imply redistribution of population from one ecological setting to another but there is a redistribution of the attitudes, behaviour and customs of the people, which produce profound effect on the whole spatial patterning of human activities, the repercussions of which may be felt long after the migration events themselves have taken place.

The study of rural urban migration is multi disciplinary and also in its widest sense interdisciplinary field. However there are various reasons why geographers devote attention to the study of migration ; for one, the territorial redistribution of population is an attractive theme for spatially oriented discipline. Secondly geographers devote attention to dynamic aspects of spatial processes and spatial interactions. Thus the following range of questions satisfy the quest of geographers in studying migration. 1. Who migrates ? 2. Why does migration occur ? 3. What are the patterns of migration ? and 4. What are the effects of migration on the areas, communities or societies of destination ? Thus the objective of geographers is to evaluate spatial flows with interaction between different places and with areal variations between two places of origin and destination.

The purpose of this paper is to examine the geographical impact of rural urban migrants in Delhi. A special feature of the present paper is to deal comprehensively the magnitude, incidence and process of migration. Vigorous attempts are made to explore how does the process of migration occur as a result of decision made by individuals in the light of what they perceive the objective world to be like. It is assumed that migrants held an erroneous view of their environment, it is that erroneous view, acted upon rather than the objective real world situation. The present paper incorporates the principal of Paulwhite and Robertwood[18] who commented that normative explanations of migration as a response to economic wage rate fluctuations, are only partial generalizations for they always neglect considerations of the perceptions prevelent among the potential migrants. As such the present paper explores the subjective appraisals of migrants whose perceptions of spatial differentiation of opportunities for different geographical locations offer different levels of potential well being to various migrants.

It is these perceived differences between places that are important rather than any "push" or "pull" mechanism propounded by economic model builders. Generalizations in the present paper are based on the presumption that so long as migrants perceive differentiation in place utility, there is likely to be greater volume of migration streams from rural to urban areas. This field of study of course owes much to behavioural psychology and to the work of Julianwolpart,[19] who introduced certain behavioural concepts to a wider geographical audience. The behaviourist approach to the process of migration has provided a useful set of concepts but it has not yet provided a satisfactory set of predictive models. Nevertheless, the analysis of the importance of individual decision maker in migration provides satisfactory clues to the understanding of the selectivity of migration.

Data set

The present study entirely relies upon the field data collected by the author during 80-81. The explanation is made on the basis of a sample of 1000 heads of households which are systematically distributed to five types of colonies in urban Delhi which receives largest number of rural migrants. They are 1. Urban Villages, 2. Squatter Settlements, 3. Regularized Colonies, 4. Old Resettlement Colonies and 5. New Resettlement Colonies.

MIGRATION IN DELHI AND URBAN POPULATION GROWTH

Migration to Delhi

There is an unchecked flow of rural migrants from villages to the small and medium class towns and from these to metropolitan cities. The migrants in their wake have brought a variety of interactable problems to these cities like Delhi, Bombay and Calcutta. In Delhi the problem is unprecedented which pertains to increasing squatter settlements, spiralling and speculation of land values and rental values, congestion of traffic, shortage of housing, shortage of civic and basic amenities etc. The planners have started thinking that unabated flow of rural migrants to Delhi has befalled the orderly growth of the National Capital and the city is running into its sorry state. For proper growth some of these migrants need to be diverted from Delhi to other towns.

Trend of population growth

There has been a significant increase in the growth of Delhi population during twentieth century. It is a truism that very few cities in India or for that matter even the world have grown so fast as Delhi.[20] Over a period of seventy years the population has increased ten times, *e.g.* in 1901 it was 4.05 lakhs whereas in 1971 it was 40.65 lakhs;[21] however the bulk of this increase occurred during the last three decades (Table 13.1). It is self-evident from the table that the population of Delhi during 1951 has recorded the highest percentage increase of 106 per cent over the previous census records. This sudden spurt was primarily due to the large scale migration of population during the partition of India and Delhi was the destination of innumerable migrants because it provided an extra ordinary impetus after becoming the capital of independent India. In the subsequent two decades *i.e.* (1951-61 and 1961-71), there has been more or less equal rate of increase (Table 13.1), approximately 64 per cent in 1961 and 54.7 per cent in 1971. The factors largely responsible for the rapid growth of population of Delhi were that there was a spurt of jobs in government and semi-government offices, there was increasing concentration of the transportation network and wholesale trade and commerce in the city. These coupled with "push" factors, operating in the rural areas have been responsible for the rising crescendo of in-migration to Delhi which have seriously deteriorated its physical, social and economic environment.

Component of urban growth

The population growth of urban Delhi is primarily due to three factors : natural increase, extension in urban boundary and migration. In the population explosion ; migration to Delhi has played a dominant role in accelerating the growth of population in the city. The contribution of net migration to the total population growth of Delhi has always been more than that of natural increase. During (1961-71) the growth of population due to natural increase was 43.33 per cent (Table 13.2). The proportion increase due to extension in urban boundary was only 5.6 per cent. The contribution of migration was 51.06 per cent. The total migrants enumerated in 1971 in Delhi were 16.53 lakhs. Bulk of migrants to Delhi poured in from four adjoining states—U.P., Haryana, Punjab and Rajasthan – which together contributed 77.8 per cent of the total migrant stream. It is an interesting fact that U.P. has send the largest contingent of migrants to Delhi which constitutes 42.5 per cent, which is being followed by Haryana 14.07 per cent, Punjab 13.01 and Rajasthan 8.16 per cent. The population of migrants from remaining other states of India accounted for 22.19 per cent only (Table 13.3).[22] It has been estimated that approximately 100,000 migrants per year are constantly pouring into Delhi.

TABLE 13.1 : **Decadel growth of population in Delhi 1901-1971**

Decade	Population of Urban Delhi	Percentage increase over the previous decade
1901	214,115	—
1911	237,944	11.13
1921	304,420	27.94
1931	447,422	46.98
1941	695,688	56.48
1951	1,437,134	106.58
1961	2,359,408	64.17
1971	3,647,023	54.57

Source : Census of India Publications, Delhi, 1971.

TABLE 13.2 : **Growth of population due to various components in Delhi (1961-1971)**

S. No.	Components	Absolute increase	Percentage increase to total
1.	Natural Increase	587,878	43.23
2.	Extension of Urban Boundary	72,278	5.61
3.	Net Migration	657,459	51.06
4.	Addition in Population	1,287,615	100.00

Source : Compiled by T.C.P.O.

TABLE 13 3 : **Magnitude of migrants in Delhi (1971)**

S. No.	Source Region	No. of Migrants in Delhi	Percentage of Migrants to Total Migrants
1.	Uttar Pradesh	636,073	42.57
2.	Haryana	210,311	15.91
3.	Punjab	194,403	13.01
4.	Rajasthan	121,951	8.16
5.	Total from four adjoining states	1,162,738	77.81
6.	Total migrants from other states	331,548	22.10
7.	Total migrants from all India	1,494,286	100

Source : Compiled from the Census Records, 1971.

PROCESS OF MIGRATION

Pre-migration status of migrants

Before we discuss the perceptive channels of migrants, it is essential to know their pre-migration social and spatial status. There is enough evidence to prove that migration is a selective process in terms of demographic characteristics of those who move.

Social Status

The character of immigrants to Delhi constitutes to be complex and heterogeneous. Socially they vary in terms of social experience. It is evident from the survey that most of the migrants to Delhi belonged to 'have not' group or poorest of all the poor, socially deprived, destitutes and economically under employed, illiterate casual labourers. It is obvious from Table 13.4, that largest stream of Migrants constitute marginal farmers and sharecroppers who are unable to earn enough to support the family. The other prominent sector of migrants belongs to landless labourers and artisan class such as carpenters, weavers, barbers, potters, cobblers, sweepers and manual labourers. While we examine (Table 13.5) it becomes self evident that rural migrants are highly selective of their caste system.

TABLE 13.4 : **Pre-migration occupational status of migrants in Delhi**

S. No.	Occupational Status	Percentage of the total respondent
1.	Marginal farmers who holds less than one acre land	40
2.	Landless labourers	35
3.	Artisans and service occupation	15
4.	Others	10
5.	Total	100

Source : Compiled from Field Survey, 1980-81.

TABLE 13.5 : **Pre-migration caste status of migrants in Delhi**

S. No.	Caste Status	Percentage of the total respondent
1.	Upper Caste Hindu	10
2.	Backward Classes	15
3.	Scheduled Caste	70
4.	Muslims	3
5.	Sikhs	2
6.	Total	100

Source : Compiled from Field Survey, 1980-81.

Approximately 70 per cent migrants belong to Scheduled Caste and 15 per cent to backward class. The higher status migrants constitutes a very small proportion.

Demographic selectivity among migrants

There is much cross cultural evidence that migration is a selective process in terms of the demographic characteristics of those who move. In general the propensity to move is greatest among young adults. The migration is selective of young adults which is most widely demonstrated preposition to be emerged from the survey. Speaking broadly persons aged 15 to 30 years old predominate in such a measure that they comprise 75 per cent of all migrants (Table 13.6). It seems that young men are often better equipped than his peers, who consciously decide to move to satisfy his aspirations and they tend to be more motivated, more aggressive, risk taking and adventurous. The flow of migrants in this age group postulates that there would be social and economic depression or decline in rural settings.

Sex selectivity

It is clear from the survey that males participate more frequently than do females in migration to Delhi. The difference is pronounced (80 per cent males and 20 per cent females). The differentiation by marital status is also demonstrated. Single male adult without marriage are more prone to move to unknown destination (60 per cent unmarried and 40 per cent married).

TABLE 13.6 : **Pre-migration age structure**

S. No.	Age of Migrants	Percentage of the total respondent
1.	Migrants 15–20 years	45
2.	Migrants 20–30 years	30
3.	Migrants 30–40 years	15
4.	Migrants above 40	10
5.	Total	100

Source : Compiled from Field Survey, 1980-81.

TABLE 13.7 : **Pre-migration educational status**

S. No.	Educational Status	Percentage of the total respondent
1.	Illiterate	65
2.	Those who can sign or write	1
3.	Primary Education	20
4.	Middle	10
5.	Higher Secondary	3
6.	More than Higher Secondary	1
7.	Total	100

Source : Compiled from Field Survey, 1980-81.

Pre-migration educational status

It seems that a large majority of migrants were illiterate when they left their villages. Approximately 65 per cent were illiterate (Table 13.7). It shows that due to sluggish economic activities in the villages, parents do not prefer to send their children to schools.

All these aspects of the pre-migration status of migrants clearly reveal that migration from rural areas to the city is highly selective. It is seen that most deprived, downtrodden, poorest of all the poor, dare to choose to leave hospitable environment of the village. Young male adults who are never married are most mobile.

Sources of migration

To ascertain the status of the migrants it is very essential to know the place of birth of migrants. From the survey, it is evident that unplanned colonies or localities of Delhi harbour 90 per cent migrants who have come from rural areas, and a very small proportion 10 per cent belongs to small cities. The regional affinities of the migrants has already been discussed, however, migrant streams from U.P. confirm that majority of migrants belongs, to the districts which are closer to Delhi, to most backward districts where there are no industries or factories in the close proximity, to districts where natural calamities occur frequently such as floods and droughts, and to districts where there is agricultural stagnation at its highest peak.

The study of sources of migration justified that there is concomitant relationship between migration and distance. It is a truism that a change of residence necessarily involves spatial consideration and cost of transportation. The study of Delhi supports one of the most familiar "laws" of migration propounded by Ravenstein[23] which states that the great body of our migrants only proceed a short distance. As a corollary, the longer the distance of migration, the less the number of people migrating between an origin and a destination. The study of Delhi supports a common conjuncture that poor migrants travel short distance or to a place which minimizes cost of transportation. It reveals that only higher socio-economic status persons, seeking better jobs or opportunities dare to move a greater distance to look for desirable opportunities whereas poor migrants move only for less desirable opportunities. Thus distance is an obvious and important factor. Delhi recruit more of its migrants from its nearby hinterland than from the remote areas because journey is so much more simple and less costly. Again the nearer areas are likely to have experienced an early and faster rate of economic development and their people have greater contacts, and hold a better perceived image of the opportunities available in the city.

The above analysis demonstrates that the process of rural migrants is important not just because of the redistribution of population perse, each migrant has certain attributes, for example, age, sex, family status, occupation, educational attainment, social and cultural attributes and regional affinities. Thus the process of migration in its wake brings much more than simple population distribution, it also leads to a redistribution of such attributes from rural areas to the city which ultimately results in to spatial structure which is neither rural nor urban.

Process of decision making

The normative analysis of migration, as a consequence to economic wage rate fluctuations provides only limited clues because they neglect considerations of the perceptions prevalent among the potential migrants. If the study of migration ignores decision of individual migrant and his motivations ; it will not only impoverishes our understanding of the migration process but also deprives us of an image of a vital element in the life experience of the migrant which will effect his own perception of the urban environment and of his activities there in.[24] In order to obtain more detailed explanations, why migration occur, consideration must be given to the process of decision making where by individuals decide to migrate and decide where to move to. Common to most behavioural work on migration is the principle of place utility which is stated to be as an individuals degree of satisfaction or dissatisfaction with different attributes of a place. The information may be biased about places, however an individual's perception of the place utility of the place he lives in, has a strong element of certainty about it, because the individual has actually experienced and evaluated the advantages and disadvantages of life existed in that place. Thus several alternatives are made by migrants before they take a decision to migrate from rural areas to the cities. Migration involves a hierarchy of decisions, each successive stage of the hierarchy involving a research within area of geographical scale. These successive stages are 1. dissatisfaction, 2. motivation and 3. attitudes of the migrants.

Dissatisfaction of migrants

In studies of migration the accent has generally been placed on the incentives provided by dissatisfaction with one's social, and economical environment. From the survey of Delhi it is quite obvious that a majority of migrants (80 per cent) were initially dissatisfied with the conditions prevalent in the villages because they obtain insufficient food, shelter and clothing (Table 13.8). Approximately 40 per cent respondent revealed that they were seasonal labourers, so it was difficult to earn enough money to support a family life which led to a lot of tension in the minds of the migrants. It is interesting that 70 per cent respondent were worried about paying the heavy debt to money lenders. 75 per cent respondent were dissatisfied because they were landless labourers. Sixty five per cent respondent reported low wages as the case of dissatisfaction. Fragmentation of landholdings caused dissatisfaction in the minds of 42 per cent respondent. The other reasons of dissatisfactions were, lack of medical facilities (20%), harassed by upper caste people (21%), crop failure (13%), insecurity (17%), fear of famine and draught (20 per cent) and unemployment (38%) (Table 13.8). So it seems that reasons of dissatisfaction are numerous which created tension and instability in the personal life of the migrants when they were living in the villages. The tension and disorganized life later on flame the fire and facilitated the migrants to take quick decision to leave the home. From the study it is clear that approximately 70 per cent migrants made up their mind to leave the village. The main reasons of their decision to migrate were the reasons of dissatisfaction. These causes of the dissatisfaction repel the migrants from villages.

The survey demonstrates a conscious desire among the migrants for economic and social mobility which provided direct motivation to seek better jobs, higher income and less social discrimination. The rural migrants in Delhi are drown from two extreme streams which face basically different problems ; one type qualitatively creame such as artisans who migrate in search of wider opportunities and second type is non-selective streams who are drown from 'have not' sector are numerically dominant, they are pushed from the villages by dearth of land and employment opportunities. A distinctive feature of rural migrants in Delhi is that they are "*Lemper* proletarial" whose problems are increasing uncertainty and insecurity. These migrants are not only related to the "bottom of the heap" in the social hierarchy of rural life but are also economically and politically deprived. So the move of migrant to Delhi was not so much of an alternative way of life rather it was an act of desperation.

Motivation

The decision to migrate involves change in place of employment and change in residence, so migrants take a judicious decision in the selection of a new place of employment. In rural communities, there is a customary resistence against mobility. If migration does occur, the kinship relationship plays an important role in guiding the decision maker. The source of information about the job opportunities prior to

TABLE 13.8 : **Percentage migrants dissatisfy with native place**

S. No.	Reasons of dissatisfaction	Composite percentage of respondent
1.	Not sufficient food, shelter an l clothing	80
2.	Seasonal employment	40
3.	Caste discrimination	45
4.	Indebtedness	70
5.	No medical facilities	20
6.	No land to cultivate	75
7.	Low wages	65
8.	Large family	35
9.	Division of land	42
10.	Crop failure	13
11.	Fear of decoids	17
12.	Flood havock	14
13.	Draught famine	9
14.	Unemployment	38
15.	Do not get sufficient price for their goods	11

Source : Compiled from Field Survey, 1980-81.

migration is a very significant contributory factor to highlight the place utility of the destination. Such information may take the form of recollection of personal visits, letters from past migrants, conversation with friends who have visited other places[25] or books, newspapers and broadcaste. However the informal system of information is more operative. This "information flow" effectively enable the migrants to develop a place utility idea of the destination.

While inquired about the source of information or agents of motivation about employment of migrants (Table 9), relatives, friends and co-villagers appears to be the major source of information. It accounts for approximately 60 per cent respondent. The relatives or co-villagers provide them incentives in terms of information, regarding better job opportunities, more wages and better residence. There are only 10 per cent migrants who sought their incentives from the labour contractors (Table 13.9), while approximately 20 per cent assessed the place utility of Delhi while they visited the city themselves.

TABLE 13.9 : **Percentage migrants according to source of motivation**

S. No.	Source of motivation	Percentage of respondent
1.	Family members	25
2.	Co-villagers	15
3.	Friends	10
4.	Relatives	18
5.	Agents	10
6.	Voluntary	20
7.	No response	2
8.	Total	100

Source : Compiled from Field Survey, 1980-81.

TABLE 13.10 : **Routes of rural urban migrants**

S. No.	Routes	Percentage of respondent
1.	Rural to Rural	10
2.	Rural to market than to Delhi	10
3.	Rural to small towns than to Delhi	25
4.	Rural to provincial centre than to Delhi	15
5.	Rural to Metropolitan City	40
6.	Total	100

Source : Compiled from Field Survey, 1980-81.

The motivation of migrants about the place utility of destination depends largely on social communication network and the formal system of information does not play an important role in terms of unskilled, illiterate migrants.

Attitude of migrant

It is an interesting finding of the survey that 80 per cent migrants shifted willingly or voluntarily and 10 per cent unwillingly who resisted and were indifferent during their initial movement from the village, approximately 10 per cent did not know any thing, they had completely forgotten the situation.

The migrants were not only motivated but they were also provided financial help to move and were helped to search jobs and residences by the fellow relations already living in the city. It is estimated that 40 per cent did not obtain any financial help to move whereas 60 per cent received financial help. Of those obtained financial help, 90 per cent received help from relatives and 10 per cent from contractors.

The causes and motivation of migration of rural poor to Delhi, as observed, may be many. However the common ones are : (1) the perceived employment opportunities in the city, (2) dissatisfaction of labourers in their native place, (3) encouragement or inducement by relations from the city, (4) offer of employment by the professional contractors, (5) age old social injustice suffered by the backward communities, (6) hopes and dreams of better life in the cities.

The rural migrants perceive better employment opportunities and higher wages in Delhi which they found in informal sector such as, construction of buildings and roads petty trades, professional services (sweepers, barbers tailors. carpenters, household and domestic servants and other odd jobs in organized commercial establishments.

The rural migrants perceived their native place unsatisfactory because they were marginal workers in the village who lived on the brink of acute distress, under compulsion left their villages and sought their fortune in Delhi. The migrants also perceived that there was a decline of employment opportunities in the villages due to erosion of traditional crafts and professions as a result of competition from the modern sector. Thus artisan communities such as potters, oilman, carpenters, blacksmith, found their professions threatened, wage a grim battle for survival so they changed their occupations and looked towards Delhi for better opportunities.

Added to these predisposing economic factors, are the social circumstances that determined the propensities to migrate to Delhi. The immediate cause of stimulation to spark off the mobility is provided by the encouragement or inducement of a city based relation who act to neutralise the risk and hesitation that inevitably preface the decision making process. The glitter of the city that these relations tell to the villagers during their short visit and boast of their prestige as being enterprising pioneers, generally allure the young adult males of the village.

There are also professional contractors who recruite labours for construction. They periodically visit the villages and encourage groups of labourers to the city under their patronage. These contractors sometimes give them advance money to be adjusted later against their wages.

Mode and patterns of migration

The rural migrants in Delhi do infact come from all areas. They leave their villages because there are so few opportunities to gain a successful living from stagnating agriculture. At first such people may migrate seasonally or target workers. As time lapses these migrants gradually gain more knowledge so will more men spend larger periods there, the successful migrants when visit the village, stimulate other fellow being to try their luck in the city. The patterns of migration are complex and bewildering. In an attempt to bring order to an apparently chaotic picture scholars search for a universal pattern of migration *e.g.*, a step migration, a chain migration and a circular migration patterns. The patterns of migration vary not only between communities but also over time. Any argument that either step or chain or circular migration provides the correct model is clearly misconceived.[26] However a hypothetical example might clarify this point. This hypothetical generalization is conceived from the recollections of migrants. It was customary in India that weekly market centres were organized where villagers from nearby areas gather to purchase. Most of the stalls in these markets were of artisans, who were the first emigrants to go to the nearby towns. They return after a few months to continue their traditional mode of life. A pattern of circular or seasonal migration is established. Some of these artisans, instead of returning home, venture further afield, and eventually reach the capital city. These men have experienced step migration. Off there a few will succeed and reports of their fortune will percolate back to the village, when they visit their village they encourage the youth of later generation to come to the city directly. Gradually the link between village and city intensify. As the new arrivals seek better fortune in the city they encourage their kin to follow them and the chain movement increases by geometric progression.

A step migration

The survey of Delhi rural migrants demonstrates that cityward migration involves a series of spatial movements. The migrants recollect that they have moved to the capital city through various stages between the first migration from their villages and the final to the city. There are various escape routes adopted by these migrants (Table 13.10, Figure 13.1). It is evident that their journey to Delhi was not straight from their village, for some it was the last stage, however they wondered far and wide from one city to another being led by the pressure of events. It is a step migration. A step migration is postulated when the migrants successively move from village to small towns than to provincial towns and from there to capital city. The survey of Delhi confirms that approximately 55 per cent migrants have experienced this process, because 10 per cent migrants moved from rural areas to weekly marketing centre than to Delhi, 25 per cent moved from rural areas to smaller towns than to Delhi, (Table 13.10), 15 per cent from rural areas to provincial large city than to Delhi (Figure 13.1).

Chain migration

The step migration is replaced by a chain migration, as successful city immigrants encourage their kin to travel directly to the capital city. The survey of Delhi demonstrates that a substantial large number of migrants have experienced chain process (40 per cent) (Table 13.10). The chain process postulates the integration of rural communities and urban communities. The relatives and friends who had migrated earlier and established themselves in the city, instigate or stimulate their fellow kin to come to the city. These new aspirants who are torn too rapidly away from the traditional cultural framework of their lives find themselves thrown to quickly as strangers into a cultural environment which is unfamiliar and thus the danger of disorganisation is great. The new comers to the city treat the immigrant community as the beach head from which they move with strength and establish themselves. This probably explains why

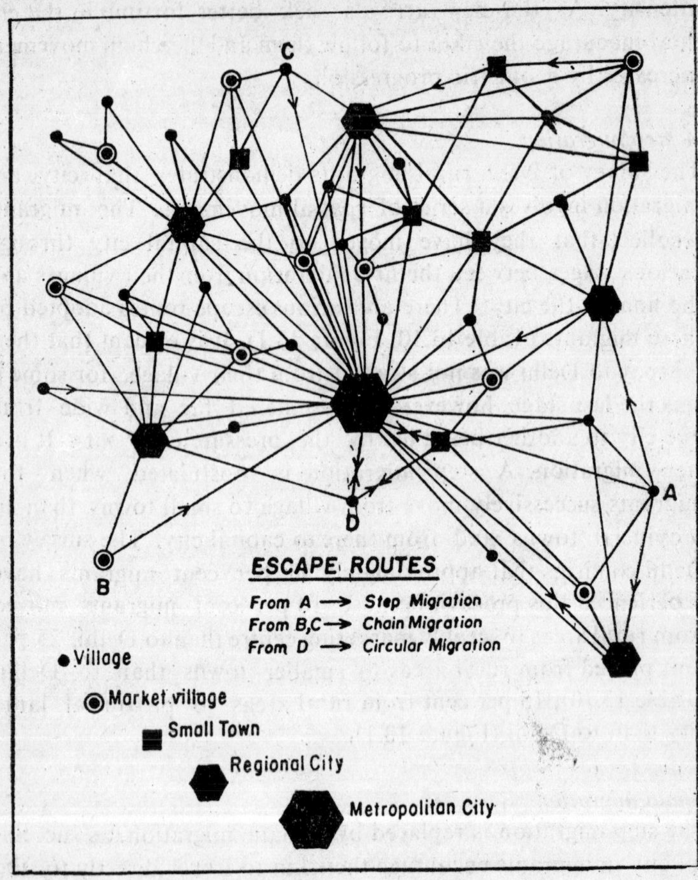

FIG. 13.1 : *Patterns of migration*

new migrants tend to go to the same places where earlier migrants live *i.e.* chain process.

Circular migration

Many a social scientist are increasingly accepting the idea that people who migrate do not always intend to remain in the place where they go, but expect to return and often do return to their places of origin. It is apparent from the survey of Delhi that approximately 90 per cent migrants have spend some period of their lives in the city, returned home and, perhaps after a further period, setting off again. The artisans or traders always see an expansion of their activities only in a larger and wealthier community. They set off tentatively to try their back. If successful, they will stay on in the city, if they fail to establish themselves they will return perhaps to try again later on in some other areas, becoming by default rather than by design, the circular migrants. Take another case of illiterate unskilled labourer who aspires for a better life in material terms—more food to eat, and an improved house. He may see this better life as being achieved in the city but he has strong bonds which do not allow him to leave the village permanently. In this case he will contemplate either one or more seasonal migration, leaving the village for a few months when agricultural activity is at its lowest to make a quick cash working as an unskilled labourer. These types of migrants carry a dual or multiple identity. The movement to cities by migrants from rural areas, who expect to return, with significantly high frequency, urbanize their lifestyles, attitudes and behaviour which in due course of time become one of the most important factor of urbanization of rural folks.

Preference for Delhi

The move of poor migrant from rural setting, primarily due to a sense of rejection, motivated them to accept the new environment. The move implies a process of dissociation from homogeneous, formal or familiar setting to a transitional, unknown environment and to a new relation of physical space. This new environment may be already known destination. The choice of migrant to move to city is entirely based on the individual's evaluation of anticipated utility which is derived from information flows facilitated a large number of prospective migrants to select Delhi as the destination for migration. Their choice was related to the perceived utility of the city. Before a final decision was taken by migrants, they went through a complex process of decision making. Initially a potential migrant gathered precise knowledge, about job's opportunities, place to stay and financial support that could be needed at the place of destination. In this process they were helped by those kin relationship who had already migrated to Delhi city. It was these links with their fellow migrants and their perception of Delhi as a

TABLE 13.11 : **Reasons, migrants prefer Delhi as their destination**

S. No.	Reasons of Preference	Composite Percentage
1.	Better opportunities in Delhi	62.2
2.	Nearest place from the Village	8.3
3.	Glamour of the City	2.2
4.	Relatives or Friends live in Delhi	22.8
5.	Higher Wages	26.5

Source : Compiled from Field Survey, 1980-81.

convenient centre of job opportunities that lurred them to select Delhi as their destination of migration.

It is quite apparent from (Table 13.11), that almost 60.2 per cent migrants chose Delhi as a place of migration because of better job opportunities. Approximately 26 per cent prefer Delhi because of the higher wages offered in different sectors of employment. A very large section of migrants considered the presence of their relatives as an additional factor of migrating to Delhi.

The aspects of prior idea of Delhi clearly reveals that a majority of migrants had prior idea of Delhi. They had acquired well in advance a perfect knowledge of the city. Table 13.12 allows to conclude that approximately 70 per cent migrants had a definite idea of Delhi, and 19 per cent had some vague idea. This justifies that majority of migrants had safe landing in Delhi city.

MIGRANTS ADJUSTMENT TO THE CITY LIFE

There is a way of adjustment of rural migrants to a stable urban culture of Delhi. Physically it is envisioned as a search for shelter and jobs. They try to assimilate into the complex system of the city. Economically the migrants make an attempt to adjust to the changed occupation and rhythm of work. Culturally they undergo a revolution in motivation, values and ideologies. While busy with these activities, the migrants shape the culture of the city as much as they are adjusting to it. Their action is neither traditional nor city like. They are largely

TABLE 13.12 : **Percentage migrants who had prior idea of Delhi**

S. No.	Whether they had prior idea	Percentage of respondent
1.	Non whatsoever	11.3
2.	Some Vague Idea	19.2
3.	Definite Idea	69.5
4.	Total	100

Source : Compiled from Field Survey, 1980-81.

TABLE 13.13 : **Duration of stay of migrants in Delhi**

S. No.	Duration of Stay	Percentage of respondent
1.	Less than 1 year	9.3
2.	1 – 5 years	27.4
3.	5—10 years	18.3
4.	10 – 15 years	22.4
5.	15 years and above	17.8
6.	Period not mentioned	4.8
7.	Total	100

Source : Complied from Field Survey, 1980-81.

ruralizing the culture of the Delhi city. Some aspects such as duration of stay, occupational mobility, links with the native place, remittances send to the native places, desirability of keeping contacts with native place, comparison of city life with village life and attitude towards city life, all reflect how migrant make an adjustment with the city life.

Duration of stay in Delhi

Majority of migrants in Delhi have opted to stay in Delhi permanently and there are no prospects of returning back to the village life. Majority of them have been staying for more than five years (Table 13.13). This reflects that they have become the integral part and parcel of the main stream of city life.

TABLE 13.14 : **Occupational status of migrants in Delhi**

S. No.	Occupation	Percentage of respondent
1.	Hawkers and Venders	12.2
2.	Construction Labourers	39.8
3.	Loading and Unloading	8.2
4.	Household Workers	5.2
5.	Lobourers in Industrial and Commercial Establishment	8.3
6.	Workers in Traditional Trade	11.5
7.	Semi-professional Workers	5.7
8.	Petty Shopkeeper	9.1
9.	Total	100

Source : Compiled from Field Survey, 1980-81.

Occupational mobility of migrants

The enormous expansion of Delhi city in terms of construction of houses, roads, commerce and industry, provide wide range of job opportunities to the migrants, who are engaged in unskilled low paid jobs, so their status in the city remains as marginal or subsistence workers. The classification of migrants in various jobs is given in Table 13.14. An examination of the table clearly reveals that a majority of migrants are engaged in unskilled low paid jobs which constitutes approximately 65 per cent migrants, they are hawkers and venders (12.2%), construction workers (39.8%), loading and unloading (8.2%) and household workers (5.2%). A relatively very low proportion of these workers (8.3%) is engaged in industrial establishments. The workers in traditional trade are only 11.5 per cent. The other sectors of employment of these migrants are semi-professional and petty trades. The survey apparently demonstrates that about 37 per cent migrants are casual labourers whereas 52 per cent are semi-permanent. Only 22 per cent are permanently engaged (Table 13.15). A majority of workers found a lot of difference between "before" and "after" situation. The monthly wages earned by these workers shows that they remain marginal workers in the city who cannot earn enough money from their wages.

TABLE : 13.15 **Percentage migrants with duration of jobs**

S. No.	Duration of Jobs	Wages	Percentage of respondent
1.	10 days a month	Rs. 150	8.5
2.	15 days a month	Rs. 225	15.8
3.	20 days a month	Rs. 300	12.7
4.	25 days a month	Rs. 375	40.2
5.	Full month but semi-permanent	Rs. 400	22.8

Source : Compiled from Field Survey, 1980-81.

TABLE 13.16 : **Linkage with native place**

S. No.	Reasons of Linkage	Composite percentage
1.	No Property or House in Native Place	30.2
2.	Possess Property	69.8
3.	No Family Members at Native Place	23.2
4.	Wife, Children and Dependent Parents at Native Place	18.3
5.	Other Family Members at Native Place	55.5

Source : Compiled from Field Survey, 1980-81.

Living conditions

When migrants enter into city, their immediate task is to explore for shelter which normally they share (in their initial stage with the host. Generally newly arrived migrants seek the assistance of relatives, friends or co-villagers, already established in the city. It is revealed by the findings of the survey that nearly 80 per cent migrants sought assistance from their relatives during their transitional period. It is also revealed that 70 per cent migrant live in a group of 4-5 persons, together in one room accommodation devoid of basic and civic amenities. Usually the low paid labourers select accommodation which is cheaper, so mostly they harbour in slum localities.

PROCESS OF STABILIZATION

The migrants in Delhi recollected that initially they shifted to the city as temporary necessitarian, however, in due course of time they gradually stabilizes them. The study provides sufficient clues that in spite of temporary involvement of migrants in the city, they are active participant in the development of the city. They serve the city by rendering various services ; they are the source of cheap labour which is essential for an effective and efficient functioning of the city. As a matter of fact they are needed by the city for the survival of its affluent society.

The rural migrants, adopt different mechanisms to cope with urban life, the earlier arrivals provide the subsequent migrants assistance in finding jobs and shelter in the city. These information links with the senior migrants play an important role in the socialization, stabilization and acculturation of migrants in the city. In the process of stabilization the "pull" of the village seems to be weakening irrespective of the fact that these migrants visit their native place, send remittances, have their property and ties with the kins.

Links with the native place

It is observed that migrants keep a close contact with their kin and family members in the village. Approximately 70 per cent migrants, in their initial stage, left their family members back at home (Table 13.16). About 30 per cent left the village along with their families. It is ascertained by the survey (Table 13.16) that nearly 70 per cent migrants possess property and house in the village, so they have reasons to visit their villages. A very large majority of respondent have larger kin group residing in the native place.

The frequency of visits to the native place measures the degree of ties with the native communities. The migrants recollect that on an average they visit their villages twice a year. In general these visits are made on the occasion of important festivals, to perform social ceremonies and in connection with the management of their property.

It is customary in the village communities that the village fellowbeings usually visit their kin in the city. It was found in Delhi that about 60 per cent migrants received visitors last year. Some of these visitors came to see their family members, some came with an idea to explore chances of migration at some future date. The migrants also keep a close link with native place by way of sending remittances. Approximately 40 per cent migrants used to send remittances.

Choice of migrants to settledown in Delhi

The migrants while leaving their native place face transitional situation in which there is loss of the one and the gradual acceptance and understanding of the other. The poor migrants of Delhi have whemently documented the complex emotional problems involved in such a transition, and there seems a sharp contrast between "before" and "after" dichotomies. The obvious question than is ; have they wipped out the old and ready to be fully socialized and assimilated to the new ?

On the basis of group discussion and frequent visit to these migrants, it is revealed that a large majority of migrants have decided to settledown permanently in Delhi. It was found that longer the duration of stay stronger is the decision of migrant to live permanently in the city (Table 13.17). It is apparent from the table that 72.3 per cent respondent have made up their mind to stay permanently in the city. Approximately 18 per cent have not taken any decision, so they have an open option to decide in future, where as 9.6 per cent have out rightly rejected to settledown in the city. New commers to the city do not take a hasty decision, until and unless they sought some period of socialization in the city.

Attitude towards city life

In effect, to make a clear distinction between the perceived and objective environment ; it is very essential to find out how migrants react to their immediate surrounding in which they are living. In the sample survey the respondent were asked to make statements about the prevailing living conditions in their own locality. This is designed to find out how rural migrants perceive their own environment and the manner in which they evaluate the living conditions in their own localities.

TABLE 13.17 : **Duration of stay in Delhi and decision to settle permanently**

S. No.	Duration of Stay	Decision to Settledown		
		% do not wanted	% not yet taken decision	% decided
1.	Less than 5 Years	21.2	35.4	45.4
2.	5 to 10 Years	4.5	14.3	84.4
3.	10-15 Years	3.2	5.7	91.1
4.	Total	9.6	18.1	72.3

Source : Compiled from Field Survey, 1980-81.

TABLE 13.18 : **Evaluation of conditions in Delhi**

S. No.	Perceived Living Conditions	Percentage of respondent
1.	Excellent	8.0
2.	Good	42.0
3.	Satisfactory	38.0
4.	Bad	10.0
5.	Very Bad	2.0
6.	Total	100

Source : Compiled from Field Survey, 1980-81.

Overall view

Interestingly enough only 20 per cent reported their localities as bad (Table 13.18) whereas 60 per cent reported their localities either good or satisfactory. The analysis emphasises that nearly 88 per cent migrants of Delhi feel quite satisfactory and there is no sense of disappointment and dejection. The migrants of Delhi city show a very high degree of tolerance to adjust themselves in an undesirable environment.

Aspects of satisfaction

The survey demonstrates that a majority of rural migrants were satisfied in Delhi because of good transport facilities (93.4%) and availability of water and electric facilities (Table 13.19). A

TABLE 13.19 : **Frequency of mention of reasons for satisfaction of Delhi**

S. No.	Reasons for Satisfaction	Composite Percentage Satisfied
1.	Good Transport Facilities	93.4
2.	Good Water Facilities	55.0
3.	Good Electricity Facilities	74.5
4.	Owned a House	88.2
5.	Low Rental Values	41.0
6.	School Facilities for their Children	65.0
7.	Market Facilities	82.0
8.	Closer to their Kin	87.0
9.	Living for a long time	42.0
10.	No interference in life	78.0
11.	No sense of dejection	78.0
12.	Better employment opportunities	90.0
13.	Higher wages than in native place	87.0
14.	Better Social Status	60.0

Source : Compiled from Field Survey, 1980-81.

very strong sense of satisfaction is mentioned by some of the migrants because they own their self made house (which was allotted to them during 1976 emergency period). The migrants also like Delhi city because it is closer to their native place (87%) some of them are satisfied because of better socio-economic status. Migrants also feel that Delhi provide better medical facilities. A very large section displays that they have less tension in Delhi city than at their native place.

Aspects of dissatisfaction

Migrants feel dissatisfied about Delhi city in many a ways. The migrants reported that their main resentment with Delhi is that they live far away from their place of work. The migrants are also aware of the prevailing congestion and insanitation (Table 13.20) in the city. Most of the migrants found Delhi a costly place. A section of 30 per cent of migrants showed the sense that Delhi is a city which is meant for affluent society. They also feel that planners and administrators do not pay attention to their problems (Table 13.20).

TABLE 13.20 : **Frequency of mention of reasons for dissatisfaction of Delhi**

S. No.	Reasons of Dissatisfaction	Composite Percentage Dissatisfied
1.	House away from place of work	80.0
2.	Congestion	20.0
3.	Insanitation	60.0
4.	Things are costly in the market	77.0
5.	Administrators do not pay attention	40.0
6.	Delhi belongs to affluent society	30.0
7.	No response	10.0

Source : Compiled from Field Survey, 1980-81.

STRATEGIES

The discussion of magnitude of migration in Delhi, the process of migration, the patterns and their linkages with Delhi, all point that for some decades large scale migration will be inevitable. The study of migration of Delhi confirm the idea of Dennis A. Rodinelli,[27] that rural to urban migration patterns have tended to reinforce the growth and dominance of primate cities in India. It has been remarked about the urbanization process in India that India is over urbanized and that its primate cities are manifestations of a pseudo-urbanization which primarily rely on tertiary sector rather than on productive economic activities. Moreover, migration from rural areas is frequently considered evils of urbanization, is not itself necessarily bad. As a matter of fact rural urban migration is an essential condition of both rural and urban development and can be an indicator of healthy economic change. In principal certain level of rural to urban migration is inevitable and must be accommodated in the cities. However, as may be the case of Delhi, the adversities of unabated streams of migration to it, combined with high rate of population increase in both rural and urban areas and skewed pattern of urbanization which is too slow and too constrained, have led in India to search for urbanization policy which will help lowering over all population growth rate and changing patterns of migration. If no solution is sought to regulate the unguided, unplanned flow of migrants, the administrators and planners will face a uphill task because these unabated streams of migrants will add more tragedy to the already existing problems. The remedy of this problem lies with the policies of urban unemployment, dispersed urbanization and housing.

The policies to deal with urban unemployment

The most obvious solution to the problem of urban unemployment is to fix minimum urban wages which will help the casual labourers. The government can force to keep the urban minimum wage by providing wage subsidies to urban employees and by encouraging and subsidizing industrial investment to expand urban employment. The most effective solution lies if government restrict rural urban migration or establish government run labour enchanges, where by only when jobs are open up in urban centers, an equal number of workers is allowed to migrate to cities to fill those jobs.

The policies of dispersed urbanization and population planning

The most promising alternative seems to be dispersed urbanization and population planning which will aim at lowering overall population growth rate. Measures should be taken to increase productivity capacity of rural areas by encouraging the growth of market centers, small cities and regional urban centers. In India it is feasible because there is an articulated national spatial hierarchy of urban centers (Fig. 13.1). In the long run such a strategy could strongly influence overall patterns of urbanization, population growth and migration.

The study of Delhi points that volume of migration does not necessarily create problems but its patterns. As several scholars have identified that in India class I cities have grown faster than their counter part small and medium cities. It is labelled against the planners and administrators that they have failed to sought ways to strengthen the economies and to promote the growth of secondary cities. It is because of this factor, rural migrants have no where to go for better economic opportunities but to already overcrowded primate cities. Because of this Delhi is receiving large number of migrants and now is unable to absorb some more number of new migrants. A crisis situation has arisen. If government will provide better infrastructure to already existing intermediate and small towns in the vicinity of Delhi than migrants will move more progressively towards smaller towns and medium size cities. The study of Delhi supports the contention that rural people always move to places offering a wide variety of services, facilities and potential employment. If intermediate cities and smaller towns around Delhi are provided these facilities, they will definitely stimulate the economics of surrounding rural areas and help to slow down migration to Delhi city and the backward regions will receive benefits of economic growth. The growth of secondary cities will definitely alter the overall patterns of rural urban migration to Delhi city. The growth of smaller cities will also redirect the direction of migrants.

Another strategy that can check rural urban migration is to foster comprehensive spatial national development plan which will involve integrated urban and rural development strategy. Plans should be prepared to make the rural life productive and satisfactory. Programms are needed to involve poor rural dwellers in a high productivity agricultural system. All efforts should be made to provide better facilities to villagers. The labourers should get higher wages, they should be absorbed in some development plans like construction of roads. The government should provide them better housing and medical facilities so that the labourers are not tempted to leave their villages. So long as there is wide gap between the development of cities and villages, the rural urban migration will be stimulated.

Urban housing policies

A very large proportion of migrants of Delhi live in slums and squatter settlements, the slums are "transitional" settlements, in the sense that their inhabitants are undergoing a social and economic change from a rural to urban life unfortunately this desired transition is associated with much human deprivation. In the process of searching for jobs and needing minimum shelter, many marginal rural migrants occupy illegally public and private land, located in a variety of places. As it is evident that slum settlement are characterised by bad physical housing composed of makeshift substandard material and are devoid of basic and civic amenities. Therefore urban housing policies should be based on the economic needs of the poor migrants. Such policies have been proposed and advocated in recent years in the U.N. Habitat conference recommendation.[28] The essence of these policies is that they propagate and emphasize to provide support and help to the migrants rather than complete solutions. They emphasize housing services rather than public housing and a wide based gradualism rather than a few immediate housing "lottery winners".[29]

A complete solution of the housing problem could be advocated on the basis of following strategies. The first step towards solving the housing problem is to ensure security of land tenure and win over the threat of eviction, as it was done in Delhi in 1976, when migrants were given land titles in resettlement colonies. Second step a government can take is to encourage self help construction of houses by the poor migrants, the government can provide assistance in management, design and execution. By doing so, the house construction will require less capital, create valuable skills and encourage community co-operation. The planners should adopt the views of Turner[30, 31, 32] who had advocated the principle of "freedom to built". His arguments for assisted self help is both simple and compelling. The proper role of the government is to ensure that those who are best able to built, either for themselves or for their neighbour, have access to the tools and basic resources for the job.

We have explored and analysed many problem areas and constraints on migration and urbanization. There are no clear solutions or guranteed successes, only some prefered direction. The government of India under 20-point programme include some of these directions ; how much is achieved is still debatable, but enough remains to be done. Therefore a dialogue and understanding is needed between various professions which are involved in migration, particularly between the government and the governed.

SUMMARY AND CONCLUSION

The rural urban migration has been one of the most dramatic occurrence of recent decades which has fostered urbanization of large segments of peasants. The process of urbanization in India is slow and concentrated. Primate cities receives more stream of migrants. In Delhi every year 100,000 migrants are pouring in who have seriously deteriorated its physical, social and economic environment. A close view of rural urban migration mechanism in Delhi provided a useful perspective of the process as a whole. Theoretically rural urban migration is not a spurious movement of a random selection of the population, but a deliberate move of select people with certain characteristics ; the social, economic and demographic elements of sending and receiving societies are affected. This mechanism leads to achieve a regional balance in terms of distribution of income and labour. However in reality it does not happen because rural migration create underemployment problems in the city and the selective out migration of the working group and labour force, hampers the development of rural areas with dependent population.

It is observed that migration of poor labourers into Delhi city is selective in terms of sex, age, education and social status. The study shows that largest number of migrants constitute marginal farmers, casual labourers, low socio status people. Young males predominates the whole stream. Delhi receives migrants from four neighbouring states. The analysis demonstrates that process of migration in Delhi is important not because of redistribution of population perse ; each migrant has certain attributes for example age, sex, family status, occupation, educational status, regional activities and its attitudes, customs and behaviour, so it also leads to a redistribution of such attributes from rural areas to the city.

The factors of decision to migrate demonstrate that there is a conscious desire among the migrants for economic and social mobility which provided direct motivation and they try to seek better jobs, higher income and less social discrimination.

The causes and motivation of migration of rural poor to Delhi are many, however the common ones are (*i*) perceived employment opportunities in the city, (*ii*) dissatisfaction of labourers in their native place, (*iii*) encouragement or inducement by relations and friends, (*iv*) offer of employment by the professional contractors from the cities, (*v*) age old social injustice suffered by the backward communities, (*vi*) hopes and dreams of better life in the cities.

The study of Delhi reveals that migrants usually follow a universal pattern of migration. In Delhi, a step migration, chain migration and circular migration are postulated.

The analysis makes it apparent that rural migrants in Delhi, adopt different mechanism to cope with urban life. The earlier arrivals provides the subsequent migrants assistance in finding jobs and shelter in the city. These information links with senior migrants play an important role in the socialization, stabilization and acculturation of migrants in the city. In the process of stabilization the "pull" of the village seems to be weakening irrespective of the fact that these migrants visit their native place, send remittances, have their property and ties with the kins. Thus the migrants represent dualistic system which is neither traditional in nature nor urban in out look rather it is transitional.

An integrated planning of rural and city development, guided migration and population planning may be helpful to redirect the streams of migration from primate cities. It is apparent that so long as migrants perceived better job opportunities in the cities they will tend to migrate, so migration is inevitable. To slow down the rate of migration efforts are needed to develop rural areas with job opportunities and provision of services and amenities.

REFERENCES

1. U.N. Population Division ; Patterns of Urban and Rural Growth (New York : Department of Economic and Social Affairs, 1980).
2. Wolpart, "Behavioral Aspects of the Decision to Migrate" : Papers of the Regional Science Association, Vol. 15, 1965, pp. 159-169.
3. Brown and Longbrake, "Migration Flows in Intra Urban Space, Place Utility Considerations", *Annals of the Association of American Geographers*, Vol. 60 (1970), pp. 368-89.

4. Cebulla and Vedder, "A Note on Migration, Economic Opportunity and the Quality of Life", *Journal of Regional Science Association*, Vol. 13 (1973), pp. 205-211.
5. Lee, E.S., "A Theory of Migration" in Population Geography : A Reader (Eds.) George, J.D., Harold, M.P. and George, A.S., Mc-Graw Hill, June 1970, p. 290.
6. Pack, "Determinants of Migration to Central Cities", *Journal of Regional Science*, Vol. 13, 1973, pp. 249-260.
7. Liu, "Differential Net Migration Rates and the Quality of Life", *Review of Economics and Statistics*, Vol. 57, 1975, pp. 329-37.
8. Sajadstad, L.A., "The Costs and Returns of Human Migration", *Journal of Political Economy, Supplement*, Vol. 70, 1962, pp. 80-93.
9. Bowels, S., "Migration as Investment : Empirical Tests of the Human Investment Approach to Geographical Mobility", *Review of Economics and Statistics*, Vol. 52, 1970, pp. 356-62.
10. Fabricant, R.A., "An Expectational Model of Migration", *Journal of Regional Science*, Vol. 10, 1970, pp. 13-24.
11. Nelson, "Migration, Real Income and Information", *Journal of Regional Science*, Vol. 1, 1959, pp. 43-74.
12. Parrish, "Internal Migration and Modernization", *Economic Development and Cultural Change*, Vol. 21, 1973, pp. 591-609.
13. Trott, "Differential Response in the Decisive to Migrate", *Papers of Regional Science Association*, Vol. 28, 1972, pp. 203-219.
14. Warriner, "Some Problems of Rural Urban Migration", *International Labour Review*, Vol. 101, 1970, pp. 441-451.
15. Zelinsky, W., "The Hypothesis of the Mobility Transition", *The Geographical Review*, Vol. 61, 1971, pp. 219-249.
16. Ravenstein, E.G., "The Laws of Migration", *Journal of Royal Statistical Society*, Vol. 48, 1885, pp. 167-227.
17. Zachariah and Bogue, D.J., "Urbanization and Migration in India", in *Indias Urban Future*, Ed. Roy Turner, Oxford University Press, 1962, p. 27.
18. Paulwhite and Robertwood, "The Geographical Impact of Migration" (Ed.).
19. Wolpart, Footnote 2, above.
20. National Capital Regional Plan Summary and Recommendation T.C.P.O.
21. *Census of India*, Delhi, 1971.
22. *Census of India*, Delhi, 1971.
23. Ravenstein, Footnote 16, above.
24. Peter Lloyd, "Slums of Hope : Shanty Towns of Third World" (1979), Penguin Books.
25. Paulwhite ahd Robertwood, Footnote 18, above.
26. Peter Lloyd, Footnote 24, above.
27. Dennis A. Rodinelli, "Balanced Urbanization Spatial Integration

and Economic Development in Asia", *Urbanism Past and Present*, Number 9 (Winlir, 1979-80).

28. United Nations, "Report on Habitat : United Nations Conference on Human Settlements", *Vancouver*, 31 May—11 June, 1976, New York.
29. Samuel Avoni, "Housing Policies, A Development World Perspective", *Housing Science*, Vol. 2, No. 4 (1978), 299-334.
30. Turner, J.F.C., "Approaches to Government—Sponsored Housing", *Ekistics*, Vol. 41, No. 242, January 1976, pp. 4-7.
31. Turner, J.F.C. and Fitcher, R., editors, *Freedom to Build*, The Macmillan Co., New York, 1972.
32. Turner, J.F.C., "A New Universe of Squatter Builders", *The UNESCO Courier*, Paris, June 1976, pp. 12-33

FOURTEEN

YORAM BAR-GAL

THE BIRTH PANGS OF A CITY
From Jaffa to Tel Aviv

A REAPPRAISAL of the contact between man and landscape took place in Geography during the decade of the seventies—marked by the appearance of the humanistic aspects, which had retreated during the previous decade, a period in which Geography stressed the positivistic approach (R.D. Sack, 1980 ; A. Buttimer, 1976).

The contact between man and landscape is frequently described (in one way or another) by writers and artists in their creative work (R.L. Heathcote, 1972 ; Y.F. Tuan, 1976, 1978). This is also true of Israel where the contact between man and landscape—the conquest of new space, the creation of new settlements, the building of a new society—has also found artistic expression. One of the interesting events in the development of the landscape in Israel over the last hundred years is the establishment of Tel Aviv as a neighbourhood of the ancient city of Jaffa and its crystallization as a city. The aim of this article is to cast this event in the light of the humanistic approach through the use of literature and art as source material. By this linear the description of the experience of the foundation and crystallization of the city during the first twenty years of the century (Fig. 14.1).

The urban landscape as experienced by Gutman and Alterman : Gutman (1898-1980) and Alterman (1910-1970) were associated with Tel Aviv for years. Both were versatile artists. Gutman achieved fame as an artist, but also did literary work

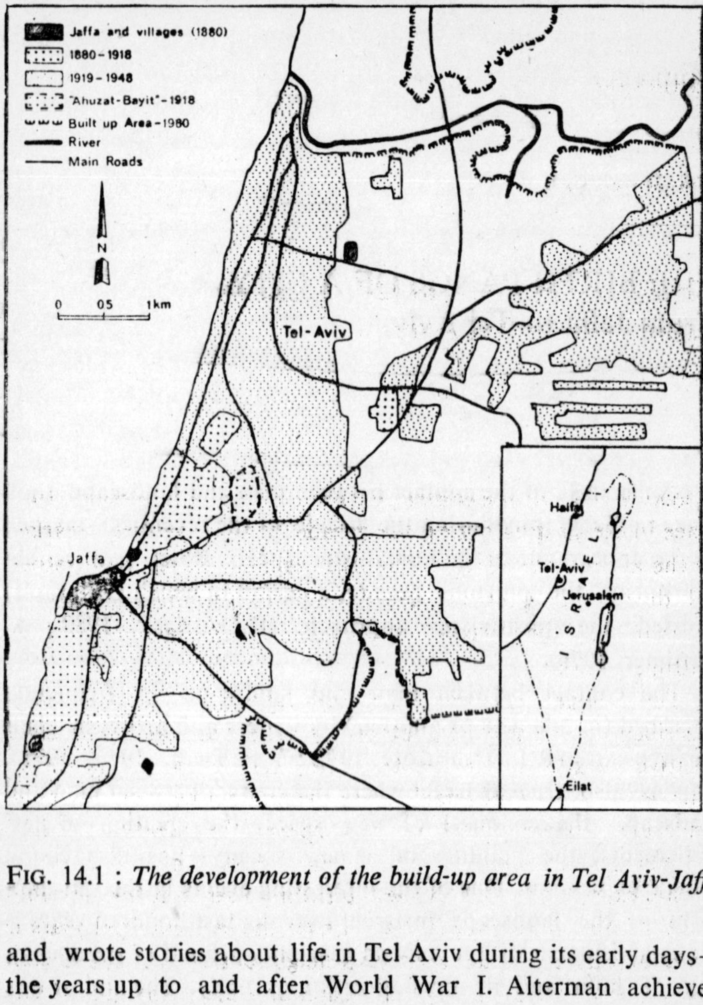

FIG. 14.1 : *The development of the build-up area in Tel Aviv-Jaffa*

and wrote stories about life in Tel Aviv during its early days—the years up to and after World War I. Alterman achieved fame as a poet but left descriptions and essays which were not works of poetry. His relationship to the city of Tel Aviv deals with the period after the First World War. The style of their prose was different. The fact that Gutman was an artist can be seen in his work as can the fact that Alterman was a poet be seen in his, and sometimes it is difficult to decide whether their writings are drawings or poems written in prose.

The urban landscape experienced by Gutman, which is primarily an optimistic experience and full of hope, is in complete contrast to the metaphors of the urban landscape described as a "concrete jungle" or an "urban wilderness". These two metaphors are typical of descriptions of cities throughout the world and they create a negative connotation for this landscape (D.L. Livingstone & R.T. Harrison, 1981). The urban landscape described as a "jungle" suggests—an enclosed place, noise, loneliness and a struggle for survival. This is a place where the fight for human existence reaches its peak ; there is a place of the greatest alienation between man and his environment.

The works of Gutman and Alterman are very sensitive to landscape. This quality of sensitivity to landscape that writers have has been pointed out by Wright (J.R. Wright, 1924) and especially in the work done by Salter and Lloyd (D.L. Salter and W.J. Lloyd, 1977). They claim that writers achieve a delicacy of observation which is greater than that of professional geographers. They claim that one should seek the "signatures" of man in his landscape and landscape in man—in literature. Life experience in landscape is a "signature" which appears in the work of Gutman and Alterman. Both of these artists have absorbed, through their senses, the birth process of the City of Tel Aviv, coming out of the ancient city of Jaffa, and they have left us their testimony of this experiece of man and his landscape.

We will concentrate on the experience of the landscape as it is reflected in Gutman's book—"A Little City And Few Men Within It" ("Ir Ktana Ve' anashim Ba Me'at"), (1959) and in Alterman's book—"Little Tel Aviv" ("Tel Aviv Hak 'tana"), (1979). Both books deal with the landscape called "Little Tel Aviv" today. This is a symbolic concept referring to a time and place—the neighbourhood called "Ahuzat Bayit" and the process of its becoming a big city. The concept contains within it—the size of the settlement, the style and form of life, the atmosphere of doing something for the first time—things different from their parallels in the present. "Little Tel Aviv" is an historical, urban, social and cultural symbol which is more than a little nurtured by the heritage left by the people who experienced it (like Gutman and Alterman) in the place at the time. The following areas seem most important as having influenced the intensity of the urban landscape experience of "Little Tel Aviv" :

(*a*) The City of Jaffa—symbolizes the old, the foreign, the strange, the cultural antithesis of the first Hebrew city.

(*b*) The birth of the new city—the house, the street, the neighbourhood, the forming of a new community—symbolizes progress and Hebraism.

Interwoven within these areas are the contacts with the social and cultural world as well as the natural world—the sand, the heat and the sycamore trees. We will concentrate on the world of culture.

THE CITY OF JAFFA AND ITS SYMBOLS

The founders and first builders of Tel Aviv came from the Jaffa Jewish community. Their motives for leaving were associated with the character of Jaffa at the end of the nineteenth and beginning of the twentieth centuries as well as the process of Jewish immigration, primarily the Second Aliya (second wave of immigration) : The Jaffa of this period was a middle-eastern city in its planning, style of housing and population. Immigration to the Land of Israel from the end of the previous century onwards brought about a growth in the city's population and the exodus of Jews and Arabs who were not happy about the urban crowding in Jaffa. New Arab neighbourhoods (Ma'nsiah) and Jewish (Naveh Isedek-1887, Naveh Shalom-1890) were built. From an historical point of view these neighbourhoods preceded Ahuzat Bayit (1909) by almost a whole generation (E. Efrat, 1976, p. 70) (Fig. 14.2).

The Jewish immigrants who arrived in Jaffa at the beginning of the century underwent a profound experience in their first contact with the eastern landscape, the pre-Tel Aviv landscape of the land of Israel. Every immigrant reacted differently in his contact with landscape ; and perceived the pre-Tel Tviv eastern city differently.

"He rose and went out and began to walk about the byways of Jaffa. He saw narrow streets, a narrow port and most of the street taken up by the chairs of coffee-houses or smelly swamps, people in wide trousers, women in billowing dresses, donkeys loaded with stores and blocks, caravans of bad-tempered camels loaded with iron pipes and boards. The passersby pressed

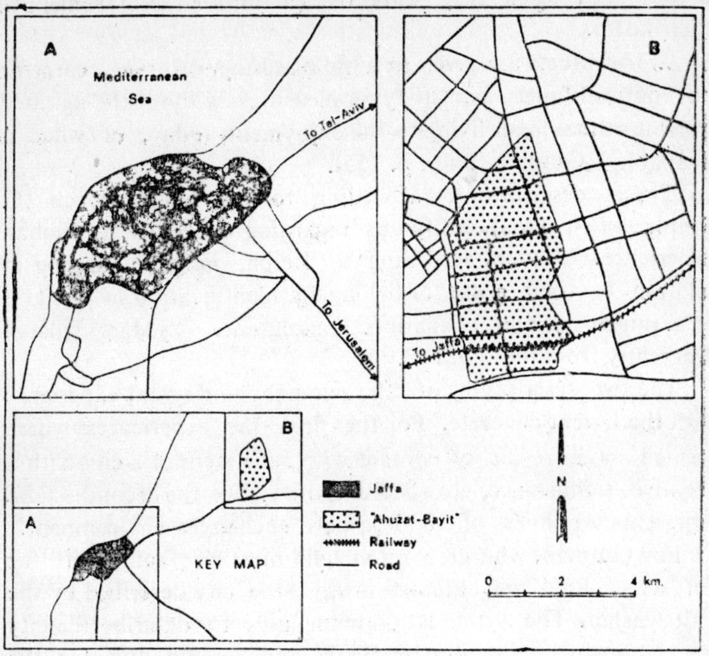

FIG. 14.2 : *The pattern of Old Jaffa* (*A*) *and new Tel-Aviv* (*B*), *1920*

themselves against the walls of the houses to avoid being crushed..." (Gutman, "Ir K'tana", p. 124).—This was the Jaffa experienced by a Bessarabian immigrant, three months after coming to Israel, who later became a wagon driver. There was yet another immigrant, from Russia, who arrived at the same period (the end of the first decade of the century) and who, after a while, became a white-washer in Tel Aviv.

"The white-washer saw the same scene differently. Clearly, people see different sides of the same things. Mustached men in silken, striped shiffs, every movement made sending the stripes into several directions, sit, reclining, playing with their toes as though they were beads, flowers behind their ears, roses decorating the pink meat of slaughtered sheep. They sell various types of food from hot, copper pans. Rich and poor sit in the same cafe, veiled women are dressed in black, wide dresses and when they walk one cannot see the movement of their knees.

...The streets are given to a life of eating, drinking, carrying out natural functions, satisfying pleasures, without the agitated pursuit of making a living-to the enjoyment, today, of what is available" (Gutman, ibid., p. 155).

These descriptions, according to Relph's approach (E. Relph, 1967, 1981), edify us regarding place as a human experience. All men, according to Relph, judge landscape in relation to their sense of belonging, identification or the level of strangeness and alienation. Immigrants "judge" places differently from the "locals".

The two descriptions of Jaffa make the immigrant experience with the Orient concrete. For the first, the experiences which formed as a result of contact with Jaffa were of a city with a negative significance, crowded and dirty. For the second—Jaffa represents a richness of colour, a new, enchanged environment.

For Gutman, who grew up in Jaffa until his family left for Tel Aviv, Jaffa was almost always the city described by the whitewasher. The symbols Gutman uses to describe the city are colourful, polar, materialistic and foreign. But for the Jewish immigrants Jaffa was symbolised by negative images. It was these images which brought about their exodus from the city and the construction of a new independent neighbourhood. This event took place in 1906, and another three years of purchasing land and the creation of a group of settlers, passed until the first families left for Ahuzat Bayit in 1909. The constructors of Ahuzat Bayit wished to cut themselves off from Jaffa and to create an independent Hebrew settled community—which evolved into Tel Aviv as the years went by.

TEL AVIV AND ITS SYMBOLS

From Gutman's descriptions, and later Alterman's, one can construct a world of symbols from which the image of "Little Tel Aviv" was formed, for example—the sand, the camels, the sycamore trees, the water tower, western technology, white houses, the high school, straight streets, Hebrew labour, building and creative activity, a new society and more.

Some of these symbols stand in opposition to the world of Jaffa's symbols—the wheelbarrow ("an improvement of western technology") as opposed to the donkey and camel, the straight "European" street as opposed to the winding "oriental" alleyways, the activity of creation and building as opposed to "oriental calm".

The major symbol—Tel Aviv (then Ahuzat Bayit), winds like a second thread through Gutman's work. This was the place where the feeling of home would develop and which would create the "feeling of Place" for the Jews—as opposed to Jaffa where the feeling was one of foreignness and alienation.

In positivistic descriptions of the construction of the city and the development of the built-up area a distinction exists between the created landscape and man. This is a typical characteristic of scientific literature. As opposed to this, according to Tuan (1976), imaginitive literature does not separate them. The house is a good example of the connection between the physical structure and man. "The house" has strong emotional significance for man (D.G. Hayward, 1975).

The subject of the house, and the feeling of "home" in Tel Aviv greatly interested Gutman, not only as one who was uprooted from one environment to another, from the old to the new, but also as one who witnessed "The Tel Aviv explosion" by the Turks during World War I. In his book, *Ir K'tana*, Gutman devotes a fair-sized section (pp. 59-120) to a description of the construction of a building in Tel Aviv, through a detailed description of the characters involved in it. And when the building is completed and the owner enters his dwelling Gutman writes, "And I say that this building is not a home, an empty shell ! Four walls and a roof are not yet a home even if little girls are standing at its windows. How can one explain what a home is ? Apart from all the confusion, a house does not, all of a sudden, become a home. It gradually grows and, suddenly, without knowing when the change took place, the building begins to be a home. And everybody knows it is a home" (*Ir K'tana*, 1.110). Gutman follows the building of the neighbourhood in a wonderful description at the beginning of the book. At first one building rose and then another but it was not yet a street. The street appeared when fences were placed between the houses and private areas could be identified ; and the area which separated the private and public sectors was formed by the fence in front of the house. And later there were other things—the watchman, water-tower, the committee, the high school—and all of these together created the neighbourhood. Despite the knowledge that a new neighbourhood was being built the first settlers could not imagine the extent of the dynamism of building a new city ; suddenly, out of nowhere, things appeared : "I didn't know that with the appearance of the first twenty houses being built between those sand dunes, before my very eyes, I could see the beginning of activity which gathered momentum like the mechanism of wheels—where one wheel drives the others, pavements were laid out between the houses, a road was made between the pavements. The streets made a neighbourhood—and the line continued developing until public life came into being with leaders, debts and regulations" (Gutman, Shvil Khpat Hatapuzim (Orange Peel Lane, p. 113).

As a youth who felt the rewards of landscape, Gutman managed to "freeze" moments in the formative process of the city. He succeeds in conveying the message better than any aerial photograph or the maps they used to make during that period.

Alterman deals with another Tel Aviv. He settled in the city in 1925 (as a lad of fifteen) and he mainly relates to the maturation of the city from a neighbourhood into a city at the end of the twenties and the beginning of the thirties. "The city is now at an age which satisfies no one, like a woman who is no longer a girl but not yet a lady. To wear high heels is to feel strange ; to wear sandals ridiculous...her body parts look stuck to each other, with no balance between form and size, some having developed early and others remaining immature (Alterman, pp. 23-25).

The change in the face of the city, the passage from the neighbourhood Ahuzat Bayit and the urban growth expressed in new streets being built in the direction of North-East, the creation of commercial centres, vehicles, multi-storeyed buildings—all these bring Alterman to the conclusion "that Tel Aviv has to grow, to be like her faraway sisters, desert-like and voluble, strange and loved, crowded and beautiful and heroic. A city ! A jungle of concrete and electricity and iron...automo-

14.1 A typcla urban landscape in Haifa area, near K. Bialik.

14.2 The contact zone between a Jewish vilage (Moshav, K. Bialik) and the urban Landscape.

14.3 The city of Nazareth, a general view.

14.4 A typicla urbanized Arab village near Nazareth.

tive leopards leaping out of corner-ambushes...on a background of desolation a new desert is coming into being" (ibid., p. 16).

Alterman's sense of city appears in the commercial centres, at the stock exchange and in the shops. He frequently describes them. In the commercial centre—Levinsky, Herzl and the Jaffa-Tel Aviv Rd., "You can wander around for an hour or so without having to say hello to anyone even once...here the noise grows louder and louder..."juice" machines gurgle, a car honks its horn, an Arab wagon driver...screeches in Arabic "Hassidah!" ("out of the way"). A cheeky, confident Yemenite assures everyone that today there is inter-e-e-esting news in Ha-a-retz! (a newspaper) and a Jewish woman loaded down with baskets shouts at the scurrying bus—"Mister-Wait!" The buses are falling apart, they jump around, they bend, they recklessly force their way through. There are pedestrians and hand carts like red threads which have been caught in an ant hill (ibid., p. 20).

Gutman lived through the passage from Yaffo to Ahuzat Bayit when Alterman was just being born in Warsaw, but their paths crossed in the mid-twenties with Gutman returning from Paris after studying art and Alterman, the youth, immigrating to Tel Aviv. In Gutman's work we have the picture of Tel Aviv as a neighbourhood frozen in time and in Alterman the feeling of being a city only begins to form at the end of the twenties. By combining their descriptions, which cover the first generation of Tel Aviv, the impression arises of a passage from the "oriental jungle" of Jaffa, from which the builders of Ahuzat Bayit escaped, to the "Hebrew Jungle" which developed in Tel Aviv. Beginning as a small community the neighbourhood became a city of thousands and its profile changed completely. Their colourful descriptions illustrate the difference in the sense of place in the growth process of the city and thus act as an additional source to the dry data available on the size of the city and the changes which took place in its social and economic patterns.

Summary

The humanistic approach, as an intellectual method in Geography, is helpful in revealing additional dimensions of the relations which exist between man and landscape. Literature, and the other forms of art which deal with landscape and man, act as a rich source for Geographers wishing to uncover "hidden dimensions" in the landscape. They do not replace positivistic methods but they may act as an addition to them. The positivist relating to landscape does so with the assistance of the rational instruments which he developed when he learned his profession, in the process discarding various tools, approaches and ideas which did not suit his approach. The writer relating to landscape does so with the emotional instruments and aides which are available to him. These approaches do not contradict each other, rather they supplement each other, and, to use Bronowski's expression—knowledge (science) and imagination (art) are common sources for human consciousness (Bronowski, 1980).

For the positivist the birth process of Tel Aviv is described with statistical data, maps, and aerial photographs : how much area has been built up ; how many roads paved ; what the rate of population growth was and its density ; how land utilization developed and so on. For the humanist the birth process of the city is the contact between man and landscape, a contact which creates feelings and a world of symbols which are passed on to the coming generations through painting, sketching and literary description. Literary description allows one to relive the contact with a world which has vanished. Nahum Gutman and Natan Alterman express, in their urban descriptions, that very same return to the past, and thus allow us to understand the landscape.

These artists reveal the "hidden dimension" of the transformation of a small group of buildings into houses, into a neighbourhood and then into a city. This is the dimension of "the sense of place" that Humanistic Geography aims to reveal as part of man's relationship with landscape.

Attention should be drawn to the contribution of Gutman and Alterman to the subjective reconstruction of time and place in Tel Aviv. This construction leaves us, people who were not then alive, a collection of images and symbols from those days. Subjective reconstruction is no less important than objective reconstruction (maps, statistical data and so on). Through these artists one can see the stages of—*experiencing* the landscape, *reconstructing* the landscape and their influence on the third stage—the public *image* which tries to preserve this landscape in different ways such as decisions to preserve sites, landmarks, movements and so on.

REFERENCES

Alterman, N., (1979), *The Little Tel-Aviv,* Ha'kibbutz Ha'meohad Publishers, Tel-Aviv (Hebrew).

Bronowski, J., (1980), *The Origins of Knowledge and Imagination,* Am Oved Publishers, Tel-Aviv (Hebrew).

Buttimer, A., (1976), "Grasping the Dynamism of Lifeworld", *Ann. Assoc. Amer. Geog.*, Vol. 66, pp. 277-292.

Efrat, E., (1976), *Towns and Urbanization in Israel,* Achiasaf, Tel-Aviv (Hebrew).

Gutman, N., (1959), *A Little City and Few Men Within it,* Am Oved and Dvir Publishers, Tel-Aviv (Hebrew).

Gutman, N., (1981), Orange Peel Lane (8th edition), Yavne, Tel-Aviv (Hebrew).

Hayward, D.G., (1975), "Home as an environmental and psychological concept," *Landscape,* Vol. 20, 1, pp. 2-9.

Heathcote, R.L., (1972), The Artist as Geographer : Landscape painting as source for Geographical Research," *Proceedings of Royal Geographical Society of Australia,* Vol. 73, pp. 1-21.

Livingstone, D. and R.T. Harrison, (1981), "Meaning Through Metaphor : Analogy as Epistemology," *Ann. Assoc. Amer. Geog.*, Vol. 71, pp. 95-107.

Relph, E.C., (1981), *Rational Landscape and Humanistic Geography,* Croom Helm, London.

Relph, E.C., (1976), *Place and Placelessness,* Pion, London.

Sack, R.D.. (1980), Conception of Spaces in Social Thought—*A Geographical Perspective,* The MacMillan Press, London.

Salter, D.L. and W.J. Lloyd, (1977), *Landscape in Literature,* Resource papers for college geography, No. 76-3, Association of American Geographers.

Tuan, Y.F., (1976), "Literature, Experience and Environmental Knowing", in Moore, G.T. and R.G. Golledge (eds.), *Environmental Knowing : Theories, Research and Methods,* Dowden, Hutchinson and Ross, Stroudsburg, Penna., pp. 260-274.

Tuan, Y.F., (1978), "Literature and Geography : Implication for Geographical Research", in Ley, D. and M.S. Samuels (eds.), *Humanistic Geography, Prospects and Problems,* Maaroufa Press, Chicago, pp. 194-207.

Wright, J.K., (1924), "Geography in Literature", *Geographical Review,* Vol. 14, pp. 659-660.

FIFTEEN

MAURO O'BRIEN-MARCHAND AND JOSEPH B. JUHASZ

AESTHETIC JUDGMENTS AND OBJECTIVE CHARACTERISTICS OF NATURAL LANDSCAPES

AESTHETIC landscape factors—those characteristics of a natural landscape that influence aesthetic judgment of an area—are not readily amenable to dollar quantification in land and resource analysis. For this reason, aesthetic factors tend to be discounted and are rarely included in land-use planning and decision-making processes. The problems inherent in placing a monetary value on landscape aesthetics, however, do not preclude numerical or other quantitative techniques. Little research has focused on quantitative evaluation of the aesthetic aspects of natural landscapes or on identification of those landscape elements that affect aesthetic judgment. This paper develops quantitative techniques to estimate aesthetic factors in a system of landscape evaluation as a first step in regional planning for parkland or open space.

Aesthetics is the study of the mind and emotions in relation to the sense of beauty. The term is used in discussing appreciation or criticism of beauty or in describing what is pleasing to the senses. Frequently the concepts of form, line, complexity, ambiguity, dynamicism, and balance interact in such a way as to influence one's aesthetic impression of an object or landscape. Landscape aesthetics are a synthesis of the physical (geological, hydrological, biological) and cultural (historical, anthropological) characteristics of the landscape. The physical and cultural aspects strongly influence but do not wholly determine how a landscape may be aesthetically perceived by an individual. It is the complex intermeshing of physical and cultural factors which create a new entity, different from the sum total of its component parts, which is then perceived through the mind of the person making an aesthetic judgment. Consequently, aesthetic judgments of the landscape must be distinguished from physical or cultural evaluations, although all of these aspects are relevant to a total system of landscape evaluation.

To use aesthetics as a means to evaluate landscape a distinction must be made between aesthetic judgment and aesthetic preference and the (influence) relationship of viewer background (demographic factors) on their aesthetic judgments must be (ascertained) established. A distinction must be made between aesthetic judgment and aesthetic preference. Aesthetic judgment can be equated to what is pleasing or beautiful on a broad, perhaps universal scale, as opposed to aesthetic preference, which refers to individual likes or dislikes: 'I like what I like". Whereas aesthetic judgment involves no connotations of use, aesthetic preference is frequently influenced by a person's concept of how that object (or landscape) might be used. Psychological research affirms this distinction between judgment and preference (Knight, 1967 ; Macdonald, 1967 ; Margolis, 1965). Craik (1972 : 256) states that "modern philosophers of aesthetics and art criticism are in general agreement in differentiating evaluative aesthetic judgments, akin to verdicts and findings, from appreciative aesthetic preferences expressing affections, preferences, and antipathies." Child's study (1968) compares individual and cultural derivation of aesthetic judgment and the universality of aesthetic judgment. He shows that there is a statistically significant degree of agreement among groups representing different cultures—Bantu tribesmen, Japanese potters, native Fiji Islanders, and Western art experts—in comparing the relative aesthetic quality of both Western and indigenous art, suggesting strong generality in aesthetic judgment. If the distinction between aesthetic judgment and preference can be made, and if aesthetic judgments to transgress social and cultural boundaries, then aesthetics may be an objective means by which natural landscapes can be evaluated quantitatively.

Aesthetics are as viable a resource in landscape appraisal as physical and cultural factors. The aesthetic importance of landscape is supported by Shafer and Mietz's (1969) study. In surveying hikers in two northeastern wilderness areas, they found that the hikers' primary benefits from the wilderness were aesthetic in nature. On an attitude scale developed by the National Advisory Council on Regional Planning, the hikers rated aesthetic benefits were ten times more important than educational or social benefits ; emotional benefits were rated eight to nine times more important and physical benefits were five times more important.

Landscape elements that actually affect aesthetic judgment have not been clearly nor completely identified. Several authors (Litton, 1972 ; Craik, 1970 ; Kaplan, 1975) have attempted to identify and classify aesthetics into attributes and Raychaudhuri (1972) has observed ambiguity, complexity, and perceptual independence as being the principal factors in aesthetic sensitivity. The study of Kaplan and others (1972) confirms the complexity factor in aesthetic sensitivity. None of these studies, however, identify what natural landscapes elements affect people's sense of beauty or ugliness, pleasantness or unpleasantness. Information is lacking regarding those specific physical or cultural aspects of a landscape which influence aesthetic judgments and an awareness of their relative importance. Linton (1968) asserts that there are two basic elements in the scenic resources of any area. The first is land-form character based on relative relief and proximity of hilltops and valley floors. The second is land-use type. However, Craik (1969) finds that scenery occurs for the human observer only through the interaction between land form and land-use. Leopold (1969) showed that at least one physical aspect of a river valley's grandeur to the viewer could be expressed as valley width/depth ratio : valleys generally regarded so scenic or spectacular as to be preserved in national parks and wilderness areas tended to be narrow and deep. Other studies emphasize relative relief, low urbanization, frequency of vistas, and presence of water surfaces as variables in landscape appraisal (Hart and Graham, 1967 ; Kiemsledt, 1968 ; Vedenin and Miroschnickenko, 1971).

The techniques that have been used to assess the aesthetic component of landscapes include photographic evaluation of the scenic quality, field evaluation, and adjectival lists, or as combination of any of the three techniques. In recent years, several attempts have been made to evaluate landscape aesthetics using photographs. Morisawa (1971) showed a set of 45 Kodachrome slides to several groups of students from high school age through graduate school. The students were asked to examine the slides and rate the scenery represented in them on a scale of six values from "extremely beautiful, breathtaking" to "very unattractive, or eyesore". Wohlwill (1973) discussed the limitation of slides in the investigation of environmental aesthetic and landscape evaluation. In his study, a group of students were asked to evaluate the natural environment in the field and then from a group of eight photographs projected in an octagonal enclosure. The outcome of the field study differed in a number of important respects from that carried out in the laboratory. The difference was particularly strong in the case of the exploration time[2] data, which not only yielded marked differences in the role of certain of the independent measures, but generally appeared to give rise to more strongly differentiated responses to the different octants than was the case in the laboratory. Wohlwill maintains that photo stills represent to a degree an impoverished stimulus field and noted in particular the absence of motion and sound.

Using photographs and adjectival lists, Peterson and Newmann (1969) identified two groups having distinctly different evaluations in a study on human responses to beach scenes. They used black and white photos for perceptions and preferences of visual characteristics, free responses to identify variables, and semantic differentials to measure selected attributes of a variety of beaches. The photographic and adjectival lists-techniques gave similar results pointing up the fact that the means of evaluation is not the distinction. However, the authors of this paper suggest that the landscape evaluation was use-oriented the two groups were selecting beaches for different purposes, an example of aesthetic preference, not aesthetic judgment.

Strong positive results from field and photographic evaluations of landscapes has been obtained by Craik (1972 : 260), however, who reports that "in the Brandywine study, two surveyors rated the attractiveness of the natural environment at 92 locations in the field. Subsequently, nine judges rated the same 92 locations on the basis of one to eight photographs taken at each location. Mean ratings of the field surveyors and of the photographic presentation panel correlated at +0.64." Similarly, Zube and others (1974), in a perception and measurement study of scenic, resources, found a high correlation between site evaluation in the field with panoramic photographic evaluation. Also Coughlin and Goldstein (1970) found responses to slides tended to be consistent with responses to the same environments rated in the field on a scale from 1 to 7 for environmental attractiveness ; however, the lowest levels of agreement were found when the evaluators were asked to rate slides with regard to functional attractiveness (for living in or sightseeing), rather than for environmental attractiveness in the abstract, again an example of preference, not judgment.

This paper compares various techniques of aesthetic evaluation of natural landscapes in a number of small, central pennsylvania watersheds. Scenic rating by socio-economic groups is contrasted and the influence on aesthetic judgment of differing photographic media (including color slides and black and white photographs) and photographic quality is examined. The paper also identifies and assesses the relative importance of some of the physical land characteristics which affect human aesthetic perception of the landscape. Quantitative techniques for evaluating physical and cultural aspects of the landscape and their use in conjunction with aesthetic ratings in an overall system of landscape evaluation will be discussed in a separate publication.

METHODOLOGY

Field area

Twenty-three small stream basins were selected for the study area (Fig. 15.1), all within the Valley and Ridge physiographic-geologic province of central Pennsylvania. The ridges and uncleared portions of the valley floors are covered by second-growth deciduous forest dominated by oak, maple, hickory, and beech, with significant numbers of pine and hemlock, the latter two being especially common in moist areas along streams draining the ridges. The cleared valleys are presently dominated by agriculture. The Susquehanna River drains the entire region and all of the streams studied here flow into the Susquehanna or its tributaries. The basins were chosen to include the widest possible

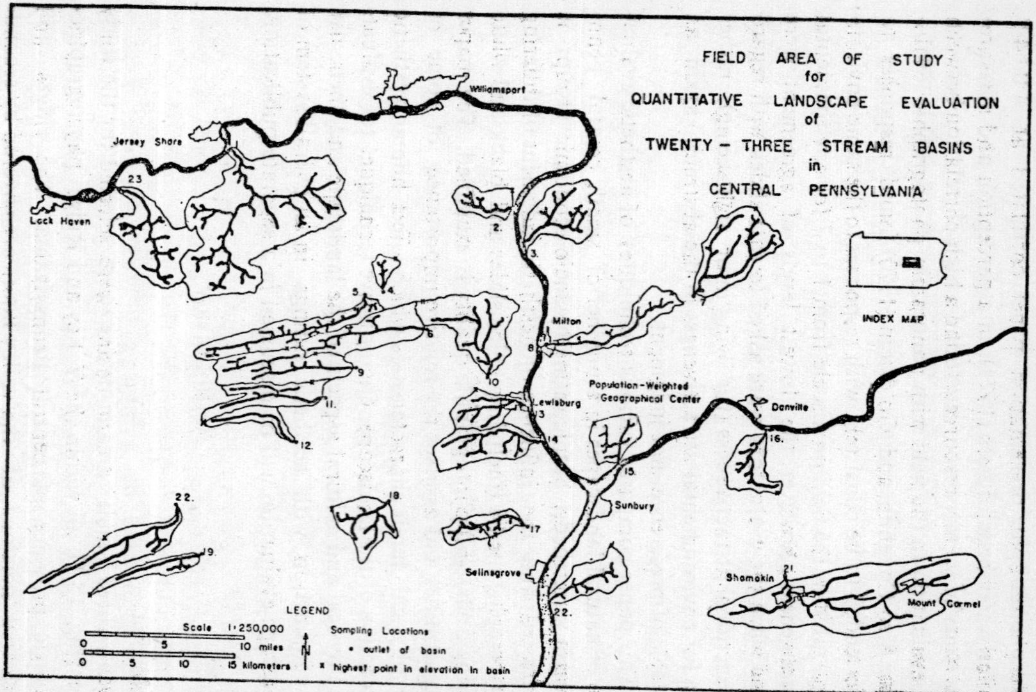

FIG. 15.1 : *Field area of study for quantitative landscape evaluation of twenty-three stream basins in central Pennsylvania*

range of land-use practices, stream sizes, landscape forms, vegetation, archaeological sites, and historical areas. They include the watersheds of such diverse streams as Antes Creek, draining limestone terrain of high agricultural potential and characterized by karst topography,[3] Shamokin Creek within the anthracite coal region, and three streams located within state parks.

Evaluative techniques

Landscape aesthetics of the 23 stream basins were evaluated as part of an overall landscape evaluation system involving three distinct rating subsystems : Uniqueness Ratio, Wilderness Potential, and General Aesthetic Impression. The components of the overall system are schematically illustrated in Figure 15.2.

The Uniqueness Ratio and Wilderness Potential are objective estimates based on defined landscape characteristics using scientific methods. Subjective elements enter only in the selection of the landscape characteristics used as parameters in Uniqueness Ratio and Wilderness Potential, and in the decision to assign equal weight to all landscape characteristics. Most data are collected from topographic maps (7½ minute quadrangles) or in the field by direct measurement. General Aesthetic Impression represents the authors best efforts to quantify those elements of the landscape pertaining to scenic beauty of that watershed. It is based on aesthetic judgments made in the field viewing the scenery, and those made viewing black and white photographs and color transparencies. The photographic evaluations were completed by a large randomly selected sample, while field evaluations were made by one person.

The Uniqueness Ratio measures how different each basin is from every other basin included in the study. It is applied only to those landscape aspects which are not *a priori* good or bad ; rather their value attaches to how different a given basin is from the usual or the norm. Six parameters were used to evaluate Uniqueness : physiography, hydrology, geology, botany, anthropology, and history. These parameters were in turn evaluated by a group of more specific subparameters. The raw data obtained for each subparameter were used to assign a value

UNIQUENESS RATIO

Physiography	*Hydrology*	*Botany+*	*Geology*	*Anthropology*	*Post-1619 History*
topography relief	stream width	successional stage	lithology	midden or camp-sites	number of pre-1850 communities
mean elevation	stream depth	dominant tree species	structure	natural sites with mystic quality	number of historic sites or structures
max. valley depth/width ratio	velocity	dominant shrub species	geomorphic process	hunting and agri-cultural sites	
drainage orientation	stream load : —sediment size —suspended load	dominant herb species	paleontology : —diversity of species —number of fossiliferous outcrops		
basin area	stream density	number of tree species			
	stream order	number of shrub species			
		number of herb species			

WILDERNESS POTENTIAL

Air Quality	*Water Quality*	*Solid Waste*	*Road Development*	*Degree of Urbanization*	*Field Aesthetic Impression*
visibility	color	quantity of litter+	miles of paved roads/basin area	land use	scenic quality+
odor+	acidity		miles unsurfaced roads/area	industry or mining	number of vistas
	nitrozen		distance from population weighted geographical center of study area	% forested area	impression of total basin
	phosphate				
	iron				
	dissolved oxyzen				
	algal abundance				

GENERAL AESTHETIC IMPRESSION

Photographic		*Field*+
Black-and-White+	Color+	

FIG. 15.2 : A graphic presentation of a system of quantitative landscape evaluation based on the rank of Uniqueness Ratio rank order + Wilderness Potential rank order + General Aesthetic Impression rank order.
+ subparameter evaluated at both the confluence and the highest point in elevation of the stream basin.

on a fivefold scale, the boundaries drawn to include the full range of data variation and to encompass five approximately equivalent ranges. From the cotegory ratings it is possible to calculate Uniqueness Ratios for each basin by subparameter. An arithmetic average of the subparameter ratios is then used to obtain parameter ratios and an overall Uniqueness Ratio for each basin. The Uniqueness Ratio is simply defined as the inverse of the number of watersheds sharing a given category. If a basin is unique, it is rated 1/1 or 1.0, if two basins share that characteristic then the ratio drops to 0.50, and from there to 0.33 with three basins sharing that category. Consequently the ratios decrease exponentially as the number of basins sharing the rating increases such that all Uniqueness Ratios range from near 0 to 1.0.

Some aspects of the landscape, however, are not well described in terms of Uniqueness because they tend to have a social value connotation. Obviously, a uniquely polluted site is of little societal value, even if it is very different from other sites in a region. Wilderness Potential is used as a measure of human impact on and alteration of each watershed, based on factors which have definite "good" or "bad" implications : air and water quality, solid waste, road development, degree of urbanization, and Field Aesthetic Impression. A fivefold rating, with category one representing least natural conditions and category five the most, was used to calculate the Wilderness Potential as the cumulative sum of ratings divided by the highest possible sum of ratings. For example, if a basin receives ratings of 4, 5, and 3 for air quality parameter then the Wilderness Potential is calculated as 4+5+3 divided by 15, the highest possible total, giving air quality a value of 0.80. The overall Wilderness Potential is computed as the mean of the parameter ratings, and follows a linear scale ranging from near 0 to 1.0. The Wilderness Potential value increases as its naturalness or freedom from human alteration increases. These two subsystems serve to evaluate, in an objective manner, the physical and cultural aspects of a stream basin landscape. For further discussion of Uniqueness Ratio and Wilderness Potential, see Marchand (1974).

The aesthetic impact of this physical and cultural landscape on the viewer is evaluated through General Aesthetic Impression, the third rating subsystem. General Aesthetic Impression of scenic quality is computed from two sources of information : 1) on-site aesthetic evaluation of the watershed in the field by the senior author, hereafter referred to as Field Aesthetic Impression, and 2) evaluation of color transparencies and black and white photographs of the watersheds by a sample of persons who had not visited the field areas but were familiar with the scenery in this part of Pennsylvania. Evaluation of scenic beauty by field and photographic technique is discussed in the following two sections. The value for General Aesthetic Impression are, therefore, a direct measure of the degree to which the landscape being evaluated is aesthetically pleasing.

Evaluation of field aesthetic impression

Field Aesthetic Impression of each watershed was rated by the senior author through four subparameters : scenic quality estimated at the highest point and at the lowest point (outflow) in each stream basin ; number of vistas ; and overall impression, irrespective of location within the basin. Scenic quality at the highest and lowest points was rated by becoming familiar with the immediate area and then taking about 10 seconds to make a judgment, such that first impressions would be recorded. Ratings were made on a fivefold scale, from 1 being least aesthetically pleasing, very unpleasant to 5 being most aesthetically pleasing then translated to a scale of 0.0 to 1.0 for comparative purposes. These ratings take into account such factors as color and color contrast ; shapes and forms of the vegetation, land, water, and sky and given inter-relations ; and the evaluator's comparative enjoyment in being at that location as opposed to comparable locations in other stream basins. A conscious attempt was made to rate the scenes such that a judgment, rather than a preference, was being recorded. Vistas were assessed by tallying the number of scenic views afforded by high points in each basin, not necessarily from the highest point. Overall impression of total basin scenic quality (subparameter four) was based on notes taken in the field at sampling sites (for Uniqueness Ratio and Wilderness Potential subparameters) and while walking and driving through the watershed. A rating was assigned by reviewing the approximately 100-word descriptions prepared for each basin at some time after the recording of impressions in the field, to minimize the influence of weather and the evaluator's personal mood variations. The Field Aesthetic Impression values thus represent what we believe to be a proper balance of rapid aesthetic impressions and longer-term reactions.

Evaluation using photographic methods

In this study, landscape scenic quality was also evaluated by randomly selected respondents who based their ratings upon black and white photographs and color transparencies. All photographs were taken over a short period of time and under clear weather conditions to minimize variations in season and sunlight. The camera location and orientation was standardized for every basin as follows : two black and white photographs and two color slides were taken at the lowest point in each basin, one viewing upstream and one viewing downstream ; one black and white photograph and one color slide were taken at the highest point in each basin with the view oriented toward the basin perpendicular to the trend of the drainage divide.

The photographs and color transparencies were exhibited for scenic evaluation to a diverse audience including metropolitan professionals, a rural college community, and rural skilled and unskilled persons. The black and white photographs shown to 181 persons were enlarged to 8″×10″ prints matted on large poster boards, and exhibited in four localities to : 1) a group of predominantly urban-suburban professional people at Bucknell University, Lewisburg, Pennsylvania, 2) local Lewisburg town residents at an arts festival, 3) local rural residents at a weekly farmer's produce market, and 4) to a group of Bucknell University geology students. The color slides were shown in an auditorium on a full-size commercial screen to a subsample of 33 participants from group (1) above. A questionnaire was used to rocord viewers' aesthetic judgments based on photographs. In designing the questionnaire, care was taken to provide clear and succinct directions for rating the photographs. Each viewer was asked to read the directions and the rating system was explained orally as well. The viewers were asked to evaluate "the scenery represented by the photographs, not the photographs themselves" on a fivefold scale. Some demographic information was also requested in addition to the viewers' ratings to identify any preference in aesthetic judgments assciated with socio-economic level, age, sex, and degree of interest in the outdoors and involvement with conservation. All ratings were converted to a 0.0 to 1.0 scale for data analysis and comparison.

The photographic evaluative techniques differ from Field Aesthetic Impression in three important ways : (1) the on-site evaluations were made by one person whereas the photographic evaluations involved 181 persons for black and white and 33 persons for color transparencies, (2) the on-site evaluator was much more familiar with the areas being compared than were those persons who made aesthetic judgments based on photographs, (3) in photographic evaluation, judgments could be affected by the character or quality of the media of representation.

Since the photographic medium is a representation of the actual scenery, the quality of representation could be a possible source of bias. An evaluation of the photographic quality of each print and slide was made by a professional artist-photographer on a fivefold scale from least quality to highest quality to ascertain the influence of technical quality on the scenic evaluation as viewed through photographs.

RESULTS AND DISCUSSION

The techniques developed to assess scenic quality are compared and contrasted. Field and photographic methods are discussed and the influence of the quality of photography on aesthetic judgment is estimated. Using landscape characteristics assessed by the Uniqueness Ratio and Wilderness Potential parameters, a statistical model was predicted for each technique. Factor analysis illustrates the underlying relationships between aesthetic judgments, the various evaluative techniques, landscape characteristics and the influence of background, socio-economic level and outdoor interest on aesthetic judgments of scenic quality. Lastly, inquiry was made into identifying and rating those elements of natural landscapes (as seen by viewers of photographs) that affect human perception of the aesthetic.

Comparison of aesthetic judgment evaluations

General Aesthetic Impression of the scenic quality of natural landscapes and the rating systems for the field and photographic techniques are contrasted (Table 15.1). The values for

TABLE 15.1 : **Aesthteic judgments of scenic quality and photographic quality ratings for each stream basin. The aesthetic quality of the scenery ranges from least aesthetic quality (0.20) to highest aesthetic quality (1.00) for field, photographic and General Aesthetic Impression.[4] The quality of photography ranges from least (0.20) to highest (1.00)**

		Aesthelic Judgments of Scenic Quality				Photographic Quality Evaluation	
		Field	Photographic		General		
Basin Number	Basin Name	Aesthetic Impression	Black and white	Color	Aesthetic Impression	Black and white	Color
1.	Antes Creek	.60	.774	.844	.739	.8	1.0
2.	Black Run	.65	.638	.582	.623	.8	.8
3.	Delaware Run	.60	.542	.666	.603	.8	.8
4.	Lick Run	.60	.780	.634	.671	.8	.8
5.	White Deer Creek	.55	.798	.814	.721	.6	.8
6.	Spruce Run	.40	.698	.744	.614	.8	.8
7.	White hall Creak	.35	.506	.614	.490	.6	.6
8.	Limeston Run, Miton	.45	.682	.594	.575	.6	.4
9.°	Rapid Run	.55	.856	.574	.660	1.0	.6
10.	Little Buffalo Creek	.35	.688	.846	.628	.6	.8
11.°	Half-Way Dam	.95	.844	.876	.890	.6	.8
12.	Buffalo Creek	.80	.776	.654	.743	.6	.8

13.	Limestone Run, Lewisburg	.60	.466	.574	.547	.4	.6
14.	Turtle Creek	.50	.548	.444	.497	.4	.6
15.	Lithia Springs Creek	.45	.650	.494	.531	.8	1.0
16.	Logan Run	.55	.574	.682	.602	.6	.6
17.	Monogahela Run	.65	.714	.746	.703	.6	.8
18.	Dry Run	.45	.554	.854	.619	.4	.6
19.°	Swift Run	.75	.870	.836	.819	1.0	.8
20.	Hallowing Run	.50	.772	.740	.671	.8	.8
21.	Shamokin Creek	.45	.458	.344	.417	.4	.6
22.	Weikert Run	.55	.806	.794	.717	.8	.8
23.	McElhatten Creek	.30	.408	.644	.451	.4	.6
Mean		.55	.670	.678	.632	0.66	0.73
Standard Deviation		.15	.139	.142	.115		
Minimum		.30	.408	.344	.417		
Maximum		.95	.870	.876	.890		
Number of viewers		1	181	33			

°Stream basins within state parks.

scenic quality evaluation range from 0.30 to 0.95 and General Aesthetic Impression has a slightly higher range. Means vary from 0.6 to 0.7 with a standard deviation of 0.12 to 0.15.

In comparing the various basins (basin #11) has the highest General Aesthetic Impression in addition to ranking first in field and color photographic evaluation and third in black-and-white photographic evaluation. The other two basins within state parks (#19 and #9) are rated second and tenth in General Aesthetic Impression. At the other end of the spectrum, basins 21 and 23 received low ratings by all aesthetic methods of evaluation, probably due to water pollution and mining activities of Shamokin Creek (#21) and artificial control of the McElhattan Creek channel (#23).

Photographic quality data were undertaken to monitor the amount of influence of the evaluative technique on the evaluation (Table 15.1, columns 5 and 6). In most cases a change of photographic quality coincides with a similar change in scenic evaluations as rated in black-and-white and color media. While landscape rating by viewers of photographs is a reasonably valid technique, it appears to be strongly influenced by the quality of the photography (see also discussion on correlation matrix below).

A correlation matrix was constructed to compare several techniques used in this study to evaluate landscape aesthetics. An examination of Table 15.2 indicates significant positive ($R=+0.555$) correlation between Field Aesthetic Impression and subjects' ratings of black-and-white photographs, accounting for 31% of the variance in the scores. It is noteworthy that the correlation between color slides and black-and-white photographs is in the same range while that between color and Field Aesthetic Impression is only 0.279. Several interpretations of these results are possible but it questions Wohlwill's (1973) belief that increased verismilitude leads to increased reliability. In fact the color photography seems to be accentuating the noise rather than the information between photographic representation and field aesthetic impression.

The finding that Field Aesthetic Impression is correlated to Wilderness Potential at 0.430 shows that some of the parameters and subparameters are redundant with aesthetic judgment. The

TABLE 15.2 : **Correlation matrix for several landscape evaluative techniques and photographic quality. The field techniques are based on several parameters assessed for 23 stream basins ; the black-and-white photographic technique is based on evaluation by 181 persons for the 23 basins ; black-and-white subgroup is a subsample of the black-and-white evaluation (above) and is the rating by the 33 persons for the 23 basins who also rated color transparencies ; color transparency technique represents scenic quality evaluation as seen thru color slides by 33 persons rating the 23 basins ; and photographic quality is an evaluation of photographic quality not scenic quality by one person schooled in photography and for each of the 23 basins**

	Uniqueness Ratio	Wilderness Potential	Wilderness Potential without Field Aesthetic Impression	Field Aesthetic Impression	Black-and-White	Black-and-White Subgroup	Color
	1	2	3	4	5	6	7
Field Evaluation Techniques :							
Uniqueness Ratio	1						
Wilderness Potential	−.176	1					
Wilderness Potential without Field Aesthetic Impression	−.190	.987	1				
Field Aesthetic Impression	−.019	.573	.430	1			

TABLE 15.2 (*Contd.*)

	1	2	3	4	5	6	7
Photographic Evaluation Techniques :							
Black-and-White	−.056	.678	.637	.555	1		
Black-and-White, Subgroup	−.031	.669	.612	.628	.971	1	
Color (N=33)	−.128	.557	.557	.279	.532	.575	1
Photographic Quality Evaluation by Artist :							
Black-and-White	.032	.461	.455	.256	.703	.668	*
Color	.276	.472	.455	.329	•	•	.379

•Irrelevant

finding of greatest interest here is that the black-and-white photographic judgments account for 46% of the variance in the expert judgment's evaluation of Wilderness Potential. It is of great practical as well as theoretic significance. Noteworthy, also, is the lack of correlation between Wilderness Potential and Uniqueness both from the point of view of the expert rater's evaluation and the photographic judgments of lay people. Aesthetics and Wilderness potential are clearly not related to the objective uniqueness of an area.

The high correlations between the evaluations of photographic quality by the artist and Wilderness Potential shows that the bothersome problem of taking out the noise of photographic quality from aesthetic judgments is extremely difficult even by a trained expert. Further work in this area is needed before higher correlations between field and photographic judgments can be obtained.

It is interesting to note that block-and-white photographic evaluation of scenic quality is the best predictor of Wilderness Potential of the variables, followed by color and Field Aesthetic Impression. This finding confirms the study of Kaplan *et al.* (1972) illustrating higher aesthetic ratings for natural views over urban or developed scenes, and demonstates the usefulness of less expensive black-and-white photography for evaluating natural landscapes.

Color evaluation has a moderately strong correlation with total block-and-white evaluation of scenic quality and Wilderness Potential. The addition of Field Aesthetic Impression contributes nothing to the correlation of Wilderness Potential with color evaluation. And while Field Aesthetic Impression has a correlation of 0.56 with black-and-white evaluation, it correlates with color only at the level of 0.28. Differences in the media (8″×10″ black-and-white prints vs. life-size projection of the color transparencies on a large screen) may account for part of this variation by rendering the scene more life-like. Possibly the viewing environment (photos on posters vs. slides shown in a darkened room) may explain some of the discrepancy. As noted below, even the photographic quality evaluation may have been affected by the media and mode of presentation. Further investigation of the differences between color and black-and-white evaluation of landscapes needs to be carried out, and, if the results of thie study continue to hold for other groups of viewers under other experimental conditions, a definitive explanation would be necessary.

The effect of photographic quality on viewer ratings is illustrated by the correlation coefficient between black-and-white scenic evaluation and black-and-white photo quality (0.703) and by the comparable coefficient for color (0.379). For both photographic quality evaluations, the correlations with Wilderness Potential are moderately strong and are similar in magnitude (0.461 and 0.472). The correlation of Uniqueness Ratio and Field Aesthetic Impression with color photo quality are moderate, but much stronger than the comparable correlations with black-and-white photo quality. The Uniqueness Ratio correlation coefficient with photo quality changes from insignificant in the case of black-and-white to significant for color, whereas for Field Aesthetic Impression the corresponding change is less dramatic, although still noteworthy. It could be inferred that in the color photo quality evaluation, factors of Uniqueness and Field Aesthetics may have entered into the assessment to a greater extent than they did in the evaluation of black-and-white photo quality. In both evaluations of photo quality, Wilderness Potential factors played a more significant role in influencing the ratings than did Uniqueness Ratios. The color photo quality assessment appears to have been carried out more independently of the scenic quality than was the black-and-white photo quality evaluation, but both ratings of photo quality appear to correlate significantly with the ratings of viewers who were asked to assess the scenic quality of the areas illustrated by the photographs. Perhaps, in the evaluation of the scenic quality represented in photographs, it is impossible to completely separate photographic and landscape qualities. It would also appear that the task of separating photographic quality from scenic quality is more difficult viewing black-and-white than for color. Again, the reasons for this contrast between the two media are not entirely clear, indicating the need for further investigation.

In capsule, the correlation matrix of scenic evaluation with black-and-white photographs differed significantly from that carried out with color slides. Significant correlations between

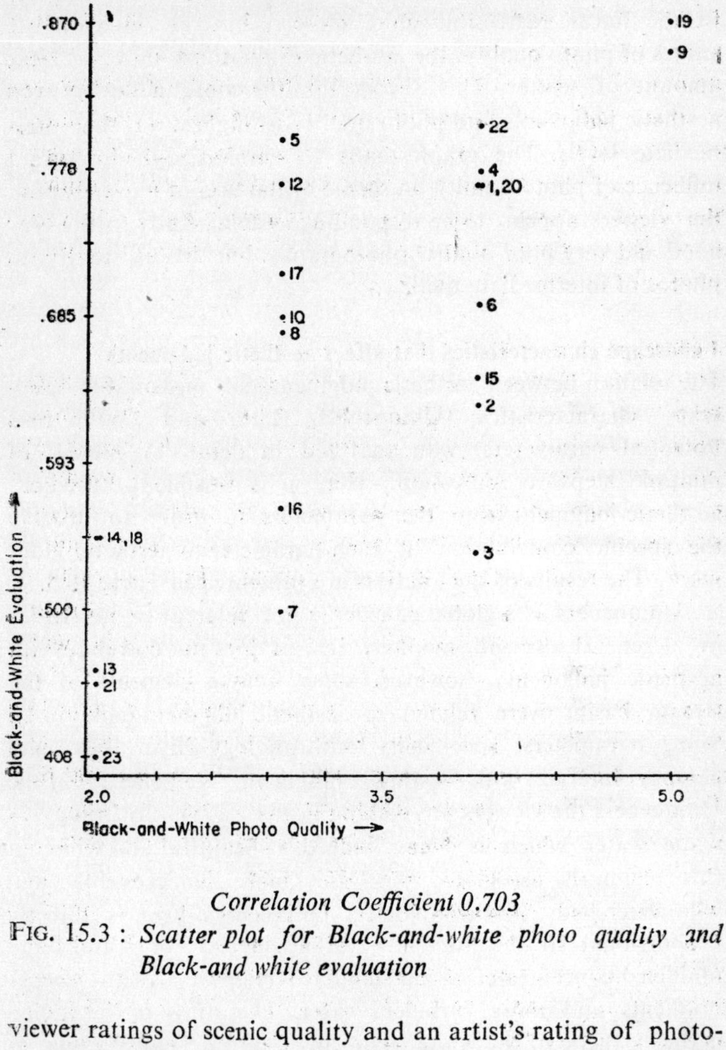

Correlation Coefficient 0.703

FIG. 15.3 : *Scatter plot for Black-and-white photo quality and Black-and white evaluation*

viewer ratings of scenic quality and an artist's rating of photographic quality suggest that the two aspects of photographic evaluation are difficult to separate. Field Aesthetic Impression shows a moderate degree of correlation with Wilderness Potential and black-and-white scenic evaluation.

The relationship between scenic quality and photographic quality for the black-and-white photographs is illustrated by a scatter plot (Fig. 15.3). For very high and very low values of photo quality, evaluation of black-and-white scenic quality fit the linear regression quite closely, but at intermediate values of photo quality, the aesthetic evaluations show a large amount of scatter. This shows that the confounding between aesthetic judgments and photo quality is highest at the intermediate levels. The graph tends to emphasize the important influence of photo quality on scenic evaluation of photographs: the viewers appear to be responding systematically to the very good and very poor quality photographs, but inconsistently to photos of intermediate quality.

Landscape characteristics that affect aesthetic judgments

The relation between aesthetic judgment and measurable landscape characteristics (Uniqueness Ratio and Wilderness Potential parameters) was analyzed in detail by means of multiple stepwise regression.[5] Here it is possible to "predict" aesthetic judgment from the parameters in order to observe the specific contribution of each parameter to aesthetic judgment. The results of the analysis are presented in Table 15.3.

Uniqueness as a global concept is not related to aesthetics in a general over-all manner, i.e., it does not correlate with aesthetic judgments, however, some unique elements of the stream basins were related to aesthetic judgment (column 1). Some parameters, specifically anthropology, hydrology, and geology interact with aesthetic judgment. We believe that the Uniqueness the viewers are picking up vis a vis hydrology is white water which is being judged as beautiful and which in this region is associated with the more unaccessible and wild watersheds. Anthropological Uniqueness here is directly proportional to the number of archeological sites (camps and middens) concentrated along smaller streamways with steeper gradients and more turbulent water. The utility of the Indian is the aesthetic of the white man, in Central Pennsylvania at any rate. Geological uniqueness is associated with sandstone and quartzite, in the more resistant ridge forming areas which have undergone glacial processes—areas suited neither to agriculture nor industry but rather to forestation and wildlife ; Indian rather than white lifestyle. These aspects of Uniqueness are then positively associated with wilderness and therefore aesthetics. We note the absence of hydrology in the data on Field

TABLE 15.3 : **Stepwise regression analysis of aesthetic judgments based on photographic and field evaluation. As each landscape characteristic (Uniqueness Ratio and Wilderness Potential Parameters) is added to the equation to Predict aesthetic judgment models, they are added cumulatively, so in column 1, A+Geology is Anthropology+Geology**

Dependent Variables Aesthetic Judgments based on	Independent Variables *Column 1*			*Column 2*			*Column 3*		
Predictor ⟶ Predicted ↓	Uniqueness Ratio Parameters	r	R^2	Wilderness Potential Parameters without Field	r	R^2	Uniqueness Ratio and Wilderness Potential Parameters	r	R^2
Black-and White	Anthropology	.412	17%	Water Quality	.664	44%	Water Quality	.664	44%
	A+Geology	.625	39%				W+Anthropology	.715	51%
	A+G+Hydrology	.685	47%				W+A+Hydrology	.742	55%
							W+A+H+ Physiography	.761	58%
Color	Hydrology	.388	15%	Air Quality	.539	29%	Air Quality	.539	29%
	H+Anthropology	.520	27%	A+Solid Waste	.633	40%	A+Solid Waste	.633	40%
							A+S+Hydrology	.655	43%
							A+S+H+History	.706	50%
Field Aesthetic Impression	Anthropology	.300	9%	Water Quality	.510	26%	Water Quality	.510	26%
	A+Geology	.520	27%	W+Degree of Urbanization	.539	29%	+Physiography	.538	29%
				W+D+Air Quality	.591	35%	+Degree of Urbanization	.591	35%
				W+D+A+Solid Waste	.633	40%	+Air Quality	.633	40%
							+Solid Waste	.664	44%
							+Anthropology	.692	48%
							+History	.728	53%

Aesthetic Impression and the lower level of its prediction from Uniqueness Ratio parameters. We believe this is accounted for by the senior author's tendency to keep uniqueness and wilderness features and their subparameters more conceptually separate than lay people would do. Our ability to predict the color judgments is similarly impaired. The explanation here, however, seems to lie in the distractions of color photography rather than conceptual clarity.

Column 2 shows the familiar association between Wilderness Potential characteristics and aesthetic judgment. Forty-four per cent of the variance in aesthetic judgment based on black-and-white photographs is accounted for by water quality (clearness, transparency) alone. It is the absence of focus on water quality (not a colorful feature) that makes the color transparencies less accurate predictors of aesthetic judgmeut, in this instance, than black-and-white photographs are. Apparently Wilderness and water quality are more unambiguously related in this geographic area than any other measured parameters. The expert rater is also influenced by degree of urbanization, something that our sample did not observe from the photographs presented. The authors are nevertheless struck again by the remarkably high correlation between aesthetic judgment and objectively measured Wilderness Potential.

With the combination of Uniqueness and Wilderness parameters (column 3) we are approaching the limits of capacity to predict aesthetic judgments from any objective, real world variables. We are now dealing with multiple correlations in the order of 0.75 and accounting regularly for half or even more of the variance in scores. Clearly, this shows that aesthetic judgments are not heedless, subjective, emotional opinions but considered estimates based on measurable features of the landscape.

Water quality holds an overwhelming importance in predicting aesthetic judgments in all instances but that of color photo quality, where the transparency of the water is apparently obscured by more colorful distractions (litter, etc.). The discussion of the inclusion of the other parameters needs to further elaboration here. We note, in the case of the black-and-white photographs the inclusion of physiography and the dropping a geology from the previous parameters. Since the two concepts are interrelated we are assuming that the inclusion of the one makes the other redundant as a predictor.

The inclusion of history as a substitute for anthropology is probably explained by the high degree of overlap, as early white settlement of the area followed the stream channels and was either exploratory or closely related to fur trapping, hunting, and other non-agricultural pursuits.

The equation for Field Aesthetic Impression includes more variables than the photographic evaluation equations. This larger number of variables suggests that Field Aesthetic Impression is not based on one dominant characteristic of the landscape as viewed by an expert, rather it tends to reflect many of the objectively measured parameters of the Uniqueness Ratio and Wilderness Potential (with the Field Aesthetic Impression parameter excluded). The best equation for Field Aesthetic Impression indicates that water quality is again the most important predictor, explaining 26 per cent of the variance. It is followed by such diverse variables as physiography, degree of urbanization, air quality, solid waste, anthropology, and history, explaining 53 per cent of the variance.

Stepwise regression equations run but not included in this paper reaffirm that artist rating of photographic quality significantly predict the aesthetic judgments made by photographic viewers. When allowed into the equation, photographic quality was the most significant variable in the black-and-white equation and accounted for half of the variance. As stated earlier this highlights the problem of interaction between photo quality and scenic content. The present results indicate that neither the artist judge nor the photography viewers were completely able to distinguish between quality and content of the photographs.

It is difficult to identify factors influencing human aesthetic perception of natural landscapes. Shafer and Mietz (1969) describe the wilderness experience as having great aesthetic value as compared to emotional, social, educational, or physical, but do not discuss what elements that contribute to human aesthetic perception of the wilderness. In this investigation, using the landscape characteristics defined by the Uniqueness

Ratio and Wilderness Potential parameters the characteristics of the water and the air appear to best explain the viewer's aesthetic judgments of natural landscapes as seen through photographs. Aesthetic evaluation in the field seems dependent on these same factors of water and air, but also on the configuration of the land and the degree of landscape alteration and urban development. Further study, will be needed to define what specific aspects of water and air affect human aesthetic judgments.

To summarize, stepwise regression analysis clearly shows that black-and-white equations account for more of the variance compared to color and Field Aesthetic judgments of the landscape. Certain variables, particularly water and air quality, anthropology, and hydrology best account for the aesthetic judgments made both by viewers of photographs and expert evaluation in the field. Some uniqueness parameters are related to aesthetics (anthropology, hydrology, and geology). Water quality is the single most important variable and is more evident in aesthetic judgments made using black-and-white photographs ra er than color slides.

Influence of demographic factors on aesthetic judgment

From the viewer background information collected with the photographic evaluation questionnaire, it was possible to observe the influence of several demographic factors on aesthetic judgments of natural landscapes. The factors analyzed include socio-economic status measured by occupation and amount of education, age, sex, and involvement in outdoor activities and conservation. Fig. 15.4 graphically represents the demographic information collected from the 181 viewers. Few consistent differences in aesthetic judgment by subgroup can be isolated. There is a fairly widespread minimum ratings in the occupational subgroups, and unskilled workers tend to give low ratings while professional people tend to rate their aesthetic impression of the scenery higher. These trends are minor and of questionable statistical significance, and in the case of the unskilled subgroup, the number of observations was 12 (7% of sample). The mean ratings based on age subgroups show some variation, but the maxima and minima are rather consistent and there is no progressive pattern of higher

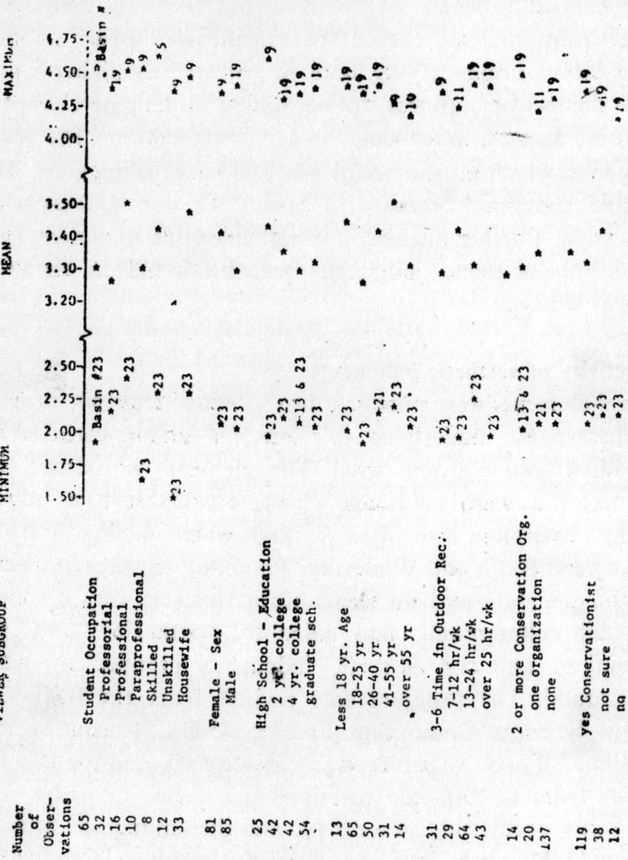

FIG. 15.4 : *Aesthetic Impression rating distribution of B&W evaluation by photographic viewer subgroup. Drainage basin numbers for minimum and maximum ratings are shown on diagram*

or lower ratings with increasing age. Similarly, little evidence can be found of any strong correlation between aesthetic judgments and degree of involvement in outdoor activities or conservation interests, except that members of two or more conservation organizations tend to give slightly higher ratings. Sex and education appear to be almost totally irrelevant as potential factors influencing aesthetic evaluation. The consistency with which all subgroups give minimum ratings to basin 23, and maximum ratings to basins 19 and 9, is especially impressive. Further discussion of influence due to viewer background on aesthetic judgments will be found in the factor analysis section.

Objectivity of aesthetic judgments

Several elements were punched into a factor analysis program to observe the underlying relationships among variables and individual sample groups used. The elements introduced into the program were landscape characteristics such as physiography, hydrology, air quality, and water quality (all the Uniqueness Ratio and Wilderness Potential parameters), aesthetic judgments based on scenic evaluation seen through black-and-white photographs and color transparencies, and field evaluation, and the aesthetic judgments grouped by viewer background. The program was revised from the BMDX 72, Health Sciences Computing Facility, U.C.L.A. using varimax rotations.[6] Forty variables were introduced and the first four factors from a 10-factor rotations are listed in Table 15.4. The factor coefficients above 0.400 and the amount of variance explained by each factor are given in the table. Each factor is defined and discussed in the following paragraphs.

Factor 1 can be defined as aesthetic judgment of the scenic quality. Particularly, it is the aesthetic judgments as evaluated by viewers of black-and-white photographs. The fact that all methods of aesthetic evaluation are loaded on this factor and 69 per cent of the total variance is associated with it underlines the importance of aesthetics in landscape appraisal. Aesthetic judgments based on color slide ratings and field evaluation show fairly significant (positive) loadings, however, much lower than black-and-white ratings. All of the viewer subgroups[7] representing different age, sex, socio-economic

TABLE 15.4 : **Factor analysis of aesthetic judgments and landscape characteristics. Four principal factors with coefficients above [0.400] are listed. Per cent of variance explained by each factor is given in parentheses. U.R. is uniqueness ratio and WP is wilderness potential parameters**

Factor 1 (68.0%)	
Aesthetic judgments based on Black-and-White photographs	.958
Aesthetic judgments based on Black-and-White by viewer subgroup	.962-.839
Education—1-2 yr college	.962
Exhibit Location—Arts Festival	.961
Sex—Female	.960
Conservationist—Yes	.957
Outdoor Recreation - 2-6 hr/wk	.956
Age—41-55 yrs	.954
Exhibit Location—Parents Weekend	.953
Exhibit Location—Farmers Produce Market	.952
Outdoor Recreation—13-24 hr/wk	.946
Outdoor Recreation—7-12 hr/wk	.946
Conservationist—Not sure	.946
Occupation - Professional	.941
Age—18-25 yrs	.935
Conservation Membership—1 organization	.935
Occupation—Unskilled	.933
Education—3-4 yr college	.933
Occupation—Professional	.928
Age—26-40 yrs	.925
Occupation—Student	.923
Black-and-White subgroup	.906
Education—High school	.905
Occupation—Paraprofessional	.885
Conservation Membership in 2 or more organizations	.883
Age—Less than 18 yrs	.866
Occupation—Skilled Laborer	.839
Water Quality-W.P.	.476
Aesthetic Judgments based on Color Slides	.413
Field Aesthetic Impression	.407
Degree of Urbanization, W.P.	.404
Factor 2 (8.1%)	
Physiography, U.R.	.879

TABLE 15.4 (*Contd.*)

Hydrology, U.R.	.830
History, U.R.	.820
Factor 3 (5%)	
Degree of Urbanization, W.P.	.883
Road Development, W.P.	.838
Air Quality, W.P.	.785
Water Quality, W.P.	.649
Factor 4 (3.8%)	
Field Aesthetic Impression, W.P.	.899

status, outdoor interest, and degree of involvement in conservation show virtually the same factor loadings as the black-and-white total sample.

The results of this study support Child's work (1968), suggesting that a universality of aesthetic judgment exists which transgresses social demographic boundaries. Evidence presented here clearly indicates that age, sex, socio-economic level or conservation interest have no significant influence on aesthetic judgment of natural landscapes as seen through photographs.

Factor 2 describes the landscape morphology and is defined at basin and stream size. Physiography, hydrology, and history all show strong positive loadings due to the fact that many of their subparameters vary in response to basin area or stream discharge. The occurrenee of only Uniqueness Ratio parameters here shows the degree of non-overlap among aesthetic judgments and uniqueness characteristics of landscapes.

Factor 3, a rotated factor is defined as a measure of human impact on the landscape. It is characterized by Wilderness Potential parameters assessing environmental quality.

Factor 4 describes the visual natural elements of landscapes as viewed and experienced in the field. It is interesting to note that Field Aesthetic Judgment as an evaluative technique or landscape element is not closely associated with other techniques or characteristics. It's independence represents a separate and distinct element of landscape beauty. Factor 4 illustrates the degree of non-overlap between the expert rater in the field and the lay people's aesthetic judgment based on photography. Whereas the | 0.4 | coefficient in factor 1 of Field Aesthetic judgment represents the degree of overlap between photographic and field evaluation of landscape aesthetics.

The first four factors account for more than 85 per cent of the variance, and each represents an evaluative technique. Field aesthetic judgment has a moderately low loading on factor 1 and splits off from the other aesthetic judgment ratings to form factor 4.

There has been much debate about the concurrence among viewer groups in aesthetic judgments based on natural landscapes. This study clearly indicates that there is no statistically significant difference among viewer groups due to background, socio-economic status nor conservation interest. The fact that all viewer groups are loaded on factor 1 with the coefficients between 0.839 and 0.962 illustrates their unanimity in making aesthetic judgments. The work by Zube *et al.* (1974) concurs with our findings. Zube *et al.* report substantial agreement among thirteen subgroups of evaluators on all measures of landscape quality using both field and photographic techniques. However, in a study on human responses, Peterson and Neumann (1969) identified two groups having distinctly different ratings. They used black-and-white photos for perceptions and preferences of visual characteristics of beaches, free responses to identify variables, and semantic differentials to measure selected attributes of a variety of beaches. It was suggested that the two groups were using beaches for different purposes, the present authors would inject that this is an example of aesthetic preference, not aesthetic judgment. In the present paper, aesthetic evaluation is not use oriented, and the broad spectrum of physiographic features, biological characteristics, land-use and human interest factors would encourage evaluation from a general perspective, that is what is pleasing to the eye or beautiful—aesthetic judgment.

SUMMARY AND RECOMMENDATIONS FOR FUTURE RESEARCH

Aesthetic judgments using black-and-white photographs confirm objectively measured landscape characteristics, while color transparencies tend to distract. Additional work is needed to clarify the discrepancy between aesthetic judgments based on black-and-white prints compared to color transparencies.

The Uniqueness parameters measure landscape characteristics other than scenic beauty and botanical characteristics function independently of all measured landscape characteristics.

There is substantial interaction of aesthetic judgments of natural landscapes and Wilderness Potential characteristics, with water and air quality being most significant. Further research needs to identify the specific elements of water and air quality that affect human perception of aesthetic judgments. Work needs to identify those landscape characteristics of on-site field aesthetic judgments that are not contained in aesthetic judgments based on photography.

The independence of aesthetic judgment from viewers' background, socio-economic level and conservation interest needs confirmation by further studies including viewer groups from diverse geographical areas and cultural backgrounds. If they continue to be substantiated, they would indicate that aesthetic judgments constitute a great common denominator among people and that the question of landscape aesthetics is not personal or subjective. An implication of these findings is that scenery may be treated by objective or quantitative methods upon which society could (at least theoretically) agree. If the value of the landscape can be described in generally acceptable and objective terms other than monetarily, then we are approaching a system of landscape evaluation, that could accurately reflect not only the practical needs but the aesthetic desires of the people.

FOOTNOTES

1. Paper is based on M.S. thesis, "A System of Quantitative Landscape Evaluation," Bucknell University, Lewisburg, Penna., 17837.
2. Exploration time is the amount of time spent viewing the scenery or photographs depicting it.
3. Karst topography results from the dissolving of soluble rock, usually limestone, by ground water, and is characterized by numerous caves, sink holes, streams that disappear beneath the surface and reappear elsewhere, and generally irregular, knobby topography.

4. Field, Photographic and General Aesthetic Impression ratings have a high occurrence of even digit numbers. This is probably due to a truncation property of the basic statistics program used.
5. Stepwise regression was performed on the DMX 1300 computer at Lehigh University, Bethlehem, Pennsylvania, with the aid of Leaps-Ver. 2.06, a program written by Frank W. Koko, Dept. Chemical Engineering, Bucknell University, Lewisburg, Penna.
6. C.S.U. Statistical Laboratory, Constant=0.001, upper limit on correlation coefficients=0.95.
7. Twenty-five of the 32 possible viewer subgroups were run in the factor analysis program.

REFERENCES

Child, I.L. (1968) "The experts and the bridge of judgment that crosses every cultural gap." *Psychology Today* 2, 7 : 24-29.

Coughlin, Robert E. and Karen A. Goldstein (1970) "The Extent of Agreement Among Observers on Environmental Attractiveness." *Regional Science Research Institute Discussion Paper* No. 37.

Craik, Kenneth H. (1972) "Psychological factors in landscape appraisal." *Environment and Behavior* 4, 3 : 255-266.

Craik, Kenneth H. (1970) "A system of landscape dimensions : appraisal of its objectivity and illustration of its scientific application." Report to Resources for the Future, Inc. Berkeley : University of California Institute of Personality Assessment and Research.

Craik, Kenneth H. (1969) "Human responsiveness to landscape : an environmental psychological perspective," pp. 168-193 in K. Coates and K. Moffett (eds.) *Response to Environment* (Student Publication of the School of Design 18). Raleigh : North Carolina State Univ. Press.

Hart, W.J. and W.W. Graham (1967) "How to rate and rank landscape." Landscape Architecture 57 : 121-122.

Kaplan, Stephen (1975) "An informal model for the prediction of preference," in E.H. Zube, J.G. Fabos, and R.O. Brush [eds.] *Landscape Assessment : Values, Perceptions, and Resources.* Strausburg, Pennsylvania : Dowden, Hutchinson and Ross.

Kaplan, S., R. Kaplan, and J. Wendt (1972) "Rated preference and complexity for natural and urban visual material." *Perception and Psychophysics* 12, 4 : 356-356.

Kiemstedt, H. (1968) "The evaluation of the natural components of the landscape for leisure." Presented at the Congress of International Federation of Landscape Architects.

Knight, H. (1967) "The use of 'good' in aesthetic judgements," pp. 147-160 in W. Elton (ed.) *Aesthetics and Language*. Oxford : Basil Blackwell.

Leopold, L.B. (1969) "Landscape esthetics." *Natural History* 76 : 36-45.

Linton, D.L. (1968) "The assessment of scenery as a natural resource." *Scottish Geographical Magazine* 84 : 219-238.

Litton, R. Burton, Jr. (1972) "Aesthetic Dimensions of the Landscape." 262-291 in John V. Krufilla [ed.] *Natural Environments : Studies in Theoretical and Applied Analysis.* Baltimore : Johns Hopkins University Press.

Macdonald, M. (1967) "Some distinctive features of arguments used in criticism of the arts." pp. 114-130 in W. Elton (ed.) *Aesthetics and Language*. Oxford : Basil Blackwell.

Marchand, Maura O'brien (1974) "A System of Quantitative Landscape Evaluation." Thesis. Lewisburg, Pennsylvania : Bucknell University.

Margolis, J. (1965) *The Language of Art and Art Criticism : Analytic Questions in Aesthetics.* Detroit, Mich. : Wayne State University.

Morisawa, M.E. (1971) "Evaluating riverscapes." in D.R. Coates [ed.] *Environmental Geomorphology.* Binghamton, New York : State University of New York Publications in Geomorphology.

Peterson, George L., and Edwards S. Neumann (1969) "Modeling and Predicting Human Response to the Visual Recreation Environment." *Journal of Leisure Research* 1, 3 : 219-237.

Raychaudhuri, M. (1972) "Some perceptual correlates of aesthetics." *Revista Latinoamericanade Psicologia* 4, 2 : 221-226.

Shafer, E.L., and J. Mietz (1969) "Aesthetic and emotional values rate high with northeastern wilderness hikers." *Environment and Behavior* 1, 2 : 187-198.

Vedenin, Y.A. and N.N. Miroschnichenko (1971) "Evaluation of the natural environment for recreational purposes." Ekistics 31 : 223-226.

Wohlwill, J. (1973) "Factors in the differential response to the natural and the man-made environment." in "Affective Response to the Outdoor Environment." Symposium held at the Meetings of the American Psychological Association, Montreal, August.

Zube, Ervin H., David G. Pitt, and Thomas W. Anderson (1974) "Perception and measurement of scenic resources in the southern Connecticut River Valley." Publication No. R-74-1. Amherst, Massachusetts : Institute for Man and His Environment.

SIXTEEN

PETER F. SMITH

THE HARMONICS OF INFORMATION IN ARCHITECTURE

THE very idea of harmony as a quality of architecture has been unfashionable for some time. It seems to have been one of the casualties of the First World War.

The question I wish to pose is this : can we apply traditional rules of harmony to the contemporary architectural and urban situation ?

Historically architects used proportional systems overtly, and the most enduring harmonic relationship has been the golden section or phi, to use its Greek shorthand. This is a mathematical ratio originating with the Pythagoreans and derived from the formula $1 : \frac{\surd 5-1}{2}$.

This ratio was popular with the Greeks ; it was employed in the middle ages, notably in that supreme work of the gothic age, the Cathedral of Notre Dame, Chartres ; renaissance architects used it extensively and in the modern era Le Corbusier claims to have subjected all his designs to the regimen of phi. So, since this harmonic relationship spans all the main European architectural ages and even present in the overall proportions of certain Islamic buildings such as the Taj Mahal, we shall use it to demonstrate the flexibility of the harmonic principle.

We are accustomed to identifying phi in, say, the ratio of height to breadth of the front of the Parthenon in Athens. But can we also identify it on the more complex and subtle levels of information ?

Before tackling this question directly in relation to buildings I need to make brief reference to the way the mind processes information. A top priority in the perception routine is the need to reduce the complexity of the sensory world by recognising patterns or systems of orderliness. A residue from our primordial past is the need to attempt to eliminate or at least reduce uncertainty in our environment. One way to do this is to reduce the gross complexity of the milieu by organising data into patterns or schemas. The more the environment can be systematised in this way, the less the uncertainty, and so the less we are likely to be taken by surprise.

One routine which the mind seems to favour is to arrange data into related pairs. This binary organisational routine is the simplest way of building up an orderly model of the world, perhaps on a hierarchical basis. First we recognise the most obvious binary relationship, say between the nave and tower of a church. Then we discern more discreet binary sub-systems, such as the relationship between window and will, or decoration and plainness, and so on.

The next important point to note is that the mind somehow attaches weight to information systems according to their complexity and mass. Furthermore, the tendency of the mind to establish related pairs extends to more discreet information matrices. Here we come to the heart of aesthetics, because the mind will make a value judgement according to the relative informational weight of the two related but distinct systems. If the relative strengths achieve either equality or harmony, then we have eliminated uncertainty. Aesthetic value has a direct correlation with the elimination of uncertainty.

Harmony as conceived in terms of phi consists of a binary relationship in which one entity is clearly dominant in terms of informational weight. However, the domination is not overwhelming ; the subordinate system retains its self-respect. The ratio of 1 : 1.618 or phi seems to satisfy this condition perfectly.

It is time to clarify all this by referring to the Greek temple. Perhaps the first visual contest which we notice is between the features which express the two axes, vertical and horizontal. The rapid rhythm of columns contribute to the informational 'mass' of verticalness, whilst the heavy entablature and portico together with the crepidoma base assert the horizontal axis.

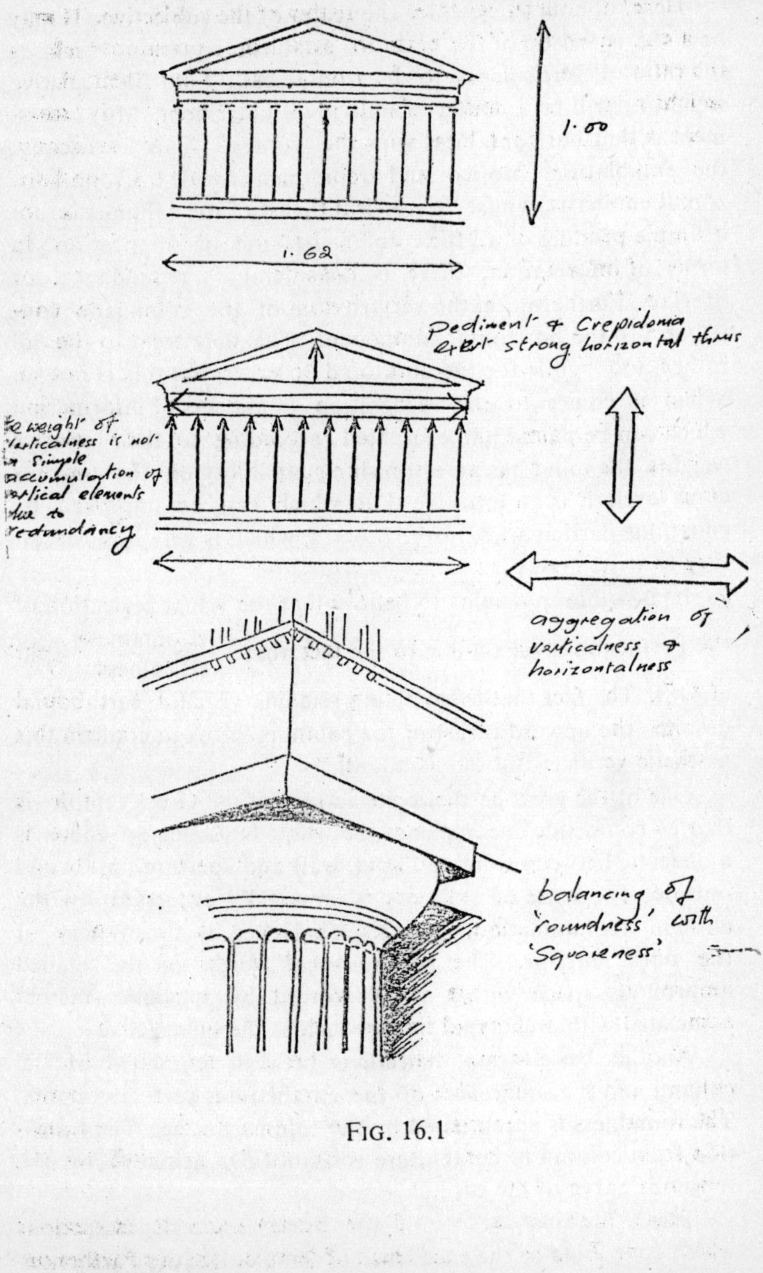
1.00
1.62
Pediment & Crepidoma exert strong horizontal thrus
the weight of verticalness is not a simple accumulation of vertical elements due to redundancy
aggregation of verticalness & horizontalness
balancing of 'roundness' with 'Squareness'

FIG. 16.1

Here, of course, we enter the realm of the subjective. It may be a characteristic of the brain to establish equations such as the ratio of 'verticalness' to horizontalness', but their relative weighting will be a matter of individual judgement. My assessment is that horizontalness wins the contest. This is because the entablature, protico and crepidoma provide a strong horizontal emphasis, whilst the vertical thrust of the columns is not a simple product of all the columns because of duplication. In terms of information, there is considerable redundancy, or overlap. Furthermore, the very rhythm of the colonnade contributes to the horizontal component. This may seem to be all rather too subtle for the untutored observer, but this is not so. When it comes to the recognition of systems of information which can be paired and evaluated according to their relative weights, the mind has an astonishing capability on the unconscious level. It is an intuitive skill which can be improved by conscious participation in the process, which is why it is necessary to write about it !

It is quite possible to believe that the visual perfection of the Parthenon is partly due to the fact that $\frac{\text{horizontalness}}{\text{verticalness}} = \text{phi}$ (1.618). The fact that the building remains visually earthbound despite the upward thrust of the columns seems to confirm this aesthetic verdict. But this is not all.

One of the great aesthetic attractions of the Greek temple is that its colonnade encompasses the whole building. So there is a dialectic between solid and void, wall and aperture, inside and outside. The sense of 'wallness' is powerfully expressed by the close intercolumniation, but this is balanced by the mystery of the dark interior. The psychological weight of the shaded amorphous space within is re-inforced by symbolic factors associated with archetypal images such as the sacred cave.

Another basic formal dialectic is between roundness of the column and the squareness of the entablature and crepidoma. The roundness is accentuated by the column fluting. The transition from column to entablature is beautifully achieved by the sensuous curve of the capital.

These are just a few of the binary aesthetic interactions which contribute to the excellence of temples like the Parthenon. From these examples it can be seen that the aesthetic measure of this building derives from an orchestration of informational dialectics or creative clashes on numerous levels. Crowning these multiple harmonics was the dialectic between the building itself and its environment. It was the jewel in the crown of the Acropolis ; sited high above the city of Athens it served as a mediator between the Polis and the gods ; a permanent reminder of the sacred amidst the secular. For in this building the aesthetic and the symbolic were inextricably combined.

This system of analysis on the basis of informational confrontation or 'diamorphism' can be applied to any style of architecture, western or eastern. For example, it may yield new insights into that classic of Indian architecture, the Taj Mahal. It ranks with the Parthenon as one of the most beautiful buildings in the world.

It may be argued that this is such an obviously beautiful building that it is pointless to analyse it. This is precisely the reason why we should attempt to make an assessment of the aesthetic resources of this building. It satisfies our intuitive aesthetic sense whether we belong to eastern or western cultures.

In its overall proportions the Taj Mahal closely approximates to phi, but this is only the start of the aesthetic journey.

As I proposed earlier, the mind tends to organise visual data into the simplest of orderly patterns, namely related pairs

FIG. 16.2 : *'Energised' space between minarets and mausoleum ensures that the minarets are perceived as part of the total architectural composition*

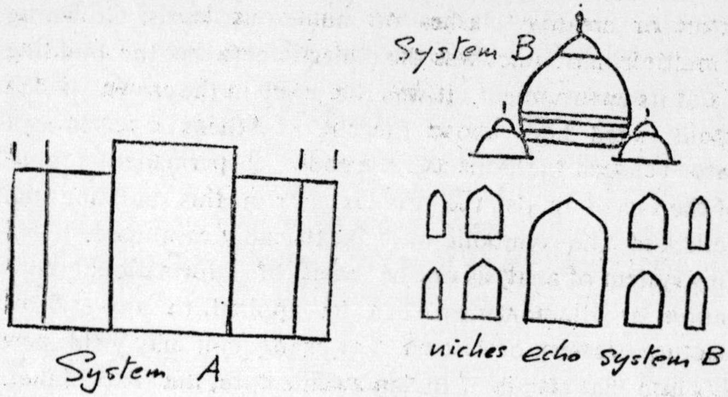

FIG. 16.3

or binary groups. In a complex building like the Mausoleum at Agra the mind works in hierarchical way, from the most obvious dialectical relationship down to the most subtle binary interaction.

In this case, the most prominent dialogue is between the Mausoleum and its garden setting. Architecture and nature have several things in common. The garden court is geometrically designed, like the architecture; nature subject to the impress of human design. In this sense the garden *rhymes* with the architecture. In the phrase of Gerard Manley Hopkins, it is a case of "likeness tempered with difference", which sums up the meaning of rhyme.

The relationship between the architecture and its setting is particularly poetic when viewed from the central pool. A reflection is, after all, a kind of rhyme.

Next in the hierarchy of aesthetic interactions is the relationship between the mausoleum and the elegant marble minarets which serve to define the boundary of the building. The space between the minarets and the mausoleum is perhaps the most highly charged space in architecture. Anyone who doubts that space can be psychologically energised should visit the Taj Mahal.

In terms of perceptual weight, the mausoleum is the dominant unit. The minarets, though subordinate in visual weight, constitute a powerful sub-dominant theme, due to their symbolic overtones.

The next contrapuntal theme involves the main body of the Tomb and the domes which form its roof. Here are two related but contrasting systems of information locked in creative tension. Theo are bound together by the materials of construction. At the same time the cavernous niches in the elevation set up a rhyme with the domes.

The relative weighting of A and B will be a subjective matter, but for many the domes will be the dominant system because of their symbolic enrichment, and because of the reinforcement given to them by the pointed niches and by the domes on the minarets. May be the perfection of the design is due to the harmonic balance between system A and system B. We might even speculate this equation

$$\frac{\text{system A}}{\text{system B}} = .618 \text{ (phi)}$$

This is one binary interpretation of the mausoleum ; another involves the harmonic balance between the central element and the side elements. Again there is a perfectly gauged aesthetic balance between likeness and difference, and between the perceptual weighting of the two systems.

The informational weight of system C is reduced by the fact that there is duplication or redundancy in information terms. Thus system D seems clearly dominant well beyond the terms of phi. On its own the central element would appear over-dominant. However, the flanking elements tend to be reinforced across space by the minarets. When these are taken into account the equation seems to approach symmetrical balance : system C is approximately equivalent to system D.

These various aesthetic interactions or contrapuntal themes orchestrate into a whole of immeasurable beauty. We may not be consciously aware of these subtle relationships, but nevertheless the mind seems able to identify them and perceive the composition as a dynamic system of forces in which the resultant is perfect harmony. Thus our 'intuitive' perception of elegance is the outcome of a highly sophisticated perception routine in which information is 'measured' for its weight of complexity or patternness and then organised into logical binary systems.

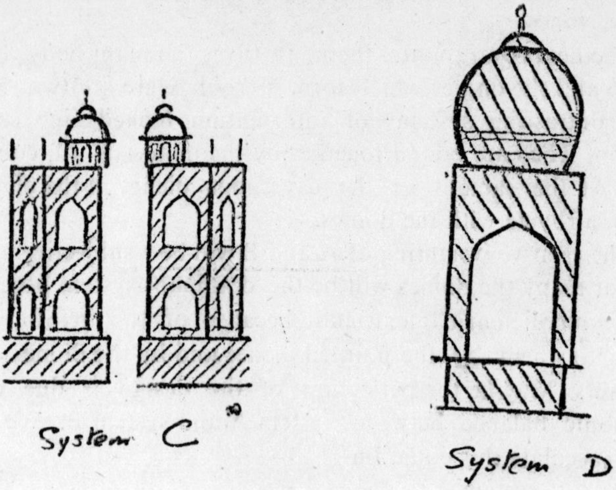

FIG. 16.4

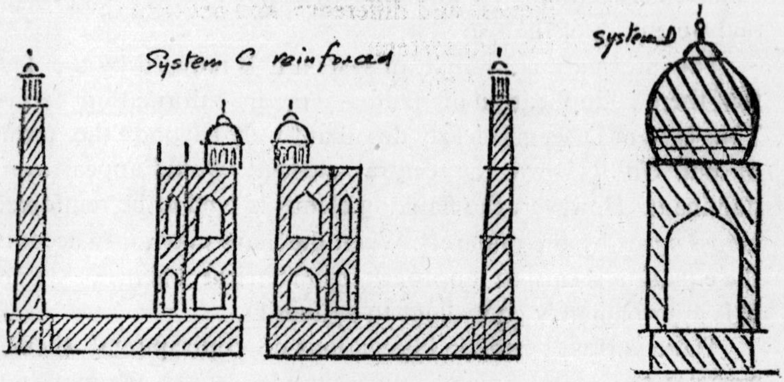

FIG. 16.5

Fig 16. 6 between Page 462-463

FIG. 16.7

These systems can then be evaluated according to the extent to which they eliminate uncertainty.

Can we apply this method of aesthetic analysis to modern buildings ? We certainly can, and it helps us to appreciate why certain buildings are widely acclaimed and others condemned.

A building which has recently startled Londoners is the new Danish Embassy, flanking Sloane Square. Designed by Arne Jacobsen, Dissing and Weitting, it is a sophisticated building in terms of detailing and finishes. The problem is that it is really two buildings trying unsuccessfully to look like one.

There is a four storey block fronting the square which has the appearance of accommodation modules stacked in threes and forming five bays. They are finished in pale yellow. It is an innocent design conceit calculated to evoke the 'high tech' image.

Rising abruptly behind this element is a skin-tight curtain wall block which houses the ambassador's apartments. The only link it establishes with the forward block is a vestigial division into five bays. In every other way it represents a total contrast in shape, colour and texture with the pavement elevation. Both units could exist perfectly well on their own. The only rhyming link is the bay division.

This is the first aesthetic problem ; the second concerns their respective visual weighting. In terms of informational 'mass' they establish a relationship undermined by uncertainty.

In terms of pure bulk the rear curtain wall unit is the dominant element. However, by virtue of its simple fenestration and evenly distributed dark tone, it is low in visual complexity.

The front unit is much smaller in size but contains considerably more information. There is complexity in the rhythms associated with windows and bay module. Colour adds further complexity.

To sum it up : we have a building comprising two major elements which, in information terms, reveal no logical reason for their juxtaposition. There is an almost total absence of likeness tempered with difference'. At the same time the composition leaves us uncertain as to which is really the dominant partner. One element is the major feature in terms of pure size, the other in terms of its rate of information. When we add to all this the fact that the building makes no attempt whatever to respect its neighbours, then, all in all, we have a recipe for ugliness.

We must quickly redress the balance with a building, which, in my opinion, achieves considerable aesthetic stature. In the Sir Thomas White building at St. John's College, Oxford, we immediately become aware of two themes running through the whole design. The more prominent is the theme of glass pavilions suspended within a delicate concrete frame. Between the pavilions are windowless staircase towers faced in stone. It is a beautiful dialogue between a heavy and opaque element and one which is light and transparent. Both units express a measure of independence, but interdependence is the stronger force.

Furthermore, it is a harmonic dialogue. The glass pavilion with its taut concrete supporting frame is the major element in terms of visual and symbolic complexity. It is symbolic of high technology, but in a manner which has total integrity. There is never phoney 'high tech.' in the architecture of Arup and Partners. The staircase towers have just the right amount of visual weight to be the minor element whilst retaining their self-respect. Perhaps here too we perceive aesthetic correctness because the ratio of the dominant to the subordinate approximates to a harmonic displacement.

What puts the seal of excellence on this building is its sensitive relationship with the surroundings. Within the College it adds a new dimension of interest to the venerable buildings,

Fig 16.8 between Page 464-465

Fig 16.9 between Page 464-465

Fig 16.10 between Page 464-465

Fig 16.11 between Page 464-465

whilst on the town side it establishes a new visual climax to a plain Georgian street. Inside and outside the College, the Stir Thomas White building has contributed enrichment to the environment. It contrasts violently with the new addition to the adjacent Keble College. Here an embattled image is presented to the city whilst inside the College a serpentine smoked-glass wall collides with the existing polychomatic neo-Gothic architecture. It is truly a clash of opposed systems which will create sparks for many years to come.

The next question to consider is whether this 'diamorphic' aesthetic mode can be transposed into the broader urban key. Is it possible for a complex urban ensemble to be rendered down into a fundamental binary situation ?

That this can be the case can be demonstrated by reference to one of the most ancient cities in England, the cathedral city of Lincoln. One of its most attractive prospects is the view along the Strait towards the central tower of the cathedral. In the foreground is a somewhat disorderly ensemble of domestic buildings flanking the steep ascent to the cathedral. There is a great deal of variety at this level of the scene, but what rivets the attention is the majestic and almost ethereal tower of one of the great churches of Christendom.

In the face of this challenge, the secular architecture on the lower slopes of this 'sacred mountain' resolve their differences to offer a united front in this monumental aesthetic confrontation.

In terms of abstract information, the brick built houses and shops present the greater weight. But they cannot compete with the Cathedral on the plane of symbolism. That great 15th century tower resonates with archetypal images of the City of God, of the temple on the acropolis marking the intersection of the cosmic zones af earth, heaven and the nether regions. Of course such primordial resonances are rarely articulated, but they are present in all of us and add considerably to the psychological weight of the Cathedral. Though smaller in terms of pure visual information it is much more heavily saturated with *symbolic* information than the buildings at its feet. So the Cathedral wins the contest ; not too easily but nevertheless convincingly.

This dialectic between the sacred and the secular has received a modern interpretation in the West German city of Köln.

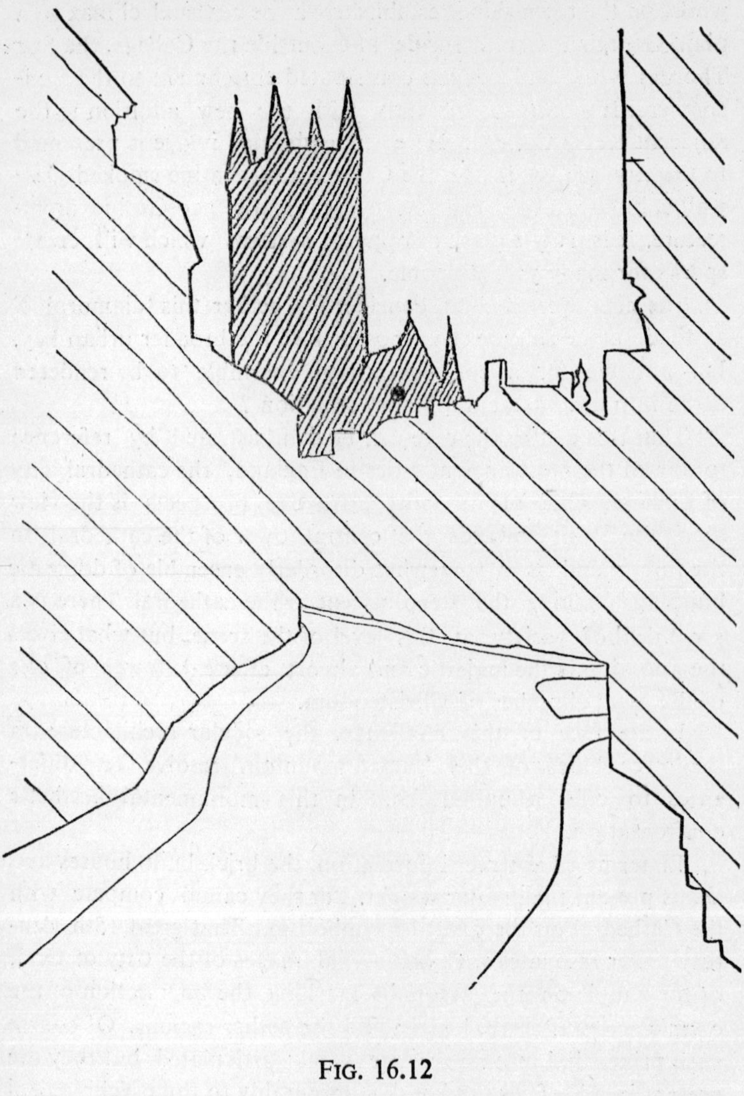

FIG. 16.12

Near the Cathedral is the massive Romanesque church of Great St. Martin. A recent development of high quality apartments forms three sides of a square enclosed on the fourth side by the great south flank of the church. It is a robust dialogue between ancient and modern. The dimensions of the square provide sufficient space for old and new to disperse their 'energy fields'. Again, the church, with its historical and religious connotations, is the dominant building but the vigorously-modelled housing, its balconies bedecked with foliage, is a worthy partner.

The complexity in the situation is made up of two main components. First there is the pure visual complexity or multiplexity in both church and housing. Then there is the complexity arising from the modernity of the housing. Novelty is a form of complexity.

How to relate the new with the old to produce aesthetic riehness is a challenge which faces every practising architect and urban planner working within all historic cultures. If we see aesthetic value in terms of the dynamics of information than this opens up new possibilities for designers to establish a vigorous dialectic between novelty and familiarity.

Aesthetic counterpoint

We have seen how aesthetic orderliness can emerge from binary relationships in which there is either perfect balance, or the tensile equilibrium resulting from a combination of dominant with subordinate. The ideal relative weighting in the latter case seems to centre around phi.

There is another historically attested aesthetic system which concerns the tension between complexity and pattern. It has long been recognised that aesthetic reward may accompany the apprehension of orderliness within complexity. The criterion seems to be that the complexity should be adequate to constitute a real challenge to our pattern-recognition skills. Orderliness should ultimately be triumphant but only after a struggle. If the orderliness is too easily accessible, then the aesthetic 'pressure' drops dramatically. This aesthetic system is most rapidly appreciated in certain historic towns, particularly those dating from the middle ages. The one which immediately comes to mind is Amsterdam. In the medieval core of the city there is a marvellous architectural mixture which at first seems to constitute total disorder. Nevertheless, the scene is 'picturesque', which means that it offers aesthetic rewards. This is because we intuitively recognise several interlocking systems of orderliness or pattern which lie discreetly behind the surface of complexity and apparent anarchy.

In the first place there is a broad consensus regarding materials. Dark brown and red brick predominates and this is a powerful unifying factor. The buildings are not all identical in colour, but, on aggregate, similarity is far stronger than variety.

The same applies to roof termination. Most buildings greet the sky with that style of gable which is characteristically Dutch. Each gable expresses its individuality, yet overall, the unifying factor of 'gableness' is stronger than the impression of variety. The resultant effect is of pattern rather than arbitrariness.

A major contributor to orderliness is the rhythm of windows. At first sight, rhythm appears to be absent. Windows are of different size ; their levels rarely correspond from one building to the next. Nevertheless, a sense of rhythm is more pronounced than a feeling of pure randomness. There are several reasons for this. Despite variations in size aud placement, all the windows fall within a size and proportion boundary which proclaims likeness rather than difference. Most are contained in groups of three, so that there is a predominant pattern of triads binding the scene together. The pattern-factor in the windows is given its final boost by the consistent system of white painted glazing bars which establish a universal module.

Lastly there is the question of building plot size. Once again we do not have strict regularity, but the variations fall within the boundaries of patternness rather than randomness.

The consequence of all this is that there is a final aggregate of complexity or multiplexity which is equated against the overall weight of patternness. When engaging in aesthetic perception, the mind has the capacity to attribute weight to these respective matrices of complexity and orderliness. Where orderliness outweighs complexity by a critical margin, then potentially we have aesthetic richness. This contest between two kinds of information is fundamental to aesthetic perception. Perhaps we can envisage the possibility of the classic equation of beauty applying to much more complex systems of information like townscape. In the case of Amsterdam the magic of the place may be due in part to the fact that orderliness outweighs variety by a ratio somewhere near the golden mean.

Fig 16.13 between Page 468-469

Fig 16.14 between Page 468-469

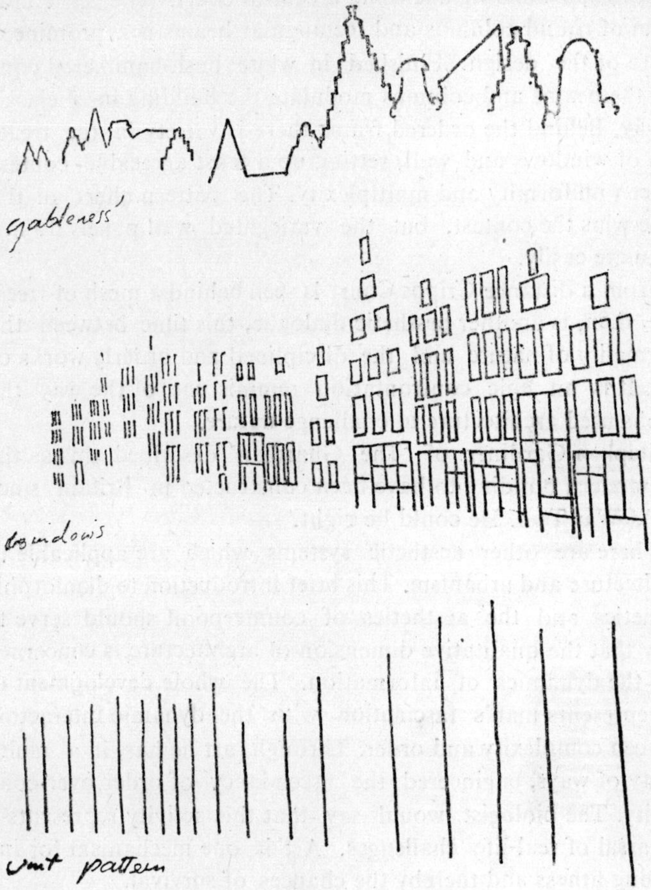

FIG. 16.15 : *Amsterdam* : *Pattern factors*

I have called this the aesthetics of counterpoint because there are two types of information engaged in continuous dialogue, so to speak. It is linear and synchronous interaction, analogous to musical counterpoint.

We may witness this aesthetic mode not only in townscape but also in the design of individual buildings. A recent striking example is Cripps Court at Queen's College, Cambridge. It is a rectangular building enclosing a central court. The structural system of round columns and rectangular beams is a prominent feature of the design. Finished in white bush-hammered concrete the beams and columns modulate the building in a classical way. Behind the ordered frame there is variety in the treatment of windows and wall, setting up a most agreeable contest between uniformity and multiplexity. The pattern effect of the frame wins the contest, but the variegated wall panels do not capitulate easily.

From a distance Cripps Court is seen behind a mesh of trees. Here, then, is another aesthetic dialogue, this time between the informality of nature and the disciplined and orderly works of man. It is an epic confrontation reminiscent of the way the Greeks used architecture to challenge nature.

Stephen Gardiner of 'The Guardian' described this as the best modern building to have been constructed in Britain since World War Two. He could be right.

There are other aesthetic systems which are applicable to architecture and urbanism. This brief introduction to diamorphic aesthetics and the aesthetics of counterpoint should serve to show that the qualitative dimension of architecture is concerned with the dynamics of information. The whole development of art represents man's fascination with the dynamic interaction between complexity and order. Through art he has, in a multiplicity of ways, engineered the ascendancy of order over complexity. The biologist would say that this activity represents a rehearsal of real-life challenges. Art is one mechanism for improving fitness and thereby the chances of survival.

Architecture, and above all urbanism, represents a giant projection of this archetypal contest between the forces of anarchy and arbitrariness on the one hand and regularity and orderliness on the other. How this contest is regulated is a matter which is at the heart of that elusive concept called beauty. This is not a new idea. It was evident to Descartes, and Leibnitz claimed that the aim of the artist is "to obtain as much variety as possible but with the greatest order that one can". He was elaborating on that medieval formula for beauty ; 'multi-

Fig 16.16 between Page 470-471

plexitas in uno'. Even that derives from Aristotle who considered that the essence of our appreciation of poetry lies in "an intuitive perception of the *similarity in dissimilars*".

Few would deny that we need more poetry in architecture and that cities should be poetic on an epic scale.

INDEX